Nazi Germany, Annexed Poland, and Colonial Rule

Modern Histories of Politics and Violence

Series Editors:
Paul Jackson *(University of Northampton, UK)* and
Raul Carstocea *(University of Leicester, UK)*

Editorial Board:
Roger Griffin *(Oxford Brookes University, UK)*
Leonard Weinberg *(University of Nevada, USA)*
Ramon Spaaij *(La Trobe University, Melbourne, Australia)*
Richard Steigmann-Gall *(Kent State University, USA)*
Aristotle Kallis *(Keele University, UK)*
Matthew Feldman *(University of Teesside, UK)*
Kathleen Blee *(University of Pittsburgh, USA)*

The book series *Modern Histories of Politics and Violence* scrutinizes diverse histories of political violence in the modern world, from the French Revolution to the late 20th century. Volumes in the series—comprising both monographs and edited collections—aim to further our understanding of violence as part of the modern experience.

The series has a global scope and seeks to challenge Eurocentric assumptions. Areas of particular interest include: modernization and violence; colonial era violence and acts of aggression accompanying processes of decolonization; political violence associated with communist and fascist movements and regimes; liberal cultures of political violence; and the use of violence to achieve emancipatory political ends.

The series aims to explore both violence "from above," directed by state institutions such as armies or law enforcement agencies, and violence "from below," developed by a wide range of individuals and groups. Volumes in the series also question the cultural foundations of violence, and how perceptions of gender, race, class, community, and memory can be used to legitimate violent acts. In line with its interest in novel methodological approaches, the series encourages volumes that seek to redefine, broaden, or challenge extant definitions of violence.

Finally, the series also examines the impact of political violence on its victims, as well as its lasting consequences.

Published:
British Fascist Antisemitism and the Jewish Responses, 1932–40, Daniel Tilles (2014)
A British Fascist in the Second World War, edited by Brendan Fleming and
Claudia Baldoli (2014)
Civil Uprisings in Modern Sudan, W. J. Berridge (2015)
*Transnational Fascism in the Twentieth Century: Spain, Italy and the Global
Neo-Fascist Network*, Matteo Albanese and Pablo del Hierro (2016)
Colin Jordan and Britain's Neo-Nazi Social Movement, Paul Jackson (2016)
The Victims of Slavery, Colonization and the Holocaust, Kitty Millet (2017)
Survivor Transitional Narratives of Nazi-Era Destruction: The Second Liberation,
Dennis B. Klein (2017)
The Image of the Soldier in German Culture, 1871–1933, Paul Fox (2017)

Forthcoming:
The Comparative History of Fascism in Eastern Europe, Constantin Iordachi
Traces of Aerial Bombing in Berlin, Eloise Florence

Nazi Germany, Annexed Poland, and Colonial Rule

Resettlement, Germanization, and Population Policies in Comparative Perspective

Rachel O'Sullivan

BLOOMSBURY ACADEMIC
LONDON • NEW YORK • OXFORD • NEW DELHI • SYDNEY

BLOOMSBURY ACADEMIC

Bloomsbury Publishing Plc, 50 Bedford Square, London, WC1B 3DP, UK
Bloomsbury Publishing Inc, 1385 Broadway, New York, NY 10018, USA
Bloomsbury Publishing Ireland, 29 Earlsfort Terrace, Dublin 2, D02 AY28, Ireland

BLOOMSBURY, BLOOMSBURY ACADEMIC and the Diana logo are trademarks of
Bloomsbury Publishing Plc

First published in Great Britain 2023
This paperback edition published in 2025

Copyright © Rachel O'Sullivan, 2023

Rachel O'Sullivan has asserted her right under the Copyright, Designs and Patents Act, 1988, to be identified as Author of this work.

Series design by Clare Turner
Cover image: Border crossing of Volhynian German resettlers at Hrubieszow, 1940
© Sueddeutsche Zeitung Photo / Alamy

All rights reserved. No part of this publication may be: i) reproduced or transmitted in any form, electronic or mechanical, including photocopying, recording or by means of any information storage or retrieval system without prior permission in writing from the publishers; or ii) used or reproduced in any way for the training, development or operation of artificial intelligence (AI) technologies, including generative AI technologies. The rights holders expressly reserve this publication from the text and data mining exception as per Article 4(3) of the Digital Single Market Directive (EU) 2019/790.

Bloomsbury Publishing Plc does not have any control over, or responsibility for, any third-party websites referred to or in this book. All internet addresses given in this book were correct at the time of going to press. The author and publisher regret any inconvenience caused if addresses have changed or sites have ceased to exist, but can accept no responsibility for any such changes.

Every effort has been made to trace the copyright holders and obtain permission to reproduce the copyright material. Please do get in touch with any enquiries or any information relating to such material or the rights holder. We would be pleased to rectify any omissions in subsequent editions of this publication should they be drawn to our attention.

A catalogue record for this book is available from the British Library.

A catalog record for this book is available from the Library of Congress.

ISBN: HB: 978-1-3503-7722-6
PB: 978-1-3503-7723-3
ePDF: 978-1-3503-7724-0
eBook: 978-1-3503-7725-7

Series: Modern Histories of Politics and Violence

Typeset by Newgen KnowledgeWorks Pvt. Ltd., Chennai, India

For product safety related questions contact productsafety@bloomsbury.com.

To find out more about our authors and books visit www.bloomsbury.com
and sign up for our newsletters.

For my parents, grandparents, and Liosa

Contents

List of Illustrations	x
Acknowledgments	xi
Introduction	1

Part 1 Looking West? Looking East?

1 "A Bigger Germany, It Shall Be!": Germany's Colonial Past in Africa and Poland 21

Part 2 The Annexation of Poland and the Restructuring of Society

2 "Our Children Will Have It Better Than We Do!": Societal Stratification and Assimilation in Poland 49

3 A German Task: The Reich German Mission 79

4 Effacing Difference and the Settler Colonial Model 107

Part 3 Aligning Overseas and Continental Colonial Aims during the Third Reich

5 "To Colonize Is to Cultivate": Colonial Overlaps between Africa and Poland 137

Conclusion	165
Notes	173
Bibliography	221
Index	245

Illustrations

Map

0.1   Map of the *Reichsgau* Wartheland and *Reichsgau* Danzig-West Prussia, and the surrounding provinces and territories, in March 1940   14

Figures

3.1   *Kampf und Aufbau im Wartheland Ausstellung* (Struggle and Development in the Wartheland Exhibition) Poster   83

4.1   The renovated Radegast (Radogoszcz) train station in Łódź   117

Acknowledgments

This book would not have been possible without the help of numerous individuals and institutions to whom I am extremely grateful. Although this book is only loosely based on my PhD thesis, my warmest thanks go to my former supervisors, Stephan Malinowski and Donald Bloxham for their encouragement and support during my time at the University of Edinburgh and in the years following my graduation. Thank you to Gerhard Wolf and David Kaufman for their helpful comments and suggestions on my thesis. I am also extremely grateful to the anonymous reviewers of this book for their useful feedback and recommendations. I have received much advice on my work during conferences, workshops and seminars, and I am extremely thankful for the opportunities I had to present my research. I would also like to thank Bloomsbury Academic and the editors Laura Reeves and Rhodri Mogford for their help in the publication of this book. My sincere thanks go to the various organizations and institutions that provided me with funding, grants, and fellowships to travel abroad and complete my research, especially the Deutscher Akademischer Austausch Dienst (DAAD) and the Center for Holocaust Studies, at the Leibniz Institute for Contemporary History in Munich. Additionally, I would like to thank all the staff at the libraries and archives I visited in Germany and in Poland, particularly Bogumił Rudawski at the Instytut Zachodni in Poznań and colleagues at the Leibniz Institute for Contemporary History. This book would not have been possible without the invaluable support of Frank Bajohr and Andrea Löw at the Center for Holocaust Studies and my amazing colleagues there; Gaëlle Fisher, Anna Ullrich, Giles Bennett, Gregor Hofmann, Mirjam Neuhoff, Tobias Wals, and Katarina Kezeric. Thank you all for your collegiality, advice, ideas, and friendship. I am also incredibly thankful to the many others who have taken the time to read draft chapters, provide feedback, give me tips and hints, or simply talk with me about postdoc life and future plans; in particular, I am immensely grateful to Michelle Gordon, Winson Chu, and Eve Rosenhaft.

My thanks also go to my wonderful friends in Dublin, Edinburgh, and Munich, principally to Caoimhe, Ashling, Catherine, and Clare, who have provided me with never-ending encouragement and, perhaps most importantly, laughter. For the emotional support, love, patience, and always showing interest in my work, I am forever thankful to my family: Jim and Catherine, Amy, James, and Katie. Finally, my deepest thanks go to Raphael Schönen—the unwavering calm to my chaos—for all his support, love, and belief in me.

Introduction

In 1942, the Polish Research Centre in London released a short pamphlet entitled *German Failures in Poland: Natural Obstacles to Nazi Population Policy*. The pamphlet began by detailing the background to the "Polish-German war," highlighting the German motivations behind invading Poland such as German migration from the agricultural areas near the Polish border, seasonal Polish immigration to Germany, and the "imperialistic principles of *Geopolitik*" and the "sophistical theory of nationality" upon which the Germans based their arguments for a German right to Polish territory.[1] In section 3 of the pamphlet, and indeed throughout the publication, the authors clearly named the German process of the annexation and settlement of the Polish territories, which had been occurring since 1939: "colonisation."[2] The pamphlet specifically described this process with a framework of removal and replacement: "The Polish lands incorporated in the Reich are being Germanised mainly by a policy of transfer of population. The Poles are being expelled wholesale and Germans settled in their place."[3] Additionally, the authors labelled the German settlers, who were transferred from territories such as the Baltic States and Bessarabia, as "colonists." For the authors, colonialism appeared to provide an apt, widely identifiable concept for describing and understanding what was happening in Poland. The native Polish population were being legally and societally subjugated, forcibly removed from their homes and land, allocated reduced food rations, and exploited as forced laborers. Though the pamphlet does not go into specific detail on the topic of violence, under the section "A Policy of Extermination," it notes how the Germans were engaging in the "most brutal methods of mass executions and of destruction of Polish youth."[4] At the same time, the Polish population was being replaced by German settlers coming from further east. The authors noted how two principles, firstly, "mass colonisation, of creating whole settlements of purely German colonists," and secondly, "granting privileges to colonists as distinct from those who live side by side with them," (i.e., the Polish population) were being applied with "ruthless consistency."[5]

Despite the analogies with colonialism that were evident to the authors of the pamphlet, since the end of the Second World War, the significance of colonialism and the concept of colonization within the academic investigation and analysis of Nazi Germany's actions in annexed Poland has been much disputed. Political thinkers, philosophers, and historians have argued for and against ways in which Nazi Germany's expansion and violence can either be traced back to colonial roots or compared with colonial contexts. The most prominent aspect in these debates has not been Nazi Germany's expansion or its settlement of Poland, rather the main focus has been the devastating violence unleashed in Poland and further east, specifically the Holocaust. The first clear allusion to the colonial roots of the Holocaust in academia perhaps stems from the creation of the term "genocide," which was later applied to the Holocaust as a new and deadly crime category. In his 1944 book, *Axis Rule in Occupied Europe*, the Polish lawyer, Raphael Lemkin and creator of the term "genocide" first described the act as consisting of two phases:

> One, destruction of the national pattern of the oppressed group; the other, the imposition of the national pattern of the oppressor. This imposition, in turn, may be made upon the oppressed population which is allowed to remain, or upon the territory alone, after removal of the population and the colonisation of the area by the oppressor's own nationals.[6]

Although the definition of genocide was adjusted when it was adopted as a legal concept by the United Nations in 1948, Lemkin's unpublished works reveal, far from solely examining the Holocaust when creating the term, he looked at many instances of colonial and imperial violence spanning across different periods and continents.[7] In addition to Lemkin, intellectuals also started to loosely connect colonial violence and the crimes of the Nazi regime. For example, in his book *Discours sur le colonialisme*, Aimé Césaire argued what the Christian bourgeois of the twentieth century could not forgive Adolf Hitler for was:

> Not the humiliation of man as such, it [was] the crime against the white man, the humiliation of the white man, and the fact that he applied to Europe colonialist procedures which until then had been reserved exclusively for the Arabs of Algeria, the coolies of India, and the blacks of Africa.[8]

Similarly, in *The Origins of Totalitarianism*, Hannah Arendt proposed that anti-Semitism, expansion, and race-thinking were not a German invention nor were they purely the policies of Nazi ideology but they had been elements present in European imperial history before. These elements had crystallized into totalitarianism.[9]

After its legal and intellectual origins in the late 1940s and early 1950s, the debate on Nazi Germany's links with colonialism resurfaced among professional historians two decades ago. These historical arguments form part of the impetus and background to this book—a publication that is thematically situated at the intersection between the history of Nazi Germany's expansion and rule in annexed Poland, the Holocaust, and colonialism. In this book, I focus on Nazi Germany's population management and the resulting establishment of a racially stratified society within the *Reichsgaue* (Reich Districts) Wartheland and Danzig-West Prussia (German: Danzig-Westpreußen) through a colonial lens. As opposed to solely concentrating on violence to investigate whether the Holocaust can be understood within wider frameworks of colonial genocide and mass killing, I adopt a broader approach by considering various aspects of Nazi Germany's rule in Poland that were directly and indirectly related to the perpetration of the Holocaust. I attempt to show the colonial similarities inherent to Nazi Germany's expansion as part of a bigger systematic effort to transform the population and territory of the *Reichsgaue*. In addition to exclusionary population policies, which sought to rid the annexed territory of undesirable population groups through deportation, segregation, and murder, I also analyze Nazi Germany's inclusionary policies, Germanization, and assimilation, and compare them to colonial contexts. As such, this book presents a new way of approaching questions on how the history of Nazi Germany's expansion, resettlement, Germanization, and violence can be viewed from a perspective other than a solely National Socialist one.

As a focal point of my study, I have chosen a topic that has not yet been thoroughly analyzed from a comparative standpoint: the resettlement (*Umsiedlung*) of ethnic Germans (*Volksdeutsche*)—groups of individuals of German descent who had lived within Eastern Europe until the outbreak of the Second World War. The ethnic Germans were the new settlers of the annexed *Reichsgaue* and their arrival laid the foundations for the establishment of German society and culture. To accommodate them, the German authorities evicted thousands of Jewish and non-Jewish Poles from their homes and businesses. I demonstrate how the Nazi regime and its expansion and settlement of territory captured the attention of thousands of Reich Germans (*Reichsdeutsche*, Germans born in the *Altreich*, or pre-1939 Germany) who came to the *Reichsgaue* to care for and guide ethnic German resettlers (*Umsiedler*) while also becoming the German cultural backbone of the settlement areas. I consider not only the fantasies that informed and justified Nazi Germany's expansionary mission but also the realities and complications of establishing a society stratified along racial lines.[10]

By investigating the inclusion of certain population groups into the fledgling German society and the establishment of German rule and culture within the *Reichsgaue*, I highlight the dual relationship between population inclusion and societal creation and exclusion and destruction. Similar to colonial expansionary missions, Nazi Germany planned to eradicate Poland, its culture, and its people by destroying and then replacing them. As such, the book highlights the two-sided nature of Nazi population policy—on one side, the weakening and attempted destruction of a country and society and, on the other side, the reshaping of these elements into the image of the conqueror. I aim to show how it is the duality and complexity, which was inseparable from Nazi Germany's expansion and rule that can best be aligned with stereotypical patterns of colonialism. By presenting how the Nazi regime was similar in its approach to population management and the establishment of society, I highlight how Nazi Germany's actions during the Second World War can be integrated into other fields of historical enquiry and show how studies on National Socialism and the Holocaust can benefit from an awareness of the significant comparative overlaps.

Resettlement and the Annexed Territories

As mentioned, this book brings together numerous topics and, as such, it builds on a wide range of historical research. In terms of places and times, the book bridges Nazi Germany, Poland, the *Kaiserreich* (German Empire, 1871–1918), and various other historical colonial examples from around the globe. Simultaneously, it touches on the debate surrounding the comparative areas between Nazi expansion and the Holocaust and colonial rule and violence. The key case study within this book is the resettlement of ethnic Germans in the *Reichsgaue* Wartheland and Danzig-West Prussia. Nazi Germany's goal of regaining the German territory lost in the Treaty of Versailles (1919), and controlling newly conquered Polish territory, was not only planned to be achieved through military conquest but also the settlement of the land by suitable Germans. The majority of these German settlers were ethnic Germans who were living in areas such as the Baltic States, Volhynia, and Bukovina before the war. Through the resettlement policy named *Heim ins Reich* (Home to the Reich), ethnic Germans could voluntarily apply for resettlement in the newly annexed territories in Poland.[11] The resettlement policy was overseen by the *Reichskommissariat für die Festigung deutschen Volkstums* (Reich Commission for the Consolidation of Germandom, RKFDV), headed by Heinrich Himmler.[12]

The resettlements began in late October 1939 and throughout the war, almost one million ethnic Germans were resettled. Thousands of Reich German men and women flocked to the annexed territories to assist with the resettlement. As highlighted by Elizabeth Harvey, women played a particularly crucial role in the care and guidance of the resettlers.[13] They often worked in roles, such as teachers, nurses, and settlement advisors (*Ansiedlerbetreuerinnen*), which allowed them intimate access to the resettlers' homes and private lives. As such, they were responsible for the cultural "re-education" of the new ethnic Germans who had spent years living in foreign territories and therefore often no longer spoke the German language nor were they familiar with German culture and traditions.

In addition to racially screening ethnic German resettlers, a topic explored in the in-depth study by Andreas Strippel, the resettlement allowed for the racial screening of local ethnic Germans who had already been living in the Polish territories.[14] Isabel Heinemann has demonstrated how the *Rasse-und Siedlungshauptamt der SS* (SS Race and Settlement Main Office, RuSHA) acted as a key institution in the racial re-categorization in western Poland and how the criteria used to judge an individual's inclusion into the Reich were the same used to judge who would be excluded. The RuSHA racial "experts" work thus had a significant impact on not only the German rule of the territory but also on the application of population policy on the ground.[15] Non-Jewish Poles who could adequately prove their political loyalty or German descent were eligible to apply for the *Deutsche Volksliste* (German Peoples' List, DVL), a set of categories that determined the German applicant's and their family's status, or lack of status. Through studies such as Gerhard Wolf's *Ideologie und Herrschaftsrationalität*, the sheer extent of the DVL and the German authorities' efforts to demographically reconfigure the *Reichsgaue* can clearly be seen—the German authorities recognized millions of people as German based on supposed racial or political criteria. As Wolf has argued, the DVL was "the largest assimilation project in modern German history."[16]

Interestingly, although the inclusion of certain population groups through such methods as assimilation was a key part of colonial and imperial rule, this aspect of Nazi Germany's annexation and control of annexed Poland has largely not been placed within such wider analytical frameworks.[17] In the majority of studies, Nazi Germany's inclusionary policies are viewed solely within the boundaries of National Socialist racial ideology; however, this book abandons such a one-sided view. Though it investigates Nazi Germany's inclusion of certain population groups as a fundamental part of the German endeavor to secure space and to provide supposed racial security, this book widens the analytical perspective and demonstrates that the National Socialist inclusionary policies operated, both in terms of the fantasy of how they *should* work and the reality of how they *did* work, in similar ways to inclusion in colonial contexts. Two elements that linked strongly to the fantasy of German rule in Poland are what I term the German self-conceived "civilizing" or "humanitarian mission" directed toward ethnic Germans, particularly the resettlers from further east. The notion of civilizing and humanitarian missions in colonial contexts is undoubtedly highly problematic and laced with ambiguity.[18] Such missions were used as the legitimization for colonial expansion and policies—implementing cultural hierarchies, promoting Western Europe as the beacon of civilization, and ultimately justifying the destruction of indigenous languages, cultures, and traditions. Within this book, I often use the adjectives "self-conceived" or "self-understood" before the terms civilizing or humanitarian missions to illustrate the complexity of the concepts and to demonstrate they were often a part of Nazi Germany's propaganda or fantasies of expansion.

Both the Wartheland and Danzig-West Prussia were significant areas for Nazi Germany's territorial expansion during the Second World War; in addition to the ethnic Germans' resettlement, which was planned to transform the ownership of the territory for years to come, the rapid escalation of the mistreatment of the native Polish population occurred in the Wartheland and Danzig-West Prussia. Both non-Jewish and Jewish Poles were, in different ways, victims of Nazi Germany's territorial acquisition and domination and efforts to racially restructure society. The German authorities forcibly removed members of the Polish population from the *Reichsgaue* whom they considered to be a racial or political threat, often simply by being Polish; their removal provided the much-needed space for the resettlers to whom the German authorities assigned the vacated homes, farms, and businesses. Against this background of eviction and settlement, the Germans legally subjugated, economically exploited, and segregated non-Jewish and Jewish Poles, they deported them to other Polish territories or murdered them by starvation, shooting, or in gas vans.[19] This mistreatment occurred at the same time as, and often close to, ethnic German resettlement—as certain individuals' lives irrevocably changed for the worst, others embarked on their promised better life as Germans. The *Reichsgau* Wartheland was a particularly crucial location in the perpetration of the Holocaust as highlighted by historians such as Michael Alberti and Ingo Loose;[20] here, the German authorities first expanded their murder program from psychiatric hospital patients to Polish Jews and Sinti and Roma at Chełmno nad Nerem (Kulmhof an der Nehr). The gas vans used at Chełmno, not far from where ethnic and Reich Germans went about their daily business, marked the beginning of the targeted extermination of Polish Jews, before also impacting Jews from other European states, such as Germany, who were brought from the Łódź (Litzmannstadt) ghetto to their deaths.

The *Kaiserreich*, Continental and Overseas Imperialism, and Nazi Germany's Colonial Planning

Within the historical debate on the potential crossovers between Nazi violence and colonial violence, German colonialism during the *Kaiserreich* and the German Army's perpetration of genocide against the Herero and Nama people in German South West Africa were notable starting points within the debate over two decades ago. Jürgen Zimmerer's work has provided much impetus for other areas of investigation; he argued through numerous articles, collectively published in his 2011 book *Von Windhuk nach Auschwitz*, that direct lines of influence existed from the *Kaiserreich* to Nazi rule in Eastern Europe and the Holocaust. Zimmerer's main thesis points to the German Army's perpetration of genocide against the Herero and Nama, which resulted in the deaths of up to 100,000 Herero and 10,000 Nama, as a genocide not only broke the taboo of mass killing but also created a "reservoir of knowledge" from which the Nazis could draw ideas.[21] Although Zimmerer avoids using the continuity thesis as a simple, mono-causal explanation for Nazi Germany's perpetration of genocide, he does place the roots of the Holocaust within Germany's previous experience of colonialism in Africa. Additionally, some of Zimmerer's articles published in *Von Windhuk nach Auschwitz* highlight parallels to broader patterns of colonial violence and highlight how "structural similarities" between colonialism and National Socialism go further than continuity from the Herero and Nama Wars (1904–8) and can be observed in Nazi Germany's expansionary and exterminatory policies.[22]

The debate on the influence of the *Kaiserreich*'s overseas colonialism on Nazi Germany's expansion became influential in the early historical debate. However, the empirical evidence that policies in German South West Africa directly influenced or informed Nazi Germany's policies in Poland, whether by personal or institutional continuities or by knowledge transfers, remains scant. Such limitations of the direct continuity thesis have previously been discussed by historians such as Birthe Kundrus, Sybille Steinbacher, Robert Gerwarth, and Stephan Malinowski.[23] This book does not deny the important historical impact the *Kaiserreich* had on Nazi Germany; nevertheless, it diverges from the argument of direct continuities and instead focuses on colonial similarities to Nazi Germany's population policies, practices, and the problems it faced during its rule of annexed Poland. Despite this study's divergence from direct continuities, the *Kaiserreich* still plays a key role in this book, but in a much more flexible, transcendent way. I explore the *Kaiserreich* in line with other scholars who have demonstrated that the *Kaiserreich*'s colonial period, albeit short and previously often eclipsed by research on Nazi Germany, was significant in its own right based on its shaping of Germany and German society as a whole. For example, Dirk van Laak has demonstrated the role of German infrastructural development and its relationship to German perceptions of colonial Africa.[24] Van Laak argues the impact of German overseas colonialism on Germany was increased due to the different generations of Germans who had contact, either first-hand or through education, with the colonies. Similarly, Susanne Zantop persuasively argued that the development of colonial fantasies in Germany occurred before the reality of the attainment of overseas territories.²⁵ Through history books and literary fiction, Germans were able to engage with colonialism without ever having to possess colonies. The desire for colonial adventure based on imaginary encounters thus shaped the German perception of not only the overseas colonial possession but also their perceptions of race. The contributions to Birthe Kundrus' edited collection *Phantasiereiche* have additionally highlighted the influence of Germany's possession of colonial overseas territory and Germany's continual dream of empire-building during the *Kaiserreich*, the Weimar era, and the Third Reich.²⁶

Another important area of influence on Nazi Germany was the *Kaiserreich*'s perception and policy toward Poland before the First World War and the continuation of such perceptions during the interwar period. The perceived threat of Eastern European expansion into German territory and fear of the "Polonization" of Germans grew after unification in 1871. The Prussian government pursued *Kulturkampf* (culture struggle) policies, aiming at the integration of the Prussian Polish minority and preventing the growth of the Polish language and culture. In 1885, Prussian authorities began to expel numerous Poles who did not hold German or Prussian citizenship from Prussian territory and from 1886, the *Königlich Preußische Ansiedlungskommission in den Provinzen Westpreußen und Posen* (known as the Prussian Settlement Commission) began attempts to settle Prussia with more Germans to weaken Polish nationalism and to stem German immigration from the east to western industrial areas.²⁷ Such policies both utilized and strengthened notions of Polish primitiveness and unsuitability to rule while contrasting the Poles with the supposedly superior Germans, thus revealing colonial perceptions of land and people. As Christoph Kienemann has shown in his study of printed sources such as scientific journals, newspapers, and magazines, throughout the duration of the *Kaiserreich*, German publications regularly framed Eastern Europe as colonial territory and this perception influenced policies related to the east.²⁸

After Germany's defeat in 1918 and the end of the *Kaiserreich*, Poland continued to be seen as a suitable area for German expansion by numerous different research groups and was framed in similar ways to the overseas colonies, both in terms of territorial reclamation after the Treaty of Versailles and expansion into new territories outside of the former *Kaiserreich* borders. The development of the academic discipline *Ostforschung* (Eastern Research) during the interwar period is also key to understanding Nazi Germany's later ideas about Poland and the East. Through such academic fields as history, population studies, ethnography, and geography, *Ostforschung* academics attempted to legitimize calls for the reclamation of German territory in Poland and German expansion further east. As demonstrated by Michael Burleigh, the *Ostforschung* academics made significant contributions to the Nazi regime's ideology and policies. Burleigh sheds light on the various areas of influence that the academics and their studies had on justifications for German control in the East, ethnic reordering, and the organization and placement of ethnic German settlers.²⁹ These academic justifications additionally led to the formation of distinct policies in Poland and the German-occupied East. Ingo Haar, Götz Aly, and Susanne Heim have similarly pointed to *Ostforschung* as a legitimizing force behind anti-Semitic policies within the regime.³⁰ *Ostforschung* not only provided the foundational information for encouraging German action in Poland and Eastern Europe, but it also contributed to the supposedly scientific or scholarly evidence behind Nazi Germany's expansion and racial reordering.

Despite Nazi Germany's lack of overseas colonial expansion, the regime's planning of future colonial policy and the perceived value it placed on overseas territories is another topic that has gained popularity as a research topic in recent years.[31] For example, Karsten Linne analyzed National Socialist organizations' plans regarding economic, social, and labor policies in the desired future colonies. He maintains that, despite some similarities between the colonial organizations' plans with that of the plans for expansion in Eastern Europe, there were also inherent differences.[32] Willeke Sandler has focused on public culture and the cultural legacies of German overseas colonialism within the Third Reich and provides a comprehensive analysis of how overseas colonialists navigated their role within Nazi Germany.[33] Such studies, among others, have demonstrated apart from any arguments on the *Kaiserreich*'s continuity or influence, Nazi Germany's overseas planning was still significant within German society at the time.

Nazi Germany ultimately concentrated its expansionary efforts on Eastern Europe and as such, the German expansion and rule there has largely become the most common territory to be investigated when searching for potential comparisons to colonialism. The two geographical end goals of German expansion, Eastern Europe and Africa, are often framed within secondary literature as having been in opposition to one another. Although this book will primarily focus on Eastern Europe, specifically Poland, a particular merit of this study is, as well as investigating Nazi Germany's territorial acquisition to the east, it also integrates analysis of Nazi Germany's plans for reclaiming former German overseas territories. I adopt a new approach that combines the examination of *Ostforschung* publications, a topic that has not yet been examined from a colonial standpoint, and publications on German overseas expansion. Through examining discourses produced in these publications, I highlight how overseas colonialism provided familiar tropes and justifications that could also be applied to Nazi Germany's eastern expansion and ultimately, to the ethnic German resettlement in annexed Poland. Though Nazi Germany only implemented its plans in Eastern Europe, this book shows the German expansionary fantasies, regardless of the location, often coincided with one another.

Frameworks of Violence and the Third Reich

The Holocaust has often been considered, by historians and the public alike, as a unique event that was as incomparable, as it was incomprehensible.[34] However, since the late 1980s, as demonstrated by the *Historikerstreit* and later publications and arguments such as those by Zimmerer discussed above,[35] scholars have increasingly begun to challenge notions of Holocaust singularity or uniqueness in both the academic and public sphere by comparing it to or contextualizing it with other examples of mass violence. The various contributors to the debate represented different institutions and historical fields, and used a variety of approaches, but the thrust of the main argument revolved around the basic question: was the Holocaust a special or more extreme type of genocide, given its scale, effectiveness, incomprehensibility, and victim group? Scholars on one side of the debate supported such an interpretation, while scholars on the other side argued that the Holocaust can be understood as an example of genocide and thus can be compared to common patterns of violence. Due to the longevity and ongoing nature of the debate, I will not endeavor to give a complete overview of all the publications that have contributed to new understandings of how the Holocaust can be analyzed. Instead, in the following paragraphs, I will highlight some of the main approaches used by historians in the past and most recently that are particularly relevant to this study.[36]

Moving away from arguments of continuity between the *Kaiserreich* and the Third Reich, historians such as A. Dirk Moses, Dan Stone, and Donald Bloxham have argued that the Holocaust must be understood in terms of wider concepts of European empire-building, racism, and violence.[37] For example, Dan Stone has highlighted the benefits of viewing the Holocaust from a comparative genocide standpoint. He argues that although the Holocaust did not look like the majority of other cases of genocides, "the Holocaust was genocide, and it shares many features with genocides that have occurred elsewhere."[38] For Stone, the acknowledgement of the Holocaust as a product of wider traditions of Western violence heightens our understanding of the specific role that Jews played within the Nazi imagination rather than diminishing it.[39] In his recent book, Moses illustrates the problems inherent in the concept of "genocide" and instead proposes "permanent security"—the driving force behind anticipatory violence perpetrated against civilians by states attempting to make themselves indestructible to threats. This argument further links to discussions on understanding the Holocaust as part of broader attempts by states to remove those whom they perceived as internal or external threats.[40] Pascal Grosse has convincingly argued that instead of seeking continuities, historians should recognize German colonialism and Nazism as part of the same conceptual framework in which other European colonial powers can be included. This conceptual framework can be understood as one that called for a racial ordering of the state and a desire for expansion. Grosse concludes, "German colonialism was less a prerequisite for the emergence of National Socialist racial policies than an expression of the same intellectual eugenicist model at an earlier time and in a different historical setting."[41]

In his book, *Hitler's Empire*, Mark Mazower emphasizes Hitler's role as an "empire-builder" and argues elements of Nazi Germany's empire, such as settlement, collaboration, opposition, and violence were also elements of empire building.[42] He argues that the constructive element of Hitler's empire-building should not be outweighed by the destructive element because for Mazower, the "war against the Jews" grew from the "war for the Germans." Although Mazower ultimately does not focus on anti-Semitism or Jews, he does recognize the Nazi brand of empire as unusual due to its restrictive defining of nationalism.[43] In the similarly titled publication, *Nazi Empire*, Shelly Baranowski also argues Nazi Germany can be located within wider imperial frameworks, including that of the *Kaiserreich*. She argues that imperial competition and security played into the German creation of empire, albeit without "the pretense of a 'civilizing mission.'"[44] Roberta Pergher and Mark Roseman have argued that the Holocaust was the first, and potentially the only, "pan-imperial genocide" as it was pursued throughout the entire empire including satellite states the imperial dimensions of the Holocaust are unusual because the Nazi breed of imperialism was also unusual.[45] Robert Gerwarth and Stephan Malinowski highlighted how the common colonial combination of "development" and "force" is all but impossible to find in Nazi Germany's rule in Poland and ultimately argued that "National Socialism and the German war of annihilation constituted a break with European traditions of colonialism rather than a continuation."[46]

Since the heightened academic debate's initial beginnings in the late 1990s and early 2000s, comparisons, overlaps, and intersections between the history of the Third Reich and other genocides or acts of mass violence have increasingly been examined in ways that have moved the focus from the Nazi regime's aims and actions. Instead, the occasionally interdisciplinary research focuses on broader viewpoints and research fields in seeking comparative or integrative examples. Approaching the debate from a literature and memory studies viewpoint, Michael Rothberg demonstrated how the collective memory of the Holocaust interconnects with the memory of other traumatic events, such as decolonization, and how the memory of one can borrow from or inform the other, and vice versa. He suggests, as opposed to understanding the collective memory of the Holocaust as competing with collective memories of other events, "we consider memory as *multidirectional:* as subject to ongoing negotiation, cross-referencing, and borrowing; as productive and not privative."[47]

Rebecca Jinks has demonstrated how the Holocaust informed and structured representations and understandings of other twentieth-century genocides by examining literature, film, and photography.[48] Kitty Millet has produced a rare example of an analysis of Holocaust victims' experiences and victims of colonization or enslavement, while Edward Kissi has recently published on African reactions and interpretations, among both colonized and sovereign people, to Nazism, the Second World War, and the Holocaust.[49] Roni Mikel-Arieli's monograph on Holocaust memory in South Africa also shows how the prism of colonialism and Apartheid shaped Holocaust memorialization within a racial state.[50] The fourth volume of the European Holocaust Studies series, titled *Colonial Paradigms of Violence: Comparative Analysis of the Holocaust, Genocide, and Mass Killing* has recently combined numerous approaches to analyzing the entanglements between the Holocaust and colonial histories from a variety of different perspectives and demonstrates how the entanglements not only exist within the academic sphere but also the public and political ones.[51]

Undoubtedly, comparisons between Nazi expansion and the Holocaust and colonialism and colonial violence have become more commonplace, and indeed more widely accepted. However, despite the longevity of the debate on comparisons, the large majority of books, conference papers, and ongoing research on the history of Nazi Germany's expansion and violence, perhaps 80 to 90 percent, do not focus on or mention potential colonial similarities, let alone analyze topics outside of a National Socialist specific sphere. This book's thesis, that Nazi Germany's annexation of western Poland, its rule there, and the population policies it enacted can be viewed from a colonial perspective, may seem indisputable to some readers. Conversely, for others, the notion of understanding Nazi Germany within wider comparative frameworks is still highly contestable or occasionally seen as controversial. This is especially relevant to discussions on the topic of the singularity of the Holocaust, which has dominated the debates.

Evidence of how some historians still staunchly reject comparative analysis can perhaps best be seen in public debates that occurred during the research and writing of this book. In May 2020, Achille Mbembe, the Cameroon-born philosopher and political theorist, was subject to accusations of anti-Semitism and relativizing the Holocaust based on his earlier work, which drew comparisons between South African Apartheid and Nazi Germany's crimes.[52] In his 2021 *Geschichte der Gegenwart* contribution titled "The German Catechism," Moses strongly criticized Germany's culture of Holocaust remembrance, which he argues promotes the theory of Holocaust singularity.[53] The contribution caused a media furor in Germany and in response, historians such as Saul Friedländer and Götz Aly publically argued through the medium of German-language mainstream media against comparative analysis on the basis that the Holocaust was "fundamentally" different from other historical crimes.[54]

Similarly, within the academic sphere challenges against comparison have been raised. For example, Steffen Klävers's recent book, *Decolonizing Auschwitz?* challenges Zimmerer, Moses, and Rothberg's arguments. Klävers maintains that the Holocaust is unique as it was an expression of "redemptive" anti-Semitism. According to Klävers, this particular uniqueness cannot be adequately captured within continuity or comparability theories and thus he questions how helpful such theories can be to studies of the Holocaust and anti-Semitism.[55] In a contribution to the journal *Vierteljahrshefte für Zeitgeschichte*, Frank Bajohr and I argued against the scandalization of comparative analysis of the Holocaust as seen in the mainstream media and in certain academic circles. In the article, we demonstrated how comparing aspects of the Holocaust and Nazi violence to other contexts is a wholly valid research approach, while simultaneously recognizing that the arguments for acknowledging the specifics of the Holocaust were equally legitimate.[56] As Michael Wildt highlighted in his final lecture at the Humboldt University in Berlin, "the Holocaust loses none of its horror when placed in the context of a European and global history of violence."[57]

A significant criticism of studies that do address colonial similarities from historians who disagree with or are skeptical of a comparative approach is that such studies often lack nuance. Often, the particular intricacies of Nazi policies and actions are glossed over and certain points, such as the colonial rhetoric and language used by leading figures like Adolf Hitler, are portrayed as evidence of influences or linkages; yet, these points are not further analyzed to see if they had any actual impact on practices on the ground.[58] This study aims to change this by offering a nuanced investigation into which elements of Nazi Germany's expansion, population policies, and the Holocaust can be investigated outside of the usual thematic, geographical, or chronological limitations without denying specificities or leaning on the continuity argument.

Moving away from the generalizations that have often plagued the debate, this book highlights the possibilities of careful comparative analysis by using specific colonial examples and drawing on concepts within the literature on colonial history, not generalized concepts. Similarly, in this study, when analyzing annexed Poland through a colonial lens, I distinguish between the National Socialist fantasy of rule and population reordering and the complex reality of what actually took place. In relation to Nazi violence and the Holocaust, as opposed to denying the specifics, this study shows how comparative analysis can better highlight these areas of specificity without cancelling out the areas of similarity. By using the approach of viewing elements of Nazi Germany's expansion, resettlement, population policies, and violence through a colonial lens, I do not attempt to in some way make the history of colonialism appear more significant or relevant. Instead, I fully recognize that the history of colonialism, and indeed colonial violence, deserves to be researched in its own right and, aside from any comparisons with Nazi Germany or the Holocaust, such research is extremely important.[59] Its importance not only lies within academia but also in understanding societal, political, and institutional structures existing to this day that were influenced by colonialism, imperialism, and racism. As such this book does not endeavor to detract any attention from studies of colonial history nor does it attempt to argue that research on National Socialism is less or more significant than such studies.

Approach, Place Names, Terminology, and Sources

As well as building on the previous research within the debate, as mentioned, this book seeks to offer new insights by moving away from a sole focus on the Holocaust and violence and instead, exploring potential overlaps between colonialism and Nazi Germany's expansion and establishment of rule more broadly. Although the search for elements of the Holocaust that can or cannot be compared to colonial contexts will not be a central emphasis of the book, the topic informs the background of my research and comes to the forefront of the analysis within the investigation of Nazi Germany's methods and policies of exclusion in Chapter 4. Within the book, I interconnect the *Kaiserreich* and the interwar period with the Third Reich and also locations such as Nazi Germany, Poland, Eastern Europe and Africa with other colonial and imperial territories. More specifically, although I do focus on official German policy and processes, I also explore examples of individuals working within the system, offering a selection of "from below" glimpses into how society functioned and how individuals perceived, portrayed, or justified their experiences in annexed Poland. I argue that we can see numerous applicable colonial similarities within many of these perceptions, justifications, and experiences.

To demonstrate such similarities, I draw transnational examples from a variety of colonial situations. The diversity of the examples, in terms of locations and periods, does not dilute the relevance of similarities; rather, it highlights general patterns that were not particular to the Nazi regime. Instead, they were stereotypical methods of inclusion and exclusion used in cases where a foreign power wished to claim and dominate territory and populations. I also engage with the field of colonial and settler colonial studies, particularly concerning racial categorization and the formation of an occupier versus an occupied society.[60]

In the final chapter, I investigate German justifications for expansion further by analyzing literary sources that provided the linguistic reasoning behind Nazi Germany's quest for both overseas and continental space. Broadly speaking, the book highlights the significant link between race and space and demonstrates how both concepts, that is, the ownership of space by the "superior" race, were inseparably linked with one another. I aim to magnify the stories of different population groups who, like in cases of colonial rule, lived side by side within a system that aimed to differentiate them, a system that intended to destroy while simultaneously aiming to rebuild and transform.

The book's main geographical focus is the *Reichsgau* Wartheland (originally called *Reichsgau* Posen until January 1940) and the *Reichsgau* Danzig-West Prussia (a joining of the *Militärbezirk Westpreußen*, or military district West Prussia, the Free City of Danzig and *Regierungsbezirk Westpreußen der preußischen Provinz Ostpreußen*, or administrative district West Prussia of the Province of East Prussia), which were officially annexed as *Reichsgaue* to Nazi Germany in October 1939 (Map 0.1). Although these locations may not seem to be an obvious choice for a study of colonial comparisons given that parts of the Wartheland and Danzig-West Prussia had been *Kaiserreich* territory and therefore German before the Treaty of Versailles, I contend the areas were still perceived and treated as colonial territories.[61] The irredentist beliefs about the reclamation of part of the territories, and their inherent German characteristics, did not contradict the notion of the territories' primitiveness. Rather, just like the former German colonies in Africa, German academics, ideologists, and planners believed the areas and the people living there had deteriorated because of foreign rule; it was thus part of the German mission to save them. Additionally, the Wartheland and Danzig-West Prussia are key locations to this study because it was there where ethnic Germans would be settled, the territory and people would be Germanized, and undesirable population groups would be removed from. As such, the two *Reichsgaue* were the locations of the initial subjugation and, later in the Wartheland, the beginning of the systematic murder of Jews.

Within the book, the terms "colonialism" and "imperialism" appear numerous times. Although similar, the concepts differ in some key ways. I define "colonialism" as a foreign power's political, cultural, and economic rule over a country or colony accompanied by often permanent settlement and exploitation of the area's resources and/or its people.[62] Whereas, I define "imperialism" as a foreign power's political, cultural, or economic rule over a country with the aid of local administration and military force but not always with settlement. As the Nazi regime did not establish an imperial-style administration in the *Reichgaue* Wartheland and Danzig-West Prussia but rather annexed the territories by installing German authorities in power positions and by settling the territory with ethnic and Reich Germans, I use colonialism as the main framework of reference for comparisons.[63] In Chapter 4, when investigating exclusion, I introduce the concept of settler colonialism as the aptest form of colonialism for comparison to the removal of certain non-Jewish and Jewish Poles. Unlike usual forms of colonialism, which relied on the colonized population for labor, settler colonialism functioned through the elimination of the indigenous population, by killing, physical removal, or assimilation, and then their replacement with settlers.[64] The indigenous population was not needed for labor demands in settler colonial systems because the settlers became the primary labor force and, with the passing of time, the new native population.

Map 0.1 Map of the *Reichsgau* Wartheland and *Reichsgau* Danzig-West Prussia, and the surrounding provinces and territories, in March 1940. Source: © Peter Palm, Berlin.

Throughout this book, I use Polish place names and provide the contemporary German name in brackets for the first usage, unless in the case of certain locations, such as camps, which are more commonly referred to by their German names in the historiography, for example, Stutthof (Sztutowo), or when I am quoting directly from or referring to a German-language source. I retain German terms that are still commonly used in scholarship, for example, *Reichsgau* and *Gauleiter* (Gau leader), and provide English translations for the first uses. For less well-known terms, I note the German in the first instance and then use the English translation of the term. Within Nazi Germany's parlance on Poland, and as such within this book, the concept of "the East" frequently occurs. This concept does not refer to a specific geographical place, but it was rather intentionally vague to convey the potential unlimitedness of the territories to which Nazi Germany could expand to.[65] It highlights the mystification of Eastern Europe within Germany and at the same time, the denial of any autonomy or individuality of the places and the people living there—the space was thus generalized and "othered."[66]

The contemporary terms for the various population groups in annexed Poland, ethnic Germans, Reich Germans, and Jews and Poles, are often problematic and were not always exact or clear population divisions. For example, "ethnic German" was a Nazi terminological construction used to identify groups of people who may or may not have identified with the term before September 1939.[67] In the case of local ethnic Germans, those who lived in Poland before the Second World War, were, like the Poles, officially members of the "native" population despite German authorities classifying them as German. Throughout the book, I use the Nazi German population group names for ease of understanding; however, I highlight through deeper analysis that the categories were not always correct, nor why they always rigidly or correctly applied. Regarding the Polish population in the annexed territory, regardless of whether they were Jewish or not, people born in Poland were largely Polish by birth. I attempt to demonstrate the differential treatment that Jewish and non-Jewish Poles received; however, when the differentiation is not needed for making sense of the analysis, I mainly refer to the native population of Poland as Poles.

The book features a variety of different sources from local, regional, and national German and Polish archives and libraries related to the resettlement of ethnic Germans and everyday life in annexed Poland, such as institutional reports, resettlement plans and reports, pamphlets, photographs and films, exhibitions, and newspaper and magazine articles. Although a proportion of the factual information in this book may not be new to the reader, the main focus of the book is not the presentation of previously unknown archival findings. Rather, it is to demonstrate an original, nuanced way of assessing the factual information alongside specific examples of colonialism and thus to show exactly which factors of Nazi Germany's expansion and population policies can be placed within wider frameworks. Shorter investigations of the resettlement of ethnic Germans can be found in many books about Nazi actions in Eastern Europe, usually in a more general sense. The majority of studies that provide an in-depth analysis of sources related to the resettlement in English are older publications, however.[68] Additionally, much of the current literature on the Nazi resettlement of annexed Poland, Germanization policies, and the DVL either does not discuss or occasionally argues against similarities to colonialism.[69]

In addition to official publications and reports, this study also utilizes scientific journals and published non-fiction literature from the time regarding the German aim of acquiring more territory during the *Kaiserreich*, interwar period, and Third Reich. These sources could be viewed as problematic given that many were instruments of propaganda; however, the analysis of such sources demonstrates how the German mentality reflected optimism for the future and reveals the German perceptions of Polish territory, the Poles, and the resettlement efforts. Although I focus on the propaganda related to the German occupation of the territory, I do highlight the problems that occurred in reality. When examining the exclusion of population groups, through their segregation, deportation, and murder, I move away from an investigation of justifications and perceptions and instead focus on the policies and methods of exclusion and the complexities that arose by examining official reports and postwar trial documents.

Structure and Outline

The book is divided into three separate thematic but related parts: Part 1: Looking West? Looking East? investigates the background of Germany's national relationship with overseas expansion and with Poland during the *Kaiserreich* and interwar period. Part 2: The Annexation of Poland and the Restructuring of Society examines the period of the Second World War and the inclusionary and exclusionary policies that occurred in annexed Poland. Part 3: Aligning Overseas and Continental Colonial Aims during the Third Reich explores the span of the Third Reich and therefore temporally overlaps with Part 2. The history of the *Kaiserreich* and Germany's first experience of being an empire and owning overseas territories is discussed first in the book, but this is not in an attempt to demonstrate any kind of direct continuity. Rather, the first chapter establishes the German mindset related to Germany's expansion and perceptions of the neighboring east; it highlights areas that would certainly influence the Nazi regime's ideology.

In Part 1, Chapter 1 briefly describes the acquisition of the *Kaiserreich*'s overseas colonies and demonstrates how the experience of becoming a colonial power impacted Germany. It shows how the memory of overseas colonialism was preserved in the interwar period and sheds light on the relationship between Germany and Poland during the *Kaiserreich* and the years between the two World Wars. The chapter also discusses the German preoccupation with the acquisition of space after the loss of German territory to Poland due to the Treaty of Versailles, the development of *Ostforschung*, and the growth of political groups that also supported German overseas and continental colonial expansion.

Part 2, Chapter 2 explores the case study of the resettlement of ethnic Germans in the *Reichsgaue* Wartheland and Danzig-West Prussia that occurred during the Second World War. Using analysis of such sources as settlement reports, books, pamphlets, and photographs, it argues that there are identifiable similarities between the treatment of ethnic Germans and the treatment of indigenous populations in colonial settings. This chapter explores how ethnic Germans were not always perceived by Reich Germans as "colonizers." Instead, they were often conceptualized as foreigners who had to be adequately Germanized. The chapter also highlights the case of certain non-Jewish Poles who were deemed suitable for assimilation. It argues that the Nazi regime's inclusionary policies and societal stratification, and the problems they created, are comparable to colonial contexts.

Chapter 3 focuses on the experiences of Reich Germans within the settlement areas. It demonstrates how societal elements and the changing infrastructure in Poland began to reflect elements similar to colonial societies. The chapter argues that although Reich Germans were not the sole destined German settlers in Poland, they occupied a place in society that was often akin to traditional colonizers. In addition to their standing within this German societal hierarchy, many Reich Germans understood and legitimized their task in Poland in a comparable way to colonial administrators and facilitators. The chapter highlights that the Nazi occupation of Poland was not devoid of a colonial-style, German self-conceived developmental mission, which, at both an individual and state level, justified the assimilation of ethnic Germans and the modernization of infrastructure in the annexed territories.

Chapter 4 addresses the segregation, subjugation, and removal of the Jewish and non-Jewish Poles by Nazi Germany in the resettlement areas. The chapter highlights how, through a variety of exclusionary policies and methods, German authorities attempted to create a homogenous society by removing population groups whom they considered a racial or political threat. It assesses whether the concept of settler colonialism, which results in the elimination of the indigenous population, is a useful model for analyzing Nazi Germany's exclusion and the Holocaust in annexed Poland. Intersecting with Chapter 2, this chapter explores the links between the inclusionary and exclusionary Nazi policies and the aims behind them. It suggests the primary areas of Nazi Germany's similarity to colonialism can be found in the interlinkage of exclusionary and inclusionary policies and the contradictions and complexities that the implementation of such policies created.

In Part 3, Chapter 5 investigates the place of overseas colonial planning during the Third Reich. It details how the reclamation of the former German colonies in Africa was seen as a legitimate plan in the early years of the Second World War and highlights how overseas colonialism was often promoted as complementary to continental expansion. It details important parallels between the goal of German colonies overseas and the goal of German expansion to the east. Additionally, the chapter combines the themes of the previous chapters and examines the overlaps between two groups of colonial discourses throughout the Nazi regime, one related to German expansion in Africa and one related to German expansion in Poland. "Discourse" can be defined as written or spoken communication that transfers information or knowledge and is formed by a particular type of vocabulary or expressions. Edward W. Said popularized the notion of colonial discourse in terms of the West's relationship to the East or the Orient. He argued that colonial discourse was in itself a form of domination of native populations. For Said, the notion of the Orient "has helped to define Europe (or the West) as its contrasting image, idea, personality, experience."[70] This can equally be applied to European colonial rule and the conceptualization of colonial territories. In Chapter 5, I will specifically interpret colonial discourses as:

> A system of statements that can be made about colonies and colonial peoples, about colonizing powers and about the relationship between these two. It is the system of knowledge and beliefs about the world within which acts of colonisation take place. Although it is generated within the society and cultures of the colonisers, it becomes that discourse within which the colonised may also come to see themselves.[71]

Although colonial discourses are usually based on strong prejudices against the colonized peoples, they still provide a significant insight into the mentality of those who were creating them. While this book will not engage in colonial discourse analysis from a linguistic or an in-depth literary standpoint, it will frame the discourse in terms of the context through which it was produced and the context in which it was then utilized. The colonial discourses investigated largely shed light on rhetoric and justifications related to German expansion and the conceptualization of future fantasies during the Third Reich, both concerning overseas and continental territory. Although the two groups of colonial discourses can be understood as developing separately (albeit simultaneously), the areas of the two groups' overlaps can be located in the Third Reich through their rhetorical and, occasionally, practical expression during the resettlement of ethnic Germans in Poland. The chapter thus highlights that a *Sonderweg* (special path) did not exist from the *Kaiserreich*'s expansion in Africa to Nazi Germany's expansion into Poland. Rather, parallels existed *between* the two groups of colonial discourses during the Third Reich.

Part One

Looking West? Looking East?

1

"A Bigger Germany, It Shall Be!": Germany's Colonial Past in Africa and Poland

In January 1932, the owner of the Berlin company Bildhauer Möbius wrote a letter to the *Deutsche Kolonialgesellschaft* (German Colonial Society, DKG) branch in Frankfurt. Herr Möbius noted that, as a member of the DKG and the creator of other colonial monuments, he would like to offer his services for the creation of a bronze commemoration plaque. The plaque would specifically commemorate the fiftieth anniversary of the founding of the DKG, and he suggested it could be placed in the meeting room of the DKG's headquarters in Berlin if the Frankfurt branch were not interested in having it. He proposed that the bigger branches could pay a contribution to the costs and, in recognition of the current "time of need," he would only charge the cost price.[1] In response, the DKG wrote to its various regional divisions requesting if they would have the means to contribute money for the creation of such a plaque. In May 1932, the head of the DKG regional division in North Rhine-Westphalia, Ludwig Pieper, replied that he had not yet received replies from the branches within his area. His letter was headed with an illustration of a map of Africa, which had the former German colonies highlighted. The illustration stated; "2,700,000 quadrat kilometres (more than five times bigger than the Motherland), German colonies are waiting for us! They are waiting for you!" Pieper ended his letter with a very thematically specific sign-off: "*Mit kolonialdeutschen Grüßen*" or "with colonial German regards."[2]

The topic of the fiftieth anniversary of the founding of the DKG was a popular one among the society in 1932 as they planned for an anniversary event to take place between October 13 and 17. Such celebrations may seem insignificant when viewed in isolation; however, when placed into a wider context, some interesting points can be observed. By 1932, Germany had been without African colonies for thirteen years and, having lost the First World War and experiencing an economically devastating interwar period, a return to an overseas empire in Africa seemed unlikely. In 1933, only a year later, Hitler would be appointed Chancellor (*Reichskanzler*) of Germany, and he would lead the country in a colonial-style expansion into Poland and further into Eastern Europe. As a result of this expansion, the annexation of territories to the east, and the violence perpetrated against the native populations of Poland and Eastern Europe, the Nazi regime remains firmly associated with its attempts to create an empire in Europe, not in Africa.

Given the strong Eastern European focus of Nazi Germany's later expansionary endeavors, why was the topic of the German colonies in Africa still under discussion in 1932? How, but also why, had a society dedicated to a German colonialism that no longer existed survived after 1919? This chapter will explore Germany's first experience of ownership but also loss of empire during the *Kaiserreich*. It investigates what impact owning and losing territory both overseas and within Europe had on Germany and the political culture at the time. The chapter will attempt to understand how and why the issue of expansion, and also the memory of the former empire, was enshrined into the German public's psyche during the interwar period and how this related to former and planned future territories in both Africa and Poland. The chapter will highlight individuals, groups, and institutions that attempted to propose solutions to interwar Germany's problems. Depending on the specific case, these individuals, groups, and institutions promoted either the reclamation of Germany's overseas colonies or Germany's continental expansion eastwards. Occasionally, groups and institutions promoted both forms of colonialism and blurred the lines between Germany's overseas and continental enlargement. Ultimately, the chapter describes the shadow the *Kaiserreich* cast on Germany to demonstrate the environment in which the National Socialist Party was founded and highlight the political discussions and ideology that circulated in Germany before 1933.

Introduction to Empire: The *Kaiserreich's* Colonial Expansion

Until the 1880s, Germany had no strong tradition of colonial expansion, and as a result, it did not possess any official colonies.[3] The German Chancellor Otto von Bismarck had declared on numerous occasions that he was opposed to large-scale overseas expansion due to the possible financial risks and threats to Germany's foreign policy.[4] Despite the official stance, Africa did not remain uncharted territory for Germans. German explorers and geographers, such as Karl Klaus von der Decken, the first European to attempt to climb Mount Kilimanjaro, Carl Peters and Gerhard Rohlfs became increasingly well-known due to their colonial careers in Africa.[5] Their travels and resulting publications recounted their experiences and helped increase the German public's awareness of Europeans exploring the African continent.[6] In addition to individuals, various missionary societies had long been established in Africa before the German unification of 1871. For example, the *Rheinische Missionsgesellschaft* (Rhenish Missionary Society) had been working in South West Africa since 1842, the *Berliner Missionsgesellschaft* (Berlin Missionary Society) also sent missionaries to South Africa in the 1830s, and the *Evangelische Missionsgesellschaft für Deutsch-Ostafrika* (Evangelical Missionary Society for German East Africa) was founded there in 1886.[7] In 1884, the *Norddeutsche Mission* (Bremen Mission) established a "missionary colony" along the coastline of where present-day Namibia and South Africa are located.[8] In addition to their aims regarding the development of Christianity in Africa, colonial societies also extensively disseminated news of their work in Germany through apologia, theoretical, and theological literature, and accounts of missionary activity.⁹ Through such material, the missionary society's work, which was based on the ideology of spreading Western religion, culture, and civilization to the native population, was available for both the German political and public spheres.

Similarly, the involvement of various merchants and trading companies on the African continent was similarly influential in spreading awareness of colonialism among Germans in the period before Germany acquired colonies given that trade demonstrated the potential for viable economic opportunities. Hanseatic merchant families had already founded trade links before German unification; for example, in 1866, Hamburg had a global network of 279 consular outposts in various locations around the world.¹⁰ Trading companies such as C. Woermann and Oloff & Sohn also operated along the African coast. By 1884, C. Woermann, the owner of the well-known *Afrikahaus* in Hamburg, owned seven trading posts in Liberia, five in Cameroon, and twelve located to the south of the Congo. Their success in importing goods from Africa, and the money such trade brought, was used as an argument by colonial enthusiasts such as Rohlfs for German colonial territory.¹¹

Although Germany initially did not have overseas territories before 1884, Susanne Zantop has demonstrated that colonial fantasies were present in Germany in the time leading up to the empire's creation. These colonial fantasies helped to create a type of pre-empire colonial culture in Germany. At the time, this culture was not impinged upon by any actual colonial action and was therefore bereft of reality. Zantop points out that this was a crucial part of German colonial fantasies at this time as Germans could create their ideal colonial empire and rectify other European empires' mistakes within a purely imaginary realm.¹² These fantasies were expressed and fostered in the pages of scientific and philosophical journals and books, and in works of fictional popular literature. Through an investigation of the Native American characters in Friedrich Gerstacker's books, Nicole Grewling has also highlighted how Germans were portrayed as more humane than their European neighbors in terms of their interactions with natives. Although the Native Americans were occasionally depicted as having admirable characteristics such as honesty and loyalty, the Germans were still shown as morally superior. Grewling argues that through fictional colonial literature, Germany could create a positive self-image of itself amid its struggle with foreign enemies and domestic problems after unification.¹³

In the early 1880s, several German colonial societies were formed, which also aimed at winning public support for colonial expansion and compelling Bismarck to begin colonial acquisition. One of the first colonial societies was the *Deutscher Kolonialverein* (German Colonial Association), which was created in 1882 in Frankfurt am Main. Two years later, the *Gesellschaft für Deutsche Kolonisation* (Society for German Colonization) was founded by Carl Peters. The founding manifesto explained that, due to the lack of German overseas colonies, Germans were emigrating to territories belonging to other nations. Thus, Germans were "foreigners on foreign land" despite the strength of the *Kaiserreich* and its position as "a leading power" on the European continent.¹⁴ In 1887, the two societies merged and became the *Deutsche Kolonialgesellschaft* (German Colonial Society, DKG) based in Berlin. The DKG's aims included: "to turn the national effort towards German colonization," "to encourage and support German-national colonizing projects," and "to maintain and strengthen the economic and intellectual connection of Germans abroad with the Fatherland."[15] By April 1898, the DKG had just over 24,000 members.[16] Although the DKG, would become one of the most prominent colonial societies, many others sprung up in the early years of Germany's colonial expansion. For example, the *Afrikanisher Verein* (African Association) was founded in 1893 and the *Nachtigal-Gesellschaft für vaterländische Afrikaforschung* (Nachtigal Society for Fatherland's African Research) in 1894.[17] As well as releasing newsletters, publishing in journals and newspapers, and holding events and meetings to attempt to raise awareness of German colonial expansion, the societies also raised money to supplement the purchase of territories abroad.

Despite Bismarck's initial reluctance, Germany ultimately acquired an overseas colonial empire within an extremely short period while Bismarck was still in power. Bismarck's change in policy regarding colonial expansion is a topic that has raised questions for historians due to the seemingly complete abandonment of his initial beliefs. Although various reasons have been suggested for this change of policy, one of the most widespread theories is that Bismarck sought to bring Germany in line with France in the hope that shared colonial interests and a shared interest in limiting English power would inhibit the chances of France taking revenge on Germany after the German victory in the Franco-Prussian War between 1870 and 1871.[18] On May 26, 1884, Bismarck announced that territories in South West Africa (present-day Namibia), which belonged to the merchant Adolf Lüderitz, would come under the "protection" of Germany. On July 5, 1884, Togoland (present-day Togo) also became a protectorate of the German Empire after Gustav Nachtigal, the German commissioner in West Africa, signed a treaty with a local chief. As protectorates, Germany indirectly ruled the two territories, but local governments and colonial organizations administered them. In November 1884, the Berlin Conference (also known as the West Africa Conference) took place after thirteen representatives of European nations were called to Berlin by Bismarck. The conference created a unified policy on European colonization and trade in Africa and was the formal beginning of the "Scramble for Africa." The conference ended in February 1885, and it resulted in the implementation of the principle of effective occupation. This meant European powers could gain colonial territories if they effectively occupied them; for example, if they created an administration or made treaties with indigenous African tribes.

Following the conference, in December 1884, Germany established official colonial rule over Cameroon (Kamerun). New Guinea and Samoa became additional German protectorates in 1884 and 1900, respectively. Within a matter of years, Germany had thus gone from having no colonial possessions, and no official desire to have any, to becoming a fledgling colonial empire. By 1904, the German overseas territorial possessions were approximately five times as large as Germany: approximately 2.5 million square kilometers.[19] Although the empire had significantly expanded, the German colonies largely remained as trade areas and not significant German settlement zones. By 1914, the white settler population of Togo was a mere 386 people while 1,871 lived in Cameroon and 5,336 in German East Africa. The largest settler colony was in German South West Africa, which had a white population of 14,830.[20] As the settlement figures indicate, German citizens apparently did not reciprocate the enthusiasm of colonial societies for colonial settlement.

However, these figures do not signify that an awareness of the German colonial overseas territories was absent in everyday society and culture in Germany. The possession of overseas territories, the supposed responsibility of caring for colonial subjects, the settling of colonies, and the continuation of colonial expansion for the empire's preservation were initially new concepts in the German public's psyche. The national possession of overseas territories allowed the German population to be exposed to certain elements of colonial ideology and colonial practices, regardless of the low numbers of Germans who were settling in the African territories. The evidence of Germany's new position as a colonial power and the development of a colonial culture that matched this new status can be observed throughout the *Kaiserreich* in a variety of different aspects of German society.

In 1896, the *Deutsche Kolonialausstellung* (German Colonial Exhibition) opened on May 1 in Berlin. The Colonial Exhibition, a part of the *Berliner Gewerbeausstellung* (Berlin Trade Exposition), was the result of the DKG's desire to transform their tactics from political lobbying for new colonial acquisitions to appealing directly to the German public. The Colonial Exhibition aimed to immerse its visitors in the colonies without leaving Berlin. It displayed life-size reconstructions of villages from places such as Togo and New Guinea. The reconstructed villages were populated by indigenous people who would act out their daily activities. In the book *Deutschland und seine Kolonien im Jahre 1896*, which reported on the exhibition, a contributor proudly noted one could say for the first time in Europe, that never had so many native people from the tropics, of different genders, ages, races, and from different climates, lived for so long in one place as they had in the Colonial Exhibition in Germany.[21] Displays also featured colonial products such as coffee, sugar, spices, rubber, and ivory, as well as maps of the German colonies and shipping routes, weapons, taxidermy animals, illustrations, and paintings. A program from the exhibition announced on August 8, 1896, the Exhibition would be closed to visitors for a day filled with a variety of events. These included a display by Herero and "Hottentots," war games and war dances by Swahili and Massai tribesmen in the reconstructed village and a "fetish dance" by the Togolese.[22]

The purpose of the Colonial Exhibition related not only to educating its visitors about the German colonies but also to justifying German possession of colonies to win more support for such endeavors. The exhibition comprised of two sections with a bridge between them. The first section was ethnographical (and contained the reconstructed villages) and the second section focused on science and trade; the bridge between them appeared to represent Germany's *Kulturarbeit* (cultural work) and illustrated how Germany was bridging the gap between the supposedly culturally backward African natives and European modernity, commercial enterprise, and culture.[23] The Colonial Exhibition was not a massive financial success, but it did prove to be popular with the public. When the Exhibition closed on October 15, 1896, it had received more than one million visitors over its five months of operation.[24] The Exhibition's public success led to the founding of a permanent museum, the *Deutsches Kolonialmuseum* (German Colonial Museum), in Berlin on October 14, 1899.

In addition to the physical visitor attractions, the increase in commercial advertisements that directly referenced colonialism to promote and sell consumer goods signified Germany's new position as a colonial ruler. The colonial-themed advertisements marketed a wide assortment of different products, from cigars and alcohol to soap, coffee, and chocolate. They often depicted caricature figures of indigenous African people, African landscapes, or exotic native animals. During the Herero and Nama Wars (1904–8), the advertisements reflected the military situation and increasingly began to show more radicalized depictions of African people. They also displayed illustrations of heroic and victorious German colonial soldiers.[25] Although the majority of Germans did not visit the colonies, the stereotypical and racialized depictions of Africans in advertisements they encountered every day meant that perceived differences between the African indigenous populations and the Germans were enhanced. Thus, advertisements informed Germans of the existence of an African "Colonial Other" and reinforced this notion by using radical caricatures. Although it is impossible to tell exactly what the German population thought of such advertisements and whether they translated into any factual desire to expand the empire, their presence in Germany is noteworthy. After 1900, every German could know what it meant to be a colonial master, not by visiting the colonies but by simply looking through newspaper advertisements or by seeing various goods available in stores.[26]

Unsurprisingly, German children learnt little about colonialism and imperialism in pre-colonial Germany. This changed in the early 1880s as a result of pressure from not only the colonial societies but also from groups of school geography teachers (*Schulgeographen*) who were not only colonial enthusiasts but also eager to strengthen their discipline for professional gains.[27] German schools introduced colonial education at all levels soon after the *Kaiserreich* was established. This usually comprised of learning about how the colonies were acquired, where they were, who populated them, and what Germans were doing there to help the natives and to benefit Germany. The school system taught young Germans about the economic importance of these overseas possessions and the significance of Germany's role in bringing civility and culture to allegedly uncivilized places. The Colonial Museum in Berlin was also utilized to enhance the children's experience of learning about the German colonies. Like the Colonial Exhibition that had gone before it, the Colonial Museum included exhibits, artefacts, and reconstructed villages with people from the African continent living in them. It was constructed in such a way that the visitors felt as if they were in a "living picture."[28] The Colonial Museum proved to be a popular destination for school tours, especially during the years of the Herero and Nama Wars. The annual number of student visitors rose from 7,134 in the fiscal year 1902–3 to over 50,000 by 1907–8.[29] In addition to the usual school curriculum, schools opened that focused specifically on preparing Germans for a life in the overseas colonies. For example, the *Deutsche Kolonialschule für Landwirtschaft, Handel und Gewerbe* (German Colonial School for Agriculture, Trade, and Commerce) opened in May 1899 in Witzenhausen. Due to the "rapid, plantation economic upswing" and the apparent lack of young Germans sufficiently trained for civil service in the colonies, the school aimed to provide students with a well-rounded education tailored to life in the colonies abroad.[30]

School education was not the sole way through which young Germans learnt about colonialism during their upbringing in the period of the *Kaiserreich*. Toy and game manufacturers, and also children's book authors began to respond to the German public's new interest in the empire. German-manufactured toys were so popular that by the beginning of the twentieth century, German producers controlled around 60 percent of the world toy market.[31] Colonial figurines, such as Native Americans, Africans, or German colonial soldiers, became common toys during this era. Children could reenact the exploration of the African continent, the Herero and Nama Wars or the journeys of cowboys across the American frontier. These toys directly related to current issues within Germany and to the subjects the children were being taught in school; hence, they could be marketed as both enjoyable and educational. Similarly, board games, such as *Durch Deutschlands Kolonien* (Through Germany's Colonies), allowed children to "experience" the responsibility and the fictional financial pressures of travelling through, purchasing, and possessing colonies.[32] Books also served the purpose of immersing young children in the world of the colonies. Fictional stories about exploration, such as those set in the American Wild West written by Karl May,[33] and also non-fiction travel accounts, like those of Hermann von Wissman, combined elements of adventure, violence, and colonial mastery.[34] Children's magazines published during the *Kaiserreich*, such as *Der gute Kamrad* (The Good Pal, first published in 1887) for young boys and *Das Kränzchen* (The Friendship Circle, first published in 1888) for young girls, also sought to prepare their readers "for their future roles of promoting the well-being of Germany."[35]

The Preservation of Colonial Memories before 1933

The First World War had a profound effect on both Germany and its population. Not only was it one of the deadliest conflicts in history, which saw the introduction of industrial warfare and up to nine million military and seven million civilian deaths, but Germany's loss in the war resulted in punishment by the Treaty of Versailles and the creation of the *Dolchstoßlegende* (stab-in-the-back legend). The loss of the war possibly delivered an even greater blow to the German population because, to many, the German Army's defeat came as a surprise. The shock of the loss coupled with the number of German fatalities (approximately two million men) was compounded by the Treaty of Versailles, which included such stipulations as the occupation and demilitarization of the Rhineland, the return of Alsace-Lorraine to France, the loss of land to Poland, and the loss of all Germany's overseas colonies. The German overseas colonial empire, which had been created extremely quickly was destroyed at an even faster pace.

The theory that the Germans were unsuitable or "bad colonizers," and that they had been uniquely brutal in their treatment of the indigenous populations in their colonies, circulated among the Allies and the European public as anti-German propaganda during the war. This theory was substantiated by accounts such as the 1918 *Report On The Natives Of South-West Africa And Their Treatment By Germany*, also known as the *Blue Book*.[36] The report, written by the South African Administrator's Office and published in Britain, detailed German atrocities in German South West Africa based on witnesses' accounts. The notion of the German "bad colonizers" provided apt justification for the confiscation of the *Kaiserreich*'s colonies and their annexation by the Allied Powers. Article 119 of the Treaty forced Germany to renounce its overseas colonies, while Article 22 established the mandate system that allowed for the transfer of German territory to the Allies for their new administration. Cameroon was divided between France and Britain; Togo was granted to France; territories in German East Africa were granted to Britain, Belgium and Portugal; and territories in German South West Africa, such as Namibia, were to be administered by the British dominion of South Africa. Overall, the treaty amounted to a total land loss of 65,000 square kilometers. For colonial enthusiasts, the loss of the overseas colonies was particularly distressing.

As well as the potential economic impact and the unfortunate situation thousands of Germans in the colonies now found themselves in, a key component to the devastation felt around the loss was related to German perceptions of their national identity that had been formed in connection with the possession of overseas colonies and the civilizing mission. For the German colonial enthusiasts, Germans, by virtue of being European, were superior to supposedly uncivilized non-European native populations. As a civilized and superior nation, Germany had "the need, duty or right" to bring civilization to other territories. By denying the Germans their overseas colonies and the means of carrying out their own civilizing missions, the Treaty of Versailles also denied the Germans a crucial part of their European identity.[37] The official German reply to the Allies in May 1919 reflected this; it noted that "as *Kulturvolk* (civilized people), the German people have a right and duty to contribute to the scientific exploration of the world and the education of undeveloped races as a collective *Aufgabe* (task) of civilized humanity."[38] The renouncement of their overseas colonies was thus a particularly bitter outcome of the war as it not only related to the loss of territory, goods, and people, but it also meant that Germany had lost their European duty and, therefore, their place among the civilized and superior nations.

The *Kaiserreich* had ended abruptly and with it Germany's respectability as a European nation; however, the memory of the German colonies and the empire was preserved in Germany, and even strengthened, through a variety of methods that kept the colonial topics alive in the public sphere between the end of the First World War and the beginning of the Nazi regime. As Geoff Eley and the contributors to the edited volume *German Colonialism in a Global Age* have highlighted, the knowledge, but also the exoticization, of German overseas colonies had deeply permeated German society during the later years of the *Kaiserreich* in a variety of ways. Through the widespread availability of colonial literature, advertising of colonial products, postcards, films, *Völkerschauen* (human zoos), and schoolbooks, German society was inundated with the topic of overseas colonialism.[39] This permeation of colonial knowledge and exoticism did not simply disappear overnight when the Treaty of Versailles terms began to take effect; instead, colonialism was enshrined into German culture and the public psyche through memorialization. The lingering colonial elements promoted by German colonial enthusiasts focused both on Germany's lost empire and the past but also promoted the idea of the reclamation of the territories and Germany's future return to power. One obvious example of the enshrinement of colonial memories is the *Afrikabücher* (Africa books) genre, which had been popular with both adults and children both before and during the *Kaiserreich*. However, their popularity did not end with the loss of the colonies; in fact, the number of publications of *Afrikabücher* increased after 1918.[40] The *Afrikabücher* continued to recount stories of colonial wars, travel accounts, diary excerpts, and stories about daily life in the colonies. The books were not only authored by men writing about exciting exploits but they were also authored by women who recounted their experiences or wrote fictional accounts. Regardless of whether the books centered on fictional or non-fiction adventures, they managed to convey a variety of themes that interested German readers. As well as popular political or nationalist themes, some of the books contained photographs and drawings that specifically catered for either adult or youth audiences. The popular author Frieda von Bülow is credited as being one of the first authors, male or female, to use the colonies as a setting for novels.[41] Her books mainly focused on fictional stories loosely based on her own travels. They promoted and legitimized the colonial cause and portrayed key ideologies related to German nationalism at the time. For example, von Bülow's novel *Im Lande der Verheissung: Ein deutscher Kolonial-Roman* (In the Promised Land: A German Colonial Novel) framed the notion of Germanness in terms of racial and moral purity. Additionally, it suggested nationalism was a factor that shaped life in the colonies.[42]

The popularity of the *Afrikabücher* in Germany can be observed in the continuation of their publication. Books such as Paul von Lettow-Vorbeck's *Heia Safari! Deutschlands Kampf in Ostafrika* (Heia Safari! Germany's Campaign in East Africa) and *Meine Erinnerungen aus Ostafrika* (My Memories from East Africa), went into several editions, while August Hauer's *Kumbuke: Erlebnisse eines Arztes in Deutsch-Ostafrika* (Kumbuke: Experiences of a Doctor in German East Africa), first published in Berlin in 1922, ran into its seventh edition in 1943.[43] Hans Grimm's *Volk ohne Raum* (People without Space), published in 1926, also fit into this category of *Afrikabücher*. The book quickly became a best seller, and just before the outbreak of the Second World War it had sold half a million copies.[44] The book tells the story of a young German who emigrates from Germany to South Africa and takes part in the Anglo-Boer Wars. Afterwards, he moves on to German South West Africa, where he prospers until the loss of the German colonies after the First World War. Upon arriving back to a changed Germany in the 1920s, he attempts to raise political support for German territorial expansion. As the name suggests, the main theme throughout the book was that Germany did not have enough space for its growing population and therefore, to provide for this population and to gain equal strength to that of other European empires, Germany had to expand. *Volk ohne Raum* appealed to the German population who were facing the harsh reality of living in a defeated, economically unstable Germany. With the tumultuous social and political period in Germany during the Weimar Republic, the fantasy of the stability of the *Kaiserreich* and the benefits of increased territorial possession (whether real or imagined) were preserved in the pages of these books and in the minds of those who read them. Britta Schilling has suggested that every time an *Afrikabuch* was read or its pages were idly flicked through, the memory of the *Kaiserreich* was "recharged."[45]

In addition to the *Afrikabücher*, other publications were available through which the German population could relive the *Kaiserreich*. For example, the DKG continued to publish its monthly newspaper, the *Deutsche Kolonial-Zeitung*. The newspaper contained pictures and articles on different geographical locations around the world with a heavy focus on Africa. It also regularly addressed the issue of *Deutschlands koloniale Forderung* (Germany's colonial claim), the argument that Germany's colonies should be returned. As well as this, they also continued to publish regular bulletins and pamphlets and promoted the publication of books on the topic. Perhaps most fascinating was the inclusion of articles and reports that focused on the subject of the former German colonies in regional newspapers. Such tactics meant ordinary German citizens, who were not part of colonial groups or organizations, could also be confronted with the discussion on the loss and reclamation of Germany's overseas colonies by the pages of their daily or weekly newspapers. German colonial enthusiasts purposely attempted to "inject" their memories of Germany's colonialism into the public sphere in a planned effort to combat the *Kolonialschuldlüge* (Colonial Guilt Lie)—a term coined by Heinrich Schnee, the former governor of German East Africa.[46]

For example, in 1921, the *Hamburger Anzeiger* featured an article titled "Kolonial- und Schifffahrtstag der Kultur- und Sport Woche" (Colonial and Shipping Day of the Culture and Sport Week), which reported on a lecture by Schnee. The article noted that the Germans must hold fast to the desire to own colonies and they must have the right to do so. It reported that Schnee, predating Grimm's *Volk ohne Raum*, said "We are too many people pressed together in too small a country." Linking work in the colonies with the German national identity, he explained, "We must be aware that we can replace the defects only by colonial cultural work, which is demonstrated by our German national character. We must learn to recognize ourselves as a united people … The activity in the colonies contributes to the recognition of unified ideas."[47] In Schnee's lecture, available to all the readers of the *Hamburger Anzeiger*, he built on the ideology that Germany needed more space and the Germans needed to feel unified once again; he argued that the colonies could provide a solution to both these problems. In a similar newspaper article, the *Freiburger Zeitung* briefly summarized what Berthold von Deimling, an Infantry General during the Herero and Nama Wars and from 1906, Commander of the *Schutztruppe* in German South West Africa, had said to the *Deutschen Demokratischen Studentengruppe* (German Democratic Student Group) at the University of Freiburg.[48] Deimling spoke about his memories of German South West Africa, including his military exploits against the Herero and Nama forces, and why Germany must have colonies again. The sound of the applause that followed his lecture supposedly gained attention from others present at the university.[49] Lectures, and newspaper reports about the lectures, were not only important in how they disseminated information but also because of the way they assisted in keeping the public's memory of colonialism alive. By utilizing colonial "celebrities," prominent figures who were well-known, the attention paid to these lectures, and what was said in them could be increased in much the same way as present-day celebrity endorsements.[50]

Literature, lectures, and newspaper articles were not the only means through which the memory of colonialism was preserved. Often physical items or places helped to solidify the legacy and remembrance of the *Kaiserreich* as they could actually be seen, encountered, or touched by individuals in Germany.[51] For example, during the *Kaiserreich*, numerous streets throughout Germany were given names such as Von-Trotha-Straße, Carl-Peters-Straße, and Lüderitzstraße. This did not only occur in main cities, but also in smaller ones. For example, there is currently a Lüderitzträße in such varied locations as Berlin, Munich, Starnberg, Karlsruhe, Lüdwigsburg, Lübeck, Kiel, Cuxhaven, and Mannheim as well as in other locations around Germany. In addition to being named after well-known colonial figures, some streets were named directly after the German colonies or towns there, such as Togostraße, Windhuker Straße, Waterberg Straße, and Swakopmunder Straße.[52]

Even during the Third Reich when German expansionist goals seemed to be firmly set on Eastern Europe, streets continued to be allocated names that recalled Germany's overseas colonial territories. For example, in the city of Łódź in the German-annexed *Reichsgau* Wartheland, there was also a Togostraße and a Windhukerstraße as well as a Koloniestraße.[53] In Poznań (Posen), there was a Wissmannstraße and a Karl-Petersstraße.[54] The presence of these streets, scattered in various locations throughout Germany and annexed Poland, is significant in that it shows an effort to maintain elements of the past. Instead of being removed after the loss of the colonies, the street names remained as public tokens to a lost empire. To those who used and observed (and still use and observe) these streets, the links to Germany's colonial past may not have been immediately obvious in that encountering them may not have inspired one to reminisce or think about the former colonies. However, by having elements of the colonial past constantly present in daily life, the street names were a noticeable part of the geography of the city and thus, small references to the former empire could still be actively used every day in Germany even if these references were removed from their original context.

More conspicuous than street names, colonial monuments specifically embodied the attempt to recall certain parts of Germany's colonial past. The colonial monuments stirred certain thoughts and feelings, but they could also bring about memories despite being far away from the actual locations or areas of the actions which they were commemorating.[55] Among other colonial monuments throughout Germany, the statue of Hermann von Wissmann was moved from Dar es Salaam in German East Africa, where it had been erected in 1909, to the campus of the University of Hamburg in 1922,[56] the *Braunschweiger Kolonialdenkmal* (Braunschweig Colonial Monument) was erected in 1925 in Braunschweig and the *Reichskolonial-Ehrenmal* elephant statue was erected in 1932 in Bremen.[57] The *Braunschweiger Kolonialdenkmal* commemorated both the lost German colonies and the German soldiers who had died fighting there during the First World War. It was funded by donations from the *Verein ehemaliger Ostasiaten und Afrikaner* (Association of Former East Asians and Africans). The meaning behind the *Reichskolonial-Ehrenmal* elephant in Bremen proved to be controversial and sparked almost six years of debate regarding which cause it should commemorate. The monument was originally proposed as a national colonial monument in 1925, and the Social Democrats in the city government wanted it to be a memorial to remember the fallen German soldiers. However, members of the colonial movement, such as the Bremen division of the DKG, wanted the monument to be a sign of protest against the Treaty of Versailles and support for the reclamation of the former German colonies in Africa.[58]

The completed monument was eventually revealed on July 6, 1932. In an invitation to the unveiling ceremony, the Bremen division of the DKG described the seven-meter-high African elephant sculpture as standing above a crypt that contained a book with the 1,500 names of "the fallen heroes" who had died in the "defensive battles of the protectorates."[59] The program of events for the unveiling included such proceedings as a performance by the military band, a speech by the chairman of the Bremen DKG division Eduard Achelis, a speech in honor of the fallen, and a speech by Lettow-Vorbeck.[60] The forms of memorialization were not only an attempt at the commemoration and preservation of Germany's past colonial exploits, they were also signifiers of a distinct attempt by colonial enthusiasts to integrate these memories or pride of the former colonies into a post-empire Germany. Physical forms of commemoration and memorialization were of course not limited to Germany and similar monuments commemorating colonial explorers or battles in the colonies were erected by other empires during their existence. A peculiarity about the German colonial monuments was that Germany was actively recalling an empire of which it no longer had a part, an empire that it had lost under dire circumstances and one that, as will be discussed in the final chapter, the new Nazi regime was hesitant to reclaim.

Events were also held in Germany after 1919, which commemorated German colonialism through celebration. For example, an event that aimed not only at remembrance but also celebration was the *Tangagedenkfeier* (Tanga Commemoration) held on November 6, 1926. The commemoration event was advertised in the *Freiburger Zeitung* on November 5, and the advert invited all "colonial friends" and Germans from abroad. Additionally, it noted that guests were very welcome.[61] The event was organized by the *Oberbadische Abteilung der DKG* (Upper Baden division of the DKG), *Frauenverein von Roten Kreuz der Deutschen über See* (Women's Red Cross Association for the Germans Overseas), and the *Verein der Kolonialkrieger und Kolonialdeutschen* (Association of the Colonial Soldiers and Colonial Germans) and was held in the *Löwenbrauerei* in Freiburg im Breisgau. After the event, the *Freiburger Zeitung* reported that a homage telegram was sent to Lettow-Vorbeck and the last governor of Cameroon, Karl Ebermaier, gave a speech.[62] The event commemorated the Battle of Tanga in German East Africa, which had taken place between November 3 and 5, 1914 during the First World War and was fought by German Askari troops and German forces against the British Indian Expeditionary Force.[63] The commemoration of such an event had a dual purpose; firstly, it commemorated a German victory in a battle of a war that would ultimately be lost. Secondly, as it was organized by the DKG and other groups and also attended by a colonial celebrity, as mentioned in the last paragraph, it acted as a platform for them to further spread their ideas and remind those in attendance, or even newspaper readers, of the former *Kaiserreich*.

In a similar way to a specific colonial commemoration event, the *Kolonialball* (Colonial Ball) was an immersive commemoration of colonialism for those who attended. The colonial balls were organized by colonial organizations, mainly the *Frauenbund der Deutschen Kolonialgesellschaft* (Women's League of the DKG, FDKG) and the *Frauenverein von Roten Kreuz der Deutschen über See*.[64] The balls gained popularity between the mid-1920s and 1930s; they were essentially an amalgamation of a colonial exhibition and a society party. The ballroom was decorated following a "colonial theme" and included tropical plants, figurines of animals and photographs and illustrations from Africa. Numerous stands displayed and sold *Kolonialwaren* (colonial products) such as fruits and rubber. Africans (or white people in black paint) served food and drink and performed dances and music. Colonial celebrities such as former governors and generals were invited to attend along with academics, artists and honorable guests.[65] The *Altonaer Nachrichten* reported the *Kolonialball*, organized by the *Frauenverein von Roten Kreuz* and the Women's League of the DKG, which was held in the Atlantik Hotel in Hamburg in 1927 was one of the most popular Society events. The newspaper reports summarize the aim of the *Kolonialball*; not only was it a festive occasion, but it also was an event for "people to come together, united by shared experiences and memories" and for the growing youth who wished to experience it and who wanted to grow into colonial pioneers.[66]

Similarly, the *Kolonialball* held by the same two organizations in February 1930 was reported on in the *Hamburgischer Correspondent* newspaper under the heading "At the Height of the Festival Season." The article described the cheerful atmosphere, the delicious buffet, the champagne bar and the tombola stand with prizes; it ended with the line "God, this is fun!"[67] Reports of colonial balls did not only appear in Hamburg newspapers but also in others, such as the *Berliner Tagesblatt,* depending on where in Germany the balls were held. As with the other facets of colonial memorialization that continued in Germany despite the loss of the colonies, the *Kolonialball* was another way in which a social event allowed for former and future colonialists to congregate and to relive German colonialism through their memories and the events' colonial décor. Although it cannot be ascertained exactly how the newspaper reports of colonial balls were viewed by those who did not attend, the presence of these articles and their representation as summaries of society events and occasions, indicate there was a public interest in the subject.

In addition to this, the newspaper reports also demonstrate another way in which the issue of German colonialism was kept in the public realm. The *Kaiserreich* may have ended, but as demonstrated by the sales of *Kolonialwaren*, the continuation of colonial advertising and the maintenance of the *Kolonialball* events, the German colonial ethos was sustained in the period between 1919 and the National Socialist Party's rise to power. Advertisements depicting colonial scenes were still present in Germany, as though Germany still had ownership over colonial territory. Monuments to the lost colonies were erected, streets were renamed, and the literature that surrounded the subject of colonies continued to be written and read. Many popular *Afrikabücher*, such as the previously mentioned *Heia Safari!* by Lettow-Vorbeck, were republished numerous times. Similarly, production companies and individuals continued to produce colonial-themed films that were about or set in Africa and explored nonfictional topics such as nature, travel, and ethnography, as well as fictional plotlines.[68] Colonial societies organized educational events and lectures and raised money for their campaigns. The various elements that kept colonialism alive in the interwar period also helped to maintain an imaginary state of affairs. The colonial novels, products and advertising all seemed to signify that Germany still was a colonial power, despite this not being the case. Although the majority of the German civilians during the interwar period had never been to the German African colonies, the importance of the colonial enthusiasts' efforts to create and strengthen collective memories related to the *Kaiserreich* should be stressed.

Collective memories of places, events, and people in a nation's history, contribute to the formation of the nation's self-identity. Such memories are created by groups of individuals, regardless of whether they were eyewitnesses to an event or whether the memories have been passed down through generations. In interwar Germany, the majority of German citizens had never visited, let alone lived, in the overseas colonies. However, remnants of Germany's past as a colonial power lingered but were also newly manufactured within the public space. As the historians Etienne François and Hagen Schulze have argued, there is "no community without commemorative events, monuments, myths, rituals, without identification with personalities, objects and events."[69] The collective memorialization of the *Kaiserreich*'s involvement in Africa was therefore aided by the various methods of commemoration and the weaving of memories of German colonialism into city maps and public spaces. Sean Andrew Wempe has argued that although colonial enthusiasts attempted to gain public support through the dissemination of materials and memoirs, in the case of the returned German settlers, certain groups also used such memorialization to distinguish themselves as unique from Germans who had not lived in the colonies. Such groups used settler memoirs as a means to criticize German collective identity and to create a new, idealized notion of an African *Heimat*, which could be juxtaposed with the economic devastation they had found upon their return to interwar Germany.[70] Regardless of whether this was the former settlers' aim or not, the post-Treaty of Versailles colonial culture in Germany was purely based on idealized, nostalgic recollections, a public collective memory semi-manufactured by colonial enthusiasts and colonial individuals' and groups' fantasies about regaining the colonies. As such, interwar Germany's colonial culture was not based on an active reality. Until 1933, the memorialization of colonialism in Germany could only exist in terms of linkages to the past; however, with the establishment of the Nazi regime and promises of a new Germany, the hope of regaining colonial territory would ultimately be strengthened.

The *Kaiserreich* and "Colonial" Poland

Germany's relationship with Poland dates back to the Middle Ages when the Teutonic Knights embarked on conquests of Old Prussian territory. The settlement of these territories by Germans (known as the *Ostsiedlung* or Eastern Settlement) soon followed the conquests as German nobles acquired land and encouraged German settlers to relocate there. In addition to the settlement in Prussia, throughout the twelfth, thirteenth and fourteenth centuries, Eastern European kingdoms experienced an influx of tens of thousands of German settlers who were invited by rulers to settle the land in exchange for special legal and tax privileges.[71] The interconnected nature of the two territories and their people continued throughout the centuries. Three partitions of the Polish-Lithuanian Commonwealth (the first in 1772, the second in 1793 and the third in 1795) resulted in the Polish territory being split between Austria, Russia and Prussia. From 1815 until 1915, a semiautonomous Polish state was created by the Congress of Vienna and ceded to the Russian Empire.[72]

After the unification of Germany in 1871, theories of Eastern European expansion, consolidation of German territories and German peoples abroad, the notion of *Kulturkampf* and the fear of the Polonization of Germans came to the forefront of the political agenda.[73] The late nineteenth century saw an increase in German nationalist sentiment concerning the need to strengthen Prussian territory against the supposed mass infiltration of immigrant workers from Polish territories. Much of the German fear relating to the Poles hinged on the question of the number of *Inlandspolen* (domestic Poles) or *Auslandspolen* (foreign Poles). The domestic Poles were those born within Prussia and typically, they had Prussian citizenship. This meant they had often been subjected to Germanization and were, to an extent, linguistically or culturally assimilated. The Prussian Germanization policy aimed at the integration of the Prussian Polish minority into Germany. It concentrated on abolishing the influence of the Polish Catholic church and education systems and attempted to curb the growth of the Polish language and culture by such measures as enforcing the use of German in schools and administration. The foreign Poles, those born outside of Prussia, were viewed as the biggest threat to the newly unified Germany due to the belief they would contribute to a Polish nationalist campaign. As the foreign Poles increasingly filled the empty agricultural positions left by German workers migrating west or to America, the belief that the Poles were forcing German workers out of Prussia also became widespread.[74]

Foreign Poles and domestic Poles, who by the early to mid-1880s not only lived and worked in Prussia and the Ruhr but also in mining areas like Upper Silesia, continued to migrate and settle despite the efforts of Germanization and *Kulturkampf*. The fear of the Polonization of these areas continued despite government attempts to prevent it. Polonization would supposedly not only cause a potential change in the language, culture and society of German areas, but it was also feared in case it led to the creation of national unity of the Polish minority within Germany which in turn would compete with German national unity. To curb the threat of foreign Poles, in March 1885 a series of expulsions of people who did not hold German or Prussian citizenship began. The following three years of expulsions were chaotic for many different reasons: local authorities only had a short period to expel thousands of people; Russia did not want to receive expellees who had no proof of Russian citizenship and refugees could be seen, starving and impoverished, at border crossings.[75] The expulsions resulted in over forty thousand Poles and Jews being driven out of the Prussian provinces regardless of status, age, or health.[76]

The *Kulturkampf* policies and the Germanization of Prussia specifically targeted people; the goal was to integrate them into the *Kaiserreich* through education, laws, and control of the church. However, as Kristin Kopp notes, from the 1880s, the German policy changed from the goal of Germanizing people to Germanizing territory instead.[77] The notion of Poland as a space for German settlement had been present since the fourteenth century, but it was reintroduced and reformulated during the *Kaiserreich*. A spate of Polish uprisings against the Kingdom of Prussia and the Austrian Empire, which occurred intermittently between 1846 and 1848 and the November Uprising against the Russian Empire in 1863, led to a distrust of Polish elites and a fear of the growth of Polish nationalism. In 1886, the *Königlich Preußische*

Ansiedlungskommission in den Provinzen Westpreußen und Posen (known as the Prussian Settlement Commission) was founded by Bismarck in an attempt to use German settlement to curb the growth of Polish nationalism in Prussia and to help stem the immigration of Germans from the east to the western industrial areas. The Prussian government tasked the Commission with reducing Polish ownership of land in Prussia and increasing German ownership. To do so, the Commission bought up large tracts of land and sold them to German settlers.

The settlement of these areas brought with it the supposed benefit of control but also a way of ensuring the areas were Germanized through the Germans who settled there. The Commission thereby had the intention of ethnically reordering the population in Prussia. By providing Germans with options for land purchase and subsidies in areas where they could create a German majority or where they could ensure the German population was not surpassed by the Polish population, the Commission hoped the Prussian settlement would encourage Germans to migrate to the Eastern borders of Germany as opposed to immigrating to America.[78] The Settlement Commission ran from 1886 until 1918 and during this time, it settled approximately 22,000 German families and purchased 828 estates (approximately 430,000 hectares) and 631 peasant farms (approximately 30,000 hectares).[79] The Commission was not an overall success; the number of Germans did not surpass that of the Poles due to the high Polish birth rate and lack of German settlers. However, when comparing the settlement figures during the *Kaserreich*, the inner colonization of Prussia was undoubtedly more successful than the settlement of German overseas colonies. More than 120,000 Germans settled in Prussia, five times more than the number of those who settled in the German colonial empire abroad.[80] After the Treaty of Versailles in 1919, more than 96 percent of the purchased land became part of the new Polish state.[81]

Despite the ultimately unsuccessful Prussian settlement mission, the campaign is significant in that it demonstrates how the German movement to Prussia facilitated a colonial perception of the territory. The idea of Germans as *Kulturträger* (bearers of culture) was not a new one; however, it was refashioned for the new settlement project. The strengths of German culture, such as intelligence, diligence, honor and stability were often juxtaposed with the weaker "Polish" images of mismanagement, unruliness and ill-breeding to legitimize German influence.[82] As Matthew P. Fitzpatrick argues, the transformation of Prussia's initial policy of protecting the Polish language and culture to that of the assimilation and displacement of Poles signified a shift from an imperial approach to a colonial approach.[83] Although the Poles were not fully subjected to living within a society based on strict racial and ethnic boundaries as they would be during the Third Reich, the German relationship with the Polish population still had identifiable colonial characteristics. The notion of differences between the German and Slavic "races" existed, as did fears regarding Polish women, in nationalist rhetoric at this time.[84] The historical exploits of Germany in Polish territory were also employed as further proof of Polish inability. Nationalists, historians and scholars reused the colonial view from an earlier period and wrote of how the Germans had once cultivated the soil, and a new, green German industriousness flourished in place of the Polish wilderness.[85]

The conceptualization of Poland as a colonial space with a supposedly inferior population can be clearly demonstrated by the portrayal of the Polish population in German literature at the time. An emerging literary genre of novels, known as the *Ostmarkenromane* (Eastern Marches Novels), exploited the perceived cultural gap between Germany and Poland for their storylines. The *Ostmarkenromane* were not unlike the *Afrikabücher* in that they had a political aim that was disguised (some less successfully than others) within the fictional stories. Like the adventure novels set in the American Wild West by authors such as Karl May, which were popular for both adults and children, they featured landscapes open for limitless exploration, excitement and lacking the constraints imposed by western society. The books depicted Poland as it had begun to be referred to in the national and political language of the time; Poland was allegedly a vast, backward, uncultivated landscape with a population in need of civilization and culture. Eastern Europe was represented as fundamentally Other and incompatible with the German notion of Self.[86]

Kopp's research of the *Ostmarkenromane* gives an invaluable insight into how the novels portrayed the Polish territories in a colonial light and how the Polish population were depicted as a "Colonial Other." For example, Kopp demonstrates how Gustav Freytag's novel *Soll und Haben* (Debit and Credit, first published in 1855) depicted Poland as the German version of the "Wild West" and she illustrates in what ways it depicted Poland as a "territory of adventure."[87] *Soll und Haben* became one of the best-selling German novels, it sold over 100,000 copies by the end of the nineteenth century, and its publication continued into the 1920s.[88] Freytag's *Soll und Haben* follows the exploits of Anton Wohlfahrt, a young German who moved to Wrocław (Breslau) in Prussia to work as an apprentice in a merchant's office. The novel demonstrates how, through hard industrial work and not by noble or aristocratic birth, Wohlfahrt manages to become extremely successful. Although the novel mostly focuses on the social aspects of Wohlfahrt's path to achievement, its setting in Prussia is important. As well as depicting Poland as an area as one for those seeking adventure, the novel also portrays the native Polish population as akin to the primitive and incapable "Colonial Other." Freytag deliberately used the exoticization of Polish Otherness and drew parallels between the Poles and Native Americans.[89] Ultimately, the novel portrayed the Poles as occupying a somewhat perplexing position located in both European and non-European realms and having white but simultaneously non-white ethnic characteristics.[90]

In his investigation of such sources as scientific journals, magazines and maps, Christoph Kienemann has also convincingly demonstrated Germany's perception of Eastern Europe during the *Kaiserreich* can be interpreted as colonial, and this perception influenced policies related to the East. By using familiar colonial tropes to describe Eastern European territory and the people who lived there, including *Ostjuden* (Eastern Jews), the Germans created an Other—the antithesis of Germany. Simultaneously, the East was portrayed as an ideal area for settlement and political and cultural plans while also being a threat to Germany and German culture.[91] Although literature may not initially seem to be powerful political influencers, as Edward Said highlighted in *Orientalism*, texts "can *create* not only knowledge but also the very reality they appear to describe." For Said, the Orient was created through knowledge from texts becoming a part of everyday life. Such a process is cyclical; the readers' experiences are determined by what they read, while the authors' selection of subjects is influenced by the readers' experiences.[92] Orientalism was "a kind of Western projection onto and will to govern over the Orient."[93] Similarly, the colonial tropes used to describe Poland functioned as a way to *make* Poland colonial through how the readers perceived Poland. The wide dissemination of texts coupled with political debates on the topic thus added to the notion that Poland was unquestionably a colonial territory. Despite the Polish territories being located in Europe, the German colonial gaze perceived the territory as equivalent to that of overseas colonial territory; the territory and its people were understood using colonial terms which in turn portrayed Poland as the perfect area for expansion, adventure and civilizing missions.

The Spatial Fantasies of Societies and Political Groups

The colonial imagining of Poland was not limited to the pages of the *Ostmarkenromane*. Research societies and radical political pressure groups strongly promoted discourses regarding Prussia (and later territories further east than Poland) as an area suitable for more intensive German settlement both during the *Kaiserreich* and in the interwar period. On April 12, 1912, Max Sering and Friedrich von Schwerin formed the *Gesellschaft zur Förderung der inneren Kolonisation* (Society for the Advancement of Inner Colonization, GFK) based on the principles of their journal called the *Archiv für innere Kolonisation* (Archive for Inner Colonization, AfiK), first published in 1908. Schwerin was the *Regierungspräsident* (District President) for Frankfurt (Oder) from 1908 till 1918 and Sering was an agrarian economist and author of the publication *Die innere Kolonisation im östlichen Deutschland* (The Inner Colonization of Eastern Germany, 1893). Before publishing the book, Sering travelled to North America in 1883 for six months on behalf of the Prussian government. It was here that he researched the American frontier settlements and supposedly first realized "inner colonization" would be the method through which Germany's problems of emigration, land and tensions with the Poles in Prussia could be solved.[94] Sering defined "inner colonization" as "the planned establishment of new settlements in the homeland of the colonizing people" with the objective of "either the expansion of the country, the full utilization of domestic resources or primarily the increasing of the national population number or to alter the distribution of land ownership."[95]

In *Die innere Kolonisation im östlichen Deutschland*, Sering discussed such topics as the historical development of German settlements in Poland, the goals of future settlements and also the work and upcoming tasks of the Prussian Settlement Commission. He concluded the book on a positive note by mentioning there was currently "a large offer of land [and] thousands of suitable applicants waiting for settlement." According to Sering, this settlement demand would increase as difficulties in finding settlement abroad also increased. He noted all the preconditions for the success of the settlement project were identifiable and the officials would "build a home for generations of free men and a protective wall (*Schutzwall*) against both the external and internal enemy of the state."[96] Comparable to the later planners of the Nazi regime,

Sering not only imagined the opportunities for settlement. He also envisioned that the territories of German settlement would create a protective boundary around Germany, which would stem the influx of foreigners from Eastern Europe.

It is clear the publications of the AfiK, and indeed, Sering, understood the settlement of the Eastern areas and the accomplishment of "inner colonization" as the most suitable use of Germany's resources.[97] However, Sering's book demonstrated how the East was strongly conceptualized in colonial terms at the time. He regularly referred to the potential of "colonies," "settlers," and the "*Kolonialpolitik*" (Colonial Policy) of the Prussian Settlement Commission and thus used colonial terminology to convey his message. As the name suggests, the AfiK also focused heavily on the notion of "inner colonization"; nevertheless, it additionally promoted overseas settlement in the German colonies in Africa as an attempt to curb overseas emigration to destinations such as America.

In an article published in 1910 in the AfiK, Paul Rohrbach, a well-known German writer born in the Kurland region, colonial advocate and the former settlement commissioner of German South West Africa (1903–6), described the conditions of the German colonies in Africa as generally poor, but he recognized their importance as settlement areas for Germans where outposts of the German nation could be formed.[98] Rohrbach noted the settlement aimed to "create powerful and unique overseas offshoots of the German nationality" and thus, "the establishment of the possession and authority of the German nation and German empire on important and distant points of the earth's surface, not only externally but also internally."[99] Rohrbach presents the reader with three options: German settlement in a destination such as America or Australia but with the risk of the settlers losing their national identity, settlement in one of the German African colonies to contribute to the preservation of German identity there (but with an acknowledgement of the hardships of the climate) and, what was only alluded to as "[settlement] internally," namely the settlement of the German eastern territories.

In another apparent attempt to present the German African colonies as a worthy settlement destination, the AfiK also published a special "*Kolonialnummer*" in February 1912, which specifically discussed the topic of settlement in the German African colonies. The foreword of the issue explained although "inner colonization is undoubtedly more important than the 'external' … the colonization of our colonies is also of great importance to our *Volk*, for our whole economy." The foreword concluded by noting that because of this importance, the Archive "should also include the settlement of the German colonies within its sphere according to the motto: A bigger Germany, it shall be!"[100] The *Kolonialnummer* gave further evidence that the GFK recognized the significance of German expansion regardless of whether it was through "inner" or "external" colonization. Although Eastern German settlement was seen as a priority to prevent further emigration and thus, a loss of Germans from Germany, the colonies in Africa presented the option of emigration while still contributing to the unity of the German empire. The overseas colonies were not portrayed as the perfect solution for settlers; however, through the texts of the AfiK, it seemed they were presented as the overseas emigration option with the best potential for maintaining an individual's connection to their homeland. The use of colonial language and terms to describe the Prussian territory and the promotion of settlement there, which ran simultaneously alongside the promotion of settlement in the German colonies in Africa, is significant in understanding how German European-based expansion could be conceptualized in colonial terms. Although they were two distinct areas, the potential for the settlement in Poland and further East, and the settlement in the African colonies were both portrayed as viable German settlement options. German expansion, regardless of whether it was overseas or continental, was explained using identifiable colonial terminology.

The AfiK is also significant due to the radicalization of its ideas during the First World War. Robert L. Nelson argues that with the successful eastward advancement of the German Army in 1915, the AfiK articles shifted their focus and began to discuss the theory that there would not be enough space for the German people's food and settlement needs within the boundaries of Germany. They began to advocate for extreme measures of clearing the intended settlement areas through the use of expulsions or population transfers.[101] The territorial advancements of the German Army allowed for the viable possibility of Germany gaining essential extra space in Eastern Europe. With the creation of the *Ober Ost* territory in 1914, the *Generalgouvernement Warschau* in 1915 and the *Polnischer Grenzstreifen* (Polish border strip), members of the GFK society found themselves to be in the perfect position to contribute to the settlement planning for the Eastern territory.[102] For example, Schwerin sent memoranda to the chancellor's office campaigning for new colonial land in the East and the removal of people from these lands through expulsion.[103] In November 1916, Schwerin travelled throughout the *Ober Ost* to collect evidence for his settlement policies. From this, he created plans for the settlement of 1.5 million Germans in the "empty" regions of Lithuania and the Kurland.[104] The plans for large-scale settlement did not come to fruition, and at the end of the war, the Treaty of Versailles resulted in the loss of German eastern territory. However, like in the case of the continuation of efforts to preserve the memory and promote the potential future reclamation of German overseas colonies, the AfiK remained in publication throughout the interwar period.

In addition to the radicalization of its theories regarding clearing space for settlement, perhaps one of the most crucial aspects of the analysis of the AfiK was its transformation during the Nazi regime. In 1933, the agrarian and colonial sciences degree holder and the soon-to-be Minister of Food and Agriculture Richard Walther Darré and Konrad Meyer, the future head of the *Reichskommissariat für die Festigung deutschen Volkstums* (Reich Commission for the Consolidation of Germandom, RKFDV) planning department, took over the journal and renamed it *Neues Bauerntum: fachwissenschaftliche Zeitschrift für das ländliche Siedlungswesen* (New Peasantry: Scientific Journal for Rural Settlement).[105] Similar to the AfiK, *Neues Bauerntum* also discussed German settlement, agriculture, economy, and the planning of new villages. However, as German settlement in Poland and further east was not only a fantasy but became a reality from 1939, the journal also recorded ongoing settlement and development projects that were occurring in the annexed Polish territories.

The GFK and its journal the AfiK were not the only methods through which ideas regarding the acquisition and settlement of Eastern Germany and Poland were disseminated to the German public and academic sphere. Similarly, it is not the only group from which discourses regarding colonial-style expansion in Poland and Eastern Europe can be observed. Political pressure groups such as the *Alldeutscher Verband* (Pan-German League) strived for expansionist, nationalist, anti-Polish, anti-Slavic and, later, anti-Semitic aims.[106] The Pan-German League was originally formed in April 1881 with the support of Carl Peters, the colonial explorer, promoter and founder of the *Gesellschaft für Deutsche Kolonisation* (Society for German Colonization), under the name of the *Allgemeine Deutsche Verband* (German General League).[107] The League was formed as a reaction to the Heligoland-Zanzibar Treaty of July 1880, which saw Germany relinquishing its rights over the Zanzibar region of Africa and conceding them to the British Empire. Friedrich Ratzel, the geographer credited with creating the term *Lebensraum* in 1897, was also one of the founders. In 1894, the German General League underwent restructuring and was renamed the *Alldeutscher Verband*. The new leader of the League was Ernst Hasse, a professor of statistics and colonial policy in Leipzig, who was a member of the board of directors of the DKG.[108]

The primary ideology of the Pan-Germans focused on the strengthening and protection of German nationality. Their goals reflected nationalist desires to politically unify Germany and German speakers, including those in Austria-Hungary and the German minorities in surrounding European territories. Although the Pan-German League is often categorized by historians as principally "an ethnic nationalist organization," the League also envisioned itself as the promoter of wider imperial solutions for Germany's current issues.[109] As well as an ethnically homogenous Germany within Europe, they strongly endorsed Germany's acquisition of overseas colonies. The League believed the strength of the nation was based on the principle of one ethnically and culturally homogenous group or *Volk*, which needed the space and resources that could be provided by both continental and overseas expansion. They saw the apparent danger and supposed linkages between an increase of Polish workers within the Reich and an increase in German emigration to countries such as America. The League's 1903 statutes reflected such principles; they stated the League was seeking an invigoration "of the German national attitude," especially in terms of creating the awareness that all parts of the German people "belong together racially and culturally." The statutes stated that the League's tasks included "the preservation of the German ethnicity [*Volkstum*] in Europe and overseas," "the fight against all forces that impede our [German] national identity" and the pursuit of German interests worldwide "especially a continuation of the colonial movement."[110]

Heinrich Claß, the leader of the League from 1908 to 1939, released numerous publications that discussed such aims. The most well-known of these was his book, first published in 1912 under the pseudonym Daniel Frymann, *Wenn ich der Kaiser wär'* (If I were the Emperor). As the book's title suggests, Claß criticized the *Kaiser* and the political system in Germany. He recommended that a reformation of the German system and a focus on the strengthening of Germanness and the German people would be the solution to Germany's problems. Claß explained that Germany's goal should be the "reform of the Reich, which would secure the future of our people [*Volk*], cleanse it of illnesses and strengthen its health … Germany for the Germans."[111] Similar to the GFK, importance was also placed on German colonial endeavors abroad as well as the settlement of areas of Prussia. The Pan-German League's close conceptual linkages between overseas and continental colonization were especially evident during their 1905 convention, which included discussions by advocates for both *Lebensraum* on the European continent and settlement overseas. As Sebastian Conrad has noted, the Pan-German League also placed a higher priority on German inner colonization as it would act as a precondition for external colonization.[112]

Despite only ever reaching a membership of 22,000 members, the Pan-German League still managed to have a significant influence on the German public and political sphere. The members of the League came from different parts of the middle class and occupied positions such as public officials and teachers. Many members were also in other nationalist political organizations and thus, the League's influence was amplified.[113] Through the members' books, articles, speeches and the official publication of the League, the *Alldeutsche Blätter*, the ideology of the Pan-Germans was disseminated throughout Germany. The *Alldeutsche Blätter*, which was released weekly, featured articles focusing on Poland or the preservation of Germanness in communities outside of Germany, such as "Die Polenfrage im Reichstag" (The Polish Question in the *Reichstag*) and "Die Zukunft des Deutschtums in den Baltischen Provinzen" (The Future of Germanness in the Baltic Provinces).[114] Additionally, it discussed news from the German colonies abroad, offered short summaries of the recent activities of regional groups of the League, and published details of new books and events.

A large proportion of the Pan-German ideology focused specifically on *Lebensraum* and, initially, the need for greater government involvement in eastern Germany. The settling of the lands in Prussia by Germans would purportedly enhance and protect the German culture, language, and social structure there. These traditional peasant farmers would form racially and culturally homogenous communities that would be self-reliant, like that of the American frontier, and they would be in command of the "lesser" race in the territory.[115] The Pan-German League's ideological discourse was no exception to the largely derogatory perception of Poland, Poles, or people of Slavic origin, which was abundant in the German political, nationalist, and public spheres both at the time of its founding and throughout its years of operation. Claß' book, *Wenn ich der Kaiser wär'*, is a particularly apt example of the early formations of the League's anti-Slavic and anti-Semitic ideology. In the book, Claß revealed a racially motivated mindset relating to Slavs, Africans, and Jews. Claß wrote, "We know what our people [*Volk*] are, with their good and bad sides" but asked:

> Where does loving humanity and the inclusion in our efforts begin and end? Is the depraved or half-animal Russian peasant of Mir, the Negro in East Africa, the half-caste in German South West Africa, or the intolerable Jew of Galicia or of Romania a member of this humanity? Whoever thinks of humanity at all, is limited to thinking of only those who are worthy of belonging to that humanity.[116]

Claß openly questioned whether members of these populations should be included in any German humanitarian efforts, and he alluded to the belief that they were potentially unworthy of belonging to the same level of humanity as the German people. Interestingly, Claß did not appear to distinguish between the native population of the German colonies in Africa and Russian or Jewish people in Eastern Europe. He questions the humanity of all named groups equally, regardless of skin color or geographical location. Claß also clarified that the measures against immigration would have to be "discerned by their racial affinity, the worth or worthlessness of the foreigners" and "their resulting treatment" would have to be organized. Claß noted that certain foreigners such as "the Flemish, the Dutch, the German-Swiss, and the German-Austrians" would be tolerated as long as their individual behavior was acceptable. However, "Poles, Jews ... Russians, Croatians [and] Italians" were deemed to be undesirable and they should be removed from the borders of the Reich immediately. Claß suggested once this had happened, the borders should then be closed.[117] Claß was not the only Pan-German League member to portray Poles, Slavs, and Jews in such ways.[118] In her article investigating the topic of anti-Slavic imagery in German radical nationalist discourse, Sylvia Jaworska concludes that the discourse is an example of a "negative other-representation and positive self-representation," which relies heavily on the use of metaphors. For example, the *Alldeutsche Blätter* described Polish people as "an unhealthy base" while other publications warned of the "Slavic tide" and "Polish flooding" which would wash into Germany and destroy it.[119] By depicting the undesirable or threatening part of the population with unsavory metaphors and thus, creating a Polish, Slavic and Jewish Other, the Pan-Germans were then able to contrast the German population to these depictions and portray themselves in a better light.[120]

The First World War and its eventual end brought with it a radicalization of the Pan-German League's ideology; for the Pan-Germans, it was "a racial war" which had then been lost.[121] The more radical ideology, which developed with the outbreak of the war and which supported the expulsion of native populations to create space on the land which was heavily linked with the new prospect of the annexation of territory. The Pan-German League was one of the first groups to publish a war aims program that they formulated in August 1914. Among territorial annexations of key industrial areas in the West, the program called for the annexation of the Polish frontier districts and Baltic regions, which were to become a settlement zone. In a sentiment that foreshadowed the Nazi plans for Poland, the League also aimed for the removal of the native populations in these territories and their replacement with Germans and ethnic Germans from abroad.[122]

Woodruff Smith has pointed out, comparable to the case of the GFK, the concept of the German annexation of Eastern European territory did not become the official rhetoric of the Pan-German League until the outbreak of the First World War. As Smith summarizes, the annexationist theories reflected plans for future-orientated migrationist colonialism aimed at Eastern Europe where it was believed there was an abundance of space available. Unlike the initially proposed inner colonization, the annexation of Eastern European territory would allow for the benefits of settlement while not disrupting the *status quo* of the *Junker* (landed nobility) interests in Prussia.[123] The First World War allowed the Pan-German League to envision vast expanses of space suitable for colonization and *Lebensraum*. Similarly, the control of these areas would allow for an imagined reordering of the population in a way that would be favorable to Germany. When the war ended in 1918 and as the Treaty of Versailles came into effect, the Pan-Germans drastically scaled back on their previous territorial aims. Its statutes, which were released in August 1919, called for the return of German territories then annexed to Poland and the annexation of Austria; however, it did not call for the annexation of the territories it had been aiming for at the beginning of the war.

As the blame for the loss of the war began to increasingly be attributed to supposed Bolshevik and Jewish conspirators in Germany, the League's statutes of 1919 reflected the belief that the Jewish people were no longer solely an external threat to Germany but an internal one. Statute 9 noted the League aimed for "the fight against all forces that hamper or harm the *völkisch* development of the German *Volk*, especially xenophilia and the Jewish hegemony which is evident in all areas of culture, business and the State."[124] Thus, the League had begun to portray even the Jewish people who had already integrated into Germany as a hidden threat that had already infiltrated aspects of German life.

Sebastian Conrad argues that although the relationship between the *Kaiserreich* and the Polish-speaking population of Prussia can be viewed within a colonial framework given such factors as the rhetoric of a civilizing mission, racial differentiation, and settlement policies, there were key differences when ruling policies and societal systems in Prussia and the German overseas colonies were compared. For Conrad, the *Kaiserreich*'s colonial attitude toward Prussia was shaped by the long-standing historical relationship and national conflicts between Germany and Poland.[125] Parallel to the GFK and the AfiK, the Pan-German League promoted the expansion of Germany both continentally and overseas. Although continental expansion was preferred, the rhetoric, ideology, and reasons behind acquiring the territory were similar regardless of the geographical location. The Pan-German League provided both spatial and racial solutions to what it perceived as Germany's problems and in doing so, it promoted racist and anti-Semitic theories.

Although the Pan-German League was disbanded by the Nazi regime in March 1939, convincing arguments exist regarding the influence of the Pan-German ideology on the National Socialists. Through an examination of the Pan-German and other radical nationalist ideology as expressed through their publications, Peter Walkenhorst demonstrates that similarities exist between the radical nationalist ideology and that of the Nazis. He explains the Nazis did not produce "ideological innovation," but rather they constructed their ideology based on an "eclectic adoption and a further radicalization of existing radical nationalist interpretative frameworks."[126] Rainer Hering has also investigated the Pan-German League by employing Benedict Anderson's concept of the "imagined community." Hering argues that the racist ideology of the Pan-German League was preparation for further racist thinking in Germany and this ideological presence represents a constant factor that projected from the *Kaiserreich* to the Third Reich.[127] Jaworska determines that there is not only strong evidence of continuity in the use of single lexical units and single metaphorical expressions between radical nationalist and Nazi rhetoric but also in scenarios and storylines that described Germany as a homogenous "*Volkskörper*" (ethnic body) whose health was threatened by "foreign bodies."[128] The National Socialist Party's discourses regarding the interlinking nature of race and space, and the potential of a foreign or Jewish internal or external ethnic threat, can thus be understood as stemming from the same political discourses and entities that often blurred the lines between overseas and continental expansion while promoting the pursuit of *Lebensraum* and the protection of Germany.[129]

Conclusion

With the unification of Germany and the creation of the *Kaiserreich* in 1871, German politicians, scientists, economists, and members of the German public began fantasizing about a strengthened empire both at home and abroad. Although Germany did not possess overseas colonies until 1884, the dreams of exploring and owning colonies, and the plans for reaping both the economic and cultural rewards from such endeavors, were still widespread in Germany. As the *Kaiserreich* gained territories overseas, the German public sphere began to reflect Germany's new place in the world. An empire with colonial subjects, access to colonial goods and the availability of land for settlement. As groups of colonial enthusiasts attempted to encourage further German expansion through publications, exhibitions, and promoting the study of the overseas colonies in schools, other groups such as the Pan-German League promoted both overseas and continental settlement as a solution to German emigration and the mounting tensions between Germans and Poles in Prussia. Like the territories in Africa, Poland and Poles became the subject of colonial othering but also colonial fantasies of civilizing missions, exploration, and expansion.

In 1919, after the First World War, Germany lost its overseas colonies and territory to Poland. For an empire that had placed a huge amount of political value on the need for acquiring space for its people, the reduction of German territory was a demoralizing blow. However, the loss of the colonies and indeed the empire did little to curb the enthusiasm of supporters of German expansion. Far from disappearing with the empire, colonial societies, and political groups increased their efforts to keep German colonialism within the German public sphere. Although they were not extensively supported by an interwar German public, facets of colonial culture, such as monuments, street names, colonial literature, products, and advertisements, lingered in Germany and were actively engaged with. Similarly, the dream of a return to empire was not wiped from the minds of such societies and the DKG, the Pan-German League or the GFK. Despite the Pan-German League and the GFK touting Eastern expansion as the best choice for Germany, they were also presenting colonial solutions to German problems, albeit with a different destination for such colonization to occur.

Historians occasionally argue that Nazi Germany was devoid of a strong colonial influence as evidenced by its attempt to create an empire solely in Eastern Europe. As opposed to arguing that there was a direct causal continuity from the *Kaiserreich* to the Third Reich, this chapter has shown colonial ideas, fantasies, and tangible elements of memorialization were still present in German society right up to the founding of the Third Reich. Discussions surrounding the reclamation of territory and German colonial expansion, whether overseas or continentally, were common occurrences within the public and political spheres and thus formed the public backdrop of the Party's creation. The National Socialist Party and indeed the number of Party supporters grew within an environment where the plans for Germany's future were pulled in different colonial directions. Simultaneously, the idealized memory of the *Kaiserreich*, the territory it possessed and the populations it controlled lingered.

Part II of this book moves forward in time to 1939 with the outbreak of the Second World War in Poland. The chapters will discuss how, through inclusion and exclusion, Nazi Germany attempted to reorder society in Eastern Europe to the benefit of the German occupiers. Although the *Kaiserreich* will not be extensively discussed, the long-standing principles of race and space, embodied in the expansion, settlement, and population policies in annexed Poland, continually resurface. Similarly, the perceptions of Poland as a colonial territory with a supposedly primitive population are also observable within the following chapters. Although it had no direct causal impact on Nazi policies, the *Kaiserreich* was a crucial precursor to Nazi Germany; the economic devastation and bitterness felt after its loss coupled, the reduction in Germany's territorial size, the nostalgic reminders of the empire's former strengths, expansionary discourses, and colonial perceptions of territories and people were all parts of its legacy.

Part Two

The Annexation of Poland and the Restructuring of Society

2

"Our Children Will Have It Better Than We Do!": Societal Stratification and Assimilation in Poland

At the end of December 1939, the German painter and art teacher Otto Engelhardt-Kyffhäuser traveled to Przemyśl on the southeast border of annexed Poland. His task was to visually record the journey of Volhynian and Galician Germans, in the form of sketches and drawings, as they trekked across the border and toward their future homes in the *Reichsgau* Wartheland. The border crossing point was the *Sanbrücke* (San Bridge), named after the San River, which it crossed. Engelhardt-Kyffhäuser waited alongside an ethnic German resettler farmer for the arrival of his six sons, who were part of a large column of traveling ethnic German resettlers expected to soon reach the border. The temperature dropped to minus thirty-two degrees. Snow lay on the ground. Finally, Engelhardt-Kyffhäuser heard the distant crunching of wagon wheels in the snow, and after a short time, an eighteen-year-old man stood before him with his horses. "Go to my uncle in the wagon behind me," said the young man; "tell him that he really is at the San, in German territory. He doesn't want to believe it." Engelhardt-Kyffhäuser recalled that the uncle, a tall farmer dressed in thick furs, looked like a huge bear. As Engelhardt-Kyffhäuser took the man's hand, he said, "Welcome to Greater Germany. You really are home with us, and the San certainly is under us – the border river." The farmer's hands clutched Engelhardt-Kyffhäuser's and he proclaimed, "Thank you! Heil Hitler!" while tears glimmered in his eyes.[1]

Engelhardt-Kyffhäuser's description appeared among other accounts of his time spent with the trek in a 1940 guidebook that accompanied a travelling exhibition containing his visual recording of the trek. The exhibition, titled "*Der große Treck: Die Heimkehr der deutschen Bauern aus Galizien und Wolhynien*" (The Great Trek: The Homecoming of the German Farmers from Galicia and Volhynia), opened from March 30 till April 28 and was held in the *Haus der Kunst* on Hardenbergstraße in Berlin. It showcased 196 sketches and paintings by Engelhardt-Kyffhäuser, which depicted people and moments from the journey of ethnic Germans. The *Hauptamt Volksdeutsche Mittlestelle* (Main Welfare Office for Ethnic Germans, VoMi) had commissioned the exhibition and the organization's head, *SS-Obergruppenführer* Werner Lorenz, opened it.[2] Engelhardt-Kyffhäuser's story of the emotional meeting with the ethnic German resettler could have happened exactly as he described it.

However, as his drawings and the resulting exhibition were destined to become Nazi propaganda tools and promote the resettlement to the German public, the story may also have been embellished. The ethnic German resettlers' return through the *Heim ins Reich* policy and their resettlement in Poland became a mass colonization movement that had a dire impact on the lives of millions of Jewish and non-Jewish Poles. The Polish inhabitants were evicted from their homes, farms, and businesses to provide accommodation and jobs for the incoming resettlers. In addition to ethnic German resettlers, the entire resettlement policy also allowed for the racial screening of local ethnic Germans who had been "stranded" in Polish territories after the Treaty of Versailles. The German authorities and settlement planners allowed local ethnic Germans to select new businesses and houses first. Then the massive influx of racially evaluated ethnic German resettlers from abroad would supplement the local ethnic Germans in populating the newly annexed territories before, finally, Germans from the *Altreich* could settle there after the war.[3] The resettlement was intrinsic to the Nazi plans for populating and securing the newly annexed Polish territories with supposedly racially valuable Germans. Although the resettlement plan appeared to be a straightforward attempt at conquest and settlement, the case of the local ethnic Germans and the resettlers was much more ambiguous. As demonstrated by the above example, ethnic German resettlers were often portrayed using idealized accounts for the benefit of the audience—the German public. However, a closer look at the resettlement and Nazi Germany's colonizing efforts also reveals many contradictions to the notion that the local and resettled ethnic Germans were stereotypical German colonizers. Similarly, the treatment of the non-Jewish Polish population who, through racial and political screening were considered "Germanizable" or "re-Germanizable," can also be compared to certain colonial contexts. This chapter provides background to the ethnic Germans' resettlement and the formation of new societal hierarchies within annexed Poland. It goes on to demonstrate how the often ambiguous status of ethnic Germans and the flexibility of Nazi Germany's inclusionary practices in annexed Poland can be overlapped with stereotypical colonial patterns related to the assimilation of certain population groups.

The Resettlements and Population Sifting

The first resettlement of ethnic German resettlers in the annexed Polish territories took place under the provision for population transfers described in the Molotov-Ribbentrop Pact. Nazi Germany and the Soviet Union signed the secret, non-aggression pact on August 23, 1939. It allowed for the division of territories in Eastern Europe between the two powers and provided for population transfers that would last from 1939 until 1941. Under the Pact, ethnic Germans who lived in territories under Soviet influence, such as the Baltic States, were permitted to resettle within the German-annexed areas. In return, Russians living within territories under German influence could return to the Soviet Union. On October 7, 1939, Hitler issued a secret decree that gave Himmler, the then *Reichsführer-SS*, certain responsibilities for the resettlement. The decree stated Himmler and his new organization, the RKFDV, had three primary tasks, firstly, they would oversee the return of eligible German citizens and ethnic Germans abroad for permanent settlement within Germany's new borders. Secondly, they would carry out the elimination of the alien parts of the population who were supposedly harmful to the Reich and the German *Volksgemeinschaft* (people's community). Thirdly, they would plan and implement the settlement of returning German citizens and ethnic Germans from abroad.[4]

Although Himmler was not authorized to title himself *Kommissar* (Commissioner), he designated his new organization as a *Reichskommissariat* (Reich Commission), and he gave himself the title *Reichkommissar*.[5] The RKFDV utilized separate state and SS organizations to carry out its tasks. The *Rasse-und Siedlungshauptamt-SS* (SS Race and Settlement Main Office, RuSHA) racially evaluated ethnic Germans before their resettlement. They worked in conjunction with the *Einwandererzentralstelle* (Central Immigration Office, EWZ), which oversaw the racial and political screening of ethnic German resettlers to determine their suitability for resettlement. The VoMi found housing and cared for the settlers in the temporary camps while they awaited evaluation and final settlement in the designated settlement areas. The RKFDV and the *SS-Arbeitsstab* (SS Task Force) carried out the task of finding suitable land and evicting the Polish owners and occupants. Through the resettlement, German settlement planners aimed for a middle-class, large-scale agrarian structure that aligned with both national economic interests and the Nazi self-perception of the Germans as the *Herrenvolk* (master race).[6]

From late October to early November 1939, ethnic German resettlers from Estonia and Latvia began to arrive in the *Reichsgau* Danzig-West Prussia. They were settled there or moved on for settlement in the Wartheland (also known as the Warthegau). As this was the first resettlement from the East, and therefore a "model" for any following resettlements, it was carried out carefully for propaganda purposes. For example, although it later became a standard practice to transport the ethnic Germans' livestock, there was a separate transport operation organized for the Baltic Germans' pets. Special effort was also made to preserve and transport Baltic German cultural artifacts, such as pictures and sculptures.[7] Between October 18 and November 15, 1939, 12,868 Estonian Germans were transported to Poland, and between November 7 and December 15 of the same year, 48,868 Latvian Germans followed them. In total, German authorities settled more than 60,000 Baltic Germans by the end of 1939.[8] Although the RKFDV planned that the first settlement of ethnic German resettlers in Danzig-West Prussia would be a model settlement, problems quickly emerged. The Danzig-West Prussia *Gauleiter*, Albert Forster, initially refused the Baltic German transfer and to arrange for their care or settlement in his *Reichsgau*.[9] He did not want elderly or very young resettlers who would hinder the economic productivity of his *Gau*. Himmler ultimately convinced him to accept some of the settlers and the rest went onwards to the *Reichsgau* Wartheland.[10]

Despite the disruption caused by Forster, the RKFDV quickly followed the Baltic German transport with other transports from various parts of Eastern Europe between December 23, 1939, and February 9, 1940. Approximately 65,000 people from Volhynia, 46,000 from Galicia, and 9,000 from the Narew district in eastern Poland arrived in Zgierz near Łódź (Litzmannstadt).[11] In October 1940, 93,548 ethnic

Germans from Bessarabia and 43,568 ethnic Germans from Bukovina left the Soviet-controlled territories; however, only a portion was approved for final settlement.[12] By the end of the war, almost one million ethnic Germans had traveled on ships, trains, or in horse-drawn carriages to annexed Poland and had resettled there.

Before the EWZ could approve ethnic German resettlers for settlement, they had to undergo a thorough examination process to determine their racial and political suitability. Despite the EWZ's best efforts, even the term "*Volksdeutsche*" or ethnic German was originally more of a general concept than a concrete definition. The term referred to a person of German heritage who was living abroad and who may or may not (depending on the various standards) have maintained linguistic, cultural, or political links to Germany. After the German defeat in the First World War and the loss of German territory in the east, ethnic Germans were portrayed as isolated ethnic minorities under foreign regimes. Hitler loosely attempted to define the term in a 1938 memorandum, which stated that ethnic Germans were German in language and culture but did not hold German citizenship.[13] Similarly, in a leaflet issued by the VoMi that described important national political terms, "*Volksdeutsche*" was defined as a German without German citizenship, "*Deutscher*" (German) was defined as a person who had German ethnic lineage, and "*Reichsdeutscher*" (Reich German) implied a German citizen of the Reich.[14]

The first resettlements of Baltic Germans from Latvia and Estonia in October 1939 were not subject to racial examination; however, the EWZ implemented a racial screening process in the following resettlements.[15] Based in Łódź (Litzmannstadt) from autumn 1940 and with branches in locations such as Gdynia (Gotenhafen), Szczecin (Stettin), and Piła (Schneidemühl), the EWZ used the screenings to ascertain not only the racial value of individual ethnic German resettlers but also their political loyalty and employment potential. They decided if the applicant would be granted German citizenship and where they would ultimately be resettled based on the evaluation results. The initial stages of screening began with an application. Every ethnic German person over the age of fourteen could apply for resettlement (in cases of families, this was left up to the head of the family), and preferably, the applicants should have possessed documents that proved their German descent.[16] Application for resettlement was voluntary; however, external pressures such as the potential of being a member of an even further reduced ethnic minority group within Soviet territories often fueled decisions to apply. Additionally, as ethnic German communities were being targeted for resettlement in groups, the social pressure of moving with one's established community was another crucial factor.[17] Specially trained EWZ members known as *Fliegende Kommissionen* (flying commissions) traveled to the various VoMi temporary camps that housed resettlers after their journey to the annexed territories, and here, they oversaw the screening process.[18] Several *Kommissionen* worked simultaneously and between 1939 and 1945, the EWZ had thirty in operation.[19] Ethnic German *Volkstumssachverständigen* (experts for regional ethnicity) supplemented the EWZ and provided specific regional information on the groups of ethnic German resettlers being evaluated.

The screening process began with ethnic German resettlers registering their personal details and religious affiliation (*Melde-und Ausweisstelle*) as individuals or as families. From there, the resettlers had their photos taken (*Lichtbildstelle*) for their identification documents and the EWZ records. The EWZ evaluated the resettlers' wealth and assets at the next station (*Vermögensstelle*) so that, should they be resettled in the East, they would be allocated property of the same value as that which they had left behind. The next screening stage was the health evaluation (*Gesundheitsstelle*) where the resettlers would not only undergo a general health examination but were also evaluated to establish their genetic and racial status. RuSHA racial experts and doctors physically checked the resettlers for signs of illness or hereditary diseases. The examination for hereditary diseases was of particular importance as doctors specifically attempted to establish the *Lebenstüchtigkeit* (vitality or capability for life) of ethnic German individuals as this related to their reproductive capabilities.[20] The doctors also determined the resettlers' blood groups and, according to Himmler's wishes, the blood group type was tattooed on their arm.[21] The doctors then measured the body, skull, and nose of the applicant and examined their eyes and hair color to establish their supposed racial value.

From this examination, the doctors assigned each ethnic German resettler to one of four racial value groups (*Wertungsgruppen*). Level I was for those of the highest racial value and classed as "pure Nordic," whereas Level II was for those of an average racial value. Level III was for those of a partially mixed racial status and Level IV was for those thought to be completely mixed or completely "Eastern," "East Baltic," or "foreign-blooded."[22] The RuSHA produced closing reports after the racial screening of regional ethnic German groups to summarize the evaluations. After the screening of ethnic German resettlers from Estonia and Latvia, the report from March 1940 noted the "racial worth" of the Baltic Germans was high in general and ethnic Germans from Estonia were slightly better than the ones from Latvia. However, ethnic Germans from the Soviet Union were found to have foreign blood from "Mongolian, Western Asian, Malay and Inner Asian races."[23]

The naturalization of ethnic German resettlers and the evaluation of their political loyalty was carried out in the next stage (*Staatsbürgerschaftsstelle und Volkstumsprüfung*). To be naturalized as a German citizen, the resettlers had to meet the criteria of German descent and political reliability.[24] The latter was judged by such factors as the ability to speak German or demonstrable proof of a commitment to Germany. EWZ guidelines issued on December 13, 1939 in Poznań (Posen) noted that language was a basic feature of German ethnicity but warned the Russian or Polish language may have influenced the ethnic Germans' dialects. Guidelines from December 12, 1939 noted in addition to statements by the applicant, other requirements, such as prior German education and attitude or membership of German clubs or associations, should be considered when assessing political alliances.[25] The final screening stage was at the Office of Labor Deployment (*Berufeinsatzstelle*) where ethnic Germans had their professional skills recorded so they could eventually be assigned work. By the end of May 1940, over 100,000 resettlers had been processed in this way.[26]

Although the racial and political criteria impacted the decision on naturalization, if an individual possessed certain specialist skills related to a particular area of use for war-related tasks, it could also influence the citizenship decision and where they would be resettled.[27] Generally, those classified as *Wertungsgruppen* Levels I or II were considered suitable for resettlement in the East, for example, in the Wartheland, and thus, they were given the *Ansatzbescheid* O (*Ost*). After January 1940, those classified as Level III were also considered for Eastern resettlement. Before this, both Levels III and IV were classified as *Ansatzbeschid* A (*Altreich*) or S (*Sonder* or special) cases. A-cases were resettled within the pre-1939 German borders and were usually put to work as industrial laborers. S-cases were sent back to their country of origin or sent to the General Government for labor. The designation of A or O settlement also influenced the financial compensation to which the resettlers were entitled after leaving their business, property, and goods in their country of origin. Regardless of the extent of their cash or property assets, A cases could only avail of debt register claims. On the other hand, O cases could be entitled to farms for compensation, even if they had not previously owned one. The reordering of the economic ownership in the territories was therefore not only achieved by the removal of Jews and Poles and the robbery and redistribution of their assets. The racial selection of ethnic Germans also extensively facilitated it.[28]

While awaiting their EWZ evaluation and their final resettlement, ethnic Germans were housed in temporary camps that were run by the VoMi. The camps were divided into three different types; the first was the *Durchgangslager* (transit camp) where the ethnic Germans passed through briefly. The second was the *Sammellager* (assembly camps), where they would be processed; stays here could last from several days to a week. The last camp in the processing stage was the *Beobachtungslager* (observation camps), where ethnic German resettlers stayed for at least four weeks. The EWZ used the last camp to observe if the ethnic German resettlers had any undesirable political inclinations or physical characteristics that they may have missed during the initial processing. The VoMi camp system was extensive; in the years 1940 to 1941, between 1,500 and 1,800 camps existed.[29] The camps were frequently established in existing buildings such as schools, churches, factories, and hotels; however, these buildings were not always suitable for long-term stays. In the *Sammellager*, resettlers were provided with straw beds, pillows made of sewn material filled with straws and blankets, which were given to women and children. Although the camps were lit by electric lights and boiled water was available, they only offered basic accommodation.[30]

In theory, the stay in the temporary camps should have only lasted just over a month. However, this was usually not the case. Delays because of a lack of available permanent accommodation or the wait for individuals or groups wanting to reunite with their families in the camps were frequent. Ethnic German resettlers, some of whom had traveled from many miles away, often felt unhappy and disappointed upon realizing they had to wait in temporary camps for weeks. Others complained about crowded accommodation, boredom, and wartime shortages and that the rooms were ridden with rats and insects.[31] As the resettlers' complaints demonstrate, despite the plans for running an efficient selection and aftercare process, camp life reality was very different. In a letter to *Reichsstatthalter Posen* and *Gauleiter* of the Wartheland Arthur Greiser's offices, an ethnic German resettler who was originally from Lublin complained about the camp conditions during his month spent there.[32] Although he had already been resettled in Swarzędz (Schwaningen) in the Wartheland at the time of writing the letter, he blamed his time in the camp for his current illnesses: tuberculosis and anemia. The man explained he had been healthy his whole life up until the point of the resettlement. He believed his ill health was a result of lying on the floor of the camps in winter with only thin straw sacks to line the ground. He further complained that his sickness was also due to cold trains and train waiting rooms that he had to use for traveling to work in Poznań. He found it nonsensical that he had been resettled in Swarzędz when there was no job for him there.[33]

Although the *Reichsministerium für Volksaufklärung und Propaganda* (Reich Propaganda Ministry, RMVP) attempted to take advantage of the delays in the camps by using the time to implement ideological mentoring program, they largely failed to have a significant impact. This was partially due to the camp conditions but also due to the majority of the resettlers' lack of German language skills.[34] During their time in the camps, the physically healthy ethnic German resettlers could be assigned work in sectors that would help the war effort, such as agriculture or industry. Although this work may have been welcomed by some to curb the boredom, Valdis Lumans notes it is unlikely they had much choice in the matter.[35] The work may have helped with the monotony of life in the camps, but it caused another problem. When the authorities eventually allocated a final settlement destination, it often caused resentment both with individual resettlers and the employer when he or she had to leave. This was avoided in the case of work that was deemed essential to the war effort as in these cases, efforts were made to allow the resettler to stay in that area.[36]

Despite efforts to find work, many ethnic German resettlers encountered problems with finding suitable jobs or receiving state payments to which they felt entitled. For example, in September 1940, Frau d'Angé, a Baltic German resettler and trained opera singer wrote a complaint letter that she addressed to Himmler. Frau d'Angé came from Latvia and was resettled in Poznań, where she hoped to find a position as an opera singer. However, she wrote that, thus far, she was unable to be admitted into the *Reichstheaterkammer* (Reich theater association) due to a delay in her final examination. She explained that as a result, she was currently unemployed. Her complaint related to an incident where she was told by the manager of the *Fürsorgeamt für baltendeutsche Umsiedler* (Baltic German Resettlers' Welfare Office) that she was committing an offense by receiving money from them. However, she felt she was justified to receive the payments given her unemployment status. In the last correspondence available regarding Frau d'Angé, the *Reichsstatthalter's* office in Poznań reported in July 1941, almost twelve months later, that Frau d'Angé was still not working as an opera singer, but she had secured a job in the office of the *Landesbühne Warthegau* (state theater Warthegau).[37] The German promise of a new and better life within the Third Reich was not an easy or quick one to fulfil. Occasionally, it was not fulfilled at all.

Even after the camp stages and their final resettlement, not all ethnic German resettlers were happy with the working or economic situation they now found themselves in. The resettlement process was extremely disruptive for the resettlers' emotional, financial, and, as demonstrated by the complaint letter, physical well-being. In postwar testimonies recorded in the early to mid-1950s, Bukovina Germans who had taken part in the resettlement aired their feelings of disappointment and resentment about the experience. Expectations, built on Nazi propaganda that promised bigger houses, land, peace, and German neighborhoods, were often not met. Although the narratives of resettlement changed over time, in the immediate postwar period, Bukovina Germans often portrayed themselves within the context of victimhood and as having been "helpless."[38] The *Heim ins Reich* policy uprooted people from their familiar environments and subjected them to camps where their freedom was restricted. The resettlement process ultimately separated families, friends, and communities, and the logistics of moving, screening, and allocating homes created tensions between the various groups of ethnic Germans and the *Gau* authorities who were overseeing their settlement.[39]

Colonizer or "Colonial Other"?

From the temporary camps, ethnic Germans were transported to their new homes which lay within the *Reichsgaue* Wartheland and Danzig-West Prussia. The forced expulsion of the non-Jewish and Jewish Poles meant that not only homes but also farms, businesses, and personal possessions were left behind for distribution among the incoming ethnic Germans. After the owners were removed from their homes and farms, young German women, many of whom were students who had been assigned tasks in annexed Poland after their graduation (*Osteinsatz*, Eastern Work Placement), cleaned and prepared the houses for the ethnic German resettlers' arrival. The initiative was run by a variety of different organizations, such as the *NS-Frauenschaft* (National Socialist Women's League), the *Bund Deutscher Mädel* (BDM, League of German Girls), the *Reichsarbeitsdienst der weiblichen Jugend* (Women's Youth Labor Service), and the *Arbeitsgemeinschaft nationalsozialistischer Studentinnen* (National Socialist Women Student Organization). They encouraged young women to move east or occasionally assigned them to specific locations to not only help with the resettlement and Germanization of ethnic Germans but also to contribute to the development of culture and community in the settlement villages.

The first group of female settlement advisors arrived in the Wartheland in December 1939. Thousands of other women followed throughout the war. To aid the settlement process, the women visited houses after (and sometimes during) the forced expulsion of Jews and Poles. The local police force usually carried out the physical evictions according to orders from the *SS-Arbeitsstab* (SS Task Force). As well as cleaning and preparing the homes for ethnic Germans, the women helped ensure the Jews and Poles did not bring any valuable possessions with them and distributed the stolen belongings to ethnic Germans. The preparations reportedly even included putting flowers on the table and cooking dinner for the new inhabitants.[40] While the Germans evicted the native population and forcibly deported many to unknown destinations, often only a few hours after the original inhabitants had left, the resettlers were supposed to be met at their new homes by a welcoming and calm atmosphere created by the settlement advisors.

However, such a welcoming atmosphere was not always achieved during the arrival of every ethnic German family. The Molotov-Ribbentrop Pact allowed for the quick transfer of thousands of ethnic Germans and, as such, they were soon arriving in Poland for resettlement. The evictions of Poles to vacate a sufficient number of homes to accommodate ethnic Germans were not happening as quickly as they were arriving. In 2009, Jana Elena Bosse conducted interviews with Baltic Germans who resettled in the Wartheland. One of the interviewees recalled that when they entered their new apartment, there was still food on the table and it was very obvious from the open cupboards, the vegetables strewn on the table, and the unmade beds that the previous inhabitants had been forced to leave very quickly. The interviewee guessed that at least two children had been pulled from their beds. Similarly, another interviewee recalled the beds in their new apartment were unmade and still warm. Cups and cutlery were still on the table. The interviewee's father complained that it was an "inhuman thing" and the family went back to the camp.[41]

Conversely, in the book *Baltenbreife zur Rückkehr ins Reich* (Baltic Letters on the Return to the Reich), which was part of the series *Volksdeutsche Heimkehr* (Ethnic German Homecoming), one of the letters from a Baltic German described their new accommodation in an inn where they had two rooms with "nice, wide beds, feather mattresses and feather bedding."[42] The letters included in the book portrayed the resettlement in the best possible light for propaganda purposes; nevertheless, Bosse's interviews also reveal that some Baltic Germans were happy with their allocated accommodation and at least one family had input regarding the size of their future accommodation. They were also permitted to decide which pieces of original furniture they wanted to keep.[43] Such conflicting testimonies highlight some factors of the variable nature of the resettlement experience. Some ethnic Germans were aware of the forced nature of the evictions of the Polish people and the true origins of their new homes and possessions. For others, it appeared they were satisfied with what they were allocated and did not openly question how the property or possessions were made available to them. Having been subjected to relocation, the VoMi camps, racial screening, and resettlement to a final destination, ethnic Germans could not establish their new lives in their assigned houses as they desired. Although the racially approved ethnic German resettlers were now administratively a part of Nazi Germany's *Volksgemeinschaft*, they still had to undergo Germanization to transform them into "proper" Germans. In light of this, the settlement advisors regularly visited the resettlers' homes and ensured they were adhering to principles of health, order, and cleanliness. Guidelines for the home visits noted that attention should be paid to such areas as the women's health, children's health, the general impression of the household and the housewife, cleaning facilities, and if there was fresh air ventilation.[44] During the home visits, the settlement advisors also checked the décor to make sure it was in a "German-style" and devoid of any objects considered to be too "kitsch." Images of saints were often removed from the homes and replaced with pictures of Hitler. Additionally, the settlement advisors discouraged the wearing of traditional dress, such as the Bessarabian German women's headscarves.[45]

Settlement advisors held courses for ethnic German women on infant care and nursing as early as in the camp stages of the resettlement process. As noted in an article in *Der Gauring*, a National Socialist Party bulletin for Danzig-West Prussia, ethnic German women were taught these techniques to dissuade them from using outdated methods.[46] In the settlement zones, the *NS-Frauenschaft* ran mothers' schools (*Mütterschule*), which offered classes for the resettlers on the subjects of infant care, cooking, and sewing. They also taught modern, German techniques for household management. According to *Der Gauring*, the mothers' schools were particularly important because, during the interwar period in Poland, the "oppressed" population were forced to ignore the simplest parts of infant care as the "most primitive needs," such as soap, were too expensive.[47]

By educating ethnic German mothers and implementing new techniques within the domestic sphere, Reich Germans not only aimed to help strengthen the health of the youngest members of the German communities. They also attempted to implant elements of German modernity directly into the homes of the female caregivers of the new settlement areas. As well as teaching ethnic Germans about hygiene and healthcare, German student doctors taking part in their *Osteinsatz* medically cared for the ethnic Germans. Although the ethnic Germans had been racially evaluated and had met the criteria for being recognized as German, and their resettlement and presence in the Polish territories was planned to contribute to the German colonization of Poland, elements of their treatment highlight that ethnic Germans were not treated as equal by Reich Germans.

In addition to educating ethnic German women, the BDM placed particular importance on the education of ethnic German children as part of the Germanization process. BDM leaders (some were qualified schoolteachers, some were not) and students on their *Osteinsatz* began establishing German schools in the settlement areas where they were assigned to. The schools provided education in reading, writing, and mathematics and they aimed to teach the ethnic German children to be fluent in German, to indoctrinate them with key National Socialist ideology regarding race, and to encourage them to support Germany. The Germans established thousands of elementary schools in annexed Poland to cater for the ever-increasing ethnic German population. For example, the number of German elementary schools in the Wartheland increased from fifty-nine in 1939 to 2,032 by April 1944, and the number of pupils in these schools increased from 4,000 to over 144,000 in the same period.[48] Conversely, in the Wartheland, Polish children were only allowed to attend school between the ages of ten and fourteen and were usually taught by poorly trained German teachers. In Danzig West-Prussia, Polish children could only attend primary schools where they would preferably only be taught in German. German children were not permitted to attend Polish schools and vice versa.[49]

The school system thus further amplified the divisions present in their society for both the children and their parents. Outside of school, guidelines for settlement advisors on home visits noted they should reinforce the notion that ethnic German children were not allowed to play with Polish children under any circumstances.[50] Thus, both inside and outside of school, Reich Germans separated ethnic German children (many of whom spoke fluent Polish as opposed to German) from Polish children while also discouraging contact, let alone friendships. The elementary schools were seen as the "focal point of the nationalist struggle for the preservation of German culture" due to the influence education would have on the next generation of Germans in Eastern Europe.[51] The very act of attending German-only schools reinforced the anti-Polish attitude that Reich Germans and the RKFDV were attempting to instill in the ethnic Germans by segregating the resettlers and offering them the "privilege" of a German education. As elucidated in an excerpt from a Reich German student's *Osteinsatz* diary, the student noted the ethnic German parents were happy their children could "finally" go to a German school again.[52]

As mentioned in this book's introduction, in the context of the debate on the potential of continuities between the *Kaiserreich* and the Nazi regime, and the debate on the similarities between Nazi Germany's expansion and colonialism, historians have largely focused on the topic of violence and as such, on the victims. Scholars have primarily sought ways in which the actions perpetrated against Jewish victims fit or do not fit into frameworks of colonial violence. For example, David Furber and Wendy Lower have argued that, because of the planned extermination of Jews, the treatment of non-Jewish Poles, can be considered as most similar to the treatment of a stereotypical colonial native as opposed to the treatment of the Jews.[53] The focus on the Jewish victim group is understandable. However, thus far, historians within the debate concerning colonial similarities have rarely incorporated comparisons related to the population group who were Nazi Germany's designated colonizers: ethnic Germans.[54] At first glance, ethnic Germans seemed to fulfil the intended function as settlers who would help colonize the newly annexed territories. The RKFDV allocated the local and resettled ethnic Germans homes, land, and businesses that had previously belonged to non-Jewish and Jewish Poles and, as a result, the native Polish population was forcibly evicted and thousands were deported. The ethnic Germans formed pockets of German settlement that supposedly protected German territory in the East. They ran businesses and farms and helped create new German societies, based on strict racial stratification, within the annexed territory. However, ethnic Germans were not "usual" colonizers when compared with colonial contexts. In addition to Jewish and non-Jewish Poles, ethnic Germans were also subjected to certain Nazi policies and treatment despite their crucial role in helping create a German community in Poland.

When viewing the work of the Reich German settlers from a colonial perspective, certain similarities arise. For example, French women were specifically encouraged to train indigenous Vietnamese, Lao, and Khmer women in French Indochina on domestic matters.[55] "The native woman needs to learn to keep house: she knows nothing of running a European house … It is in the home that a woman can be an aid in Frenchification," one writer noted.[56] Comparable to the settlement advisors in Poland, domestic standards were directly associated with the central characteristics of the ruling European power. At the 1931 Paris Colonial Exhibition, groups and societies encouraged French women to participate in work in the colonies especially in the area of educating the native women on hygiene and childcare.[57] Medicine and healthcare in a colonial context connected with the civilizing or humanitarian mission by aiding the native population, but aid was given in ways which clearly labelled the indigenous population as unhygienic.[58] Thus, medicine and the stereotypes it legitimized assisted in enforcing differentiation between the colonizer and the colonized. In addition to humanitarian missions, Roy MacLeod notes that "European medicine, and its handmaiden, public health, served as tools of empire."[59] Medical aid was a means to persuade the native population of the benefits of life as colonial subjects, which in turn could reinforce societal control and encourage political loyalty. Furthermore, under the façade of medical care, colonial powers and the Reich German settlement advisors in Poland were able to further infiltrate the citizens' private lives.

As Nancy Reagin has demonstrated, the Nazi regime radicalized both domesticity and gender within the private sphere and, as such, homemaking and family life became a fundamental part of both national identity and belonging.[60] The role of women within the home was closely linked with Nazi ideology regarding hygiene and racial purity but also self-sufficiency. The domestic training of ethnic German women was thus a mirroring of national expectations. Such a mirroring of national policy and colonial policy and an intrinsic connection between these policies and the topic of the home was not unusual in colonial contexts.[61] However, the training provided to the ethnic Germans did differ slightly from such tasks within the *Altreich* because the area of their implementation was geographically distant from German metropoles. The supposedly German principles of order and cleanliness in the home could be contrasted with the homes of Poles, those considered to be culturally or ethnically inferior. Common colonial tropes of colonizer superiority could therefore be reinforced through the lens of homemaking. German national identity and domestic order and cleanliness were closely interrelated during the Third Reich; therefore, the principles were fundamental to the Germanization of ethnic Germans in Poland.[62] Nazi Germany thus assigned the tasks an added layer of urgency and gravity given that they were fulfilled in foreign territories where German settlers' culture needed to be protected but also transformed.

Similar to colonial contexts, the ethnic German children's education was not only used as a method to provide them with essential skills and to assimilate them into German life. It was also a method through which they could be introduced to crucial details regarding the new structuring of society. Education in colonial settings had far more widespread aims than those in the metropole, and this type of education took place both in and out of the school. The broader educational aims included altering various social, religious, and ideological interactions, practices, and beliefs of both children and adults.[63] During the 1830s, the British Empire's establishment of a national school system in Ireland was driven by a need to create links between the Irish people and the empire with a view to better controlling them.[64] While different colonial and imperial powers had numerous approaches to educational policies and also different goals, similar to the education of ethnic German children in Poland, education in a colonial context was not only a way of teaching new skills for potential economic contribution. Certain colonial educational approaches reflected a paternalistic mindset. This mindset aimed at elevating the population through education, while also integrating them into the ruling power's culture for the achievement of both present and future aims. It was also a way of incorporating children into societal systems, making them aware of their particular societal standing, and creating political loyalty to the ruling power.

The provision of healthcare and education, but also the Reich Germans' perception that the ethnic German resettlers were primitive, is to an extent comparable to nationalizing processes. The Nazi assimilation process was undoubtedly a type of nationalization, it gave individuals German citizenship; however, I would argue that the process was more similar to a colonial one than standard nationalization as it did not occur within the borders of Germany and the *Altreich*, rather it occurred in recently conquered foreign territories. In France, for example, the attempts at nationalizing peasants were linked heavily with industrialization and urban and rural tensions. Peasants were drawn to cities and towns where a preestablished French community and institutions or institutional representatives such as doctors, clubs, and civil servants facilitated the nationalizing process. Interestingly, in his well-known investigation of the nationalization of peasants in France, Eugen Weber notes "what happened was akin to colonization, and may be easier to understand if one bears that in mind."[65] In annexed Poland, German communities and institutions or institutional representatives were largely established or strengthened after the German conquest had taken place and the transformation of the areas began. As such, although the processes of nationalization may appear similar to the policies related to ethnic Germans, the Nazi process of Germanizing and assimilating them in Poland was strongly linked to foreign expansion, settlement, securing land, the removal of the indigenous Polish population, and, perhaps most importantly, the eradication of racial threats. Through the racial and political screening described earlier in this chapter, ethnic Germans could also be denied acceptance into the upper levels of the German racial hierarchy. Additionally, the privileges offered to ethnic German resettlers who did make it to Poland were colonial in nature because many of these privileges relied on the subjugation and mistreatment of Poles and were shaped by German continental colonial objectives to secure territory.

As demonstrated by the examples presented, although the German authorities may have considered racially valuable ethnic German resettlers, and indeed local ethnic Germans in Poland, as German, in reality, Reich Germans did not treat them as equals. Ethnic German resettlers were not automatically permitted to self-integrate themselves into society despite the German fantasy of them being fellow countrymen returning home to the Reich. The treatment of ethnic Germans was, given the attempts to assimilate them into German culture and society, more comparable to the treatment of indigenous populations in colonial settings. Ethnic Germans were not only required to be officially evaluated to determine their suitability for resettlement; after resettlement they also had to be observed, looked after, trained, and educated by Reich Germans. The Germanization of ethnic Germans, or the effort to assimilate them into German political, ideological, and cultural norms, can be thus understood as a process that aligned with a more wide-ranging colonial framework of assimilation processes and the colonizers' self-perceived civilizing missions, not solely a Nazi German one.

Germans or Foreigners? Public Depictions and Private Perceptions

The ethnic German resettlement was not kept secret from the German public. On the contrary, the resettlement policy and photographs and descriptions of ethnic Germans featured heavily in newspaper and magazine articles, books, exhibitions, postcards, and official government organization pamphlets throughout the war. Such communication channels acted as propaganda for both the resettlement and the Nazi regime, as they were crucial in conveying how elements of German conquest and rule were being implemented in the annexed territories. Similarly, the material which was released to the public legitimized the German involvement in Poland by highlighting the work performed by Reich Germans to help ethnic Germans. Publications such as Engelhardt-Kyffhäuser's *Das Buch vom großen Treck* made for popular reading. It became a bestseller and within one year, it had sold 45,000 copies.[66] The popularity of both the topic of resettlement and Engelhardt-Kyffhäuser's work can also be seen from the number of cities his exhibition traveled to throughout the war. The public viewed Engelhardt-Kyffhäuser's exhibition in such cities as Krakow between February 2 and 12, 1940; Görlitz in June 1940; Munich in July 1940, 1941, 1942, and 1944; Poznań in March 1941; Saarbrücken in July 1941; and Łódź in December 1941.[67] By holding exhibitions, publishing resettlers' portraits and personal stories (or at least stories that claimed to be personal), reporting on the progress of the resettlement, and reiterating the importance of it, German authorities and resettlement groups attempted to solidify the resettlement into the collective consciousness and emotions of the German nation.

The public depictions of the resettlement not only adhered to geographical or statistical facts about the movement and settlement of ethnic Germans. They also commented on the ethnic German resettlers' personalities, as well as their physical appearance. One of the most prominent approaches was in-depth descriptions of the physical struggles that the resettlers had suffered during their voluntary move to German territory. This move was also framed as a direct answer to Hitler's call. For example, the publication *Völkerwanderung im 20. Jahrhundert* (Migration in the Twentieth Century) began with the notion that Hitler had tasked ethnic Germans with resettling. It proclaimed "Hitler orders – we follow!"[68] Similarly, the VoMi pamphlet *Der Führer hat uns gerufen* (The Führer has called us) reminded the reader that the Volhynian Germans, currently housed in camps, had voluntarily left their homes, farms, and fields to travel home to the Reich.[69] The pamphlet asked whether there was a more open declaration of willingness, a lovelier, or a more devout commitment to the German Reich.[70] Its back cover explained that the resettlers had traveled 250 kilometers in snow and ice through Volhynia. The pamphlet concluded with a call to the German people to go toward these Germans, to talk with them, and to always keep in mind that "these men and women had to struggle more for their Germanness than any German in the Reich."[71]

In another publication, *135,000 gewannen das Vaterland* (135,000 Gained The Fatherland), which was part of four volumes in a series entitled *Volksdeutsche Heimkehr* (Ethnic German Homecoming), the author similarly described the hardships ethnic Germans had to face. He mentioned that ethnic German resettlers often traveled day and night in temperatures as low as minus forty degrees.[72] Once again, the author highlighted how ethnic Germans voluntarily left their "homes and farms, on fields and meadows," and they were already joyful about building a new life once they were allowed to come "home" to the Greater German Reich.[73] The language used in such publications continuously reiterated the resettlement's voluntary nature and the sacrifices ethnic Germans had made to travel to and eventually settle in the Reich. By demonstrating ethnic Germans' nationalistic pride, the publications appeared to attempt to create pride in the ethnic German resettlers' patriotism. They presented the resettlers as German heroes who, after facing years of adversary under foreign powers, were now sacrificing their homes and possessions and enduring an arduous journey to reunite with Germany.[74]

Publications also attempted to demonstrate similarities and, in turn, to foster connections between ethnic German resettlers and Germans in the *Altreich*. They frequently mentioned that the resettlers were German in appearance, with blue eyes and blond hair. A short article in the *Hamburger Anzeiger* in March 1941 described the arrival of ethnic German resettlers from Bessarabia to the Wartheland. The author noted that the Bessarabian Germans were "wonderful people." The men, especially, were "imposing" and had "angular faces" with the "natural, proud demeanor of farmers."[75] Publications also described the resettlers as German speakers who occasionally even had German dialects. In a short anecdote in his book about the resettlement of the Bessarabian Germans, Andreas Pampuch recounted a story from his time with a column of resettlers and the *SS-Umsiedlungskommando* (SS Resettlement Command) who were overseeing the journey. Pampuch witnessed a German from the *SS-Umsiedlungskommando* and an ethnic German man from the Black Sea talking with one another. Before long, the two realized that the ethnic German man's ancestors came from the same region in Swabia as the German man came from. Pampuch described how 125 years ago, both the men's ancestors had emigrated and now their descendants were meeting again, speaking the same dialect and carrying the "same name as their old *Heimat*." He wrote "he would never forget this moment."[76]

Pampuch's story demonstrates not only an interesting coincidence of two men who serendipitously discover familial links. It also highlights the idea that ethnic German resettlers were not so different from the Germans of the *Altreich* and some were still very aware of and connected to their German heritage. In a similar attempt to highlight similarities and links, Helmut Sommer, the author of *135,000 gewannen das Vaterland* described how he visited the children's playroom in one of the temporary camps. The room was furnished with small chairs, benches, and colorfully varnished tables. A young girl with long, blonde plaits hugged a doll tightly to her chest while boys examined toy trains and cars. Before long, the author began to talk to the children's mothers. He noted how they spoke perfect German. Common German family names such as Schmidt, Schulze, and Bavarian names like Huber often cropped up in the conversation.[77] Similarly, in the publication *Das Buch vom großen Treck*, Otto Engelhardt-Kyffhäuser also attempted to create bonds between the reader and ethnic German resettlers. He described the Volhynian Germans as the "German brothers and sisters" who greeted the welcoming party with a "Heil Hitler" as they crossed the border.[78]

The modesty and hardworking attitude of ethnic Germans was also a feature in publications. In *135,000 gewannen das Vaterland*, Sommer wrote that although the ethnic German resettler mothers were grateful for all that the Reich Germans were doing for them, the ethnic German women often asked the Reich Germans not go to so much trouble on their behalf. The author explained despite their abundance of children, the female resettlers were still accustomed to working in the fields. According to the author, they could hardly wait to return to work on the land with their husbands.[79] Ethnic German resettlers were portrayed as similarly hardworking in the book *Der Zug der Volksdeutschen aus Bessarabien und dem Nord-Buchenland*.

The book explained that the ethnic German resettlers found the time in the temporary camps to be particularly hard. Previously, they had worked like their fathers and had not known holidays or inaction. Now, they wanted to return to work.[80]

Undoubtedly, the historical analysis of such sources as those described is not straightforward. The authors and photographers who recorded the resettlement were likely to have been fully aware of how their material would later be used or into what context it would be placed. Therefore, authors and photographers produced the material with this in mind. Conversely, some may not have been aware of where such material would eventually appear and so the intent behind such contributions may genuinely have been to capture and preserve visual or anecdotal records of the resettlement. Elizabeth Harvey argues that in the case of photographs, the resettlement had to appear as though it was the "unfolding of destiny, a logical end to the German 'cultural mission.'"[81] The majority of texts and pictures thus appear to attempt to capture the historic nature and the resettlement's significance as a national, German event that needed to be documented. Similarly, the portrayals attempted to highlight the inherent Germanness of the new settlers, as well as their patriotism and heroism. They had to create empathy among the viewer or reader while simultaneously legitimizing the resettlement policy that had led to the resettlers leaving their homes and traveling through the adverse weather conditions.

Despite the themes that are apparent in propaganda material related to the resettlement, a further examination of sources reveals portrayals of ethnic Germans by Reich Germans working in the *Reichsgaue* and by photographers and authors that seem to contradict the portrayal of ethnic Germans as suitable or "ready-made" German citizens and colonizers. As previously mentioned in this chapter, ethnic Germans first had to undergo Germanization before they could be fully integrated into the Third Reich and certain elements of this treatment are comparable to the treatment of indigenous populations by colonial powers. Similarly, ethnic Germans were often perceived by Reich Germans in a way that is comparable to the perception of colonial subjects, as opposed to fellow German citizens.

The theory of the supposed primitive nature of Poland and Poles was present in German politics and literature since the *Kaiserreich*; however, during the resettlement of ethnic Germans, they were also portrayed as primitive or backward and consequently, in need of German help.[82] Martha Michelsohn, a German woman from Laage who volunteered as a settlement advisor in the Wartheland, appears as one of the interviewees in Claude Lanzmann's momentous documentary *Shoah*. Michelsohn firstly went from Münster to Koło (Warthbrücken), then on to Chełmno (Kulm), and finally to Chełmno nad Nerem (Kulmhof an der Nehr).[83] In the interview transcript, Michelsohn explains that the ethnic Germans who arrived from Volhynia were "very poor people" and, although they had been provided with land, equipment, and seed from the government, "they were not used to modern equipment."[84] In a similar observation, the ethnic Germans' primitiveness was partially blamed on their succumbing to foreign influences. A female student noted that ethnic Germans who had previously "lived only among Poles and Russians are not used to the German work tempo and also are not fully familiar with German order and cleanliness."[85] One settlement advisor's description of the resettlers in Toruń (Thorn) portrayed them as almost childlike; she described how when she returned to inspect the ethnic Germans' houses after her Christmas break, one family was disappointed because she did not check all their rooms.[86] Similarly, a settlement advisor in Lipno (Leipe) described the success of the cooking course in the *Mütterschule* and mentioned that most of the settlers showed a great deal of interest in anything new and unknown.[87] Another explicitly illustrated the paternalistic attitude of Reich Germans when she referred to the Volhynian settlers she was helping as "my problem children."[88]

Interestingly, the Reich German's paternalistic attitude toward ethnic Germans was also evident to the Poles. One Polish witness recalled from personal observations and from hearing stories that Reich Germans did not trust ethnic Germans. The witness remembered how the Reich Germans had "despised" the ethnic Germans and they frequently referred to Baltic Germans as "the stupid Hottentots."[89] The term "Hottentot" originated from the Dutch language and was used from the seventeenth century to describe people from the Khoikhoi indigenous population of south western Africa. However, from the eighteenth century, the term began to be more widely used as a synonym for a barbarian, a person belonging to an inferior culture or of an inferior intellectual level.[90] Thus, its wider use throughout Europe took on a racially, offensive meaning. The word "Hottentot," which clearly references colonial contexts, further highlighted the supposed primitiveness of the Baltic Germans while also acting as a verbal iteration of the perceived cultural and social standing differences between Reich Germans and Baltic Germans.

Such testimonies demonstrate the relationship between Reich Germans and ethnic Germans was not always harmonious. A report on the mood of ethnic Germans in Bydgoszcz (Bromberg) from March 12, 1940 also offered an insight into a particularly tense incident. The report recounted a fight that broke out in a restaurant between a Reich German railway official and an ethnic German who was the Head of Propaganda for the local National Socialist Party group. The railway official had initially started making comments about ethnic Germans which no one paid attention to. However, the situation soon escalated and the Reich German railway official ranted and raved and made humiliating insults about ethnic Germans in general and those present. The altercation became physical and the Reich German continued to brag that he had been a Party member since 1929 and he was a member of the *Reichsbund der Kinderreichen* (Reich's Union of Large Families).[91] He apparently went on to belittle the ethnic Germans' experiences and curse at them. During the fight, the observing crowd of ethnic Germans shouted words of encouragement such as "throw the Danziger out!"[92] The report highlights how the Reich German seemed to believe his Germanness and loyalty to Germany (by virtue of his membership to the simple party and the *Reichsbund der Kinderreichen*) was of greater worth than that of the ethnic Germans around him. The incident demonstrates that not every Reich German was accepting of the newest members of the Third Reich and, in this case at least, a differentiation appeared to exist between the Reich and ethnic Germans in the mind of the Reich German railway official. He did not keep this opinion to himself; instead, he publically expressed it.

Apart from such physical altercations, problems with the ethnic Germans also arose in other areas. In 1940, the Head of the *Oberpostdirektion* (Main Post Administration) in Poznań, Fritz Richter, wrote a letter to the *Reichsstatthalter*'s department of teaching, culture, and community. Richter expressed problems he was encountering with young postmen he had hired that spring. The majority of the postmen came from local ethnic German families and during their time in school, they had received a "very inadequate" education in the German language. Richter complained that the "horrible colloquial language of these young people is still Polish."[93] The problem was that a prerequisite for adopting post office regulations was a written and spoken command of the German language. Richter noted he had already requested that post offices pay special attention to this and, in the bigger locations, they should allow the local ethnic German and Baltic German members to attend German language courses. In the medium- and smaller-sized locations where there were no immediate German courses available, Richter had asked the post offices to request that local teachers privately teach the ethnic German and Baltic German employees German for two or three hours a week. Richter requested "in the interest of a speedy Germanization of the Eastern territories," the teachers be approved to hold the lessons.[94] Although Richter was able to propose a solution to the problems encountered, and his request was approved by the *Reichsstatthalter*'s office, the letter gives an interesting insight into complications faced by Reich authorities.[95] The local ethnic Germans and the resettlers were supposed to be employed just as Reich Germans would be. Ethnic Germans were, after all, the future of Germanness in the new territories. However, as noted by Richter, language barriers posed an immediate hurdle to the ethnic Germans' integration into the workforce and thus, they needed to learn the German language as soon as possible.

In addition to Reich Germans portraying or perceiving ethnic Germans as primitive, uneducated, juvenile, or inferior, they were also occasionally perceived and portrayed as being negligent. A German woman from Jena who worked in a kindergarten in Gostynin (Waldrode) in the Wartheland reported she had experienced countless situations during her work where one had to laugh but in fact, these moments were sad examples of the "*völkisch*" (ethnic-nationalist or ethnoracial) alignment or the irresponsibility of some mothers.[96] One settlement advisor in Kępno (Kempen) complained that one could almost despair with some ethnic German women's indifference to their households.[97] In addition to their personal views, settlement advisors were not averse to imposing their ideas on ethnic Germans. One settlement advisor went against the parents' wishes and sent their sick child to the hospital; the child later died there.[98]

Reports by settlement advisors were only intended for their supervisors and not meant to be read outside of Nazi organizations. However, a chapter in Andreas Pampuch's publically available book, which was written by two *Nationalsozialistische Volkswohlfahrt* (National Socialist People's Welfare, NSV) nurses, indicated a similar sentiment. In their text, the nurses described how a baby was born on the boat that was taking the Bessarabian Germans on part of their resettlement journey. The baby was named Clemens and his birth supposedly brought a great sense of pride to everyone on board, including the captain. The nurses noted several people remarked that one of the NSV nurses, Carola, was even prouder of the child than his own mother.[99] The story is followed by a picture of six nurses holding young ethnic German children, two toddlers stand in the foreground. One woman holding a child stands in the background, almost obscured by the Reich German nurse in front of her. Another woman wearing a headscarf sits on the right behind the nurses and observes the scene. These two women, who both have covered heads and are not wearing uniforms, are presumably Bessarabian German mothers. One nurse at the front of the photo, who is wearing an NSV armband, gazes at the small baby she is cradling. There is no caption beneath the picture so it is unclear if this is Carola and Clemens. Regardless, the picture is thought-provoking in another way. The NSV nurses stand at the forefront of the picture. Each nurse holds a child and, dressed uniformly in bright, white overalls with pinned hair, they appear as figures of cleanliness and authority. On the other hand, the ethnic German women, dressed in darker colors, almost disappear into the background.

Undoubtedly, written portrayals were not the only way through which perceptions of ethnic Germans were conveyed and resulting stereotypes were constructed. Such photographs, which highlighted the ethnic German's physical appearance also played an important part in the visual recording of the resettlement. The photographs commonly depicted female resettlers wearing traditional headscarves and male resettlers wearing traditional hats, boots, and clothing. The general impression from such photos was that the ethnic Germans appeared different or foreign. Elizabeth Harvey has argued how the photographs of the resettlement conveyed subtle messages to the viewer regarding the hierarchy between Reich Germans and ethnic German resettlers. In her analysis of a photo of a Bessarabian German mother, her baby, and a nurse, Harvey points to certain subconscious messages. In the photo, the nurse leans over in front of the mother to attend to the baby who holds onto her finger. The nurse, dressed in white, disrupts the picture as she sharply contrasts with the mother, who is dressed in dark clothing and wears a traditional headscarf.[100]

This style of picture, with the Reich German nurses in the forefront and administering care while the ethnic German mothers look on or, occasionally, are completely absent, was not unusual.[101] Photographers thus captured the Reich German woman in their authoritative role as the helpers or guardians of the ethnic Germans and visually reinforced these ideas. Simultaneously, ethnic German mothers who represented old-fashioned methods of care faded into the background. Perhaps paradoxically, other photos in German propaganda materials, or sketches like Engelhardt-Kyffhäuser's, focused on the ethnic German resettlers' desirable Aryan characteristics, such as their blond or fair hair and blue eyes. As Miriam Arani has noted:

> The visual culture of Nazism popularized in accordance to its *völkisch* (ethnoracial) ideal the utopia inhabited by an ethnically homogenous, racially "pure" population, which was labelled "Aryan" and visually imagined according to an aesthetic ideal of the Nordic body.[102]

Photographic portraits of resettlers could thus convey two different messages that ultimately both aligned and legitimized Nazi Germany's inclusion, albeit in different ways; the first was that the ethnic Germans were physically identical to Germans from the *Altreich* and therefore, they were already inherently German, and the second was that ethnic Germans were the "other" but still suitable for Germanization and integration into the Reich.[103]

Private perceptions in settlement reports and interviews and subtler depictions in published material for the public, coupled with the supposed urgent requirement to educate the resettlers and monitor their homes, displayed a paternalistic approach toward ethnic Germans by Reich Germans. The language used described ethnic German adults as childlike, naïve, inexperienced, or undomesticated. Although some photos portrayed ethnic Germans as physically identical to Germans from the *Altreich*, others visually differentiated them. Similarly, photos often highlighted the difference between Westernized Reich German nurses, who were shown as eagerly helping, and ethnic German women who often were presented as idle observers. The public literary depictions of ethnic Germans as brave and loyal played into a crucial narrative that legitimized German involvement in Eastern Europe and highlighted ethnic Germans as worthy of integration into the Reich. On the other hand, private perceptions of ethnic Germans and certain public, visual depictions of them contradicted this and instead portrayed them as primitive or in need of help. However, this too played into Nazi narratives. Reich Germans were needed in Poland to assist in the resettlement, set up schools, and provide medical care. Thus, such depictions also aimed at evoking sympathy and inspiring action among Germans in the *Altreich*. Additionally, by juxtaposing modern Nazi German healthcare, education, and culture, and the old-fashioned techniques or appearances of the ethnic Germans, authors and photographers were constructing a distinctive German identity of cultured modernity in the eastern space.

Similar depictions were not uncommon in colonial settings where, for example, even the indigenous adults were often considered "perpetual children."[104] The infantilization of colonial subjects heavily tied in with not only racist prejudices regarding "lower" cultures. It also connected with the European civilizing mission and the notion of a European duty, or a "White Man's Burden," to rule, educate, and guide the destiny of colonized populations.[105] To use the African continent as an example, European colonists infantilized African natives when writing about the colonies because, by doing so, they were legitimizing European intervention there.[106] Africans were often depicted as children in advertisements for colonial products widely circulated in Germany during and after the *Kaiserreich*.[107] The portrayals allowed colonial natives to be perceived in direct opposition to the colonizers; while the colonizers were civilized, responsible, clean, and educated, the colonial natives were supposedly lacking in these qualities. Comparably, by infantilizing ethnic Germans, the Reich Germans could strengthen their position as the experts on matters of German hygiene, culture, and tradition. Contrary to usual colonial circumstances, both ethnic Germans and Reich Germans had been legally and racially designated as being German. However, by perceiving and portraying ethnic Germans as not only childlike but also primitive, unhygienic, or naïve, Reich Germans legitimated the Germans' self-perceived developmental mission in Poland.

United or Divided? The Settler Hierarchy

In his study of the Volhynian Germans, Wilhelm Fielitz highlighted that the "trek" became a central symbol within National Socialist propaganda regarding resettlement.

The word "trek" originated from the Dutch language in the context of the movement of the Boers to South Africa between 1835 and 1838, however, it was also heavily associated with the colonization of the American West. The connotations with American colonization were minimized and instead, the links with the Boer treks were more strongly clarified.[108] However, despite the frequent use of the term "trek," "pioneers," or "colonizers" to describe ethnic Germans and despite the many photos showing ethnic Germans traveling in cloth-covered, horse-drawn wagons not unlike those used by settlers in the American West, the Nazi regime did not always treat nor perceive the resettled ethnic Germans as equal to the Reich Germans, or colonizers, in the *Reichsgaue* Wartheland and Danzig-West Prussia.

An *Ordnungspolizei* (Order Police) bulletin from December 1940 declared Germans in the Wartheland should be aware that the differences between ethnic Germans, Baltic Germans, Volhynian Germans, Galician Germans, and Reich Germans had to disappear as soon as possible. According to the bulletin, every misunderstanding among Germans and every instance of segregation was a hindrance to German strength.[109] Despite such a bulletin, as discussed in this chapter, significant problems existed between the different groups. Predictably, the tensions between Reich Germans and ethnic Germans became obvious to the Reich authorities. In a report on student assignments in Danzig-West Prussia from 1942, the report writer recorded that Reich Germans treated ethnic German resettlers very harshly and Reich Germans showed little understanding for the often very difficult position of the resettlers.[110] A comment by a female Bessarabian resettler in another report was indicative of the situation between the resettlers and the district offices. After speaking with German authorities concerning the complaints she had, she noted "they do not feel sorry for us at all."[111]

In addition to the inequality between Reich Germans and ethnic Germans, despite the German aim of uniting and settling groups of ethnic Germans who were to be hoped to be ethnically and culturally homogenous, in reality, significant divisions existed between ethnic Germans in Western Poland, those from Central and Eastern Poland and ethnic German resettlers from other states. Local ethnic Germans in the west of Poland, who once had German citizenship, were resentful that they were now grouped with the allegedly inferior ethnic German resettlers from the east. These already strained relationships were further aggravated by the perceived differential treatment between the groups, especially concerning rations and work placements.[112] An excerpt from the diary of a Baltic German resettler in Łódź explained that the resettlers were "too German" for the local ethnic Germans. In what seemed to be an attempt to further verify her statement, she repeated the widely used death toll of the *Bromberger Blutsonntag* (Bromberg Bloody Sunday), which in reality was much lower.[113] The female resettler wrote that a Reich German had said the 58,000 ethnic Germans who had been murdered in Bydgoszcz (Bromberg) were the "real" Germans and the ones who had been left behind were almost all "Pole-friendly, if not half Polish."[114]

A report by the *Deutsches Frauenwerk* (German Women's Association), an organization that worked alongside the *NS-Frauenschaft*, further demonstrated differentiation between the resettlers from the east by the settlement advisors. The report noted the Baltic German resettlers in *Kreis* Wielun (District Wieluń) were clean, approachable people, and, in four weeks, they had managed more on their farms than the Volhynian resettlers had managed in one year. The report also noted how work with the Baltic Germans was going much better than with the Volhynian resettlers or ethnic Germans of the *Kreis*.[115] Such a report contrasts with the example of the Reich Germans calling the Baltic Germans "Hottentots" mentioned earlier in this chapter. This thus demonstrates the lack of uniformity in attitudes toward the ethnic German groups and further highlights the disparities within the Nazi inclusionary practices on the ground.

As opposed to the removal of differentiation between ethnic Germans and Reich Germans, the treatment and perceptions of ethnic Germans were similar to those to which indigenous populations in the context of colonial civilizing missions were subjected. The treatment and the perceptions similarly demonstrate a societal "otherness" between Reich Germans and ethnic Germans. Though many ethnic Germans were eventually granted German citizenship, the process was one of selection and simply resulted in an ethnic grading system and a hierarchical society.[116] Nazi Germany's propaganda disseminated the fantasy of populating the *Reichsgaue* with German settlers who were the human future of Germany's rule, tradition, and culture in the East. The ethnic Germans were foreseen as the settlers who would replace the native Polish population. On the contrary, the reality of the implementation of the inclusionary policies on the ground shows that ethnic Germans, potentially irrespective of success in racial or political screenings, were often perceived by Reich Germans as culturally or intellectually inferior.

Such inconsistencies within the colonizer group were not unusual within colonial contexts, however. The anthropologist and scholar of colonialism, Ann Laura Stoler, has convincingly demonstrated that in colonial spaces, even the European colonizers' society was "internally stratified." Colonial communities were artificial creations with distinctive criteria for gaining membership to the colonizer group.[117] Within different colonies, the meaning of the term "European," and indeed belonging to this category, could differ. Similarly, in annexed Poland, the term "German" was assigned a certain value but then, in practice, it was spread and applied across numerous ethnic, cultural, and societal levels.

The thorough racial and political screenings of the ethnic German resettlers were extreme and certainly specific to the particulars of National Socialist ideology, and the case of the *Heim ins Reich* resettlement. However, the presence of criteria for settlers and the actual practice of screening settlers for suitability were not. For example, during the *Kaiserreich*'s settlement of German South West Africa and also the German settlement of Prussia, German authorities discussed not only the quantity but also the quality of the settlers.[118] The settlers should be *Kulturträger* and therefore, embody and support "Germanness" abroad. Questionnaires introduced for those wishing to settle in Prussia asked applicants about issues such as the applicant's financial situation, languages spoken at home, and agricultural work experience; conversely, Theodor Leutwein, the governor of German South West Africa, simply indicated that settlers should be of a decent, frugal, and perseverant character.[119] Interestingly, although they were German and white, the colonial administration in German South West Africa used words such as "troublesome," "useless," and "degenerate" to describe individual settlers who did not meet the standards of what was considered respectable settler society. Not unlike the criticism of ethnic Germans by Reich Germans, the lifestyle and morals of such undesirable settlers in German South West Africa, such as poor whites and criminals, were occasionally depicted as being similar to those of the indigenous Africans.[120] German authorities planned that Reich Germans, local ethnic Germans, and the resettlers would be a unified group in their securing of not only territorial but also racial security. Nonetheless, different ethnic groups could often not escape recognizing, following, and indeed attempting to instigate the very racial and political divisions the National Socialist classification system created. This hierarchical system, founded on notions of race, ethnicity, and culture, largely accentuated and preserved divisions, not unity. Thus, when viewed from a colonial comparative perspective, the similarities to colonial contexts, where differences existed not only between the colonized and the colonizers but also between the colonizers themselves, are evident.

The *Deutsche Volksliste* and the *Wiedereindeutschungsverfahren*: Assimilation of the Polish Population

The ethnic German resettlers and the local ethnic Germans were not the only population group in the *Reichsgaue* to be subjected to treatment that was comparable to colonial inclusionary policies. Although differentiation and legal subjugation of the non-Jewish Polish population were fundamental parts of the German occupation of Poland, it was not exclusively exclusionary. Reich officials undertook processes to evaluate the local ethnic Germans and the non-Jewish population of the *Reichsgaue* in addition to screening incoming ethnic German resettlers. From the end of October 1939, the German authorities introduced the *Deutsche Volksliste* (German People's List, DVL) into the Wartheland. The DVL was a register of people within the *Reichsgau* who, after extensive racial and political screening, were recognized as German. In addition to this, the DVL also stipulated different categories of German. In May 1941, the Interior Ministry introduced a new version of the DVL across all the *Reichsgaue* in an attempt to standardize the screening process. Applicants registered in the first category were those who were German by commitment as demonstrated by proving their loyalty to Germany before the outbreak of the war through membership of German organizations, speaking German at home, and sending their children to German schools, for example. Applicants in the second category were German by descent but, they also had to prove their loyalty and commitment to Germany. Members of the first two categories were awarded *Reichsbürgerschaft* (Reich citizenship). German descent was not necessary for inclusion in the first category; however, a demonstrable commitment to Germany was. For the second category, German descent was a necessary but not a sufficient condition.[121] The third and fourth categories were more ambiguous. These two categories comprised of, for example, people who were of mixed Polish and German descent and, in the case of the fourth category, people of German descent who were found to be former members of Polish national organizations or considered hostile to Germany. The third category was granted provisional citizenship but the fourth category was not.[122] Registration for the DVL was voluntary and many who registered did have authentic claims of German ancestry or a desire to support and thus potentially profit from the new regime. However, intimidation and force were also certainly influencing factors in some cases, given the nature of the Nazi regime. Likewise, thanks to the dangers posed by holding any impression of national allegiance to Poland, registering for the DVL was often a way to protect one's self and one's family.[123]

By the end of the Second World War, German authorities had registered roughly three million people on the DVL.[124] Through the DVL, Nazi Germany embarked on the official Germanization of non-German people; however, it was not consistent throughout all the annexed territories.[125] Despite attempts to standardize the DVL's categories, massive discrepancies still existed between the *Reichsgaue*. Fourteen percent of the population in the Wartheland was registered with the DVL by the end of the war, compared to 70 percent of the population in Danzig-West Prussia.[126] Additionally, the grounds behind the decisions taken by the DVL examiners were unclear to the applicants. For example, an ethnic German teacher in Łódź questioned why he had been assigned to category three when he had actively worked for Germandom during the time of Polish rule. He mentioned such proof as he and his family were of German descent, he had taught for twenty years at a German school, his children had gone to German schools, his son had joined the Hilter Youth and volunteered for the *Wehrmacht*, and he and his wife were involved in National Socialist organizations.[127] The fantasy of Germany becoming a homogenous nation comprising of racially superior and politically loyal German individuals seemed, in theory, to be relatively straightforward. However, the realities and feasibility of implementing racial and political screenings in separate *Reichsgaue* with separate *Gauleiters* and *Gau* authorities, while furthermore protecting economic stability, was problematic and plagued with complications.

Such complications can be seen in a 1943 report on the mood of the Polish and the *Eingedeutsche* (Germanized). The report noted how, despite the screenings, there seemed to be little difference between Poles and the *Eingedeutsche*, especially those in the DVL category three. They spoke Polish in public, had relationships with Poles, and displayed a defiant attitude toward other Germans. One woman refused to use her DVL identity pass, and another would not learn German because, according to her, "the Germans are losing the war"—she would rather learn English or Russian.[128] Meanwhile, sources show that occasionally even those defined as *Deutschstämmig* (of German descent), or those likely to be counted as DVL category two, did not always want to be registered on the DVL. For example, a man who was found to be of 75 percent German descent with a wife who was of 100 percent German descent wrote that he refused to register for the DVL as he felt and wanted to stay Polish.[129]

As well as assimilation through the DVL, German authorities also created the RuSHA-controlled *Wiedereindeutschungsverfahren* (re-Germanization procedure, WED), which allowed for racially valuable foreigners who were officially not suitable for inclusion in the DVL and those who were in the third DVL category to be assimilated through placements with German host families in the *Altreich*. WED candidates were employed on German farms or as household help. Here, they were required, with the help of their hosts, to fully integrate themselves into German society. The German hosts were required to facilitate the WED candidates' societal and cultural inclusion, and they were instructed by Reich authorities to provide them with household furnishing and clothes and to treat them "as German nationals."[130] However, this did not always happen. Bradley J. Nichols has demonstrated how the hosts and other Germans often treated the WED candidates as inferior. They were segregated from Germans at mealtimes, provided with inadequate housing and clothing, or verbally insulted, for example. Insults frequently targeted the WED candidates' inability to speak German or their supposed lack of German work ethic.[131] Like criticisms against the Reich Germans for their lack of sympathy toward ethnic German resettlers in annexed Poland, a Nazi Party deputy criticized the *Betriebsführer* (area managers) in his district for their inadequate sensitivity to the needs of the WED participants.[132]

The treatment of the WED participants by their German hosts in combination with the treatment of ethnic Germans by Reich Germans shows that though the official Nazi Party stance was that the individuals and candidates were either ethnically German or should be treated as such, the perceived ethnic or cultural differences or the audible linguistic differences prevented some Germans from fully accepting a new racially homogenous society. Nichols employs the postcolonial theory of "hybridity" to explain this. Hybridity is "the state of belonging to two distinct races or cultures at the same time, or possessing characteristics attributed to both," which in turn leads to a blurring of the characteristics that initially distinguished them.[133] Thus, as opposed to assisting their integration, the potentially blurred ethnic and cultural belonging the WED candidates, the local ethnic Germans and the resettlers personified, possibly hindered their acceptance.

The implementation of DVL screenings differed between the two *Reichsgaue* and not every DVL member was willing to completely embrace becoming German; similarly, the WED was not a smooth process for those involved. Despite these problems, the existence of the DVL and WED illustrates the attempts on behalf of the German regime to allow suitable candidates to be recognized as German. Gerhard Wolf has argued that given the extent of the DVL inclusionary policies in annexed Poland, it can be understood as "the largest assimilation project in modern German history."[134] Assimilation was undoubtedly not a German phenomenon, and different colonial powers had varied approaches to the assimilation of colonial natives into their society. The French Empire applied an assimilation policy in its African colonies through which Africans could become French citizens once they had adopted the French language and French culture. The Portuguese Empire used an analogous policy in Africa where Africans could apply to become Portuguese citizens or *Assimilados* once they demonstrated several factors including their written and spoken command of Portuguese.[135] Conversely, the British Empire did not have a specific assimilation policy that required the adoption of British culture to become a British subject.

As will be discussed further in Chapter 4, although assimilation is occasionally considered part of wider civilizing or humanitarian missions as it did not involve violence or killing, assimilation was in effect a means through which to incorporate target groups into the occupier society and erase differences between the groups. Nazi Germany's approach to the Germanization of ethnic Germans and the members of the DVL and WED, and indeed colonial and imperial powers' assimilation policies, cannot be mistaken as purely benevolent. Assimilation was used as a colonial tactic to destroy native populations by facilitating their cultural, linguistic, or religious transformation out of existence. As Paul Bartrop has pointed out in the case of the Australian state taking "mixed-race" children away from their indigenous mothers, although there was no killing involved, the goal was the same as Nazi Germany's plan for the Jews; they would disappear.[136] Similarly, by "making" Poles into Germans through the DVL or by "re-Germanizing" individuals through the WED, Nazi Germany could destroy Poles and other Eastern European population groups without murdering them.

In the context of comparisons between colonialism and the Nazi occupation of Poland, the fact that the Nazi regime was not solely exclusionary but also had inclusionary policies, like in colonial and imperial situations, is significant. The complications in defining who was German or not were an unavoidable part of attempts to neatly assign individuals to DVL categories. German descent was not always the initial deciding factor in judging an applicant's suitability to be approved; rather, their political, linguistic, or cultural ties to Germany were seen as crucial factors. As Devin O. Pendas has summarized regarding racial categorization:

> Because racism presupposes that races are real, rather than social categories constituted and made real by racial ideologies, it is constantly disappointed by external reality's failure to live up (or down) to its expectations. Since races do not exist independent of racisms, the presumptive homogeneity of races at the heart of racism must be constantly reasserted in a futile quest to create the reality that purportedly lies outside the ideological frame. The unreality of race means that racist policy is always less than fully consistent or coherent, even on its own terms, shot through with definitional conundrums and genealogical paradoxes.[137]

Such complications in striving to define people's race based on predefined or occasionally redefined categories, as seen in the case of the DVL, are also relevant when drawing colonial comparisons.[138] Despite the presence of allegedly distinctive racial categories in certain colonial contexts, an individual's racial origin was often too difficult to conclusively determine. Resultantly, in certain colonies such as Central Mexico in the sixteenth and seventeenth centuries, the boundaries between racial categories were extremely flexible and an individual's belonging to a certain category was often subjectively decided by factors such as language, dress, and religion.[139] Problems with categorizing population groups were also encountered by the British Empire, for example, in the case of the definition of the terms "native" and "non-native" in British Central Africa.[140]

In German South West Africa, the categorization of "mixed-race" individuals also proved difficult. Although the administrative reliance on racial or biological categorization was more stringent than in many other colonies, it was no less complex. For example, certain members of the settler community deemed themselves to be white and German based on their skin color, their one German parent, or their German grandparents. They owned land, fought in the German Army, or studied at German schools. However, on occasion, if the individual was found to have an African or mixed-race ancestor this could lead to the individual's white status being revoked regardless of their skin color.¹⁴¹ Such legal rulings caused instability in the colony and as such, the administration had to ultimately accept that those initially categorized as "natives" could prove they were German if they could demonstrate it through culture and behavior.¹⁴²

Ethnic and cultural blending through assimilation, and the societal problems it created, were thus not only something faced by colonial powers. In the Nazi regime, which outwardly appeared to operate along strict racial guidelines based on supposed scientific and medical principles, the reality of interterritorial and therefore interethnic mixing meant that, on the ground, even the system of inclusion did not and could not always operate smoothly. Although the majority of the native Polish population was not intended to be included in the DVL or the WED, the German attempts at inclusionary policies and the administrative and societal problems they created, highlight that, in much the same way as the ethnic Germans, the members of the first two DVL categories and the WED candidates can also be compared to the treatment of indigenous people in colonial contexts. They were subjected to variations of assimilatory or inclusionary policies, which often further highlighted or exacerbated the obscurity of ethnic boundaries as opposed to clarifying them.

Conclusion

Within the debate on the potential similarities between Nazi expansionism and colonialism, historians have often argued that German tactics in Poland differed from standard colonial practice as Nazi Germany's treatment of Poles was devoid of any kind of civilizing or humanitarian-based missions. For example, Thomas Kühne has noted that although Hitler made references that compared Nazi Germany's eastern conquest and rule to the British rule of India, unlike the British in India, Nazi rule in Eastern Europe was not built on the principles of Westernizing or educating the indigenous populations.¹⁴³ Similarly, Stephan Malinowski and Robert Gerwarth have highlighted that the common colonial combination of "development" and "force" is all but impossible to find in the German treatment of the native population in Poland.¹⁴⁴ The Germans did not plan on building new roads, schools, hospitals, libraries, or museums for Poles. Instead, amenities and cultural and leisure activities would be solely for the Germans who settled in the area.

Such observations are correct concerning the treatment of many of the indigenous Polish population in the *Reichsgaue*; however, I suggest that through this examination of the treatment of ethnic Germans and the DVL and WED, a specific Nazi German version of a self-perceived developmental mission did exist in annexed Poland. This developmental mission, which was carried out by Reich Germans but facilitated by official German policies, assumed the primitive nature, and cultural inferiority of its subjects. The mission was both legitimized and fortified by the association of ethnic Germans and certain members of the non-Jewish Polish population with characteristics that were similar to colonized indigenous populations in colonial contexts. In contrast to a traditional colonizer, ethnic Germans were assumed to require help and this help would ultimately facilitate their assimilation into the Reich. Thus, they occupied an almost paradoxical position of being both a colonizer and also being subjected to similar treatment and perceptions as a "Colonial Other."[145] The German case, therefore, initially appears to strongly differ from stereotypical colonial contexts given that the self-conceived developmental mission was largely not intended to benefit the native population of Poland. However, many of the local ethnic Germans who had lived in Poland before the outbreak of the Second World War had considered themselves Polish until it was detrimental to outwardly do so. They had been born in Poland, lived in Poland, potentially spoke Polish, and mixed with Poles. Similarly, the ethnic Germans from the east were not necessarily homogenous German communities and had been born in non-German territories. To understand ethnic Germans, as National Socialist ideology would have us do, solely as "ethnic Germans" is therefore incorrect. They were ethnically and culturally heterogeneous groups who, by birth, can also be understood as "native" to the territories that were either conquered by Nazi Germany or ruled by the Soviet Union. As such, by investigating the case of the resettlement and Germanization of the ethnic Germans through a colonial lens, their paradoxical position as both colonizer and colonized can be illuminated, as can colonial similarities.

In terms of other colonial contexts that offer further perspectives on Nazi Germany's inclusionary policies aimed toward the ethnic Germans, DVL members and WED candidates but not the whole Polish population, Penny Russell has highlighted how establishing "civilization" in colonial Australia was seen as an accomplishment regardless of whether it benefited the Indigenous Australians or not. According to contemporary commentators, violent conquest and dispossession could be offset by bringing civilization to the land, not necessarily the people.[146] The notion of a civilizing or developmental mission repeatedly served to legitimize and also obfuscate colonial expansion and violence; thereby, the presence of ideology related to such missions did not automatically imply that the native colonized populations benefited from them.

Certain members of the DVL and the WED were also subjected to assimilation policies, regardless of their ethnic heritage. This assimilation aimed at creating Germans out of Poles and, not unlike colonial situations, once the subject met certain cultural or political criteria, they were approved for assimilation into the colonizer's society. However, also akin to colonial contexts, an individual's belonging to the category "German" was often not enough for them to be considered or treated as equals to the colonizing power's citizens. As this chapter has demonstrated, the German system of screening and categorization, which not only aimed at exclusion but also at inclusion, attempted to create a homogenous society based on racially and politically sound individuals. However, given that the nature of the system was based on a grading of "Germanness," the system resulted in creating hierarchies among the very people who were supposed to be included in the Reich. Nazi Germany had, since the first Nuremberg Laws of 1935, shaped its society in the *Altreich* and educated its citizens on the topics of racial belonging and exclusion. The territories in annexed Poland were no different; however, here the status of "being German" took on new meanings and significance.

The history of the British Empire, the *Kaiserreich* or French rule in Indochina all paint vastly different pictures of conquests and policies but, as Jürgen Osterhammel has highlighted, "colonialism is a phenomenon of colossal vagueness."[147] The definitions of colonialism, colonization, and, indeed, colony, are wrought with complexity and the various colonial subcategories, such as internal colonization or reverse colonization, which are proposed by colonial scholars add to its ambiguous nature.[148] Nevertheless, in the case of this investigation, what we can separate from the many individual intricacies of the colonial situations is the certain shared intrinsic elements that surface relating to the treatment of different population groups. In the colonial cases mentioned, and indeed in most colonial contexts, the colonizing power imposed their self-perceived superior ideals upon the colonized population.

Although ethnic Germans, certain DVL members and WED candidates did differ in certain instances to a stereotypical "Colonial Other," and they were treated better than non-Jewish and Jewish Poles, the examination of the German inclusionary practices in annexed Poland within the framework of the traditional treatment of indigenous populations in colonial contexts demonstrates that overlaps did exist. By highlighting the DVL and the WED, the German inclusionary policies, which ultimately aimed at eliminating ethnic differences, but often resulted in further complexities, can also be compared to colonial situations. Undoubtedly, the Nazi regime's inclusionary, or developmental policies had the dual purpose of not only assimilating individuals into the Reich but also gaining political support and national loyalty. This was, however, also the case in colonial contexts where such missions were not purely for humanitarian reasons. In Chapter 3, the idea of a self-perceived developmental mission will be further investigated through the lens of Nazi Germany's plans for the transformation of the annexed territories, the Reich German's experiences in Poland, and their understanding of their national duty.

3

A German Task: The Reich German Mission

On April 12, 1942, the daily German-language newspaper the *Litzmannstädter Zeitung* was published as usual. Like most newspapers, the back pages were filled with personal advertisements nestled among the classifieds. The personal postings included job vacancies, apartments for rent, and items for sale. The swimming pool at Hermannsbad appealed for applicants for an array of positions including two cooks, waiters and waitresses, and two confectioners. A bank on Adolf-Hitler-Straße needed an office assistant for an immediate start. In the side columns, businesses advertised everyday items such as toothpaste, washing detergent, and cigarette paper.[1] At first glance, the newspaper's back pages painted a picture of a normal, modern German city inhabited by civilians who needed jobs, visited cafes and swimming pools, and bought household products. However, Litzmannstadt was not a normal German city. The inhabitants who swam in the pool, ate in the cafes and restaurants, and worked in the various businesses were not only participating in everyday routines. Like those who lived and worked throughout annexed Poland, the Germans in Litzmannstadt had been exposed time and time again, through such means as pamphlets, newspaper articles, books, films, and exhibitions, to the message that they were completing a crucial German mission in Poland. Regardless of their positions, whether it be as Party officials, doctors, nurses, teachers, or typists, the Germans' ultimate mission was the transformation of the territory, the economy, and the society in Poland. Through their presence, their work, and their political loyalty, they were to undertake the task of the complete Germanization and, thus the eventual eradication, of Poland.

The *Reichsgaue* were locations where the Nazi German concepts of race and space could be put into practice, often in their most extreme form, while also realizing irredentist fantasies of a reclamation of the formerly German parts of Poland. Despite the irredentist fantasies, Poland was almost paradoxically perceived as a *tabula rasa* where Nazi Germany could wholly reorganize and restructure the land, industries and people. For this to be a success, Nazi Germany needed Reich Germans to both facilitate the resettlement of ethnic Germans and supplement the increasing German population. Enthusiastic engineers, architects, and administrators were required to transform the Polish towns and villages into German ones. Similarly, teachers, doctors, and nurses would establish schools and healthcare facilities. The stakes were extremely high as, for both the Nazi regime and German civilians, the war was being waged to protect ethnic Germans in foreign lands, reclaim old territories, acquire new *Lebensraum*, strengthen the German race, and enhance the physical and racial security of the Reich. The resettlement of ethnic Germans in Poland thus created both a heightened ideological environment and a heightened ideological mindset; it was the crux of this supposedly historic German conquest of Poland.

Through an examination of the German attempts to transform the Polish territory, create a German society, and help the arriving ethnic Germans, several colonial similarities come to light. The idea of a colonizer's task in newly conquered territories was not an unusual one. Colonial powers encouraged civilians of the metropole to become pioneers, to travel to foreign lands, and to do their duty for empire building. Like the colonial "White Man's Burden,"[2] Nazi Germany encouraged its citizens to undertake nationalistic tasks in Poland. Albert Forster, the *Gauleiter* of Danzig-West Prussia, highlighted the importance and honor of the tasks for those working in Poland, regardless of their job: "Every man who is sent to the German East in the future, no matter what post, must regard this transfer as something honourable. It must be, for each person, a special joy to be able to work in the East for Germandom."[3] These nationalistic tasks did not just apply to men but also to women who, akin to those working in overseas colonies, could avail of newfound freedom away from the constraints of their hometowns and families. Unlike the previous chapter, this chapter explores the fantasies surrounding the resettlement of ethnic Germans and the establishment of German society as opposed to focusing on the realities. It demonstrates how, through certain justifications for German involvement in the territory, colonial similarities can be observed in greater detail even if such justifications were pure propaganda. Ultimately, it shows how Nazi Germany promoted "ordinary" Reich Germans in annexed Poland and how these Germans conceptualized their new roles.

Planung und Aufbau—the Planning and Development of Towns and Villages

The planning (*Planung*) of the new settlement villages, their development or construction (*Aufbau*), and the rebuilding of existing Polish infrastructure were not only key factors in the establishment of the German administration and settlement in annexed Poland. They also heavily tied in with the Nazi regime's fantasy of a massive German empire that would spread across Central and Eastern Europe. Architects, builders, and engineers flocked to the annexed territories to participate in the planning, designing, and building taking place there. In the *Reichsgaue*, these experts took up positions in such offices as the *Stadtplanungsamt* (City Planning Office), *Bauverwaltung* (Building Authorities), *Amt für Wohnungs-und Siedlungswesen* (Office for Housing and Settlement), and the *Stadtsanierungsamt* (Urban Sanitation Office). They ardently began redesigning cities and towns and planning new apartments and houses that would be the future homes of German settlers. The sheer number of plans they created signaled their optimism; in the summer of 1941, the plans for twenty-six cities in *Regierungsbezirk* (administrative district) Posen, twenty-six cities in *Regierungsbezirk* Hohensalza (Inowrocław), and thirty-three cities in *Regierungsbezirk* Litzmannstadt were completed.[4] Unlike in the *Altreich* where they were constrained by the current infrastructure and property owners, the annexed territories offered the planning experts ample opportunities for redesign and reorganization.[5]

Articles in newspapers and architecture, engineering, and technical journals, such as *Neues Bauerntum*, originally the journal of the *Archiv für innere Kolonisation*, discussed and described the construction of German villages in both Poland and further east.[6] They included sample village layouts, photos of small-scale village models, and mock-ups of house interiors. In *Neues Bauerntum*, an article titled "*Der Stand der Raumordnungsplanung für die eingegliederten Ostgebiete*" explained that the two foundations of public life for the future villages were people and space, then administration, economy, and culture.[7] The settlement planners envisioned German villages built in areas of fertile land that could be divided up among the resettlers to secure livelihood for their families and would thus contribute to the strengthening of the peasantry. According to the article, the villages should not be viewed as single entities but rather in conjunction with the surrounding landscape and associated living and economic space.[8] These newly built villages included a *Dorfhaus* (village house), in which public space for the community was available, as well as such institutions as kindergartens, the NSV office, and libraries. One contributor to the journal *Der Deutsche Baumeister* (The German Builder) mentioned that the *Dorfhaus* should be connected to a tower that would serve as the village landmark. A restaurant, a general store, a blacksmith, and a repair shop should also be included in the village.[9]

The construction of new villages and towns and the remodeling of Polish ones began very soon after the annexation of the *Reichsgaue* by Nazi Germany. The aim of this "construction" was to make the towns in the *Reichsgaue* look German in appearance and to modernize them to a standard that the Germans saw fit. In September 1940, Greiser issued a directive that created the working group for the *Baugestaltung und Baupflege im Reichsgau Wartheland* (building construction and maintenance in the *Reichsgau* Wartheland). In the directive, Greiser specified that since Germany had taken possession of the German East "for all time," the main duty of those in the construction industry was to ensure that the essence of German construction remained as evidence of the current tremendous upheaval for centuries to come. Additionally, Greiser ordered that the new buildings should fit in aesthetically with German buildings from the past centuries that were already in the East. He stipulated that "even the smallest building must be decent, clean and orderly" and "through changes and redevelopment, ugly buildings would be redesigned and adapted to the new, orderly surroundings."[10]

As well as the reconstruction of "ugly" buildings, the German planners intended to remove the buildings' and towns' Polish characteristics and replace them with features that would make them German in appearance. Some of these changes were simply changing Polish place names and street names to German ones. The renaming gave the areas instantaneous German status and it strengthened the idea of the German ownership of the territory as the significant identification features of the areas, the Polish names, were replaced. Other external features, such as monuments or memorial plaques that the German authorities considered signifiers of Polish elements, were also removed. The German Propaganda Ministry clearly articulated what the German intentions concerning the Polish culture were; Poland could no longer be known as a "cultural nation" within the European people's community and that its "existence as a nation was over."[11] Accordingly, cultural artifacts, art, and books were taken from Polish museums, universities, libraries, and churches, and some of these items were sold to or simply stolen by German officials in the *Reichsgaue*.

The Germans occupied buildings of cultural and historical importance and modified their holdings and interiors. For example, the Imperial Castle in Poznań (Zamek Cesarski w Poznaniu) underwent extensive renovation to transform it into one of Hitler's official residences and *Reichsstatthalter* offices for Greiser. By December 1943, Greiser's offices, living quarters, and a casino had been installed in the castle at a cost of twenty million *Reichsmark*, a large sum of money to be spent during an ongoing war.[12] The Polish Muzeum Wielkopolskie was replaced by the Kaiser-Friedrich-Museum on January 21, 1940. In a letter to Greiser and for the attention of one of his aides, the new German director of the museum Siegfried Rühle mentioned that after a request he had made, the building that housed the Museum of the Polish Society of Friends for Art and Science had been taken over by the Kaiser-Friedrich-Museum, as had the whole museum collection. Rühle requested that the museum's book collection was also be quickly transferred into the Kaiser-Friedrich Museum's possession for its reading room.[13] In addition to public collections, private art, furniture, and jewelry collections were confiscated from individual residences. Reports sent to the RKFDV *Bodenamt* (Land Registry) by various offices and museum staff detailed the inventory lists of numerous valuable items from locations throughout the Wartheland.[14] The historically valuable items were added to the museum's holdings. For example, in October 1941, Rühle sent another letter to the *Reichsstatthalter*'s offices. This letter noted that the collection from the castle Adlershorst in *Kreis* Jarotschin (Jarocin) was to be transferred to the Kaiser-Friedrich-Museum. The collection included such items as furniture, vases, porcelain, and paintings. A subsequent inventory list recorded that paintings by the Flemish Baroque artists Anthony van Dyck and Peter Paul Rubens were among the transferred items.[15]

As well as expanding its collections, the Kaiser-Friedrich-Museum held various exhibitions that promoted the German work in the Wartheland, such as "Das deutsche Wartheland" (The German Wartheland) in 1940 and "Kampf und Aufbau im Wartheland" (Struggle and Development in the Wartheland) which was initially held between January 30 and February 28, 1943 before being extended to March 21. The promotional poster for "Kampf und Aufbau" (Figure 3.1) advertised that the exhibition covered such topics as the "Führer's Resettlement," "Village and Farmyard in the new East," "German Students on Eastern Placement," and "The German Woman helps manage the *Heimat*."[16] In a letter sent to various *Gau* offices, the deputy *Gauleiter* of the Wartheland Kurt Schmalz announced the exhibition and described how it gave an "overview of the national struggle and a report on the work of the Party department who dealt with the settlement, care and consolidation of Germans." He wrote that the exhibition was open to everyone and a guided tour of the exhibition could be booked in advance for groups.[17] The exhibition proved popular and attracted 21,000 visitors during its opening dates.[18] A small piece in the *Litzmännstadter Zeitung* titled "With 21,200 Covered Wagons to the New Eastern Homeland" advertised the extension of the exhibiton till March 21, 1942. It featured a picture of part of the exhibiton, a covered wagon like those used by ethnic German resettlers to travel to the annexed territories, and noted that the exhibiton included such displays as pictures from the resettler camps and a plastic depiction of "the great trek."[19]

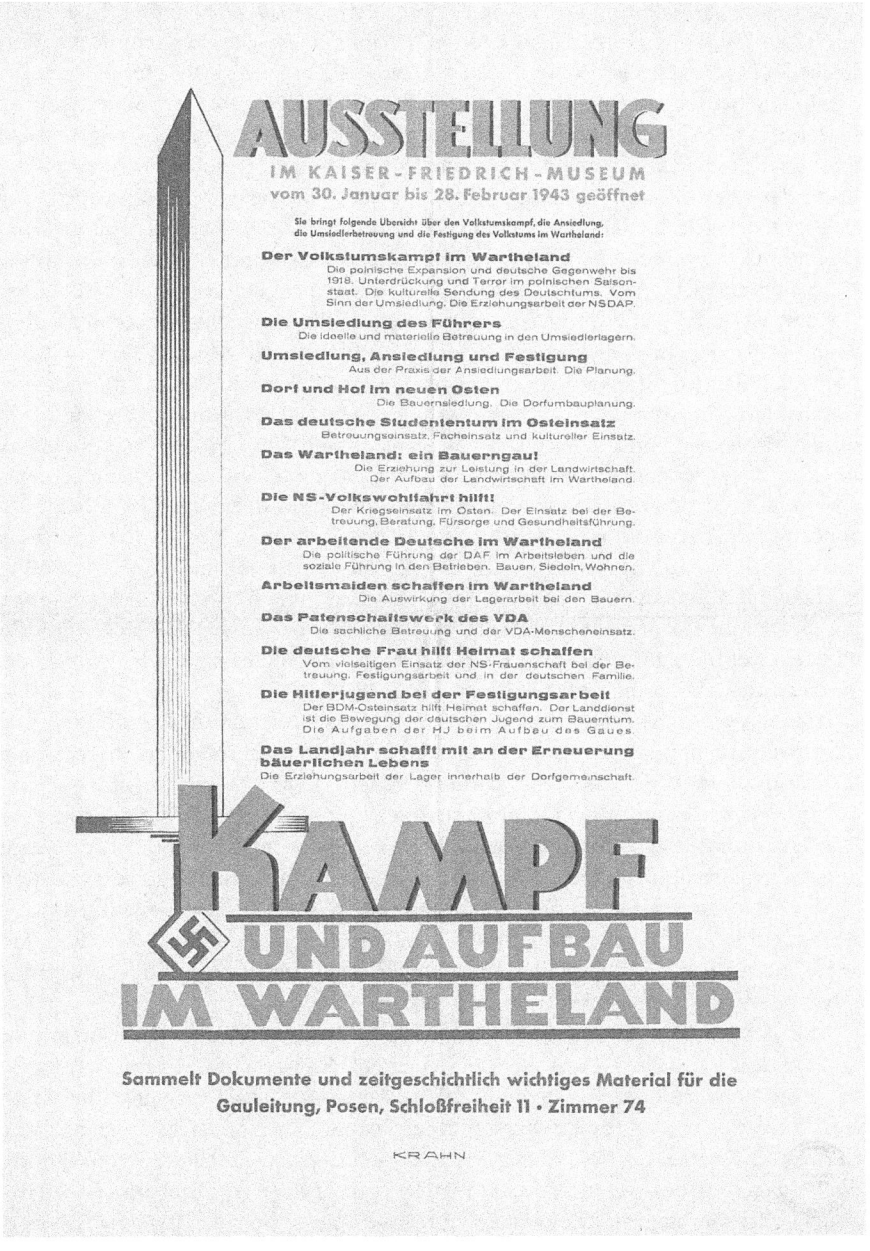

Figure 3.1 *Kampf und Aufbau im Wartheland* Ausstellung (Struggle and Development in the Wartheland Exhibition) Poster. Source: Archivum Instytut Zachodni Poznań, Dok. I-27, 21.

A similar exhibition organized by Konrad Meyer's RKFDV planning department and titled "Planung und Aufbau im Osten" (Planning and Development in the East) opened on March 20, 1941 in Berlin and was also held in Poznań in October 1941. The exhibition focused on the plans for "the fundamental redesign of German settlement." It featured maps, sketches, plans, and models of how the settlement villages would look after their redevelopment.[20] A separate *Heimatschau* (exhibition) named "Der Osten des Warthelands" (The East of the Wartheland) was held in Łódź and opened by Greiser on March 9, 1941. The opening was announced on the same day on the front page of the *Litzmännstadter Zeitung*. The newspaper also published a feature on the exhibition under the heading "German spirit and German culture shape the *Ostraum* (eastern territory)." The feature described each of the exhibition spaces; numerous rooms focused on the long history of German settlement and culture in the east, while others highlighted German monuments in the Wartheland and German farmers as *Kulturträger*. Unsurprisingly, other rooms were dedicated to the ongoing resettlement of the Wartheland and the "*Neubau* (new construction)" of Litzmannstadt.[21] A book marking the occasion of the exhibition included numerous pictures of German-style buildings, factories, and landscapes. Photographs of dilapidated farm buildings appeared, which the author described as "Polish farmhouses," and on the next page, it contained pictures of new "German" farmhouses under construction.[22] According to the publication's opening page, which featured a quote by Greiser, the exhibition highlighted the German leadership of the space in photos and text. It aimed to inform all visitors of the significance that the territory around Litzmannstadt had within the Wartheland and the whole of the "German East."[23]

Exhibitions, such as the those discussed, acted as an important way of conveying information to the public by visually displaying information and photographs regarding the Germans' work in Poland. They permitted visitors to personally see pictures, plans, and models that demonstrated how German development was currently shaping the *Reichsgaue* and promoted the expected future results of the development. Although how such information was viewed by the visitors is difficult to analyze, an examination of how the information regarding the transformation of the areas was presented to the public is still significant. Through the exhibitions, German expansion was depicted as an ordered and civilized modernization effort that directly corresponded with the German mission to transform Poland into German territory.

The settlement planners and *Gau* officials understood the construction or development of Polish towns in the settlement *Reichsgaue* as a crucial part of the ethnic and cultural war that the Nazi regime was waging against the Poles. Administrative reports, newspapers, journals exhibitions, and speeches framed the German involvement in Poland as a necessary intervention so that they could secure the land and infrastructure for future German generations. As Elizabeth Harvey has noted in her thorough study of females in the German-occupied east, many Germans considered Poland to be an extremely alien and primitive place despite its geographical proximity to Germany. This view became so widespread that the Party press began to criticize sensationalist depictions of the East as being overly backward or dangerous. They stressed that instead Poland should be portrayed as an area that was quickly being modernized and brought to order by the Germans.[24]

Despite the frequent portrayals of Polish backwardness in German media, these depictions helped justify the supposed redevelopment of the areas. For example, a contributor to the *Völkischer Beobachter* wrote about the ethnic German resettlement in the Wartheland. He painted a bleak picture of what Poland had supposedly looked like before the Germans began their developmental construction work. The author explained how the Poles were "unable to deal with water, swamps and sand" and how they let their forests deteriorate. He went on to describe the riverbanks as "overgrown with reeds and the river beds were silted." As for the villages, the author wrote that they were "grey," "dirty," and "structurally damaged," while the settlements were "primitive."[25] However, despite such an unwelcoming environment, the author described how the Germans were undertaking important planning and construction of transport networks, street improvement, and water resource management. He ended the article with an optimistic view for the future; he anticipated a *Gau* with natural resources that were best utilized and a landscape that would be well-balanced in terms of the distribution of people in the city and the countryside.[26]

Buildings, such as Polish shopfronts, underwent renovation and were rebuilt with exteriors and signs that gave them a German façade. In some areas, Polish buildings and dwellings were initially not considered to be fit to be used and inhabited by Germans. In *Regierungsbezirk* Zichenau (part of the *Provinz* Ostpreußen, Province of East Prussia), it was noted in a staff report from the RKFDV Planning Department that "the buildings are very poor, even by Polish standards."[27] Similarly, in the press materials for the "Planung und Aufbau" exhibition, an article by the architect Werner Lindner featured comparison pictures of doorways and shops as they had been with Polish owners and after German redevelopment. The article noted that the towns and villages of the new German Eastern territories would, through radical transformation and large-scale redevelopment, obtain a German visage. Lindner also noted that German influence could be seen in the construction of some of the existing buildings, but that this was hidden by neglect. However, with minor improvements and a little effort, these qualities could be brought to light, and they could even reach a considerably higher standard.[28] Such "improvements" were also noticeable to local ethnic Germans. For example, in a letter, an ethnic German from Łódź commented on the eight months of transformation that had occurred in the city. He described how "we are now in riches and our city is gradually adopting a German character: the shop signs are all in German, almost eight hundred streets have been renamed and already many of the signs with new street names are mounted." He went on to note how "in the main streets, the majority of Jewish shops have disappeared. The German schools are housed in the nicest buildings."[29]

Through the *Aufbau*, the German architects, engineers, and city administration were implanting German infrastructural elements into Poland and in doing so, they aimed to change the Polish landscape. Germany was the supposed bringer of modernity in the form of paved roads, electricity, and water. German authorities planned for bigger towns and cities to be linked to the *Altreich* by *Reichsautobahns* (RAB) and travelers from major German cities, such as Frankfurt and Berlin, could travel to the far corners of the new German empire. A *Generalplan Ost* (GPO) memorandum titled "Rechtliche, wirtschaftliche und räumliche Grundlagen des Ostaufbaus" (Legal,

Economic and Spatial fundamentals of Eastern Development) by Konrad Meyer, the leader of the Planning Department of the RKFDV, predicted similar modernization for the areas further east after the war.[30] The memo provided tables and graphs on a variety of issues, such as construction costs for streets, waterways, and electricity supplies.[31] Another major planned project whose scale indicated the strength of the belief that Nazi planners had in the future success of their eastern endeavors was the preparation of the Vistula River for use as an industrial waterway. New ports were planned for along the river and dams and canals would allow for the creation of more agricultural land for settlement by Germans.[32]

In addition to redesigning and constructing new German infrastructure in the conquered territory, other elements of Nazi Germany's construction efforts strengthened the German societal hierarchy in annexed Poland. For example, the *Deutsche Häuser* (German Houses) were seen as being so crucial to the strengthening of community that Greiser issued instructions to the *Regierungspräsidenten* (District Presidents) of Poznań, Kalisz (Kalisch), and Inowrocław (Hohensalza) in April 1940 for the establishment of *Deutsche Häuser* in their districts. The instructions were signed by August Jäger, the Deputy *Reichsstatthalter* and therefore Greiser's representative. The letter noted how every single German national must become "increasingly involved in the great aims and tasks of government." It also explained, "It is necessary that he be informed of these goals and tasks as well as the development and progress of our work in the Wartheland." It warned that the Germans in the Wartheland were still largely scattered throughout a "foreign country" and that for them "to remain conscious of the great ethnic community and its tasks, the collective still needs more than the Germanness of the closed settlement area." Jäger instructed that a *Deutsches Haus* should be created in all of the larger municipalities and that, since the war meant only limited resources were available, they should be established in existing buildings where possible.[33] Jäger also advised that each of the *Deutsche Häuser* should have a large meeting room that could accommodate at least 60 percent of the German population in the area and that, if possible, there also should be a room available for the Party and the *Hitler Jugend* (Hitler Youth).[34]

The *Deutsches Haus* was therefore not only assigned the role of a community center, but it was also to be used as a political venue. Attendance at the *Deutsche Häuser* functioned as a means to include oneself within a community of fellow expatriates segregated from their native homeland. Just as colonial clubs "represented an oasis of European culture in the colonies" during the nineteenth and early twentieth centuries,[35] the *Deutsche Häuser* could offer a similar oasis for Germans in Poland. In German-occupied Poland, they were a method of social support as well as physically bringing Germans together as part of a united group, thus enforcing the ideology of the *Volksgemeinschaft*.[36] As Stephan Lehnstaedt notes, the *Deutsches Haus* in Warsaw in the General Government was a symbol of the cultural hub of German life within the city.[37] In a similar way to newspapers, magazines, and journals, the club could provide both a sense of home and a sense of inclusion in the *Reichsgau*. Additionally, as the official instructions regarding their establishment in the Wartheland noted, the *Deutsche Häuser* were politically important for distributing news on the progress and tasks of the Germans in the *Gau*.

The efforts of the German architects, engineers, and planning authorities to transform Polish towns and villages were not dissimilar to colonial occupiers, who also attempted to create European-style infrastructure in colonies. In his study of settler building handbooks in the German colonies in Africa, Ithohan Osayimwese has highlighted how colonial and commercial interests intersected. Akin to German architects', builders', and engineers' enthusiasm in annexed Poland, colonial and imperial expansion facilitated the notion of unlimited spatial and design opportunities. Coupled with the lack of building constraints typically found within European cities, the supposedly limitless construction opportunities meant that colonial and imperial powers, and the architects, builders, and engineers who were among them, often viewed the colonies as perfect locations for building projects.[38] Colonialism often brought with it the modernization of roads, water, and electricity supplies, sewage systems, and facilities such as hospitals, universities, and libraries. Such modernization was often part of a general colonial civilizing mission, which legitimated colonizer policies and was framed as an effort to improve the lives and health of the indigenous population. Although on the surface, this goal of colonial modernization was dissimilar to the case of the Germans in Poland as the Germans were not introducing new infrastructure for the benefit of all the local Polish population, if one considers, as argued in Chapter 2, that the treatment of ethnic Germans was similar to the treatment of a "Colonial Other" and that certainly the local ethnic Germans who had always lived in Poland were also members of the native population to an extent, then such improvements can still be understood to align with colonial contexts.

In addition to infrastructural changes, the renaming of places and streets was, as Jillian Barteaux argues, a colonial method of converting supposed "empty space into a useful, meaningful, culturally relevant place."[39] Renaming towns, villages, and districts in the language of the colonizer signified ownership of the territory. More importantly, however, the renaming of places and streets in colonial locations meant that the new incoming settlers could experience a feeling of familiarity and belonging in their new environment. Barteaux has pointed out in her study of Fremantle, a settlement in Western Australia, that the British aimed at creating a landscape where the settlers could be reminded of home. Similarly, familiar names would also act as marketing for other settlers and investors.[40]

In annexed Poland, certain places and towns were renamed according to the long-standing German version of their name, for example, Poznań to Posen or Gdańsk to Danzig. However, on other occasions, there was a concerted effort to distance the name from the original Polish, for example, the renaming of Łódź in honor of the Prussian First World War general Karl Litzmann. Like Barteaux's example of Fremantle, the street names in the *Reichsgaue* were named under different categories.[41] Many of the street names were eponymous, like Robert-Koch-Straße and Friedrich-Nietzsche-Straße in Poznań or Adolf-Hitler-Straße and Hermann-Göring-Straße in Bydgoszcz (Bromberg).[42] Others were associative and reflected the purpose of the street or areas, such as Fischmarkt (Fish Market).[43] Several streets were named after locations in the *Altreich* like Bayreuther Straße and Oberbayernstraße in Łódź. Other streets such as Dornröschenstraße (Sleeping Beauty Street) and Froschkönigweg (Frog Prince Way), also in Łódź, were whimsically named after well-known German fairy tale characters.[44]

The Germanized street names were therefore similar or identical to street names in other German cities. They recalled particular locations and figures from history and the contemporary public sphere. For Reich Germans living and working in annexed Poland, and for ethnic Germans who were resettled there, German places names served to not only foster a sense of familiarity. They helped to create the perception of a burgeoning German community within a previously foreign territory, solidify the transformation of the territory, and portray the predicted permanency of the German settlement there.

Another element of the German redevelopment of Polish towns that was similar to the colonial transformation of the territory was that the architecture of colonial cities and the surrounding landscapes often began to reflect the style of the colonial rulers. As Kahina Amal Djiar argues about Algiers in French Algeria, "the re-construction of the city in a French style was supported by a colonial discourse that infected all forms of architectural representation with decidedly prejudicial implications."[45] The demolition of palaces and mosques representative of Islamic power and the architectural redesign of Algerian cities both highlighted and reinforced the French perception of their cultural superiority over the indigenous population. Howard Spodek has highlighted that urban planning in British India was often contradictory depending on the local circumstances and budget. Although sanitary and civil engineers were important figures as they insured such measures as clean water supplies, town planning, like in England at the time, was still in its infancy. Nevertheless, the town planning that did occur in India in the 1880s and 1890s was principally about solidifying the imperial presence by constructing impressive buildings for British rulers and officers.[46] Similarly, the Germans transformed Polish towns to allow for an improvement of living standards for ethnic Germans and Reich Germans who were settling there and for future German generations, but they were also transforming cities, and removing the elements of Polish history to visibly demonstrate their ownership of the territory.

The *Deutsche Häuser* were, like such establishments as colonial clubs, only open for members of the occupier group and, therefore, they also served to enforce the societal hierarchy in the areas. Colonial clubs, largely popular in the British Empire during the nineteenth century, were spaces in which the gentlemen or the elite of colonial society could meet, socialize, and reminisce about their home country with their fellow nationals. These clubs were scenes of social events, discussions, casual meetings, and sometimes alcohol-fuelled excess.[47] Simply by being German, Reich and ethnic Germans were afforded a higher legal and social status than Poles. The *Deutsche Häuser* signified this status and enhanced the visual and physical segregation of the new communities as well as affording Germans the chance to reimmerse themselves in German culture, albeit away from the *Altreich*.

It is worth noting that although colonial similarities are identifiable within the transformation of the former Polish towns and villages, officials within the Nazi regime rarely used the terms "colonies" or "colonization" when publically discussing the resettlement. This is most probably due to the association of the word "colony" with overseas territories and not continental territorial possession but also due to the potentially negative connotations, the word could have.[48] Birthe Kundrus notes that, for the colonial enthusiasts, the terminological differentiation may have been a conscious effort to assert the independence of their campaigning from the Eastern expansion, whereas the proponents of Eastern settlement probably wished to distinguish themselves from the colonial enthusiasts' "heavy-handed propaganda."[49] As early as May 1937, Albert Brackmann, the well-known *Ostforschung* (Eastern Research) academic, advised the Reich Ministry of the Interior that the word "colonisation" should not be used in relation to Poland.[50] He suggested that the term "resettlement" (*Umsiedlung*) should be used instead because "the Poles could reach certain conclusions from this [the term colonisation] that might not be very politically satisfactory for us." Similarly, he advised the editor of the publication *Deutsches Archiv für Landes-und Volksförschung* to replace terms such as "history of the colonisation" with "settlement history" in their publications.[51]

Although officials did not wish to openly use terms that would associate German Eastern expansion with overseas colonialism in public matters, colonial comparisons were still used in many reports, and personal correspondence to express perceptions of Poland and the efforts to Germanize it. For example, the colonial resemblance of the transformation of Polish cities and towns and the perception that they were populating empty or underutilized space were not overlooked by the settlement planners. As early as June 1934, Ewald Liedecke, the head of the planning office in East Prussia, described Poland and the East as "abundantly colonial" in comparison to his native Baden-Württemberg.[52] During the war, Wilhelm Hallbauer, the *Stadtbaurat* (head of municipal building) for Łódź, described how the Germans would use local resources to turn this "*Kolonialgebiet*" (colonial territory) into a living member of the German economy and the German Reich in as little time as possible. German housing could be acquired through the deportation of Jews and Poles and the use of their robbed property and so, for Hallbauer, Nazi Germany could create the required space for the *Volk ohne Raum* (People without Space) from the new *Raum ohne Volk* (space without people). He added that the "*Kolonisation*" (colonization) of areas that had never been German before would be conducted by uncommon methods.[53] A map by an unknown creator promoted the *Heim ins Reich* policy by also using similar referencing to colonialism. The map loosely depicted the ethnic German resettlers' places of origin, and in the included descriptive test, the map explained that the Führer was calling the ethnic groups back to "the homeland of their fathers." These ethnic groups would help with the expansion and consolidation of the Reich, and "their colonizing abilities [*kolonisatorische Fähigkeiten*] [would] be particularly effective in the construction of the Warthegau."[54] In a 1942 report about the work of the *Gendarmerie* (police), Fritz Klipfel, the commander of the *Gendarmerie* in the Łódź district, similarly utilized colonial terminology when referring to official activities. He ended the report with the advice that "a good, but hard will, as well as the comradeship of all gendarmes, bearing in mind their proud tradition, will also help in the (*Kolonisationsarbeit*) colonization work here."[55]

Moving away from similarities in linguistic terminology to colonial knowledge exchange, the historian Patrick Bernhard has discovered concrete links between Nazi Germany's town planning in Poland and another colonial power. Bernhard has argued that the growing Italian empire in Africa had a profound influence on Nazi settlement planners. Through direct contact links, Nazi urban planners and SS officials gained information on the Italian settlement model in Africa and created plans that reflected this. The Italian colonization of Africa acted as a justification for Nazi Germany's expansion into Eastern Europe for a variety of reasons. Like Germany, Italy was also a fascist state and had been late to the colonial and imperial race. After being one of the territorial "losers" in the Treaty of Versailles, Italy was now trying to establish an empire. This justification is demonstrated in a range of factors; for example, the belief by German writers that Italy also had a lack of "living space" (*Raumnot*), the positive German reviews and quick translation of Italian books that detailed the violent nature of Italy's war, and the frequent referencing of Italian strengths by Hitler.[56]

Additionally, according to Bernhard, Italy provided a definitive influence on the planning of urban settlement. The plans for German villages and the plans for Italian villages in Africa were remarkably similar; both were required to have the same list of facilities, public and administrative buildings and also a village tower. The German settlement planners' observations of Italian settlements also highlighted that their plans were missing a key feature that would help develop a sense of community in the new villages. The village square with Party buildings surrounding it was added to German plans so that it would become a crucial feature for public gatherings and for centralizing the important community buildings in German villages, like that of the *piazza* in Italian towns.[57] The contact between the German academics and planners and the Italian officials who were implementing the development and building in Africa, coupled with the similarity of the two country's plans for settlement towns and villages, demonstrates significant evidence for a link between a European empire, and the burgeoning German empire in Eastern Europe.

Advertising the East

Nazi Germany's expansionary mission required manpower. With numerous ethnic German resettlers arriving from Eastern Europe every day, German authorities needed Reich Germans to prepare their homes, help them adjust to their new lives, and, perhaps most importantly, integrate them. Similarly, Nazi Germany relied on Reich Germans and their language skills to adequately begin to establish a functioning, economically productive German society in Poland. As mentioned in the last chapter, snapshots of the resettlement in the form of personal stories, pictures, and drawings were used within Germany to elicit feelings of sympathy and kinship with ethnic German resettlers. However, other themes were also used to appeal to young and enthusiastic Germans.

For example, an article written by the economist Ernst Wagemann, the founder and president of the *Deutsches Institut für Wirtschaftsforschung* (DIW, German Institute for Economic Research), featured in the *Schlesische Tageszeitung*. The article was titled "*Geh' nach dem Osten, junger Mann!*" (Go East, Young Man!); it noted that Europe's future no longer lay overseas, but instead in the space that lay beyond Vienna and Danzig and stretched as far as into the Asiatic continent. Wagemann proclaimed that "the way it looks, 'go east, young man' will be the watchword for ambitious talents for decades to come."[58] Wagemann's phrasing is interesting in two ways. Firstly, the phrase "Go East, young man" was a modification of the phrase "Go West, young man," which was attributed to Horace Greely in 1851. Greely was an American author who was a supporter of westward expansion because of the belief that the American West offered freedom, new beginnings, and the chance to avoid economic instability and unemployment, which was rife in bigger cities.[59] Wagemann's choice of phrase, therefore, reflects a linkage to a period of American expansion and the notion of the Western frontier. Wagemann appears to be drawing allusions between the American case and the German case of expansion by using an example of a mainland-based empire and not one that expands to overseas territories. Secondly, Wagemann's article is noteworthy in how he says that the phrase will be "the watchword for ambitious talents for decades to come." Wagemann is calling on, but also enticing, a generation of young Germans to move to the East. An article written by the founder of the DIW, a notable institution of experts who published research and data on current economic situations and forecasts, was likely to be noticed by those searching for employment opportunities and advancement. If the founder of such an institution was predicting that to "go East" was a catchphrase for the future, it is plausible to see how this appealed to a German audience seeking career opportunities.

A further example of such propaganda was the *Kulturfilm* (culture film, akin to a documentary) *Mädel verlassen die Stadt* (Girls Leave the City), which was released in 1943 by Universum Film AG (UFA), a film production company that was under the control of Goebbels' Propaganda Ministry.[60] The unnarrated film, which is just over thirteen minutes long, follows a group of *Reichsarbeitsdienst der weiblichen Jugend* (Women's Youth Labor Service, RADwJ) girls on their journey from Hamburg to Alsace and then to a village near Łódź (a road sign shows Litzmannstadt as being 10 km away). The film depicts such scenes as girls receiving their uniforms and medical checks. It then goes on to document them undertaking a variety of activities. The girls mop the floors, do some gardening in the sunshine, hang laundry, and plant seeds with civilians. They excitedly receive postcards from home and ride their bicycles through a village, occasionally waving at people they pass. In the Wartheland, the film also shows the girls cleaning out a home where a decorated sign hangs above the door. The sign proclaims "Bessarabiendeutsche Willkommen in der neuen Heimat" (Bessarabian Germans, welcome to the new home). Shortly after, the RADwJ girls greet horse-drawn carts containing the Bessarabian German family with smiles, waves, a bunch of flowers, and handshakes.[61] Later scenes show the girls teaching ethnic German children and helping ethnic German resettlers with farming tasks. The film's final scenes show the *Arbeitsmaiden* dancing and serving food and drinks to people, presumably ethnic German resettlers, at an event. The RADwJ *Führerin* (group leader) makes a speech in front of a flying swastika flag. She notes that, after half a year of working together, the farmers will stay on the farms that they created out of Polish mismanagement and the *Arbeitsmaiden* will join the *Kriegshilfsdienst* (military service).

A film such as this portrayed a structured and seemingly regimented lifestyle, but as is the case with propaganda films, the girls shown in it appeared to be happy, hard-working, and dedicated. The film illustrates the fulfilling nature of the work that was available for women in Poland: working as a team, helping civilians, welcoming families, and playing with and teaching children. In a similar film from 1940 named

Ostland—deutsches Land (Eastern land—German land), the focus is initially on the suffering of ethnic Germans at the hands of Poles. The film notes that German villages were destroyed and it alludes to the *Bromberger Blutsonntag* by mentioning the widely circulated inflated death toll of 58,000 murdered Germans. The film goes on to depict examples of German buildings in Poznań, Malbork (Marienburg), and Grudziądz (Graudenz) before showing pictures of German-style houses. Like in *Mädel verlassen die Stadt*, newly arrived ethnic German resettlers are energetically greeted, and Reich Germans are depicted as if they are on some kind of working holiday. Young German women work in fields, hang out clothes, and groom small white rabbits while Hitler Youth boys plough fields, drive tractors, mend socks, and tend to horses. They gather together to race, box, and play a ball game. The film also records a village get-together where the women laugh and hold hands with men in SS uniforms. Surrounded by villagers, the young women and Hitler Youth members partake in traditional dancing, and a young child toddles across the screen in traditional German clothing. The film ends with the two phrases "Der weite Osten braucht eine landwillige Jugend" (the vast East needs youths willing to work the land) and "Er ruft auch Dich" (it's also calling you).[62] Such propaganda films demonstrate how the Nazi administration wanted the resettlement and the work of Reich Germans to be perceived. The films portrayed the supposed stability and achievements of the Nazi regime in Poland. The people are depicted as happy and relaxed as they carry out routine tasks, but the viewer is acutely aware that these routine tasks have some sort of wider significance by virtue of them being undertaken by teams of orderly people in smart uniforms and the presence of flags emblazoned with swastikas in numerous shots.

In addition to documentary-style films, *Die Deutsche Wochenschau* (The German Weekly Review) newsreels also featured the resettlement in many of its screenings. It presented the widely circulated images of the cloth-covered horse-drawn wagons, accompanied by women wearing headscarves, and men wearing traditional hats beside the VoMi camps.[63] Ethnic Germans were shown registering for the resettlement and cheerfully welcoming the *Umsiedlungskommando*. An *Abschiedsfest* (farewell party) also featured in the reel; the ethnic Germans went to their local church for the last time, gathered together, and danced while wearing *Tracht* (traditional costume) associated with their original German homeland.[64] Another reel showed Bessarabian Germans viewing their new farmhouses in Poland and Reich German women pouring the resettlers tea and offering cake.[65] Such updates from the resettlement allowed German citizens within the *Altreich* to stay updated with what was happening in Poland, but it also alluded to justifications of why the war was being waged. The ethnic Germans abroad, who had maintained their German culture, were now willingly returning to the Reich to take part in the settlement of the annexed territories. At the same time, such publicity for the resettlement could also have acted as encouragement for Germans to join in with the resettlement and to assist their fellow countrymen and women.

Further to non-fictional visual reports, the fictionalized and dramatic retelling of the ethnic Germans' plight and their resettlement featured in the cinematic film *Heimkehr* (Homecoming). *Heimkehr* was released in 1941 and directed by Gustav Ucicky; like *Mädel verlassen die Stadt*, the Propaganda Ministry-controlled UFA distributed the film.[66] *Heimkehr* depicts an ethnic German family in Volhynia who are, along with other ethnic Germans, subjected to increasing oppression and violence at the hands of Poles. For example, the German school is burnt down by Polish youths, the father of the family is attacked and blinded, and ethnic Germans are refused admission and treatment in the Polish hospital. When Germany invades Poland in 1939, the family is overjoyed. However, their joy is short-lived when they are discovered by Poles and arrested. The family manage to escape the prison and abusive prison guards and are saved by *Wehrmacht* soldiers. At the end of the film, they trek across the border into the German Reich to begin their new lives in the *Heimat*. The film strongly portrays the supposed violence and cruelty of the Poles while also demonstrating the loyalty of ethnic Germans to Germany and their struggle to preserve elements of German culture abroad. As the film was released when the resettlement was ongoing, it clearly attempted to evoke feelings of national pride but also sympathy for ethnic Germans.[67] *Heimkehr* thus tied in with the numerous newspaper articles and reports in circulation by visually depicting, and in turn legitimizing, the resettlement in a dramatized form. While the film demonstrated an individual family's (fictional) story of perseverance and overcoming, it also subtly alluded to the significance of resettling ethnic Germans, and therefore, the urgent need for Reich Germans to engage with work in the annexed territories to assist their return to the Reich.

In addition to the ending of *Ostland— deutsches Land*, the idea that the East was calling to Reich Germans, as opposed to the Führer calling ethnic Germans, which was discussed in Chapter 2, was prevalent in a variety of literature. For example, the first volume of the series *Die wirtschaftlichen Entwicklungsmöglichkeiten in den eingegliederten Ostgebieten des Deutschen Reiches* (The Economic Development Possibilities in the Annexed Eastern Territories of the German Reich) was titled *Deutscher! Der Osten ruft dich!* (German! The East Is Calling You!)[68] The book begins by explaining that the current generation of Germans is living through the greatest goal that Germans could be given, the establishment of the Greater German Reich.[69] It details various points such as the current population, economy, and industry in the Wartheland as well as German progress and plans for these sectors. Like many books and newspaper articles, the author, Walter Geisler, reiterates the idea of a German "*Aufgabe*" (task) numerous times. He highlights that one part of this task was to settle the *Raum* in Poland because, as the author explained, the unsettled *Raum* was like a blank piece of paper and thus, nothing more than a foundation. Everything depended on who is the one writing on it.[70] In the book's last chapter, Geisler emphasized that the "development of the German East is a task of the entirety of the German *Volk*."[71]

Similarly, in the fourth volume of the series, the author Georg Blohm wrote about the economic potential of the *Reichsgau* Danzig-West Prussia. Like Geisler, Blohm further elucidated the idea of a purely German task in the East. "Only the farmer could recapture the land for Germandom," Blohm wrote.[72] In a short publication about *Gauleiter* Albert Forster, the author Wilhelm Löbsack also utilized the idea of personal tasks. He described Forster's rise in the ranks of the Nazi Party and his prewar attempts to spread the National Socialist ideology in the Free City of Danzig in a chapter named "*Der große Aufgabe*." As *Gauleiter,* Löbsack noted that Forster's responsibilities were, firstly, to gather all of Germandom and to unify them within National Socialist ideology. Secondly, he was to clarify the question of the population; the end goal was the enforcement of Germandom and the removal of foreign Polish people.[73]

Like *Mädel verlassen die Stadt*, certain publications targeted women directly. Wolfgang Diewerge, the *Gaupropagandaleiter* (Head of Propaganda for the Gau) for Danzig-West Prussia, wrote of "special" tasks for the women of the *NS-Frauenschaft*, which were revealed through taking care of ethnic Germans and the return of Baltic and Volhynian Germans. Such tasks included the cleaning and debugging of vacated Polish properties and the erection of care stations for the newly arrived ethnic Germans.[74] In another publication, the head of the *Reichsarbeitsdienst* (Reich Labor Service, RAD), Konstantin Hierl, was quoted as highlighting the particular role that women would play in Poland. He addressed the women who were helping ethnic German farmers and noted that:

> You know that you should be more to the families you look after than just economic support … You have the great task of being particularly helpful to the mothers, who are twice as burdened by the departure of the men, not only able helpers but also faithful, affectionate pillars in all spiritual distress and worry.[75]

He went on to say that "wherever you are, the sun must shine."[76]

Another important feature of the propaganda utilized by the Germans when referring to Poland was their usage of irredentist referencing. Certain elements of Germany's use of irredentist referencing coupled with referencing more common to colonialism are unusual and can, at times, appear to be paradoxical. Poland was often stylized as being backward, primitive, and in need of German intervention. However, parts of Poland were still depicted as being German and they were frequently discussed in terms of their German character. The notion of Germanizing and developing primitive territory and people appear to contradict the notion of the territory already being fundamentally German. One way to possibly explain this, as noted in the introduction, is that the concept of irredentism can be understood to contain or promote elements of colonialism. Therefore, although the two concepts are not identical, they can be linked in terms of the desire for expansion and the ownership of territory. Another potential explanation for the paradox relates to the German idea that during the interwar years, the Polish state had allowed the former German territories to go into decline. Like ethnic Germans who had been potentially influenced by a foreign power, the territory, which was considered to be German at its core, had undergone a detrimental change.[77] Thus, German irredentist claims on the territory could still exist alongside a colonial perception of the territory; for example, it was backward and in need of modernization.

The German occupation of Poland and the creation of German towns and villages had a crucial dual purpose. It both reclaimed territory that had been German before the Treaty of Versailles and expanded past these territories to further enlarge the newly established Nazi German empire in Eastern Europe. Much of the language surrounding the resettlement refers to this dual purpose; often it does so explicitly and other times it is less obvious. An example of a fleeting reference to irredentist claims on the Polish territory can be seen in an article from *Der Gauring* titled "The German Women in Ethnic Work." The article explains how the women of the *NS-Frauenschaft* contributed to the painstaking task of building the cultural foundations of the *Reichsgau* while also participating in the ethnic struggle. The article ends by stating that the Polish language and economy shall disappear once again and its closing statement notes that "this country remains German."[78] This sentence is only a passing reference to the territory of the *Reichsgau* Danzig-West Prussia and it seems to merely convey a future intention, that the country will stay German. However, a closer examination also shows that it discloses a strong indication of irredentism in the use of the word "remains," especially when coupled with the preceding sentence, which notes the Polish language and economy will disappear again. The author is passively signaling the belief that the country was not Polish, it was German, and now that the Germans were engaging in the cultural and ethnic struggle there, the country would remain German.

Similarly, the contributors to the book released as part of the previously mentioned exhibition "Der Osten des Warthelandes" also expressed irredentist discourses regarding the Germans in Poland. In addition to covering the history of German settlement in the Łódź region, the book also features photos of archeological finds, which include an urn decorated with swastikas. The section is titled "the Litzmannstadt area is German native homeland (*Urheimat*)."[79] Another of the book's contributors reiterated that Litzmannstadt and the space surrounding it was German land for 150 years.[80] Discourses that highlighted the previous German ownership of the territory and the supposed right that Germans had to the territory because of this were common within literature relating to Poland and the East. The German invasion could be framed as the reclamation of territory while the work of the Germans could also be linked to the historical work of prior generations of Germans.

Germany's irredentist aims could also be merged with colonial ones as demonstrated in a speech given by Himmler in October 1942 in Madrid at a reception of the Party *Landesgruppe* there. Himmler's speech covered the topics of modern settlement problems and the question of the European eastern space. Himmler noted that the redesign of the territories was already underway, that Germany would be the most powerful country in the world, and the German people would be the healthiest and most capable. Himmler then referred to the settlement as "this large internal colonization."[81] The use of the word "internal" in this instance is noteworthy in that in the context it could apply to both Nazi Germany's internal colonization of Europe, but also that it could refer to the idea that the colonization was taking place largely within areas that were considered to be inherently German. The notion of internal colonization, the colonization that took place within Germany's territories to simultaneously regain land and create an empire, thus adds another level of understanding to the links between the concepts of irredentism and colonialism.

The linking of these concepts, both practically and rhetorically, was not unusual in traditional examples of colonial expansion. For example, the Italian colonial occupation of Libya (1911–43) was often described as a "return" or "re-birth" and was linked to the notion that the territory, as well as the wider Mediterranean, had once been part of the Roman Empire. This historic possession was framed as a justification for the Italian retaking of the territories.[82] Like the efforts of German planners, academics, and Nazi Party officials to promote the inherent Germanness of parts of Poland, which in turn legitimized the conquering and settlement of the territories, as pointed out by Stephanie Malia Hom regarding Italian tourism in colonial Libya, a variety of propaganda materials highlighted Libya's "Romanness."[83]

In addition to the promotion of the historical German interventions in Poland, publications, films, exhibitions, and newspaper articles advertised Eastern Europe and the contemporary resettlement to Germans citizens living in the *Altreich*. By creating the idea of a specifically German task that was not only linked to German historical conquests and lost German territory in the East but also the preservation of the German population in the future, such propaganda attempted to appeal to individuals' sense of national pride. The notion of a German task in Poland meant that every German, regardless of their gender or profession, could envision themselves as a crucial part of building a new German society. Additionally, the continued use of the sentiment that "all" German people must participate, tied in with the ideology of belonging to the *Volksgemeinschaft*. The tasks in the German East could only be completed by the German people to secure their survival in the future. Thus, it was each individual's responsibility, whether they were the *Gauleiter* or a settlement advisor, to take part.

The Reich German Eastern Experience

The changing city and village landscapes existed alongside the changes to the population of Poland. Along with qualified and politically reliable ethnic Germans who had been resettled, the German civil administration in the *Reichsgaue* was staffed by Germans from the *Altreich*. Although German propaganda attempted to frame the work of Reich Germans in Poland as part of a wider German humanitarian mission, in reality, the reasons for Reich Germans to move to Poland were varied. Occasionally, the Reich administration ordered temporary service transfer to Poland to combat staff shortages, other times individuals volunteered and this often reflected a desire for personal gains and privilege. In the case of administrative transfers within the public sector, the orders for personnel to be sent East often became a method for offices to remove unproductive or disliked people from their staff. For example, when the Erfurt city administration was told to send someone for eastern duty, they sent Reinhold Schreiber, an alcoholic.[84] This was not an isolated incident and eastern duty would be continually exploited as a convenient way to deal with certain staff members throughout the war.

The motivations behind Reich Germans' voluntary relocation to Poland are of greater importance than the involuntary transfers when examining the similarities between the case of Nazi Germany's expansion into Poland and European colonialism. The voluntary relocations to the East demonstrate why German citizens would become involved in the Nazi German empire-building enterprise; instead of solely showing the aims of the regime, it demonstrates the goals, hopes, and fantasies of the everyday, normal people who would occupy the upper level of the societal hierarchy in Poland. As a seemingly natural aspect of human life, the aspiration for personal achievement was present both in the German population willing to move to Poland and in Europeans willing to settle in distant colonies. The German occupation and rule over Poland, like that of the rule of European powers over colonies, allowed for notable benefits for members of the occupier population. Because of the low wages paid to the Poles, almost all Reich Germans could afford to employ someone to help with household duties.[85] This domestic set-up served as a reminder to Reich Germans, even within their own homes, of their privileged status in annexed Poland.

Outside of the home, employment in the German civil service in Poland often led to quicker than average career progression, an avoidance of army service, and, due to the high demand for personnel, those with a criminal record were not excluded from employment.[86] In addition to employment benefits, Reich Germans in Poland could look forward to the availability of bigger properties; the increased obtainability of wartime luxuries, like meat and vodka; and opportunities to buy jewelry, gold, artwork, and furniture at low prices as the majority of it had been stolen from Jews and Poles. The extra household items and cheaper luxury goods, known as "the eastern supplement" that Reich Germans had access to amounted to the equivalent of their salaries being doubled.[87] Despite being away from Germany, more often than not, Reich Germans were the ones to send packages from Poland back to family and friends in Germany because of the access to desirable items there.[88]

Although additional rations were one aspect, undoubtedly certain Reich Germans embraced the additional privileges afforded to them without paying much regard to how their new status impacted the Polish population. For example, a typist in Poznań named Frau Tolz wrote a letter in March 1941 to the accommodation provision department of the *Reichsstatthalter*'s office. The letter is very revealing in that it reflects the privileges that Reich Germans could avail of, or at least the privileges they believed they were entitled to. Frau Tolz wrote that, as she had the intention of staying in the Wartheland, she had found an apartment that was sufficient for her needs. She provided the exact address of the apartment and noted that it had two rooms and a kitchen. She then noted that currently the apartment was inhabited by a Polish family. Following this information, she wrote: "I request that this apartment is vacated by the Poles and allocated to the *Reichsstatthalter*. After this allocation, I ask that the apartment is assigned to me." She went on to note that in the *Altreich*, she currently pays a monthly rent of 33.50RM with no additional costs.[89]

A letter by a Reich German city administration worker in Łódź in December 1942 reflected a similar situation. Herr Minkes wrote to the Mayor of Łódź that he had been waiting for the last nine months for an apartment and that he was registered with the *Amt für Raumbewirtschaftung* (Office for Spatial Management) as seeking housing. As he was employed by the city, he was also allowed to apply for housing through the city's *Wohnungsfürsorge* (Housing Provision). Despite his enquiries, he still had not received what he considered to be adequate housing. His current apartment was too small with no oven and for the last few months, his bedroom furniture, which he had paid for, was still waiting to be collected from the furniture shop. He noted that so far the only advice he had received was that if he requested that a Polish person be relocated, then he would have a claim on their apartment. Herr Minkes took this advice and requested that the Office of Spatial Management carry out the relocation of a Polish engineer. Unfortunately for Herr Minkes, he was then told that the Polish man would not be relocated as there was a lack of housing for Poles. In the meantime, Frau Gauding, the German owner of a public house at the same address, had also put a claim in for the same apartment. The Polish inhabitant was moved out of his apartment and it was ultimately put on hold for Frau Gauding. Rather ironically given that he had attempted to take the apartment from the Polish inhabitant, Herr Minkes expressed disbelief at how a person, who was not even registered as seeking housing, could simply put an apartment on hold just because it suited them. He noted that this was "unexplainable."[90]

Although it is unclear whether Frau Tolz or Herr Minkes were eventually allocated the apartments they desired or not, their letters demonstrate the position of Reich Germans in Poland. In the case of Frau Tolz, she did not provide any reasons as to why she required that specific apartment and so it appears that she seemingly did not believe that she needed any better reason, other than that she found the apartment to be sufficient for her needs, for the Polish family to be evicted. Herr Minkes encountered a bureaucratic struggle when it came to his chosen apartment; however, his sense of entitlement is clear. In both cases, the Polish owners or inhabitants of the apartments are invisible. Reich Germans did not appear to consider the lives of those whom they wanted to evict. These examples demonstrate the duality of German involvement in Poland; on one hand, the German groups portrayed Reich Germans' work in Poland as contributing toward a selfless, specifically German task or mission, and that it was beneficial for Germany and the new *Reichsgaue*. On the other hand, Frau Tolz, Herr Minkes, and many others working in Poland were using their positions as Reich Germans for personal gain when the opportunities presented themselves on the ground.

David Furber has thoroughly investigated which Reich Germans, based on such criteria as age, religion, and birth region, worked in the Wartheland. The majority of Germans who voluntarily went to Poland at the early stages of the occupation were originally from Poland or the Baltic States and were eager to return; the results from his samples also demonstrate how most male Reich Germans were in their late thirties to early forties, more likely to be Protestant, and eight times more likely to be a member of the National Socialist Party than average Reich civil servants.[91] As previously mentioned in this chapter, men were not the only ones to go east. Women undertook jobs, not only as settlement advisors and teachers but also as nurses, secretaries, office clerks, and typists. Wendy Lower estimates that since there was at least one female Reich German administrator in every office of the Reich and if, on average, each female administrator reported to five male administrators, the figure of females in the civil administration in Poland would be approximately five thousand.[92]

Despite the propaganda to inspire Germans to move to Poland and further east, the Nazi regime, and indeed other businesses in the annexed territories, still needed a vast amount of personnel. The regime struggled to encourage sufficient numbers of Reich Germans to resettle in the East. As a result, personnel shortages were commonplace. The German civil administration in the east was between 50 percent and 75 percent understaffed. For example, in Koło, in the Wartheland, fifteen of the thirty-nine required civil servants and thirty-seven of the sixty projected employees were actually in employment.[93] Positions within the German administration were certainly available; however, the vacancies in annexed Poland were not just limited to such jobs. As the German population, supplemented at various times by arrivals of ethnic German resettlers, became more settled in the Polish settlement areas, an array of businesses needed staff to run them. For example, a small sample from the current vacancies section in the *Litzmannstäder Zeitung* in December 1941 and April 1942 reveals the types of establishments that were hiring and which roles they offered the German population. The vacancies included accountants, sales assistants, an electrical engineer, a German-speaking delivery boy, a dentist, a telephonist, and a cashier at a film theatre.[94]

Even organizations crucial to the German-desired reordering of Europe by their involvement in the evaluation and naturalization of ethnic Germans, such as the EWZ, suffered from understaffing and a high personnel turnover rate. Between April and June 1941, half of the EWZ administration personnel were replaced. Similarly, the lack of doctors available for health screenings led to the personnel office issuing a request in early 1941 for all commissions to report the location of any doctors who were among the resettlers.[95] As will be detailed later in this chapter, some Reich Germans genuinely wanted to move to Poland to help ethnic Germans and some did benefit from relocating. However, as demonstrated above and in the previous chapter, the fantasy and the rhetoric surrounding the notion of resettlement areas populated by both Reich Germans and ethnic Germans and the ideas of Reich Germans contributing to the supposed German mission in the east were harder to create in reality.

One of the best-known accounts of life in the Wartheland from the viewpoint of a Reich German official is the *Warthelӓndisches Tagebuch* (Watheland Diary) written by Franz Heinrich Bock under the pseudonym Alexander Hohenstein. While working as the mayor and commissioner of the town of Poddębice (Poddembice) in the Wartheland from 1940 until 1942, Bock stenographically recorded his time in office. After the war, he converted the records into writing for publication with the Institut für Zeitgeschichte (Institute for Contemporary History) in Munich. Throughout the diary, Bock illustrates his daily activities as well as his perceptions of Poland and his interactions with Germans, ethnic Germans, Poles, and Jews. Undoubtedly, an ego document, such as a diary, which was retyped after the war is potentially an unreliable source given that individual perception or retelling of events can be influenced by the passing of time. Such concerns are particularly relevant for how the issues of the persecution of Jews and the Holocaust are dealt with in rewritten, postwar ego documents. Despite this, Bock's *Tagebuch* still provides an interesting insight into the more mundane activities in annexed Poland that reveal the Reich Germans' experiences and their self-perception of societal status.

Bock's interactions with both local ethnic Germans and resettlers clearly disclose the superiority that Reich Germans felt over the newest members of the German social hierarchy. As alluded to in the previous chapter regarding the paternalistic treatment of ethnic Germans by Reich Germans, Bock also appeared to see ethnic Germans as simpler, uneducated, and primitive in their farming methods. On a visit to a local ethnic German's farm, Bock noted that although the farm owner did not speak German as he had never attended German classes, his mother could. Bock wrote that she made "a surprisingly intelligent impression." He felt that it was a shame that the family did not speak German at home as the mother's German skills were very good.[96] During a drive through farming settlements, Bock noticed that the isolated German farmers and "resettlers from Russia" looked cleaner, but otherwise not much different from the Poles.⁹⁷ Stumbling upon a local ethnic German throwing dung into a river, Bock immediately questioned the man and informed him that the dung was the best fertilizer for the land. He asked if no one told the man this before, and according to Bock, the man answered that he had probably heard about it, but it was something he was not used to.⁹⁸ Such an anecdote, coupled with similar ones recorded by Bock, gave a distinct impression that ethnic Germans were insular or old-fashioned.

Whether subconsciously or not, Bock was occasionally confronted with reflecting on his own status as a Reich German. For example, upon arriving in Łódź, Bock noticed with distaste how the trams had separate carriages "For Germans" and "For Poles." Later in the diary, Bock's deputy commissioner, an ethnic German who spoke "the awkward German of foreign Germans with a strong accent," told Bock not to clean his motorbike outside the house in case Poles saw him. If they did, then they may think that Bock was poor and could not afford to hire someone to clean it or indeed, that he had so little authority that he did not trust anyone else to do it. The deputy commissioner arranged for two Poles to clean the motorbike instead and they did so extremely fast. Bock finished the diary entry with the line "I have definitely learnt something."⁹⁹ A comment by Bock on a visit to the post office was, however, perhaps most telling about Reich German perception of how ethnic Germans' perceived the Germans from the *Altreich*. He observed the ethnic German personnel working in the post office and how they took great care of Reich German customers. According to Bock, "the Reich Germans were viewed by [the ethnic Germans] as like little gods."¹⁰⁰

Apart from the professional, economic, or societal benefits, some Reich Germans were drawn to Poland because of the promise of adventure. Despite its geographical proximity to Germany, Germans often considered Poland to be extremely vast and uninhabited, but also backward and unmodern. As Martha Michelsohn mentioned in her *Shoah* interview, she perceived Poland as a spatially liberating environment. She explained, "This freedom and this space (*Weite*), something one did not know anymore in the West. The unending space, right? That tempted me ... Here [the West], everything is so compressed, man by man. And there was this immeasurable space."¹⁰¹ Similarly, Elissa Mailänder Koslov has also noted how Poland was perceived to be further away than it was. Rudolf Höß, the commander of the Auschwitz–Birkenau camp between 1940 and 1943, began his autobiographical notes with the statement that Auschwitz "was far away, back there in Poland."¹⁰² In reality, Auschwitz was located in the Province of Upper Silesia (*Provinz Oberschlesien*), which had been annexed to the Reich since 1939. Although this example does not relate to the settlement areas that are the focus of this study, it sheds light on common perceptions or misconceptions of Poland by Germans. The status of the territories, that they were under German occupation, and that Poland neighbored Germany was irrelevant in light of the preconceived ideas that the areas were isolated or in the middle of nowhere. Poland fitted into the notion of a frontier for the German people; the unknown, primitive space beyond civilized, western Germany.

As opposed to dissuading people, such perceptions could encourage people to move to Poland. Martha Michelsohn expressed the sense of adventure that motivated her to leave Germany. When questioned as to why she chose to go to the Wartheland, Michelsohn noted that she had "*Unternehmungslust*" (a desire for adventure) and that she was young at the time.¹⁰³ This testimony fits in with the idea that a relocation to the East was an adventure, a life step that was exciting, new, and not always purely driven by the hope of economic gain. Dietrich Troschke, a thirty-four-year-old economist, was chosen to go east by his company. Even though Troschke did not volunteer to go, his diary entries reveal some of the reasons why others may have been motivated to relocate and also why he was happy about his new assignment. He noted that:

> Those who are on service in the East find themselves in a unique situation. Every individual is confronted with extraordinary opportunities. Nobody could ever have imagined a posting that offers so much more in the way of challenges, responsibilities and scope for initiative than anything else they have done in their entire lives.¹⁰⁴

Although men and women had coinciding interests in relocating to Poland, women often had additional motivations for moving. For many young women sent east on their *Osteinsatz* or for those who volunteered to go, it was to be their first time away from their families. Relocation to Poland or areas further east offered women the chance to be independent while still being watched over by official Reich organizations. A move to the East was not the equivalent of running away from home as they did have official roles and tasks, but the move would offer a certain degree of freedom to a generation of young women. In her study of women in the German-occupied East, Elizabeth Harvey explores the varying reasons why women were motivated to move from Germany during the German occupation of Poland. Some of these reasons pointed to the fact that the East offered more independence for women and also the chance for exploration. The notion that men had the opportunity to travel as soldiers but women were not, was also present. One teacher noted that "I actually wanted to see something of the world as well, and the boys got to go as soldiers – wherever, to France or to Finland … and that wasn't on offer for us." Other motivations for relocating echoed German propaganda; that there was a German task or job to be undertaken and that the women would help German people to find a homeland.¹⁰⁵ Martha Michelsohn also noted a similar sentiment. She agreed with Lanzmann when he asked her if she thought it was her duty to her country to help in Poland.¹⁰⁶

In addition to women's contribution to the resettlement of ethnic Germans, Wendy Lower has demonstrated that it was not only German men who were part of the Nazi SS institutions and who participated in violence or were complicit in the mistreatment of Jewish and non-Jewish Poles. Lower describes how the sense of liberation found in the East facilitated women to be complicit in and to perpetrate violence during the war and that the East was a "European stage where Hitler and his supporters fulfilled their imperial fantasies."¹⁰⁷ She highlights how women worked in administrative positions, such as typists and secretaries, and how they contributed to the production and administration of orders and records regarding the robbery, deportation, and murder of Jewish and non-Jewish civilians. Similarly, German women were employed as camp guards for female sections of concentration camps. Wives of SS men, female nurses, and other female Reich German civilians were witnesses to ghettos, expulsions, and, occasionally, they attended mass shootings.¹⁰⁸

The East did not only present opportunities and freedom for men, but it also appealed to women in both similar and dissimilar ways. For both sexes, the relocation to the East was something that could produce curiosity, excitement, the anticipation of opportunities for personal gain, and the expectation of an immense adventure. For women who potentially felt that they were prevented from offering as much to the Reich or from seeing as much of the world as men could because they were unable to take up arms and become a soldier, an assignment in the Polish settlement areas or further afield could help them to both gain life experience and contribute to the creation of a new German empire. As Christian Ingrao has highlighted in his study of how Nazi Germany promised the German people a "utopia" and how they were included in building it, historians "should not deny the emotional dimension of the *Osteinsatz*."[109]

As will be further discussed in Chapter 5, the allocation of specific roles to women, which would supplement settlement and the spread of colonizer culture, was also present within colonial expansion. European women contributed to colonial societal infrastructure by working in such professions as nurses and doctors. Perhaps most significantly, they helped further the civilizing mission by working as teachers for both indigenous and settler women and children; thereby, they conveyed the information needed to maintain the specificities of racially stratified colonial societies.[110] Similarly, by being homemakers, wives of settlers, or mothers of children, women also contributed to the preservation of the colonizer's traditions and culture within the home. As such, women who advocated for a female presence within the colonies promoted and carved out specific female roles that were in keeping with preexisting domestic gender norms, while simultaneously endorsing these roles as no less significant than male ones.

As Lora Wildenthal points out, the motto of colonialist German women became, "The man can conquer and subjugate territories in the world for the German idea, but only the persistence of women can implant and preserve the German idea abroad over the long term!"[111] As discussed in Chapter 2, women were assigned the tasks of educating local ethnic Germans and ethnic German resettlers both in terms of formal education and regarding domestic and health matters. Akin to colonial circumstances, women were able to create a specific area of expertise for themselves, which both reflected policy within Nazi Germany concerning the importance of homemaking and the expansionary policy of teaching, guiding, and preserving German culture in the annexed territories.

The German occupation of Poland not only provided Reich Germans with ample employment advantages and opportunities for travel and adventure, but it also allowed for unique experiences in terms of daily life and society. As noted earlier in this chapter, Reich Germans were members of a new societal hierarchy and they occupied its top level. They were notably privileged in that they benefitted from the segregated society. They had access to the best jobs and properties, discount luxuries, and the availability of solely German parks, restaurants, schools, and swimming pools. In a replication of colonial society, many Reich Germans employed domestic servants and farm laborers. Despite the settlement areas becoming increasingly more German in appearance, the hierarchical society, the notion that employment was in some way more important, the feeling of being far away from Germany, and the constant reminders of German domination over Poles and Jews meant that life in the settlement areas was not the same as life within the *Altreich*. The Polish settlement areas comprised of certain structural and societal elements that centerd on race and ethnicity. This was decidedly similar to the settler colonies where laws governing daily life existed as a means to preserve the *status quo* of segregation. Reich Germans, facilitated by the implementation of laws and new societal hierarchies, were the physical human implantations of the new German Empire in Poland. They were the supposed adventurers, pioneers, and humanitarian carers who were tasked with helping and educating ethnic Germans and establishing themselves, their families, the economy, and the society to ensure German ownership of the areas for future generations.

A German Humanitarian Mission?

The physical transformation of Polish towns and villages and the wide-ranging desires that encouraged the Germans to move to annexed Poland can be compared with colonial contexts. However, a more controversial area of potential colonial comparison is that of the self-conceived civilizing or humanitarian missions. As mentioned in the last chapter, historians have previously disputed the suggestion of similarities between Nazi expansion and colonialism, especially in relation to colonial development or the pretense of such.[112] In contrast to most modern colonial contexts, the Nazi regime did not embark on a civilizing or humanitarian mission for the majority of Poles. The German authorities instead selected particular groups and individuals from the Polish population who would "benefit" from Germanization—local ethnic Germans and Germanizable Poles. Subsequently, Reich Germans who were working in annexed Poland understood their work within the realms of a German humanitarian mission, which also brought them a sense of accomplishment.

In her study of midwives in Western Poland, Wiebke Lisner describes a German midwife named Ingeborg M. who voluntarily moved to the district of Konin in the Wartheland in the autumn of 1941. As revealed in a piece she contributed to the journal *Die Deutsche Hebamme* (The German Midwife) in 1942, Ingeborg M. was enthusiastic about her work. She wrote that although she had told herself "what everyone who decides to work in the East does: that everything is primitive and that no demands on civilization can be made," she explained that she became completely happy in Poland by bringing her "love for my profession, for the Germans who live among the Poles [and] all of my idealism."[113] A kindergarten teacher similarly recorded her happiness in Gostynin. According to her report, the children were gradually learning German and that every day and every hour, one could see success in the work. She wrote that it was always a great joy when suddenly another child had learnt a few words in German.[114] In comparable a report from Sępólno Krajeńskie (Zempelburg) in Danzig-West Prussia, a settlement advisor noted how her work made her happy and that she was aware that she was making a small contribution toward making people feel at home.[115]

Undoubtedly such articles and reports from the settlement advisors were often depicting an idealized situation for their supervisors or propaganda. Nevertheless, the mention of the personal value that the work brought to the individuals employed in annexed Poland is notable. These glimpses into the feelings of Reich Germans highlight how the treatment of ethnic Germans was not always exclusively conceptualized by individuals in line with propaganda on the German political or racial task in Poland. Individuals used language and mentioned feelings, which demonstrated the private benefits gained from working with ethnic Germans. One settlement advisor recalled her time in Poland as the "best years of her life."[116] Such recounting of the personal value gained from tasks was also not unusual in colonial contexts. For example, a nurse working in British Honduras from 1929 to 1932 wrote that "I have been comparatively happy here and love the people very much indeed, and for their sakes would like to return."[117] Ideological influences or the potential for personal gain would certainly have played a part but, parallel to those who contributed to colonial missions, certain individuals who took part in the various schemes did so because they felt they had a worthwhile individual contribution to make.

The promotion and perception of a self-perceived German humanitarian mission in Poland appeared numerous times in literature, newspaper articles, and films. However, the truth of this self-perceived humanitarian is riddled with complexities. While Reich Germans helped settle ethnic Germans in their new homes and contributed to the new German society, the Nazi regime in Poland aimed at the destruction of the Polish people and their culture, similarly it aimed for the eradication of Jews.[118] The ethnic German resettlers may have received healthcare, help with childcare, new jobs, and bigger homes and farms, but they were also subjected to the Nazi ideological system, separated from family and friends, and often left at the mercy of Nazi Germany's bureaucracy. As Harvey has noted, "the ethnic German resettlers were treated as the human material for a project of settler colonialism"—they were, often simultaneously, the victims and the benefactors of Nazi Germany's policies in the *Reichsgaue*.[119]

To become an integrated member of the Nazi German community, ethnic German resettlers had to undergo certain transformations at the hands of Reich German men and women. Parallel to many colonial contexts, the provision of healthcare, education, and housing was dependent on the willingness of the individual to engage with and adapt to the rules of the colonial power. In their article about social work in the Canadian settler-colonial project, Craig Fortier and Edward Hon-Sing Wong highlight that social work and benefits were employed as a means of state control over indigenous people.[120] In the case of ethnic Germans, such a tactic was perhaps used more subtly. However, despite the probable presence of individuals with a genuine humanitarian desire to help, it is still evident that in general, Reich Germans were engaging in a nationalist, state attempt to win "hearts and minds" when it came to integrating ethnic German resettlers.

The interplay between a supposed humanitarian task, on the one hand, and manipulation, destruction, and violence, on the other, was not unusual in colonial contexts. If we examine Jürgen Osterhammel's three basic elements of colonial thought, for example, Osterhammel argues that the second element is that the colonizer believed that the lower races or civilizations needed guidance and that this guidance would benefit both the lower civilizations and the world economy, this belief in mission was held as being a justification for colonialism.[121] Historically, despite the intentions of some colonizers or religious groups, the colonial civilizing or humanitarian missions were not always peaceful and were often interwoven with subjugation and violence. Penelope Edmonds and Anna Johnston have argued that as opposed to being contradictory, humanitarian actions and acts of physical violence could be "complementary modes of colonial governance" in colonial territories.[122]

Violence was often seen as a way of achieving the civilizing mission. Thus, the potential for a self-perceived German civilizing or humanitarian mission in Poland, which simultaneously occurred with violence against Jews and Poles can still fit in a colonial paradigm. Furthermore, as indicated in the introduction to this book, benevolent humanitarian missions were frequently based on the notion that the colonizer's culture, infrastructure, educational system, and healthcare were superior to that of the indigenous people. Thus, even the desire to help the indigenous people could come from an assumption of their inferiority. Therefore, similar to the Reich German treatment and perceptions of ethnic Germans, the colonial civilizing and humanitarian missions were a double-edged sword. On one side, they aimed to improve the lives of colonized individuals. On the other side, they attempted, through the installation of the colonizer's societal, cultural, and medical norms, to wipe out long-held customs and traditions.

Conclusion

Despite the façade of a normal German society, the cities and towns of annexed Poland were anything but normal. Their shops, monuments, roads, and even street names were the end products of Nazi Germany's extensive transformation mission. This mission aimed to change the territory from Polish to German and, in the process, wipe Poland from the map. Like in colonial contexts, the transformation was portrayed as something desirable. The newly formed German societies were supplemented by German men and women from the *Altreich*. Their desire to move to Poland, whether it be for economic gain or purely for adventure, was notably similar to European colonial pioneers. Each sought to gain something worthwhile for themselves, to enrich their lives in some way, in a place which was far (or perceived to be far) from home. This enrichment was often achieved by aligning oneself with the virtues of empire-building, not only was one benefitting themselves, but they were also taking on the burden or task of the empire.

For the Reich Germans, they were helping to preserve a territorial future for Germany. Also, parallel to colonial pioneers, any employment position could be envisioned as being a contribution to the German mission or task in the east as their very presence there was in keeping with the German colonial notion of *Kulturträger*. Jobs in Poland, like that of a farmer, civil servant, or secretary, were suddenly allocated greater importance because of how they contributed to the implementation of German rule and the development of German society in the new territories. One of the opening pages of the General Report on student *Osteinsatz* in the Wartheland and Upper Silesia noted a quote by Hitler: "The German student is always to be found where the plight of the people is greatest and the assignment is most dangerous."[123] Common jobs in the Reich undertaken by students, trainee doctors, nurses, and school teachers, for example, also began to be viewed as crucial to the Reich's security in terms of both racial and cultural ideology.

Lora Wildenthal has highlighted that in the African "colonial space, women's work promised direct participation in the German community."[124] Similarly, the work of female settlement advisors, school teachers, and nurses in Poland allowed for such direct participation. Through their work in Poland, women could be liberated from societal norms and live independently. The positions that brought Reich Germans into daily contact with ethnic Germans were assigned the multilayered significance of helping fellow Germans while simultaneously taking up the German task of spreading culture. For Reich Germans, as with many colonists throughout the history of European expansion, the contrived principles of strengthening the empire, humanitarianism, and spreading culture and civilization fitted comfortably with fantasies of exploration, adventure, and personal or economic gain.

Akin to many examples of traditional colonial expansion, however, the conquest and rule of foreign territory were not achieved without the use of violence. Although the previous chapters have largely focused on Nazi Germany's inclusion of various population groups and propaganda related to a supposedly positive transformation of the *Reichsgaue*, undoubtedly the Nazi regime in annexed Poland cannot simply be reduced to inclusionary policies and self-conceived national developmental missions. Rather, one of the defining features of Nazi Germany, and a popular focal point for histofirical research, is the exclusionary tactics perpetrated by the Germans in the form of deportations, segregation, and murder, which will be investigated in the next chapter.

4

Effacing Difference and the Settler Colonial Model

Like Nazi Germany's expansion into Poland, colonial conquest and settlement were rarely devoid of violence. However, as discussed in the previous chapter, it was this violence that was often legitimized by inclusionary policies and "civilizing missions"—the latter goals could not be fully achieved without the former. For the purpose of this chapter, I do not only define exclusion as the physical exclusion of a population group. Rather, I also use it in reference to the exclusion of certain population groups and individuals from society, from assimilation into the hierarchical system, and from availing of the benefits afforded to others. Exclusion can be taken to mean initial physical removal but also the ultimate removal of population groups through murder. In the case of these exclusionary policies, the intentions and legitimizations that led to and facilitated their implementation were just as significant as their results.

Building on various elements of the arguments to date, this chapter will approach comparisons between Nazi Germany's exclusionary policies and colonial exclusionary policies in two ways. The first part of this chapter highlights a selection of specific legal, societal, and physical methods of exclusion that Nazi Germany utilized in annexed Poland. The selection of examples will be brief, and I will not attempt to provide a complete, comprehensive description of Nazi exclusionary policies and their results; such in-depth research on the treatment of Jewish and non-Jewish Poles has been done in many other studies both within and outside of the debate on colonial similarities. By using a shorter selection of examples, I will instead discuss the areas of colonial comparisons that are also most relatable to the previously discussed inclusionary policies and thus tie into the overall comprehensive system of Nazi Germany's domination of the Polish people and society.[1] The second part of this chapter will approach the question of comparisons by embracing a broader context of colonial violence and placing Nazi Germany's population policies in annexed Poland within such a framework. Specifically, in this part of the chapter, I will demonstrate how Nazi Germany's conquest and settlement of the *Reichsgaue* Wartheland and Danzig-West Prussia can be compared to settler colonial models. I highlight how Nazi exclusionary policies were heavily interlinked with inclusionary policies and how, akin to settler colonial models, both policies aimed at the destruction of difference and the annihilation of the "Other." By employing these two approaches, I not only demonstrate how certain methods that facilitated or contributed to the Holocaust are comparable to colonial methods of exclusion. I also detail in what ways it, and Nazi

Germany's control of annexed Poland, can be understood in relation to wider patterns of colonial violence.

Legal and Societal Exclusion

As the Germans transformed Polish towns and villages and began to establish themselves there from October 1939, the German authorities imposed segregation laws on both Jewish and non-Jewish Poles. The laws regarding the Jewish population in the occupied territories after September 1939 largely stemmed from the anti-Semitic measures that were already in place in the *Altreich*; the German authorities forcibly separated Jews from the rest of the population and enforced special regulations, which meant Jews were no longer part of the legal system. Additionally, following the regulations in the *Altreich*, Jews were also obliged to use the name Israel or Sara in official communication with the German authorities in the Wartheland.[2] Throughout the war, the Germans established a variety of new decrees, such as the *Polenstrafrechtsverordnung* (Polish Criminal Regulations) in December 1941, which resulted in differential legal treatment for all Poles.[3] The laws meant that minor misdemeanors committed by Jews or Poles, such as stealing, undermining German authorities, or insulting a German, could be punished with extremely harsh penalties—often death sentences. As well as forced labor for all Jews over the age of fourteen, the German authorities began seizing Jewish property and businesses and restricting professional employment and the possession of cash.[4] From the beginning of the annexation, both Jews and Poles were also subjected to threats of violence in the form of beatings or indeed murder by shooting at the hands of the German *Wehrmacht*.[5]

Ethnic Germans and Reich Germans arriving to and living and working in the settlement areas were encouraged to keep their distance, both physically and emotionally, from the Poles. From as early as November 7, 1939, *Gauleiter* Greiser had ordered that if possible, there should be no marriages between Germans and Poles in the Wartheland. From September 1940, sexual relations between Poles and German women were punishable by death and in April 1943 marriages between Poles and Germans but also between foreigners and so-called stateless people in the annexed eastern territories were prohibited to prevent unapproved racial mixing.[6] Additionally, German authorities in the Wartheland raised the permitted age of marriage for Poles from twenty-five to twenty-eight in January 1942.[7] Such measures caused discontent among Poles and correspondence from the *Reichsstatthalter*'s office in December 1942 reflected this. A district head doctor phoned the *Reichsstatthalter*'s office and suggested that it would perhaps be advisable to waive the marriage age limit in specific cases based on employment grounds. The output from work assignments needed to be strengthened, and it was conceivable that the Poles' desire to work would increase, for example, crucial Polish workers in munitions factories, if they were allowed special approvals to marry earlier.[8] However, the response from the *Reichsstatthalter*'s office demonstrated German intentions behind raising the permitted marriage age. The policy toward Poles was not a political power debate, rather it was a biological one. The policy's ultimate goal was for Poles to have fewer children than the Germans.[9]

Since the invasion of Poland, members of the *Wehrmacht* and the SS were forbidden to have sexual relations with Poles; however, as Maren Röger has highlighted, consensual, forced, and commercial sexual contact between the soldiers and Polish women was frequent in the first months of occupation. These forms of contact continued throughout the war and occasionally resulted in the German partner attempting to secure better jobs or inclusion into the DVL for their female Polish partner.[10] Similarly, although the German authorities legally forbid marriages between Germans and Poles, records of marriage applications demonstrate that couples attempted to push the boundaries of the laws to secure marriage approval. In cases where the Polish partner was found suitable to be included in the DVL, marriages were permissible, and they did occur in annexed Poland.[11] However, marriage applications were anything but an exact science, and the various terms and categories used to describe the applicants' ethnic or racial category, such as "Pole," "stateless," "ethnic German," or "of German descent," were often haphazardly applied—occasionally, the same applicant would be referred to using a variety of different and sometimes even contradictory terms in different documents within the same file.[12]

An example of a marriage application submitted to the Bydgoszcz (Bromberg) registry office, *Reichsgau* Danzig-West Prussia in June 1941 demonstrates the inefficient bureaucracy of the system and indeed, a potential lack of communication between the two *Rechsgaue*.[13] The male applicant, Stephan H., was born in Berlin but living in Bydgoszcz and working as a salesman. His female partner, Wanda Z., was born in Łódź and was working as a sales assistant. The Bydgoszcz registry office sent the pair's marriage application to the *Gesundheitsamt* (health office) in Łódź as that was where Wanda Z. was born. During the examination of her suitability for marriage by a medical officer, Wanda Z. indicated on the form about her family history that she was born in Łódź. In the top right-hand corner, someone (presumably the medical officer) had written and underlined in red pencil: "Polin!" (Pole).[14] After the examination, the medical officer sent two letters; one to the *Sicherheitsdienst des Reichsführers SS* (Security Service of the *Reichsführer*-SS, SD) office in Łódź and one to the Bydgoszcz registry office.[15] He explained that due to his findings, the marriage could not be approved on ethnic grounds. However, he wondered if Germans could marry Poles in *Reichsgau* Danzig-West Prussia, given that it was forbidden in the Wartheland, and asked for a response to his query. In his letter to the SD office, the medical officer additionally asked if Germans and Poles could have sexual contact with one another in Danzig-West Prussia. If so, he suggested that the SD should advise the *Gauleiter* and *Reichsstatthalter* that measures should be put in place to prevent such marriages and sexual contact given that in the Wartheland such preventative measures were seen as essential to maintain and strengthen the German race in the eastern territories.[16]

Ten days later, and three days before the planned date of the wedding, the registry office in Bydgoszcz replied to the *Gesundheitsamt* with a curt response. It stated that the marriage application in question "does not relate to Germans, both of the engaged partners are Polish" and added that "also here [in Danzig-West Prussia] marriages between Germans and Poles had been banned following the decree by the Ministry for the Interior since 24 December 1939."[17] It is unclear from the records why the registry office in Bydgoszcz had now categorized Stephan H., who had listed his birthplace as Berlin, a Pole, or why they initially sent the application to the *Gesundheitsamt* in Łódź if they knew or suspected that the marriage applicants were not Germans. In any case, the example demonstrates how the system appeared to show problems, not least because the medical officer in Łódź appeared to be unaware of the neighboring *Reichsgau*'s marriage policies.

In addition to relationships, the everyday lives of Poles were also restricted. For example, Poles were not permitted to use the trams in Poznań during the morning rush hour. During the hours they were allowed to use it, they had to give up their seats to Germans if the tram was full. Throughout the Wartheland from 1942, Poles were only permitted to use the lowest class of rail travel.[18] Additionally, instructions sent by the *Reichsstatthalter* offices in the Wartheland in June 1940 stipulated, non-Germans were only allowed to use public transport when they had received permission from the German authorities.[19] Tickets were only to be sold to those who had a valid permission slip with an accompanying personal identification card. The instructions were clear: "without question, Germans should not be unnecessarily bothered" by the transport inspectors.[20] Furthermore, the German authorities placed restrictions on Poles riding bicycles. Police orders from July 1941 specified that Poles were only permitted to ride bicycles to and from their home to their place of work over two kilometers away. The only exception was in an emergency. While riding their bikes, they were also required to carry a bicycle pass.[21]

Poles were required to greet German officials and to move off pedestrian paths to allow Germans through; they were also forbidden from wearing any form of badges or medals to avoid any confusion with German ones.[22] Certain establishments, such as restaurants, swimming pools, playgrounds, and even park benches, were designated as being specifically for Germans or Poles; although Poles were forbidden from entering German establishments, Germans could enter Polish ones thus further highlighting supposed German superiority.[23] Such rules also applied outside the *Reichsgaue*. In an official letter to the Police Chief in Poznań, the Police Chief of Sosnowiec (Sosnowitz) in Upper Silesia, noted that under instruction from the Führer and the Reich Minister of Propaganda Joseph Goebbels, "Poles and Jews should be excluded from cultural activities, especially cinema visits." As a result of this, cinemas in the area had been forced to close as the small number of German visitors was not enough to sustain them economically.[24]

As mentioned in Chapter 3, almost all Reich Germans were able to afford some form of Polish domestic help. However, despite working in German homes, Polish domestic workers were required to have an *Einkaufsausweis* (purchase pass) for buying goods in German shops.[25] Additionally, a curfew was in place, which forbade Poles to be outside of their homes at night. For example, an order from the *Regierungspräsident* of Posen Viktor Böttcher in April 1943 stated that Poles were not allowed out between 9.00 pm and 5.00 am and that between May 1 and August 31, 1943, they were not allowed outside between 10.00 pm and 4.00 am. Poles also had to leave bars or restaurants by 8.00 pm during this time frame.[26]

To physically distinguish ethnic and Reich Germans from the Polish population, both groups of Germans in the Wartheland (who were not already in uniforms such as members of the SS or resettlement organizations) wore a badge. In a letter addressed to all departments of the authorities in the *Reichsgau* Wartheland, the Deputy *Reichsstatthalter* August Jäger, reminded the recipients that "the special circumstances in the *Reichsgau* Wartheland make it necessary for all Germans to be openly recognizable as Germans by wearing badges, especially the party badge."[27] The badge allowed the wearer to enter public areas reserved for Germans and it also identified them as members of the occupier group. As well as badges, German authorities planned that language was to become a distinct indicator of where an individual stood within the German societal hierarchy in Poland. It was difficult to eradicate or legally ban the use of the Polish language completely given that many local ethnic Germans, as well as some ethnic German resettlers, were fluent in Polish and only spoke limited German. Similarly, any interaction with the Polish population would have been greatly hindered if the Germans completely banned the Polish language.[28] Perhaps most importantly for the German authorities in annexed Poland, if Polish was forbidden, then an important sign of differentiation between the German population and Poles would be lost.

In the Wartheland, Greiser found a solution to the problem of recognizing German as the official language without banning Polish completely. Greiser issued a circular to all the major authorities in the *Gau* on the usage of the Polish language on February 23, 1943. He stated that the German policy in Poland in 1914 was incorrect because it attempted to Germanize Poles. Nazi Germany's policies, however, reflected *völkisch* and racial necessities and thus, recognized that "there is no community between Germans and Poles."[29] According to Greiser, Polish could not be banned and it would be impossible to force any German official to learn it so he advised that German was only permitted to be spoken by Poles in the presence of German authorities and employees of the Party and the State. Any Pole who could not speak German during official interactions would need to bring a translator. Signposts should be in German and be understandable for the Polish people. On the street, Poles were permitted to speak Polish "as much as they like" and no penalties would apply. In Polish schools, the German language should only be taught to the extent that the Poles could work. They were permitted to learn vocabulary but should not be able to speak it with any grammatical proficiency.[30] In this way, the German authorities planned to keep the Polish population linguistically distinct from the higher echelons of society. Not only would basic German language skills signify that an individual was not a German citizen, but it would also prevent the individual's professional or societal advancement and acceptance.

Relating to the issue of language, the German school policy for Polish children also further strengthened societal exclusion. As described in Chapter 2, the German authorities founded numerous schools for local ethnic German and ethnic German resettler children. However, for Polish children, formal education above a primary school level was abandoned in Danzig West-Prussia and only permitted between the ages of ten and fourteen in the Wartheland. As a result, numerous Polish schools were closed. The various measures between 1940 and 1944 clearly show the exclusionary treatment that the Polish children received. For example, once the *Reichsstatthalter* had instructed that Polish children in the district of Gniezno (Gnesen) should be educated, the *Schulrat* (Education Board) sought school helpers who were of German ethnicity with "impeccable morals"; however, as opposed to hiring qualified teachers, there were no special requirements for candidates to have previous experience or education.[31] A letter from the *Reichsstatthalter* offices to the *Regierungspräsidenten* in Litzmannstadt, Hohensalza, and Posen in May 1943 noted that the current use of alphabet books in Polish schools was not permissible. If Polish schools used these books, there was a danger that a large number of German school children would begin the new school year without them. The letter called on the heads of Polish schools to not place any more book orders.[32] In addition to the rudimentary education provisions, Polish school children were also deemed to be suitable for work assignments on weekday afternoons. A letter from the *Regierungspräsident* to the head of the local *Landjahrlager* (agricultural year camp) noted that the work should be suitable for the age level of the children, for example, weeding and hoeing or keeping the village clean.[33]

Although other factors such as forced labor, the confiscation of property, and the harsh punishments Poles received for minor offences could also be included in the category of legal and societal measures that furthered Germany's exclusionary processes, the policies discussed above are significant for a selection of reasons. Marriage laws, restrictions on the use of public transport, and the limitations put on the education of Polish children were not as outwardly violent or extreme as the physical exclusionary measures, which will be discussed in the next section. However, such measures were in direct contradiction to inclusionary policies. Those deemed unsuitable for integration into German society were treated as the lowest members of the societal hierarchy and the laws put in place were designed to systematically embed racism into everyday life. The differentiation that the Poles were subjected to was not solely to ensure they remained excluded from German society, it also served to reinforce the Germans as the occupants of the highest levels of society. Through mundane daily encounters, such as journeys on the tram or passing Poles in the street, both Reich and ethnic Germans bore witness to the subjugation of the native Polish population. It was through this everyday subjugation that the Reich and ethnic Germans could be reminded of their status in society and Nazi Germany's control over the territory.

Physical Exclusion: Deportation, Segregation, Murder

In addition to the discussed societal and legal exclusionary policies utilized by Nazi Germany to control who was permitted to integrate into society, exclusionary policies were also created that resulted in the physical exclusion of population groups. One significant method used by Nazi Germany throughout the war was the physical removal of Poles and Jews to allow for the reallocation of land, the resettlement of ethnic Germans, and the fulfillment of labor needs. In the Wartheland, the deportations were initially run by Wilhelm Koppe, the *Höhere SS und Polizeiführer* (Higher SS and Police Leader, HSSPF), and carried out by the *Reichssicherheitshauptamt* (RSHA) according to a series of plans. Koppe announced that as well as all of the Jews, Poles who were members of the intelligentsia or whose national-political alignment could disrupt the work of the Germans in the Gau would be deported.[34] The first *Nahplan* (short-range plan) began at the end of November 1939, when it was proposed by Reinhard Heydrich, the head of the RSHA. The plan ran until December 1939, and was aimed at the removal of the Polish intelligentsia and Jews from the Wartheland. Although it was planned that 80,000 Poles (both Jewish and non-Jewish) would be deported, a total of 87,883 were moved to the General Government to create space for the Baltic German resettlers. Contrary to Himmler's wishes for the deportations to include mainly Jews, only approximately 5,000 Jews were deported during the first deportation action.[35] The plans were geographically extended to include all of the annexed territories and not just the Wartheland, the following two plans would concentrate on the deportation of non-Jewish Poles. The initial removal of the non-Jewish Poles was more urgent for the resettlement of ethnic Germans as houses, larger apartments, and farms were needed to accommodate them. Jewish tenement buildings were deemed unsuitable for resettlement purposes and many Jews had already lost their businesses and properties in 1939, and so seizing their assets was of less benefit to the incoming ethnic Germans.[36] Additionally, correspondence between the *Reichsstatthalter's* labor department and the labor authorities in the Wartheland highlighted the importance of suitable Polish workers for Germany's agricultural self-dependence. The correspondence stipulated that workers between the ages of sixteen and forty-five were required; they should be of suitable physical health and there should be no political objections to their work placement. Due to a current lack of female workers, they were especially valuable.[37] Guidelines were also issued to doctors for checking the health of potential workers and travel to the *Altreich* was only permitted for workers who came from areas with no typhus or other infectious diseases.[38]

The *Zwischenplan* (interim plan) from February 10, 1940 till March 15, 1940, saw a further 40,128 people deported. From April 1940, the *Umwandererzentralstelle* (Central Emigration Office, UWZ), based in Łódź under the control of Hermann Krumey, oversaw the following deportations. The second *Nahplan* was carried out between May 1940 and January 20, 1941. This plan facilitated the resettlement of ethnic Germans from Volhynia, Galicia, and the Cholmer and Narew districts and led to the deportations of 133,506 people. Some of them were deported to the General Government, and non-Jewish Poles who were deemed suitable were sent to the *Altreich* for work. The third *Nahplan* ran from January 21, 1941 to January 20, 1942. Under this plan, the UWZ reported they deported 130,326 people deported.[39] From January 1942 till the end of 1942, the Germans deported approximately 99,000 people as part of an extended third *Nahplan*. By December 31, 1943, the UWZ reported that they had deported and expelled a total of 534,384 people from the Wartheland.[40]

A UWZ 1940 report from *Kreis* Birnbaum (Międzychód) in the Wartheland provides some details on the eviction process. On October 1, 1940 at 5:30 am, the eviction of Polish-farming families in the area began. The evictions went smoothly and by midday, they were finished.[41] In total, the German authorities removed seventy-four families from their homes and sent them to the train station at Pniewy (Pinne) for "evacuation."[42] The report detailed how one family objected to the eviction because they were ethnic Germans. The father of the family was currently interred in the Dachau concentration camp, but his wife and her sister protested on behalf of the family. The report noted that the family did not have ethnic German identification papers and had not submitted an application. The report ended with the line: "The [family] do not have a good reputation."[43]

Although the report does not give much information on the finer details of the evictions, it does provide an insight into the ease with which the German authorities removed Poles from their homes for their replacement by ethnic German resettlers. *Sicherheitspolizei* (Security Police, SiPo) and UWZ guidelines for police carrying out the evictions shed light on further information regarding the removal of the Polish residents and property seizures by the Germans.[44] The Poles would be given one hour to pack their belongings; the police authorities were to ensure that, if possible, each person had food for fourteen days, warm clothes, a wool blanket, cutlery and food and drink utensils, identification, and their birth certificate. The luggage should not exceed twenty-five to thirty kilograms per person and bringing animals of any kind was not permitted. The guidelines also noted that locking containers or cupboards and the taking of keys should be prevented. Money and jewelry were to be left to the Poles but bank savings books, commercial papers, and valuables were to be recorded by the police authorities and packed into envelopes that were to be signed by the owner. The guidelines also instructed the police to draw up a register of the property left behind by the evicted Poles with the help of an interpreter.[45] Once evicted from their homes, the Poles were transported to a transit camp in Głowno (Glowno) and from there, they were transported to the *Altreich* or the General Government in unheated cattle cars. Reports from Arthur Greiser's trial, held in 1946, recorded that it was not unusual for people to freeze to death on the journey.[46]

As mentioned, the deportations from annexed Poland initially focused on the removal of non-Jewish Poles to make sufficient room for the influx of ethnic German resettlers. Although German authorities had not made an official decision on whether the deportations would impact mainly Jewish Poles or mainly non-Jewish Poles, in December 1939 officials already began making plans for the remaining Jewish Poles in the *Reichsgaue*. On December 10, 1939, Friedrich Uebelhoer, the *Regierungspräsident* of Kalisch (later included as part of Litzmannstadt) issued a circular titled "Formation of a ghetto in the city of Lodsch." The circular noted that approximately 320,000 Jews were living in the greater city of Lodsch and that their "immediate evacuation" was not possible. Consequently, Uebelhoer called for the Jews in the north of the city to be accommodated in a ghetto and for the rest of the Jews in the city, who were capable of working, to be accommodated in guarded barracks.[47] The German authorities officially established the ghetto on February 8, 1940 and April 30, they sealed it to further isolate the ghetto's Jewish population.[48]

As the founding of the Łódź ghetto demonstrated, the initial logic behind establishing ghettos in annexed Poland was a method to quickly segregate the Jewish population from the rest of the population until a longer-term solution for their relocation was found. The ghetto in Łódź would eventually become the second largest ghetto next to the Warsaw ghetto; by August 1940, it is estimated that up to 160,000 Jews were already living there.[49] Other ghettos were formed in smaller towns throughout the Wartheland; for example, in Pabianice (Pabianitz) in February 1940, in Kutno in June 1940 and Koło in December 1940. In contrast to the Wartheland, the Germans did not establish ghettos in the *Reichsgau* Danzig-West Prussia as the *Gau*'s Jewish population was significantly smaller than that of the Wartheland; the main city of Danzig was home to only approximately 1,660 Jews by the end of August 1939.[50]

The National Socialist Party had already begun to assert its influence and implement anti-Semitic measures since the 1930s; hence, many Jews who had the financial means had managed to emigrate from the city of Danzig and its surroundings by the time the war broke out.[51] Those who did not manage to emigrate were largely deported to the General Government or were murdered at the beginning of the war and so the need to establish ghettos was not as great there as it was in the Wartheland.

Primarily between 1939 and 1942, hundreds of ghettos were established throughout the rest of Poland in both small and large towns. Although the ghettos differed in location, type (namely some were open ghettos, some were closed), and size, they controlled the Jewish Polish population by concentrating them in specific areas away from the rest of the population. Living conditions in the ghettos continually worsened as the war progressed and, as the German authorities filled the ghettos with more and more people due to the continuing need for accommodation for ethnic German resettlers (especially in the Wartheland), overcrowding became a massive issue. The German administration controlled the food supply and this usually amounted to less than what was needed to sustain the population. As a result, thousands died of starvation. The ghetto inhabitants lacked medical supplies and due to overcrowding and terrible conditions, mortality rates from diseases such as tuberculosis, typhus, and dysentery increasingly rose.[52] Oskar Rosenfeld, an inhabitant of the Łódź ghetto, wrote about daily life in the ghetto in his diary. He noted the health problems he and others were experiencing: hunger, the bitter cold, neuralgia, a neck abscess, weight loss, fingernails and toenails dying, and women no longer menstruating.[53] Overall, an estimated 43,000 inhabitants in the Łódź ghetto died of starvation and disease.[54]

In certain ghettos, the inhabitants were forced to work in ghetto industries to supplement the Reich. In Łódź, Jewish workers produced such items as clothes, shoes, and textiles, and uniforms, weapons, and equipment for the military. The head of the *Judenrat* (Jewish Council), Chaim Rumkowski, justified his efforts to create work for as many people as possible with the argument that the productivity of the ghetto and the high employment figures impacted food allowance and, later, the number of people deported from the ghetto. Between April and June 1941, Rumkowski reported an increase from twenty workshops and business operations to forty-two and that the number of people employed increased from 9,305 to 9,820.[55] A more complete list from August 1941, which included Jews employed in administrative roles, transportation, or as kitchen staff, counted 39,993 people in employment.[56] In addition to the manufacture of new goods, clothing and valuables that had belonged to Jews who had been deported from the ghetto to be killed at the extermination camps were returned to the ghetto for sorting and repairs.

Reports of criminal proceedings against individuals accused of crimes in Chełmno nad Nerem (Kulmhof an der Nehr, now more often referred to as Chełmno) detailed how ghetto inhabitants recognized the clothes of fellow inhabitants who had been removed from the ghetto. According to reports, letters or notes that detailed what was happening at the extermination site were occasionally hidden in the clothes.[57] The shoes left behind by Jews who had been evicted from their homes in the Wartheland were also collected and sent to the ghetto in Łódź, as were the shoes of Jews murdered in the extermination camp in Chełmno. The shoes were sorted and, where possible, repaired; by May 1944, the so-called *Altschuhlager* (old shoe warehouse) had repaired 110,000 pairs of old shoes for the requirements of the ghetto. The leather from shoes that could not be repaired was collected and utilized in shoe production.[58] Despite the macabre origin of such materials as shoe leather, through the industrialization of the Łódź ghetto and its productive capacity, the ghetto managed to continue running until August 1944 when it was the last of the large ghettos to be cleared.

As the overcrowding of the ghetto continued with the arrival of Jews in the autumn of 1941 from western states, such as Germany, Luxembourg, and Austria, solutions were sought to control the number of inhabitants and to ensure that the ghetto space was reserved for those who were also suitable for labor purposes. Through correspondence throughout the summer and autumn of 1941 between Greiser, Himmler, Koppe, Heydrich, Hitler, and other regional heads, a decision was made to extend the murder of psychiatric hospital patients in the Wartheland, which was already underway in mobile gas vans, to Jewish men, women, and children. The *SS-Sonderkommando Lange*, a group specially formed for such euthanasia programs under the leadership of Herbert Lange, was ordered to begin exterminating the Jews in the Wartheland who were unfit to work.

During the German invasion of Poland, Lange had been a member of *Einsatzgruppe* VI until it was disbanded in November 1939. Alongside August Becker, an SS chemist, he had initially helped conduct murder experiments on Polish prisoners in Fort VII, officially *Konzentrationslager* Posen, using gas.[59] In December 1941, having received the orders to begin killing Jews from the Wartheland's ghettos, Lange established an extermination camp at the site of an old manor house in Chełmno nad Nerem, where victims would be gassed in vans. It is unclear if Lange received a direct order from Greiser to establish a stationary extermination camp, but as historian Patrick Montague points out, Greiser probably only cared that the task was completed and not about how it was done.[60] In March 1942, Lange was replaced by Hans Bothmann.

At Chełmno, the members of the *Sonderkommando*, who were aided by Jewish and Polish men forced to work at the camp, received extra pay and an extra allowance of food, tobacco, and alcohol for the task they were carrying out.[61] Using the vacated manor house (known as the *Schlosslager* or manor camp) as an area for the victims to undress, the *Sonderkommando* and the Jewish and Polish workers loaded the victims into the vans to be gassed. German *Sonderkommando* members were in charge of operating and driving the vans. After the gassings, the vans drove to a nearby forest (known as the *Waldlager*, or forest camp) for the bodies to be deposed of by Jewish and Polish workers. In total, fifty to sixty Jewish workers were forced to assist the *Sonderkommando* and were shackled with iron ankle chains while doing so. Approximately thirty Jews worked in the *Waldlager*, while others sorted the victims' belongings at the *Schlosslager*. If they became too weak to work, they were shot.[62] Initially, the victims' bodies that were unloaded from the vans were buried in large trenches, but from the summer of 1942, the bodies were cremated in open-air crematoria. After the removal of the bodies, the vans were driven back to the *Schlosslager* and cleaned by Jewish workers.

The *Sonderkommando Lange* initially began murdering Jews from surrounding villages such as Koło. In January 1942, they began to receive transports of Jews and Sinti and Roma who had camps within the Łódź ghetto. Continuing into March

1942, the victims, most of whom were the unemployed young, elderly, or sick, were selected for deportation by ghetto doctors based on medical examinations.[63] They were transported from the ghetto via the Radegast (Radogoszcz) train station (Figure 4.1). Outside of the Łódź ghetto, Jews from other ghettos in the Wartheland such as those in Ciechocinek (Hermansbad) and Włocławek (Leslau) were transported to and murdered at Chełmno during the spring of 1942. Only a few hundred Jews from these areas were assigned to labor camps or transferred to the Łódź ghetto for work.[64]

Himmler travelled to Poznań on April 16, 1942 to meet with Greiser and later, he journeyed through the Wartheland with Koppe. It was most likely during this visit that Himmler ordered the murder of 10,000 western Jews who were unable to work, as well as Polish Jews unable to work, the further liquidation of the Watheland's other ghettos, and the transfer of Jews suitable for work to the Łódź ghetto.[65] From May 1942, the German authorities began to send the Western Jews who had arrived in the ghetto from Germany, Luxembourg, Prague, and Vienna in the autumn of 1941 to Chełmno. The murder of the western Jews was followed by further deportations of the ghetto's young, elderly, and sick inhabitants, as well as Jews from surrounding districts in the Wartheland. On April 7, 1943, the Germans stopped Chełmno's operations and the camp's first murder phase.[66] The *Schlosslager* and the crematoria in the *Waldlager* were destroyed. By this stage in 1943, the majority of the ghettos in the Wartheland had been emptied and those who were not directly engaged in

Figure 4.1 The renovated Radegast (Radogoszcz) train station in Łódź. Source: Rachel O'Sullivan, February 2020.

labor assignments, for example in the Łódź ghetto, had been murdered. However, in June 1944, the extermination camp at Chełmno was reopened for the liquidation of the Litzmannstadt ghetto and the *Sonderkommando*, still led by Bothmann, returned. In his extensive study on the extermination of the Jews in the Wartheland, Michael Alberti estimates that during the initial phase between December 1941 and March 1943, 150,000 people were murdered at Chełmno, 96 percent of whom were Jewish. The number does not include the thousands of Jews who were murdered during the Łódź ghetto liquidation.[67]

The Łódź ghetto and the extermination camp at Chełmno, both located in the Wartheland, are perhaps the most well-known locations of the segregation and extermination of Polish Jews in annexed Poland. However, in addition to other ghettos previously mentioned, forced labor, and concentration camps, which contributed to the deaths of Poles and Jews, as well as other population groups, also existed in Danzig-West Prussia. The Germans established a camp at Stutthof (Sztutowo) on September 2, 1939 making it the first civilian internment camp to be established outside of the *Altreich*. The prisoners were initially Poles and Polish Jews who were displaced by the establishment of German rule, but by the end of the war, the prisoners came from numerous other countries and included Soviet Prisoners of War (POW). Although the camp was founded as a civilian internment camp, it later expanded to become a labor camp with numerous sub-camps in the surrounding areas. These sub-camps included a female camp, Bromberg-Ost, established in 1944 in Bydgoszcz, and, until 1941, the Potulice (Potulitz) concentration camp, which also acted as a detention center for Polish children who had been approved for Germanization.

The Stutthof camp became an official *Konzentrationslager* (concentration camp, KL or KZ) under the control of the WVHA from 1942.[68] As part of the KL system, Stutthof began to receive an influx of prisoners from other camps, including Auschwitz, as well as Jews from the Baltic States and Hungary due to the labor demands of the shipbuilding and armaments industry. These prisoners included a large number of Jewish women, who were housed in a new extension of the camp. The conditions in the Stutthof main camp were terrible, food provisions were low, and diseases were rife; the sanitary conditions in the female camp were particularly bad as there was no sewage system, water pipes, or washing facilities.[69] A statement from Paja Pavlowskaja, a former prisoner of the camp, described how the prisoners were starving and had to eat grass. The guards hit the prisoners and lashed at their faces and heads with straps. The ill and weak were taken away every day under the pretense of being brought to do easier work assignments but later, the other prisoners saw these people being led in the direction of the crematoria.[70] In early 1944, Stutthof held no more than 7,500 prisoners, but by late summer 1944, the prisoner numbers had dramatically increased to over 60,000.[71] In 1944, the Germans added a small gas chamber to the camp for the murder of prisoners; however, shooting and lethal injection remained the main killing methods.[72] One way in which the shooting was carried out was using the *Genickschussanlage* (neck shooting facility). The victims were taken for a supposed medical examination; instead, they were shot in the back of the neck using specially adapted equipment while having their height measured.[73] In total, approximately 61,500 people died in Stutthof.[74]

Although perhaps the most chilling advancements in Nazi Germany's implementation of technology for rapidly murdering Polish Jews and Jews from other European states came about at Chełmno, the use of gas vans was not the only way through which the Germans conducted their murder campaign. After the German invasion in September 1939, a notable example of the mobile part of the murder campaign was the *Einsatzgruppen* who initially travelled throughout Poland behind the *Wehrmacht*. The *Einsatzgruppen* were tasked with dealing with "elements hostile to the Reich and Germany in enemy territory behind the troops engaged in combat." A note by Heydrich in July 1940 explained; their instructions were "extraordinarily radical (e.g. the order to liquidate numerous Polish ruling circles, which affected thousands)."[75] "Ruling circles" referred to Polish intelligentsia, such as professors, priests, journalists, and lawyers, whom the *Einsatzgruppen* would eliminate in an attempt to prevent the organization of Polish resistance to Nazi Germany's rule (known as the *Intelligenzaktion*).[76] The *Einsatzgruppen* were assisted at different times by the *Volksdeutscher Selbstschutz*, *Waffen SS*, the *Wehrmacht*, and the police, and they not only targeted members of the Polish intelligentsia, but also Jews, Sinti, and Roma, the mentally ill, and other Poles throughout the war. Using the method of shooting groups of people, who were often forced to dig their own mass graves beforehand, the *Einsatzgruppen* murdered tens of thousands of people. Although the use of gas as a murder weapon and cremation as a means to dispose of bodies were potentially less psychologically strenuous for the perpetrators and more efficient, the *Einsatzgruppen*'s tasks were not outsourced to stationary extermination camps, and they largely continued their campaign throughout the war.

Despite the aforementioned differing approaches to murder throughout Poland and the Soviet territories, Nazi Germany's intention after 1942 regarding the fate of the European Jews was clear; they would be completely eradicated. German planners intended that non-Jewish Poles who were not eligible for inclusion in the DVL would be physically removed after the war as per the GPO (*Generalplan Ost*). The GPO was not one singular entity but rather a series of plans produced between 1940 and 1942 under Himmler's instruction. To coordinate the planning for future German spatial goals, Himmler installed Konrad Meyer, one of the most prominent agronomists and a professor at the University of Berlin, as leader of the Planning Department of the RKFDV in 1939.[77] Meyer led SS-affiliated academics from such fields as agricultural science, race sciences, and geography in the creation of various plans collectively known as the GPO.[78] Throughout the war, the various plan iterations were added to, adapted, and ultimately radicalized in reflection of Germany's progress during the war. Although a complete version of the GPO has yet to be found intact, it can largely be pieced together from these different variants of the plan created by Meyer's Planning Department and the RSHA *Amtsgruppe III B*, under the leadership of Hans Ehlich. For example, information on an iteration of the plan produced by the *Amtsgruppe III B* in 1941 has been gained from an analysis of it written by Erhard Wetzel and dated April 27, 1942.[79] Wetzel's analysis relayed that the RSHA's GPO plans to deport thirty-one million members of the native Eastern European population and the settlement of ten million Germans in the thirty years following the war.[80] In the section "*Zur Lösung der Polenfrage*" (For the Solution of the Polish Question), Wetzel estimated that 80 to 85 percent or approximately twenty million of those to be deported were Poles and approximately 3 to 4.8 million would be permitted to remain in the German settlement areas for Germanization. Those who were not suitable for Germanization could be deported to Western Siberia.[81] Chillingly, Wetzel noted that it was obvious that the Polish question could not be solved by them being "liquidated," like the Jews were, because neighboring populations may then suspect that they too would be treated this way.[82] A later version of the GPO was reworked by Meyer at the request of Himmler and a newer version known as the *Generalsiedlungsplan* was completed in late 1942.[83]

In summary, the various iterations of the plans plotted the deportation of approximately thirty to forty million so-called racial undesirables, mainly Slavs, and the use of fourteen million people for forced labor.[84] Like what had occurred when with numerous Poles at the beginning of the war, deportation, or "evacuation" was more likely to be code for the removal of populations to territories where they would ultimately be eradicated through harsh transport conditions, forced labor, disease, starvation, or sterilization. Nazi Germany's planners thus envisioned the complete removal of the Polish population in the years after the war. As opposed to a quick annihilation, like with the extermination of Jews, Poles would be used for labor before being gradually pushed out of their land. Through the exclusion of Poles not deemed to be racially suitable, but also through the inclusion of Poles suitable for Germanization, Nazi Germany planned the destruction of Poland and its people.

Colonial Exclusionary Measures

Unsurprisingly, the Nazi regime was not the only European power to harness exclusionary methods to manage populations during expansionary missions. Such measures not only allowed for the stratification of society but also the control and domination of population groups in colonial contexts. Analogous to Nazi Germany's laws relating to sexual contact and marriage between Germans and Poles, colonial powers also used legal measures as a method of present control, by preventing marriages and sexual contact between the colonizer and colonized, and as a method of future control, by preventing the birth of children from "mixed" relationships. Although some colonial powers accepted mixing between European settlers and the indigenous population, for example, concubinage in the Dutch East Indies, others adopted a variety of different tactics to prevent such mixing.[85] For example, Germans and Africans were forbidden to marry from 1905 in German South West Africa, from 1906 in German East Africa, and from 1912 in German Samoa.[86] In the early twentieth century, the British and Dutch colonial governments banned concubinage, but this proved difficult to enforce. In Ethiopia, during the Fascist Italian rule from 1936 to 1944, interracial sexual activity was tolerated as long as there was no intent or attempts at making the relationship exclusive or long-term. Emanuele Ertola highlights that in Southern Rhodesia, for example, the preexisting societal stigmatization of relationships with Africans meant there was not an explicit need for a legal marriage ban. However, as the settler society in Ethiopia was a newly founded one, the idea of marrying Ethiopians was not yet socially stigmatized enough to deter it from happening. Therefore, the Italians introduced laws to legally punish such behavior.[87]

The ban on so-called mixed relationships and marriages in colonial territories and Nazi Germany's introduction of laws banning sexual contact and marriage between Germans and Poles are similar in numerous ways. The impetus behind the introduction of such laws was multilayered. As well as reasons such as supposedly preventing the transfer of diseases or the protection of women, such laws attempted to enforce structure and homogeneity within racial hierarchies. The colonizer deemed the colonized or indigenous population to be inferior and so they could not be afforded the status to marry a member of the supposedly superior population. Accordingly, racial boundaries and indeed the categorization of populations, could be upheld and reinforced. By preventing sexual contact, such laws also attempted to minimize the number of mixed-race children.

Such children did not fit neatly into the racial categories predefined by the ruling power; as Ann Laura Stoler has highlighted, these children "straddled the divisions of ruler and ruled" and "threatened to blur the colonial divide."[88] Overall, sexual contact between the colonizer and the colonized was seen as a dangerous threat to the empire, it threatened the racialized foundation upon which the empire was based and the means through which it functioned. Sexual contact between racial or ethnic groups, which undermined the societal hierarchy, meant it was conceivable that a European could "feel desire, affection or intrigue for those beyond the racial divide." Such situations could destabilize the imperial and colonial hierarchies by proving that the racial divides on which empire and colonial rule were based were false.[89]

It is interesting to note that the laws regarding sexual contact and marriage in both colonial contexts and annexed Poland were not only similar in that they controlled the indigenous populations, but they also controlled the colonizers or, in the case of annexed Poland, Reich Germans and ethnic Germans. Colonial exclusionary politics not only set external boundaries but also internal ones. Similarly, the condoning of certain marriages was as related to the hierarchies of privilege and power as the condemnation of other marriages was.[90] Maren Röger's study of relationships between the German occupiers and Poles during the Second World War proves that despite German bans on such intermixing, sexual contact and relationships still existed.[91] Like in many colonial situations, although the laws attempted to uphold certain racial standards and strengthen the fantasy of a racially stratified society, in reality, neither the colonizers nor the colonized consistently adhered to the rules of the colonial or imperial power. Colonial social boundaries were not static despite attempts to make them so; rather, colonial society existed alongside constantly shifting binaries between different population groups who were brought into contact through expansion and domination.[92] The same was true of Nazi Germany's annexation of Polish territories and the Germans' attempts at the categorization and separation of certain population groups.

Parallel to the *Reichsgaue* Wartheland and Danzig-West Prussia, other legal and societal restrictions on indigenous people's integration into occupier society existed as well as those placed on marriages. For example, curfews were also imposed on indigenous populations in certain colonial territories to control their movements. Such curfews similarly served the purpose of limiting the indigenous population groups' freedom to partake in leisure and cultural activities or to socialize with others. For example, in Italian Ethiopia, Italy enacted laws in September 1938 that decreed that shops run by Ethiopians had to close by 8.30 pm and Ethiopians were not allowed to be in the city after 9.00 pm. Some Ethiopians were allowed outside after curfew but only if they were employed by the Italian authorities.[93] Devin O. Pendas has highlighted significant similarities between the Nazi regime's racially based social stratification to apartheid-era South Africa and the Jim Crow Laws in the United States.[94] Comparable to the treatment of Poles, Africans and African Americans experienced legally enforced societal and political segregation in multiple areas of daily life including public transport leisure activities, and education. Although Pendas also notes where each regime had elements of specificity, he highlights that such regimes had a common feature; through the segregation and dominance of the supposed lower racial groups, the privileged members of society could sense race as a unifying force.[95]

Restrictions on language and education were also colonial exclusionary tactics that prevented indigenous populations from rising within social or professional hierarchies. In annexed Poland, the education of Polish children was specifically aimed to keep them separate from the Germans, not only physically but also regarding language and employment skills. Segregated schooling for indigenous children was largely a colonial norm, for example, in the Belgian Congo or the initial years of rule in French Algeria. The subjects taught in such schools were either aimed at assisting the assimilation of the native population or strengthening differences depending on the individual colonial powers' aims. In annexed Poland, Nazi authorities did not emphasize German-language education for Polish children to assist their integration into German society. Rather, the limited education they received was intrinsically linked to providing them with the minimum amount of skills for their future ability to supplement the labor force. Comparably, the modification of educational policies for native populations in a response to their planned or assumed future as laborers was not unusual in colonial settings.[96] Aboriginal Australian children were expected to learn the "habits of useful industry" and in Adelaide, for example, they were only educated through vocational training.[97] During the Fascist Italian rule of Libya, the Italians decreed in 1924 and 1928 that Libyan children should be educated separately from the Italians. The specific task for the native schools in not only Libya but also in Somalia and Eritrea was to produce workers for the colonies.[98]

Historically in European-ruled colonies abroad, unlike in annexed Poland, wearing a badge was not necessary as members of the ruling colonial elite and the native population were often physically identifiable by skin color. However, it is significant to note that within the context of physically identifying who was German and who was not, the Germans simply created a visible difference, a badge, between the Germans and Poles when one had previously not existed.[99] Similarly, the limited education that Polish children received in German meant that the ability or the inability to speak the German language fluently would also be ultimately used as an identifying factor. A point of potential differentiation to colonial situations was that the Germans and the Poles had the same color skin. However, as evidenced by the case of the initial English colonization of Ireland, the British treatment of the Irish during hundreds of years of British rule, and contemporary historical studies and debates on Irish immigrants' status in America during the nineteenth and twentieth century, the fact that the Irish were white did not automatically allow them access to membership in the higher echelons of society.[100] In relation to understandings of race in America, for example, racial classification was never as unambiguous as simply a division between white and non-white.[101] As alluded to in Chapter 2, even within colonial categorization and the integration of individuals, skin color, or indeed ethnic descent, was not always deemed a reliable identifier of ethnic belonging. Correspondingly, in the case of annexed Poland, for the Germans, skin color could not be a categorization tool for deciding who was to be included or excluded from society.[102] This does not make the German situation in Poland any less similar to colonial contexts; instead, it makes it similarly complex.

As with the German annexation of the *Reichsgaue* Wartheland and Danzig-West Prussia, legal and societal measures were not the sole colonial tactics that colonial powers used to control and exclude indigenous populations. The physical exclusion of population groups through population transfer, forced removal, or mass deportations were not uncommon methods in such situations. They allowed for the dual results of both removing the indigenous population from the territory to segregate them from the colonizers while simultaneously clearing space on which the colonizers could settle. For example, the Indian Removal Act of May 1830 formalized previous policy relating to the removal of Native Americans and their transfer to territory west of the Mississippi River. Although the initial removal policy was envisioned as "voluntary," under the presidency of Andrew Jackson and Martin Van Buren, the removal of Native Americans was also carried out using force. From the late 1840s, the American policy changed to that of creating reservations for the Native Americans. Those living in such reservations often struggled against diseases and inadequate supplies of food rations.[103] From a global comparative viewpoint, such methods of physical removal had a devastating impact on the ability of population groups to acquire food and shelter. Removal dispersed long-standing communities, broke social and familial ties, and disrupted many traditions and cultural practices inherent to group identity. The new locations, and with them the new systems of living, created both social and psychological destabilization. As communal activities, such as seasonal hunting, festivals, or social gatherings disappeared, the sense of belonging, group cohesion, and individual meaning related to such occasions also began to vanish.[104]

The physical exclusion of the indigenous population through the use of concentration camps was not a unique factor of Nazi Germany's policies against Jews, Poles, and supposed political enemies.[105] Rather, civilian concentration camps were a population control method within colonial powers' arsenals. One of the most notable uses of civilian concentration camps before the Second World War was during the Second Anglo-Boer War (1899–1902). Approximately 40,000 people (both Boers and their native African servants) died during their interment in the camps due to appalling living conditions, such as overcrowded tents and inadequate food, sanitation, and medical care.[106] In the concentration camp at Swakopmund in German South West Africa, the male and female prisoners were provided with inadequate shelter and clothing during the wet and cold winter months. Despite being subjected to hard, physical labor, they were not provided with enough food to sustain them. A report from the time noted that between 1904 and 1907, 45.2 percent of the prison population in German South West Africa had died.[107] Prisoners from the Shark Island concentration camp were used to construct a new railway at Lüderitz Bay; however, little thought was given by the German Army to providing them with enough food or medical care. Between January 1906 and June 1907, 67 percent of the prisoners died.[108]

Certain historians have disputed the similarities between colonial concentration camps and Nazi Germany's camps due to the varying purposes of colonial camps or the occasional effort, for example in the case of the British in South Africa, to improve conditions for those imprisoned there. Iain R. Smith and Andreas Stucki argue that colonial concentration camps differed from the "camp culture" of Nazi Germany and in this case, despite the colonial origin of the term *Konzentrationslager*, it was used to describe "differing phenomena in different contexts and eras."[109] Using more detailed arguments, Jonas Kreienbaum rejects comparisons between the concentration camps in South Africa and German South West Africa and specifically German extermination camps such as Sobibór, Auschwitz, and Chełmno.[110] For Kreienbaum, colonial concentration camps' three main purposes were the total control of the colonized population, educating or civilizing the inmates, and obtaining a labor force. Although Kreienbaum notes that similarities may have existed between Nazi Germany's labor camps and British camps for Africans during the Second Anglo-Boer War, he argues the differences still outweigh the similarities.[111]

Indisputably, there were differences between Nazi Germany's concentration camps and their colonial counterparts. However, investigations of colonial concentration camps have also shown differences in both the goals of the camps and how they functioned. For example, Smith and Stucki distinguish the concentration camps in Cuba, South Africa, and the Philippines from those in German South West Africa as the former were part of an anti-guerrilla strategy whereas the latter was focused on the punishment of an already defeated enemy. In his book, Kreienbaum also distinguishes the camps in German South West Africa from the camps during the Second Anglo-Boer War and the camps for white Boers from the camps for the Africans. Additionally, within his argument on the camps main purposes, he recognizes differences between the camps in South Africa, German South West Africa, and Cuba.

Such analysis that highlights the differences between colonial concentration camps, both in their purpose and in how they treated the inmates, suggests that there was no standard model for colonial concentration camps. Certainly, there were norms, but there were also specificities. If we utilize a comparative framework to investigate both Nazi Germany's concentration camps in annexed Poland and the ghettos the Germans created as a method of physically excluding Jews through segregation, they were undoubtedly not an anti-guerilla or a military solution, nor had they educational or civilizational aims. Nevertheless, they did aim at securing a supposed threat to occupier society and controlling the Polish Jewish population, supposed political enemies, and Sinti and Roma during a military offensive.

Although colonial administrators used concentration camps for anti-guerrilla means or, in German South West Africa, punishment, it was often the case that the civilian population and the resistance fighters could not be distinguished from one another. This was not only the case in colonies with concentration camps but also throughout European colonial history. The colonized civilian population could aid fighters by hiding weapons or fighters, passing messages, providing food and medical care, or being fighters disguised as civilians and thus colonial authorities consequently viewed them with suspicion and considered them to be a potential threat. The differences between civilians and fighters were frequently so blurred that in German South West Africa, for example, German soldiers often fired at whatever targets they saw regardless of whether they were unarmed men, women, or children.[112] Thus the idea that colonial concentration camps were used to eradicate a military threat is one factor, but the imprisonment of civilians including women and children also demonstrates that they were perceived as a potential or future threat. Like the segregation of Jewish civilians within camps and ghettos, the Germans utilized techniques to control a threat embedded within civilian society. Regardless of the military aims, men, women, and children were all considered dangerous and needed to be contained.

Akin to colonial concentration camps, Nazi Germany also harnessed the imprisoned "threat" for labor purposes both in concentration camps and ghettos. As was the case with the Łódź ghetto, the provision of food for the concentration camp inmates was largely related to their employment as slave laborers. Although the civilian population of Poland was unlikely to pose a significant military threat to the Nazi Germany authorities, German racial ideology stipulated that those who were considered a racial threat were just as dangerous as a military one. As has been highlighted in this chapter, the Germans deemed such racial threats as particularly insidious. Without question, death was a major part of the Nazi Germany concentration camp and ghetto system. But, as this chapter has shown, the Germans established camps that had the sole purpose of extermination, such as Chełmno, and it was in these camps where the systematic murder of Jews began in early 1942. Therefore, while the intended outcome of concentration camps and ghettos was not necessarily the direct murder of Jews (as specific locations were later created to do this), mass death of the camp and ghetto inhabitants due to starvation, disease, overworking, or physical violence was an outcome that did not cause concern to the German authorities.

Correspondingly, colonial concentration camps, which were not specifically designated extermination tools, were sites of mass death. This comparison does not suggest that there were links or transfers between colonial concentration camps and Nazi camps and ghettos, as Benjamin Madley has proposed, for example.[113] Nor does it suggest that these locations were identical in aims and functions. Rather, an examination of the occupiers' attitudes to the inmates of such camps raises questions regarding not only the similarities between Nazi camps and ghettos and colonial concentration camps but also about what historians of colonial violence can learn from studying the exclusionary methods utilized by Nazi Germany. Even if the deaths of colonial camp prisoners were officially unintentional, it is unclear how truly unintentional such mass deaths can be when the colonizer's overall intention is to quash a threat supposedly hidden within or aided by civilian populations. Similarly, as can be seen in the case of Nazi Germany's camps and ghettos, questions should be asked about the extent to which the dehumanization and othering of the inmates influenced the occupiers' ambivalence regarding whether the inmates lived or died. The occupiers' apathetic approach to the loss of life, regardless of whether it was in annexed Poland or colonies on the African continent, was unequivocally interlinked with the supposed racial inferiority of the victims.

The defining feature of the Nazi regime's physical exclusion of the Polish Jews and other population groups not considered suitable for integration into society was targeted annihilation; the Germans planned the permanent removal of certain population groups during the war and established designated locations in an attempt to proficiently carry out these crimes. As detailed in this chapter, the escalation of industrial-style methods of physical exclusion at designated extermination sites such as Chełmno and Auschwitz was part of a gradually accelerating process that increased the Nazi regime's capacity for mass murder. The topic of Auschwitz-Birkenau especially, but also gas chambers in other camps, has often dominated public and academic narratives of the Holocaust. These narratives portray the Nazi murder campaign as an efficient, industrial process carried out via a disturbingly well-organized system of gas chambers followed by crematoria.[114] Auschwitz's dominance within the historical landscape has also emerged within the debate on continuities and similarities between colonial violence and violence perpetrated by Nazi Germany. For example, publication titles such as Madley's article "From Africa to Auschwitz," Zimmerer's *Von Windhuk nach Auschwitz* and Steffen Kläver's more recent publication *Decolonizing Auschwitz?* strongly allude to Auschwitz's long-standing significance.[115]

However, as Frank Bajohr and Andrea Löw have highlighted, in the last two decades, an increasing number of historians have begun to move away from focusing on the impersonal, bureaucratic, and mechanical processes of killing during the Holocaust. Instead, scholarly attention has begun to address the face-to-face nature of many killings and massacres that the Germans, and collaborators of other nationalities, committed in Eastern Europe.[116] For example, Christian Gerlach has noted that the prevalence of theories on the mechanical or industrial aspects of extermination camps not only overlooks the frequency of other murder techniques but also the lack of centralization or unification of these camps and the frequent operational problems faced there. In the Soviet territories, approximately two million Jews were shot, not gassed. Similarly, half of all Jews who died during the war did not die in gas chambers—many succumbed to illness or starvation in ghettos, or the terrible conditions during deportations or on death marches at the end of the war.[117] The camps were administered by the SS and the police, not by Heydrich and the RSHA, and there was no standardized murder apparatus; for example, the Germans used gas vans in Chełmno, engine gas in gas chambers in Treblinka, and prussic acid in gas chambers in Auschwitz-Birkenau.[118] Similarly, the individual perpetrators within annexed Poland cannot be reduced to one particular homogenously German group. Certainly many were Reich German SS members, but the murder and betrayal of civilians were also carried out or assisted by other groups including ethnic Germans, Polish police, and Polish civilian collaborators.[119]

Although chemical weapons were used in military combat within colonial contexts and this impacted civilians, large-scale killing by gas vans and stationary gas chambers were not established colonial killing methods.[120] Harnessing these specific methods was unique to the Nazi regime's selection of methods for annihilating population groups they deemed racially undesirable. Despite this area of specificity, the recognition of the prevalence of the other methods of killing still allows for comparisons to colonial killing where shooting but also starvation, exhaustion by labor, and a lack of medical provision to combat deadly diseases were also common murder techniques.[121] Similarly, the research, creation, and introduction of new killing technology, for example, the mobile gas vans in annexed Poland, for the removal of a supposed threat was not a factor specific to Nazi Germany. In colonial conquests, the colonized population often fell outside the parameters of the rules for "civilized" warfare and so the creation of new weaponry specifically for use against the supposed inferior colonial threat, such as exploding bullets, was not unusual.[122] Concerning the British Empire, for example, Michelle Gordon has highlighted how empire "was connected as part of a broader framework of British colonial military behaviour and an acceptance of a particularly brutal type of warfare against one's colonial 'enemies.'"[123] In Nazi Germany, Jews were seen as *Untermensch* (subhuman) and thus dehumanized. As such, newly created killing techniques, which would ordinarily not be used against "superior" population groups within European territory, could be used against Jews and other population groups within the supposedly primitive territories once belonging to Poland.

Although the killing methods may have differed depending on specific contexts, as did the specifics of the ways and means through which the targeted group was excluded by the occupying power, ultimately, legal, societal, and physical methods of exclusion were utilized in both Nazi Germany's conquest and annexation of the *Reichsgaue* Wartheland and Danzig-West Prussia and in occupied colonial territories. Such methods of exclusion prevented the integration of specific population groups into occupier society and served to solidify hierarchies. Nazi Germany's annexation and rule in Poland were certainly complex given the variety of stratified ethnic groups (for example, Reich Germans, ethnic Germans, the members of the DVL, Poles, and Jews), which all shared the same skin color. However, this does not mean that the situation in annexed Poland was unique. In fact, the creation of artificial racial categories and the attempts to organize society along racial lines was just as complex and problematic for the German occupiers as the attempts at population inclusion and exclusion by European powers in colonies were.

Often, discussions of whether colonial mass killing can be classed as genocide revolve around whether the "intent to destroy, in whole or in part, a national, ethnical, racial or religious group" can be proven.[124] In colonial examples, where military aims dictate violence and civilian loss of life equates with collateral damage, such an intention to destroy can be difficult to substantiate. Resultantly, scholarly discussions of whether the Holocaust and colonial mass killing can be compared to one another often return to the issue of a proven or unproven intent to destroy. Raphael Lemkin, the creator of the term "genocide," initially defined it in 1944 as always encompassing some form of colonization through "the imposition of the national pattern of the oppressor"; in his definition, Lemkin did not include reference to intent.[125] As A. Dirk Moses has argued in his recent publication *The Problems of Genocide*, the legalization of the term "genocide" by the United Nations in 1948 significantly narrowed the definition and, as the UN delegation wanted to encapsulate the crimes of Nazi Germany within the definition, the legal term positions Holocaust memory at its center. Moses poses significant questions as to why should intent be privileged when deciding what is an act of genocide as surely whether civilian deaths were caused with military intent or genocidal intent matters very little to those who are being killed.[126]

The exclusion of population groups through murder, regardless of the method, was a crucial part of the establishment of occupier and indeed settler society and power. By removing supposed military, societal, or racial threats, real or imagined, irrespective of if they were resistance groups or civilians, the ruling power's domination of the territory and its security could be fortified.[127] Tied with the notion of the inferiority of the occupied territory's population and the resulting indifferent approach to the loss of life, or indeed specific plans to murder, the exclusionary methods of colonial mass killing and the Holocaust can and should be compared.

Certainly, the Nazi regime's attempted annihilation of the European Jews, along with other population groups such as the Sinti and Roma, was a crucial moment in the escalation of racial violence within Europe during the Second World War. However, the methods through which the Holocaust was facilitated and conducted, for example, deportation, segregation, apathetic murder (through indirect methods such as starvation), and intentional murder (through direct methods such as shootings and gas chambers) were also present in colonial conquest, mass murder, and genocide. I argue that although the Holocaust cannot be considered a colonial genocide in and of itself, given that German Jews within the *Altreich* and Jews outside of Poland, for example, French Jews, were also targeted, it was perpetrated using methods that are also present in colonial frameworks of violence and rule.[128] The Holocaust was a process that began and was facilitated through expansionary conquest, annexation, and domination of territories external to Germany and the othering of population groups who were deemed inferior and unsuitable for inclusion into German society.

Interlinked Settler Colonial Inclusion and Exclusion

Although the Holocaust was not a colonial genocide, in addition to comparisons to colonial exclusionary methods there are approaches that still allow the integration of the Holocaust into broader colonial frameworks. Nazi Germany's mass extermination of the Jews began in annexed Poland in the shadow of expansion and conquest. As opposed to murdering the German Jews within the borders of the *Altreich*, the murder was exported to the new "colonies" of the Reich. Additionally, the extermination was carried out within the dichotic atmosphere of resettlement and deportation, inclusion and exclusion, and development and destruction. Despite appearing to contrast with one another, the act of including certain individuals while excluding others worked in almost constant tandem during the war. As Isabel Heinemann has described, the same apparatus of racial categorization used by RuSHA racial experts to filter the racial eligibility of ethnic German resettlers was also employed to determine who was racially ineligible.[129]

Another obvious example of the interlinked nature of inclusion and exclusion within annexed Poland was that the German authorities expelled Poles and Jews from their homes and farms so that the arriving ethnic German resettlers would have somewhere to live and work. The ethnic Germans' resettlement did not have a direct causal impact on the extermination of the Polish Jews, but the speed at which the resettlers could be allocated permanent homes largely depended on the speed at which Polish and Jewish occupants could be evicted and moved away from the territory.[130] The physical exclusion of the Polish population functioned alongside and facilitated the inclusion of ethnic Germans. The interconnection can be seen within reports on the evictions of Poles, which not only listed the number of Poles who were expelled, but also the number of ethnic German resettlers who were settled. For example, the UWZ report from Kreis Birnbaum, which was mentioned earlier in this chapter listed that seventy-four families were removed from their homes and seventy-one Volhynian German families were resettled in their place.[131]

The eviction of Poles from their homes was one factor, but the exclusionary tactics toward Jews, such as their segregation in concentration camps and their deployment as forced laborers, can also be linked to the Nazi regime's inclusionary elements. After a visit to Stutthof in November 1941, Himmler wrote a letter to Oswald Pohl, the head of the *SS-Wirtschafts- und Verwaltungshauptamt* (SS Main Economic and Administrative Office, WVHA). Himmler emphasized that due to its locations, production capacity, and creation of workshops on-site, the Stutthof camp was of great importance to the settlement of the *Reichsgau*.[132] Jewish labor, and their deaths, facilitated the inclusion of ethnic Germans into society through the macabre reuse of Jewish victims' clothes after their murders. Initially, the clothes belonging to Jewish victims at Chełmno were deloused in the gas vans as they could be fully sealed, and then the German authorities redistributed them to ethnic German resettlers in the surrounding areas.[133] However, by April 1942, the Chełmno clothes storage area was already full and supposedly a fire risk. Hans Biebow instructed that two nearby Polish churches were to be used as storage facilities.[134] The clothes were brought to and sorted in the ghetto and then sent to separate men's and women's tailors to be repaired. Due to the lack of suitable facilities in the ghetto, the clothes were taken by the VoMi *Einstazstab* (task force) for delousing. From the beginning of May 1942, some clothing items were distributed to Jewish laborers in camps while others were allocated to the NSV for redistribution to other authorities.[135]

A 1942 report from the VoMi *Einsatzstab* in Łódź demonstrated that the VoMi, the offices responsible for the welfare of ethnic German resettlers, were not just delousing clothes but also receiving them for distribution to ethnic Germans.[136] The report noted that although the allocation of shoes and material for spinning through the NSV and the main clothing warehouse had been working well and were regularly delivered, the clothing allotments had become slower toward the end of the year. It explained that since November or December, nothing had been delivered. The sporadic nature of the deliveries in the autumn and winter of 1942 can be linked to the reduction in gassings at Chełmno from late summer of 1942. Between December 1941 and June 1942, an estimated 97,000 to 100,500 people were killed but between June 1942 and December 1942, 48,000 were killed in a fewer number of transports.[137] According to the UWZ report, without the existence of the clothing warehouse up to that point, it would have been impossible for the VoMi to provide the most necessary support. To fill the "noticeable gap" in the deliveries, the report instructed that old clothes from the *Aktion*

Reinhardt (Operation Reinhardt) in the east that had arrived in Łódź for processing should be used.[138] The report followed with a list of the specified items; they included such textiles as 43,006 pieces of men's clothing such as suits, shirts, trousers, vests ,and hats, 14,358 household textiles such as bedsheets and towels and 22,296 pairs of women's, men's, and girls' and boys' shoes, slippers, summer shoes, and sandals.[139] The items left behind by the ultimate exclusion of the Jews, their murder, were thus been reused to provide for the population group whom the Germans were including in the Reich—ethnic Germans.

One argument occasionally used against comparing Nazi Germany's exclusionary policies and colonial exclusionary policies is that colonial and imperial powers rarely attempted to annihilate their labor source. Economically, the elimination of a source of cheap slave or forced laborers would seem to make little sense for the productivity of fledgling colonies. Similarly, the murder of the entirety of the colonized population was in direct contradiction to overarching civilizing missions that purported to bring the colonizer's superior religion, culture, or language to other populations. Ulrike Jureit has argued that Nazi Germany's territorial goals, pursued under the concept of *Lebensraum*, differed from colonial territorial expansion because "it represented a new and unprecedented model of domination, one that did not imagine, in colonial fashion, the spaces conquered as being empty, but rather that intended to empty these spaces and radically reorganize them for the purpose of racial selection."[140] She notes that colonial rule did not aim to homogenize territory but rather it used heterogeneity as a "structural principle" to economically and politically subjugate.[141]

In some ways, this is correct. Colonizers usually sought to impose and maintain a status quo that relied on the domination of the colonized population to benefit from their labor while also keeping them at a lower societal status. Such systems functioned through a racially ordered hierarchy of colonizer versus colonized. Nazi Germany's conquest of *Lebensraum* would seem to differ in that it aimed for the Germanization of the people and the territory and the complete removal of those who were deemed racially unfit for inclusion. However, not all forms of colonialism equally impact the treatment of the indigenous populations and not all colonizers envisioned the territory as empty to begin with. Namely, settler colonialism functions through the elimination of the indigenous population, by killing, physical removal, or assimilation, and their replacement with settlers instead of long-term exploitation for labor. The settlers colonize the territory intending to stay there. Consequently, the settlers eventually become the new population.[142] As Patrick Wolf has highlighted, settler colonialism "destroys to replace"; the colonial inclusionary policy of assimilation can thus be understood as one of a range of tactics used for the eventual elimination of the indigenous population and thus also qualifies as destruction.[143]

Parallel to the nature of settler colonial endeavors, which linked the acquisition of territory to survival, Nazi Germany had no intentions to rule territories that included Jews or the majority of Poles. Although both Jews and Poles were exploited for labor, Jews were not economically essential for labor purposes as Poles could be used for such tasks.[144] Following the GPO, after the war, the Polish nation would also disappear through both the physical removal of those deemed unsuitable for inclusion and the Germanization, or assimilation, of those who were deemed suitable through the DVL and WED. The population groups whom the Germans were physically removing were directly replaced by ethnic German resettlers. This replacement occurred both societally and economically, as ethnic Germans would populate the new German societies and take over businesses and farms, but also physically. Both Jewish Poles and many non-Jewish Poles were replaced with resettlers who were directly assigned their homes, their furniture, and, even in some cases, their clothes.

Historians have previously linked Nazi Germany's resettlement, and indeed genocide, to settler colonial models. For example, Caroline Elkins and Susan Pederson highlight that Nazi Germany's expansion into Eastern Europe grew, like Japanese expansion into Taiwan, Korea, and Manchuria, from the idea that "international standing and regional hegemony" would be achieved by the attainment of territory and the utilization of settlers.[145] Carroll P. Kakel has also utilized settler colonialism in his work; albeit, he argues that American settler colonialism was the inspiration and foundation behind Nazi Germany's ethnic cleansing and settlement in Eastern Europe and systematically compares the two cases.[146]

Leaving direct comparisons with examples of settler colonialism aside, the use of the settler colonial analytical model can greatly assist in understanding Nazi Germany's seemingly extreme use of inclusionary and exclusionary tactics for the Polish population. In his book on the topic of settler colonialism, Lorenzo Veracini highlights numerous settler colonial "transfer," or removal, strategies inflicted upon the indigenous populations by settlers. Settler colonial projects worked toward the fantasy of "cleansing" society; unlike colonialism, the occupier in settler colonial models does not dominate to exploit the indigenous population but dominates with the aim of transfer.[147] Transfer strategies that are particularly applicable to comparisons to the case of Nazi Germany's expansion into Poland include necropolitical transfer (when the indigenous population is annihilated),[148] ethnic transfer (forcible deportations of the indigenous community), and settler transfer (the movement of settlers into the territory "to create a population economy that is characterized by no indigenous presence").[149]

Apart from the physical transfer approaches, perhaps the most useful transfer strategies to apply to Nazi Germany's inclusionary and exclusionary population policies, and the establishment of population categorization, are transfer by assimilation and transfer by racialization. Veracini describes assimilation as indigenous populations being "uplifted" out of existence and that, although assimilation is often equated with absorption, the latter relates to the settler entity while the former relates to the indigenous population. Assimilation does not depend on indigenous performance. Rather, it is the settler society that ultimately controls the assimilation and as such, the need to establish assimilatory policies can exist alongside the need for policies that establish "unassimilable differences."[150] Transfer by racialization signifies the tactic of creating racial categories and "recoding" the indigenous population as racially different or "something else." This transfer strategy destroyed the indigenous population's indigeneity by codifying them according to the colonizer's categories and thus assigning them new defining features.[151]

Jureit's argument that Nazi Germany's concept of *Lebensraum* was distinct from colonial expansion in that it sought to empty territory is correct when compared to certain cases of colonialism. Settler colonialism, however, explicitly intended to empty territory to plant settlers there. In the context of Nazi Germany's population policies within annexed Poland, patterns which align with the three aforementioned settler colonial transfer or removal strategies that had a physical impact on the indigenous population can most certainly be observed. Additionally, the assimilation of Poles and other foreign nationals, through the DVL and WED or the Germanization of local ethnic Germans, and indeed the removal and murder of other Poles can be aligned with the two non-physical transfer strategies mentioned in the last paragraph. The colonizer, in this case, Nazi Germany, controlled the categorization of the population. Like colonial regimes, Nazi Germany was a "taxonomic" state—obsessed with classifying.[152] By defining and then sorting the population into supposed ethnic groups, the Germans robbed Poles of their indigeneity by assigning them to categories such as "ethnic German," "Jew," or "Pole."

Even if an individual was labelled as a "Pole" by German authorities, this was not an attempt to recognize the person's nationality due to their links to the territory. Rather, the term "Pole" was reassigned as a specific racial category that could be further broken down to investigate whether they were suitable for assimilation or not.[153] Nazi Germany utilized settler colonial transfer strategies, to borrow Veracini's term, to carry out its inclusionary and exclusionary population policies in annexed Poland. Inclusion and exclusion fed into one another; the attempted destruction of the non-Jewish and Jewish Polish population, through removal, murder, and assimilation, occurred simultaneously with the creation of the German population, through the resettlement of ethnic Germans and the Germanization of certain Poles. Akin to settler colonial projects, Nazi Germany initially created racial difference in an attempt to ultimately efface it.

Conclusion

After the invasion of Poland in September 1939, Nazi Germany undertook a policy of population reordering that, unlike the case of ethnic Germans, employed methods of the legal, societal, and physical exclusion of Jewish and non-Jewish Poles. The utilization of legal measures to instigate societal separation in everyday life facilitated an instantaneous subjugation of the majority of the Polish population. Daily activities such as going to school, riding a bike, eating at a restaurant, or visiting a cinema were redefined by who could partake and who could not. The private sphere was also encroached upon in the form of laws that dictated marriages and sexual contact. Perhaps unsurprising given the variety of failed attempts to regulate contact between colonizers and colonized in colonial territories, both Germans and Poles living under the Nazi regime did not always follow the rules despite the supposed racial threat such contact posed. Although Nazi Germany aimed for a homogenous society within Poland, a goal that was not unusual within certain types of colonial rule, German authorities struggled to achieve this during what was planned to be the founding years of German rule in Eastern Europe. As this chapter has demonstrated, race was an artificial construct and therefore categorizing people according to racial criteria could not be an exact science. The daily interactions and mixing between various population groups, despite the laws in place to try to prevent it, meant Nazi rule in the annexed territories would have most likely remained a colonial-style hierarchical, heterogeneous society comprising of Reich Germans, ethnic Germans, and non-Jewish Poles for many years if the war had not ended in 1945.

Nazi Germany's exclusionary measures extended to deportation, segregation, and mass murder, demonstrating the progressively escalating removal of the population groups perceived to be undesirable to the German *Volksgemeinschaft*. As opposed to continuing to deport or segregate the Jews and other population groups, like the Sinti and Roma, Nazi Germany embarked on their total elimination while also utilizing their labor where possible. However, this utilization did not have a sense of urgency. If members of the undesired population groups died, it was of little concern to the German authorities. Although German policies spilled out of annexed Poland and into the Soviet territories, the genesis of Nazi Germany's extreme exclusion, which included murder, first occurred in the annexed *Reichsgaue* of Danzig-West Prussia and the Wartheland. Additionally, the first target group toward which Nazi Germany aimed their aggression was not the Jews, but members of the Polish population in these areas. In particular, the Wartheland is "the key" to understanding Nazi Germany's occupation and population policy as well the beginnings of the Holocaust.[154] It was here that Nazi Germany implemented inclusionary policies toward ethnic Germans and certain Poles within the shadow of its exclusionary policies against Polish Jews, Sinti, and Roma and racially unsuitable Poles. As opposed to being paradoxical policies, the boundaries of inclusion, or who could be integrated into the German *Reich*, informed and defined the boundaries of exclusion, who would be removed, and vice versa.

Unlike many of the previous arguments that have been put forward within the debates on the comparisons between colonial violence and the Holocaust, this chapter has not solely focused on the policy of extermination or on one victim group. It has not concentrated on the familiar example of Auschwitz or gas chambers. Rather, it has presented the Holocaust as a set of escalating exclusionary policies and processes that often worked in tandem with inclusionary ones. As opposed to generalization, the chapter has applied colonial and settler colonial literature to the investigation of the Holocaust to show how the processes that led to it and the Germans' aims behind it can be aligned with broader patterns of conquest and violence. Like settler colonial endeavors, the Nazi regime aimed to secure territory through the removal of the indigenous population and their replacement with settlers. To carry this out, the undesired population became, according to Zygmunt Bauman, "the strangers." The strangers were dealt with in two ways:

> One was *anthropophagic*: annihilating the strangers by *devouring* them and then metabolically transforming them into a tissue indistinguishable from one's own. This was the strategy of assimilation – making the different similar ... The other strategy was *anthropoemic*: *vomiting* the strangers, banishing them from the limits of the orderly world and barring them from all communication with those inside. This was the strategy of exclusion – confining the strangers within the visible walls of the ghettos or behind the invisible, yet no less tangible prohibitions of

commensality, *connubium*, and *commercium*, expelling the strangers beyond the frontiers of the managed and manageable territory; or, when neither of the two measures was feasible-destroying the strangers physically.[155]

The Holocaust was Nazi Germany's attempt to "cleanse" German society. Steps were taken to make German Jews "strangers" in their own homes in Germany before the war broke out. However, the real "cleansing" of German society, that is, the physical exclusion of Jews through deportation or murder, began in annexed Poland at the same time as the establishment of German settler society in the *Reichsgau* Wartheland. Fundamentally speaking, the Holocaust was not a colonial genocide and its areas of specificity cannot be denied. However, the specificities do not cancel out the similarities that can be found between the Holocaust and the subjugation of Poles and (settler) colonial contexts. These similarities lie in the comparable nature of the policies and methods used to achieve the separation and removal of population groups. Additionally, settler colonial similarities can be seen in Nazi Germany's overall amalgamation of inclusionary and exclusionary measures with the ultimate aim of the acquisition of territory for a racially homogenous society.

Part Three

Aligning Overseas and Continental Colonial Aims during the Third Reich

5

"To Colonize Is to Cultivate": Colonial Overlaps between Africa and Poland

In his 1964 book *Dream of Empire*, the historian Wolfe W. Schmokel noted that it could be questioned whether there had ever been a nonexistent empire that had been so well administered as that of Nazi Germany.[1] For years, Schmokel's book has been one of the key texts on the theme of Nazi Germany's overseas colonial planning during the Third Reich. Such research on Germany's "nonexistent" overseas empire was largely eclipsed by studies that focused on the Nazi regime's expansion and rule in Eastern Europe and the very real damage and destruction it inflicted. Nazi Germany's colonial planning for expansion overseas was viewed by historians as a side note. As Geoff Eley highlighted, a dichotomy often existed between stressing the thinness of colonialism's impact inside the home society and seeing its depth, especially in the case of the German overseas colonial empire, which was unusually short (1884–1919).[2] Similarly, many historians assume overseas colonial planning was wholly insignificant to Nazi Germany or it was seen as a direct contradiction to the annexation of Poland. Overseas colonial planning during the Third Reich had fallen victim to the enhanced academic focus on the Holocaust and other more extreme aspects of the Nazi regime. However, scholars such as Karsten Linne, Willeke Sandler, Britta Schilling, and Birthe Kundrus, among others, have reexamined the longevity of colonial and imperial culture and fantasies in Germany and also Nazi Germany's own case of extensive colonial planning, propaganda, and education, which was fostered both before and during the war.[3] Such research demonstrates that even though the overseas colonies were lost and not regained, the topic remained a significant political discussion point and a way through which certain German individuals envisioned the shaping of German national identity and patriotic duty.

Overseas colonial planning can be viewed as an intrinsic part of Nazi Germany's opposition to the Treaty of Versailles, its ability to transform people and organizations for common political goals, and its plans for further acquisition of space, resources, and a human labor force after the war. By examining the ideas regarding overseas colonialism that circulated throughout the Third Reich, a more thorough understanding of the driving forces and fears behind Nazi Germany's ideology, as expressed by those who attempted to find a solution in the reclamation of former German overseas colonies, can be gained. This chapter will firstly investigate the attempts of colonial enthusiasts to keep the topic of German overseas colonialism in Africa relevant during the Third Reich despite the ongoing settlement in Poland. Far from being completely disregarded, colonial fantasies and the planning for a future German return to Africa were circulated both within official government departments and the public sphere throughout the Third Reich and indeed, the Second World War. Despite Hitler's doubts regarding the usefulness of overseas colonies, the reclamation of the African colonies was not solely seen as political rhetoric or as simply defiance of the Treaty of Versailles by the many who seriously engaged with the idea. Rather, these colonial enthusiasts and government planners helped create policies for Germany's overseas colonial future and they wholly considered the African colonies to be legitimate areas for the future provision of raw materials to Germany. Interestingly, overseas colonialism was not always viewed as being at odds with continental colonialism and, as this chapter will show, the two types of colonization did have similarities and were occasionally proposed as complementary to one another. Additionally, this chapter will highlight how discursive rhetoric related to the reclamation of the African colonies and discursive rhetoric related to German eastern expansion often overlapped. These overlaps can additionally be placed within the context of the resettlement of ethnic Germans during the war to further understand where certain similarities lie.

Overseas Colonialism during the Third Reich

From approximately 1935 onwards, Hitler repeatedly called on the Western powers to return the African colonies to Germany. His demands for the return of the colonies were strongly interlinked with both calls to abandon the Treaty of Versailles and attempts to absolve Germany from accusations that claimed they were "bad colonialists."[4] Although negotiations appeared to gain some traction by late 1937 and early 1938 and the British government began to discuss making possible colonial allowances to Germany, Hitler's prior views on the African colonies had largely been negative. In *Mein Kampf*, Hitler wrote:

> The former German colonial policy, like everything we did, was a half measure. It neither enlarged the area of settlement of the German race, nor did it make an attempt, criminal though it would have been, to bring about a strengthening of the Reich through the introduction of black blood.[5]

He further elucidated that the overseas colonies did not "appear suitable for settlement with Europeans on a large scale" and Germany should "terminate the endless German drive to the south and west of Europe, and direct our gaze towards the lands in the east."[6] The topic of the African colonies was largely used as a strategic political maneuver by Hitler but was not something that he deemed necessary or that he was willing to actively pursue while he was fully concentrated on establishing a continental empire.[7]

Despite Hitler's lack of enthusiasm regarding the pursuit of overseas territory, the Nazi regime permitted colonial enthusiasts to continue their promotion of colonial issues, albeit under certain restraints. Under Heinrich Schnee's presidency, which lasted until 1936, the DKG merged with several smaller organizations in 1933 to form the *Reichskolonialbund* (Reich Colonial League, RKB). The RKB managed to maintain independence from the National Socialist government for three years; however, as they were a group of private citizens with political aims and operating within a totalitarian state, the Party began to exert more control over the group.[8] In 1936, the RKB was reorganized by order of Joachim von Ribbentrop, the later German Foreign Minister, and Rudolf Heß, Hitler's deputy at the time. The reorganization led to the abandonment of the individual colonial societies and groups and united them under one organization, also named the RKB. In May 1934, the *Kolonialpolitisches Amt der NSDAP* (NSDAP Office of Colonial Policy, KPA) was formed as the official government office for colonial matters.

Both the RKB and the KPA were led by Franz Xaver Ritter von Epp, a leading colonial enthusiast, decorated military figure, and early member of the National Socialist Party.[9] Epp first joined the Bavarian Army in 1887 and volunteered in China during the repression of the Boxer Rebellion (1899–1901). Later, he served as company commander in German South West Africa during the Herero and Nama Wars (1904–8) and fought in various locations during the First World War such as Sarrebourg and Verdun. Epp was awarded the Iron Cross in 1914 and the Knight's Cross (*Ritterkreuz*) in 1916; thus, allowing for the addition of "Ritter von" (Knight of) to his surname and thereby classing him as a member of the *Persönlicher Adel* (Personal Nobility). During the German Revolutions (1918–19), Epp formed the *Freikorps Epp* voluntary paramilitary group that took part in defeating the Bavarian Soviet Republic (*Bayerische Räterepublik*). The *Freikorps* gained members, such as Ernst Röhm, Rudolf Heß, and Hans Frank. Later, the *Freikorps Epp* combined with the *Reichswehr-Schützen-Brigade* 21, a Rifle Brigade, under Epp's leadership. Himmler and his older brother Gebhard joined this brigade in November 1919. Epp went on to join the *Reichswehr* before leaving in 1923 to enter politics. Epp originally joined the Bavarian Peoples' Party but left in 1928 and joined the National Socialist Party on May 1. Later that month, Epp was elected to the *Reichstag* as a representative of the Party. Thanks to his numerous military exploits, Epp was well-known by the citizens of Bavaria and was a welcome reinforcement to the National Socialist Party. During the Third Reich, Epp attempted to use his public and political standing to promote plans for Nazi Germany's expansion overseas. In a speech published in 1939, which marked the anniversary of the *Deutsches Ausland Institut* (German Foreign Institute), Epp compared the reclamation of the colonies by Hitler to the historical situation of Bismarck acquiring the colonies during the *Kaiserreich*. According to Epp, Bismarck had recognized the increase in the German population, but also their industrial and political rise, and he had thus placed the necessary territories under German protection.[10]

Under Epp's leadership, the KPA conducted all official tasks related to planning colonial for the future reclaimed colonies and it distributed press guidelines and instructions on the topic.[11] The primary goals of the RKB, on the other hand, were to produce propaganda, raise awareness, and educate the public under the KPA and Ministry of Propaganda guidelines. In December 1933, Goebbels issued a memorandum on the *Kolonialfrage* (colonial question) in which he instructed that the question of colonies could not be discussed in conjunction with that of *Ostraumpolitik* (Eastern policies) due to "political reasons." Although some National Socialists desired the reclamation of colonies for settlement, he explained the notion of mass settlement was not a possibility. RKB propaganda and information dissemination were thus limited to combating the colonial guilt lie (*Kolonialschuldlüge*), advertising for the return or compensation of the "stolen" protectorates, and promoting the idea that future overseas colonies would be used for raw materials and colonial products, not as a settlement area for German farmers.[12] In a letter from Hans Lammers, the State Secretary and Chief of the Reich Chancellery, to Epp, Lammers explained that Hitler wanted central management and intradepartmental cooperation on the colonial issue.[13] Lammers further stressed that the government was keen to distinguish between preparations for a future colonial administration and actually attempting to regain the colonies. Epp was in charge of the former, while the Reich Foreign Ministry was responsible for the latter.[14]

Despite the unlikelihood of German settlement in Africa, the RKB energetically pursued its tasks and began to expand during the early years of the war. Adhering to the official Party guidelines, the RKB published newspapers, magazines, held various events, and ran its own youth group throughout its operational years. Its membership figures were initially limited to one million people. Despite the limit, the registration of potential members was not discouraged. For example, in 1937 the Bavarian Interior Ministry (*Bayerisches Staatsministerium des Innern*) encouraged members of the police force to join the RKB. In a letter sent on December 7, 1937, to various police departments and police schools in Bavaria, the Ministry noted that 55,000 members of the German police force outside of Bavaria were members of the RKB.[15] The letter stated that 80 percent of the police in Berlin and 75 percent of the police in Saxony were already members and explained "in the ranks of the Bavarian police, a strong and constant promotion of the aims and purposes of the RKB has to be achieved." The letter also discussed the appointment of liaison officers who would act as a contact to the RKB, provide education on colonial topics, and promote cooperation.[16]

By 1938, the RKB had already reached its membership limit. As a result, the restriction was abandoned and by early 1943, the RKB had a membership of 2,100,000 people.[17] Thanks to the recent German military successes in the west in 1940, the repossession of the former overseas colonies in Africa appeared to be a future certainty as opposed to a future dream. The KPA's budget reflected such optimism; it rose from 157,428 *Reichsmark* in 1939 to 6,379,678 *Reichsmark* in 1940 and 29,942,060 *Reichsmark* in 1941.[18] The prospect of regaining overseas colonies appeared to have such a strong potential that during a conversation with the *Reichsstatthalter* of Hamburg Karl Kaufmann, Epp announced that he had begun to develop his plans for a future *Reichskolonialministerium* (Reich Colonial Ministry). Alongside this, Epp envisioned himself as the future colonial minister for the overseas territories.[19]

Even after Poland was conquered and occupied by Nazi Germany (subsequently presenting areas for potential settlement), the RKB's actions reflected those of people who were truly convinced that the African colonies would be regained. Other subtle clues also pointed to the notion that German interest in Africa did not disappear during the Third Reich. Passenger ships regularly left Germany to take German citizens to the former colonies, which were still advertised as *Schutzgebiete* (protectorates). For example, in 1939 the *Deutsche Kolonial-Zeitung* listed weekly trips from Hamburg to and from Cameroon on motor ships. In February, there were four departure crossings (and one from London) available and in March, there were five. There was also the availability (two in February and two in March) of passenger steamships to South West Africa.[20] Additionally, the continuation of colonial research and education also demonstrated colonial enthusiasts' intentions regarding colonialism in Africa and the extent to which they believed their campaign would be successful. For example, on May 10, 1940, a piece appeared in the *Hamburger Anzeiger* on the founding anniversary of the University of Hamburg. The piece detailed how the *Hamburgisches Kolonialinstitut* (Hamburg Colonial Institute) had reopened almost a year previously and that they were back to working on the topic of the colonies in Africa. The Institute had originally been founded in 1908 but was amalgamated with other institutes in 1919 to form the University of Hamburg.[21] In April 1938, the Colonial Institute reopened for teaching and research and, according to the *Hamburger Anzeiger*, it began its new agenda with a special lecture attended by 400 students. As of May 1940, the Institute had thirty-one academic staff members, eleven employees, and fifty-four men with colonial expertise on the advisory board.[22]

Certain institutions that moved beyond teaching and research and actually provided specific colonial training for future colonialists continued their work. The *Kolonialschule* (Colonial School) located in Witzenhausen had been founded in 1898 under the name *Deutsche Kolonialschule für Landwirtschaft, Handel und Gewerbe* (German Colonial School for Agriculture, Trade, and Commerce).[23] The school operated until 1944, and during this time it trained Germans, not only for the African continent but also for Asia. As well as preparing young men for the potential regaining of the German colonies, its students also emigrated to other colonial territories. It offered a two-year course with subjects such as agriculture, horticulture, animal husbandry, forestry, colonial policy, ethnology, and also "native" languages like Swahili, Hausa, Malay, and European ones such as English, Dutch, and Portuguese. The school's facilities included a tropical climate glasshouse with tropical plants like palm trees, banana trees, sugarcane, cacti, and coffee plants. It also had its own museum, which displayed "weapons, musical instruments, drums, headdresses from Africa and the South Seas, dance masks and straw huts, pith helmets, spears and rear-loading rifles, elephant skulls and giant snakes in alcohol, wooden figures from Mexico and Abyssinia, canoes and real human heads which some savage tribe had captured and preserved as a trophy."[24]

In addition to the colonial school at Witzenhausen, there was also a colonial school for women, which was opened in Rendsburg in 1926.[25] The *Koloniale Frauenschule* Rendsburg offered a course in keeping with the gendered role of women; the students would be in the colonies as the wives and mothers of the colonial pioneers but not quite colonial pioneers themselves. Instead of skills that applied to solely colonial situations, the female students studied domestic subjects that could be used regardless of whether they were living in a colony abroad or not. For example, the practical subjects included housekeeping, tailoring, childcare, beekeeping, and gardening while the theoretical courses included nutrition, tropical hygiene and illnesses, bookkeeping, shorthand, and typing.[26] Hanna Reitsch, one of Germany's most famous pilots during the late 1930s and 1940s, spent one year between 1931 and 1932 at the *Koloniale Frauenschule* to prepare her for her initial career goal of becoming a doctor in Africa.

She noted in her autobiography that apart from her homesickness, the year she spent in Rendsburg was "one of the loveliest and happiest years of her youth."[27] A colonial school for women was not particular to Germany; similar examples of such schools and training courses can be seen in other empires. A description of Swanley College in Kent, England, which ran a colonial training course for women from 1903 sounds strikingly similar to the *Koloniale Frauenschule* at Rendsburg. The Guardian reported that the women learnt skills such as horticulture, seed-sowing, planting, jam-making, dairy work, beekeeping, carpentering, cooking, colonial hygiene and sanitation, native languages, and "such excellent details as driving and the harnessing and tending of horses."[28]

As with the colonial lectures and events of the pre-1933 period, the colonial schools' portrayal to the public during the Nazi regime is significant. In an article that appeared in 1933 in the *Hamburger Nachrichten* titled "Der deutsche Kolonialgeist lebt!" (The German Colonial Spirit Lives!) the author mentioned the question, which he posed to the then director of the colonial school in Witzenhausen Wilhelm Arning (1865–1943); "Kolonialschule ohne Kolonien?" (Colonial school without colonies?) Arning answered, "We believe in a German colonial future," but the students did not need to wait for that as there was a demand for efficient Germans abroad.[29] In his summation of the school's aims, Arning thus redirected the German colonial vision of the past to that of a colonial vision in the present and future. He noted that at the school they did not "hang onto any sentimental memories of the good old days but work for the practice of today" and they saw their task "as directing the sons of the middle class to new goals."[30]

The *Koloniale Frauenschule* was also the subject of media attention. For example, an article published in the *Hamburger Anzeiger* in 1941 detailed how the students of the *Frauenschule* must have a brave heart and "contempt for a comfortable life," to use a phrase attributed to Benito Mussolini during his visit to Berlin, given the physicality of their tasks both in their training and in the future German overseas colonies. The article's author clarified that the students must be healthy, in heart and soul, and have a good and swift working mind. In other words, they "must be German through and through."[31] As if to prove the practicality of the education provided, the author noted that "one must learn to iron not only with an electric iron but also with a simple coal iron" and "one should not only learn to cook on an electric stove but also coal, petrol, oil, gas and perhaps even an open fire."[32] Such articles did not portray the colonial schools as outdated institutions despite the German expansion eastwards instead of in Africa. Instead, the schools were depicted as current and timely; places that provided the relevant skills and learning for present-day situations and aligned with the theory of German health, family, and work ethics.

Two culture films, produced in 1937 by Paul Lieberenz, also promoted the colonial schools to the public.[33] The colonial school at Witzenhausen was the focus of the nineteen-minute-long *Der Weg in die Welt* (The Pathway to the World) and the women's colonial school at Rendsburg was the subject of *Die Deutsche Frauen-Kolonialschule Rendsburg*.[34] Although it had a less inspirational sounding name, *Die Deutsche Frauen-Kolonialschule Rendsburg* showed the female students partaking in certain activities identical to those of their male counterparts. However, *Die Deutsche*

Frauen-Kolonialschule Rendsburg also demonstrated the more domesticized activities that the women were taught; for example, it showed the students typing, arranging flowers, sewing, ironing, baking, and having a horse-riding lesson.[35] The "traditional role of women" was thus depicted in keeping with the themes of farming families, folklore, and local customs, which were frequently highlighted in culture films during the Third Reich.[36] Katharina Walgenbach notes women, and their work in households in the German overseas colonies, were often lauded as the best mediators between the colony and the homeland. They were also seen as a suitable intermediary between the colonized and the colonizers and devotion to the education and welfare of the native population were viewed as tasks that belonged to a female remit.[37] In the *Reichsgaue*, as depicted in films such as *Mädel verlassen die Stadt* (Girls Leave the City) discussed in Chapter 3, women were also portrayed as being crucial to the resettlement of ethnic Germans due to their ability to bridge the gap between the newly arrived resettlers and Germany.[38]

Newspaper articles and films featuring colonial themes like *Carl Peters* (1941), *Ohm Krüger* (1941), and *Germanin* (1943) may not have inspired audiences to become colonial settlers; however, they demonstrate the particular ways in which colonial enthusiasts marketed German overseas colonialism to the public. The subject matter of such promotion can also be compared to other facets of German expansion. For example, the colonial schools linked with the crucial concept of a "German task" in the former and future colonies. This notion of "*ein deutscher Auftrag*" (a German assignment) similarly crossed over into the resettlement of ethnic Germans and the Germanization of Poland. As described in Chapter 3, during this period in annexed Poland, common professions like doctor, accountant, teacher, or housewife, now took on a massively increased level of significance if this job was conducted in the new *Reichsgaue*. These jobs were now deemed crucial in the context of the German expansion, regardless of the geographical location, and so those who did them also understood them as being part of a specifically German task.

The RKB continued its promotion of Germany's claim to overseas colonies through mediums that appealed to the German public during the Nazi regime. One of these tactics was the use of colonial exhibitions; an estimated 1.7 million people visited colonial exhibitions between 1933 and 1938.[39] Similar to the exhibitions focusing on the resettlement of ethnic Germans and the supposed German redevelopment of Poland, the colonial exhibitions provided an amalgamation of history, culture, contemporary politics, and current problems, and they combined these factors with the idea of a day trip or a family day out.[40] Between 1933 and 1943, the DKG and RKB held six official colonial exhibitions in Germany. Numerous others were also held by smaller branches and other colonial support organizations. The exhibition in Cologne held from July 1, 1934 until September 2, 1934, included areas with subjects such as colonial history, colonial economy, colonial schoolwork, the DKG, the Women's League of the DKG, the colonial schools, the various former colonies, and a section dedicated to honoring the fallen men. A quote by Schnee in the exhibition's pamphlet appropriately summarized one of the main aims of the exhibition. He noted that "it is designed to help plant colonial thoughts in hearts and minds so that the German people recognize the tremendous significance of overseas possessions for Germany."[41]

Events in the period before the outbreak of the war, such as the RKB *Reichstagung* (Reich congress), also attracted attention in the cities in which they were held. Although the congresses were for RKB members, they were accompanied by parades through the city, exhibitions, events, and lectures. As such, the colonial enthusiasts' presence and the surrounding fanfare could not be missed by the local citizens. The congresses were held in various cities around Germany; for example, Frankfurt in 1933, Kiel in 1934, Freiburg im Breisgau in 1935, and Vienna in 1939. The congress, which was held in Bremen in 1938 and ran from May 24 till 29 included a lecture by Frau L. Diel, the first woman to travel through "new" Ethiopia, on the subject of "Tour through Mussolini's empire of work." The next day, Epp also gave a speech. The commemorative publication of the congress included articles on the RKB's work, pictures from the former colonies, and information on the exhibition "Bremen, Schlüssel zur Welt" (Bremen, Key to the World), which ran from May 25 until June 19. The exhibition held displays on the acquisition of colonies, treatment of the natives, transport in the colonies, and a display on tropical medicine by the pharmaceutical company Bayer.[42]

Before 1933, certain colonial celebrities often helped colonial organizations by appearing at events, giving speeches, and writing or contributing to books. Correspondingly, during the Nazi regime, these colonial celebrities were still publicly acknowledged. For example, Paul von Lettow-Vorbeck experienced a final high point in his popularity during the later years of the 1930s. Sales of his book *Heia Safari* increased and it went into reprint. Until 1933, there was only one street named after Lettow-Vorbeck (Lettow-Vorbeck-Straße in Bad Oeynhausen); however, between 1934 and 1939 an additional twenty-eight cities and towns around Germany also had a Lettow-Vorbeck-Straße. The street locations ranged from bigger cities such as Berlin, Frankfurt am Main, Hamburg, and Cologne to smaller ones like Fürstenfeldbruck (near Munich), Enger (near Bielefeld), Saarlouis (near Saarbrücken), and Gleiwitz (now in Poland).[43] The newly built army barracks in Hamburg, also the home of the *Deutsch-Ostafrika-Ehrenmal*, and an additional two barracks in Bremen and Leer were named after Lettow-Vorbeck between 1937 and 1938.[44]

Likewise, Epp was also a colonial celebrity, but his involvement in the Nazi regime differed slightly. As an early National Socialist Party member with an impressive military career, Epp was given positions of status in the Nazi regime as the *Reichsstatthalter* of Bavaria and as head of the KPA and RKB. However, Epp's efforts to push overseas colonial expansion onto the Nazi government's central agenda ultimately failed. Rather paradoxically, despite the inaction of the Nazi regime in terms of acquiring or providing a definite timeframe for reacquiring the African colonies, Epp remained a celebrated individual within the Party. He was a conspicuous figure in the upper echelons of the regime, both Epp and Hitler were witnesses at Josef Goebbels' marriage in December 1931. He often made appearances at events, featuring in the background of photographs with Hitler, or sitting alongside other high-ranking officials such as Hermann Göring and Himmler.

Like Lettow-Vorbeck, Epp had several streets named after him during the Nazi regime. For example, there was a Von-Epp-Straße in Dortmund, a Ritter-von-Epp-Straße in Passau, a Franz-von-Epp-Straße in Neunkirchen, an Eppstraße in Würzburg, and a Ritter von Epp-Platz in Munich. Epp was also celebrated in various newspapers and publications. On August 16, 1937, the fiftieth anniversary of Epp joining the army was celebrated with a memorial day which Hitler attended. The Munich edition of the *Völkischer Beobachter* noted that "General von Epp is a beacon for us. His face, under the steel helmet, is familiar to every German. He symbolises for us the hard fist, the power of our idea."[45] On November 17, 1942, the *Völkischer Beobachter* also reported on the twenty-fifth anniversary of Epp's knighthood, and in 1943, the *Münchner Neuste Nachrichten* published an article to mark Epp's seventy-fifth birthday.[46] Although the actualization of Eastern European expansion replaced Epp's plans for German territory in Africa, as a public personality in the Third Reich, he was not forgotten. As a decorated war hero and colonial celebrity, Epp was initially used by the National Socialist Party for gaining support. As the planning for overseas colonies was gradually surpassed by the expansion in Eastern Europe, it seems that although he predominantly represented overseas colonialism in Africa, Epp was still seen as a stalwart, German general who was an example of strong German will and determination.

Not unlike the colonial celebrities' continuing presence in Nazi Germany, the colonial balls which were popular events during the years before 1933, were still held during the Third Reich. In December 1938 and January 1939, approximately 12,000 people attended three colonial balls in Berlin.[47] The balls signified an active, publicly accessible promotion of colonial themes, and memories created and organized by German colonial societies. Even if an individual did not attend the colonial balls personally, the advertisements for such events were still significant in that they reached a larger audience of non-attendees and thus, still managed to convey many of the key messages of the balls. Such colonial balls were held to celebrate *Fasching* (Carnival) in February 1936 in the *Deutsches Theater* in Munich and 1939 in Munich. Another was held in February 1937 by the *Kriegerschaft Deutscher Kolonialtruppen* in the Hotel Wagner in Munich.[48] The 1936 and 1939 posters featured caricatures of naked African women, exotic animals such as snakes and a monkey, and advertised the "Nachtlicher Tanz in Afrika."[49] The 1937 poster advertised a "Ngoma Tanz in Afrika" (Ngoma Dance in Africa), "exotische Masken" (exotic masks), and "Kriegstanze der Eingeboren" (War Dances of the Natives).[50] The posters promoted the idea that the events would transport the guests to Africa, thus appealing to notions of exoticism and adventure.

Despite the increased membership of the RKB, the extensive official planning by KPA and the elements of overseas colonial remembrance and culture that continued during the Third Reich, both the beginning of the Soviet campaign in June 1941 and its aftermath would drastically change the possibilities of Germany regaining territory in Africa. Although the KPA continued its activities throughout the campaign and into 1942, the invasion of the Soviet Union created an opportunity for envisioning the attainment of a significantly larger expanse of Eastern European territory than had initially been planned. In 1941, the conquest of Eastern territories was already underway and thus, the likelihood of the GPO's future projections coming to fruition seemed increasingly likely given the initial German military successes. However, by late 1942, German fortunes in the war changed on both the Western and Eastern Fronts. Consequently, the KPA and RKB suffered a definitive blow as all activities deemed non-essential to the war effort were ordered to be discontinued. Earlier, in July 1942, Hitler commented that in light of the raw materials in the Eastern territories, he could not see any need for colonies. In September that year, he noted that what Germany could receive from colonies around the world, could not compare to the East.[51] Hitler's sentiment regarding the resources available in Eastern Europe was substantiated by the gradual movement of economic plans from an African focus to an Eastern European one. For example, the *Gruppe Deutscher Kolonialwirtschaftlicher Unternehmungen* (Colonial Economic Enterprises Group) increasingly turned their attention toward the resources available in the subtropical climates in territories in the German-occupied east, which included cotton. The KPA's agricultural department even drew up reports on growing cotton, rubber, tea, and oil-producing plants for the head group of agricultural economists for the East in summer 1942.[52] In January 1943, Epp received a letter from Martin Bormann, Head of the *Parteikanzlei* (Party Chancellery) and Hitler's secretary, who informed him that by February 15, the KPA and RKB should have ceased all activities. Although Epp succeeded in keeping a portion of his administration running as part of the Foreign Office, all colonial preparations ended in 1943.[53]

Colonialist Enthusiasts and the East

As demonstrated, German overseas expansion was not completely abandoned despite the National Socialist rise to power and Nazi Germany's drive into Eastern Europe. However, the two realms of expansion were often viewed as competing with each other; either Germany could expand further into Eastern Europe, or begin expansion into Africa. It could not expand simultaneously in both locations. As highlighted in Chapter 1, such discussions on the best location for German settlement were not new in Germany. However, prominent figures in the Nazi regime continued to research and openly discuss the advantages and disadvantages of German expansion in Eastern European versus German expansion in Africa. For example, since the 1920s, Richard Walther Darré, the prominent supporter of the *Blut und Boden* (Blood and Soil) ideology and the *Reichsminister für Ernährung und Landwirtschaft* (Reich Minister for Food and Agriculture) from June 1933 until May 1942, extensively wrote about German settlement.[54] Although Darré had studied at the colonial school at Witzenhausen and had a *Diplom-Kolonialwirt* (Colonial Sciences), Darré believed the East offered better opportunities for German settlement than Africa did. In one of his essays, Darré utilized the well-known title of Hans Grimm's book and noted that Germans were the "people without space" (*Volk ohne Raum*). Darré proposed four possible solutions to this problem: (1) the German population should be reduced so that they are in harmony with the space, (2) the German people should surrender their population surplus to other races who do not possess the same mental capabilities, (3) the Germans should settle their population surplus in colonies, or (4) they should attempt to gain the missing space "where it offers itself to our [German] homeland in a natural manner, namely in the East."[55]

Similarly, in 1931 he wrote an article titled "Ostraumgedanke oder Rückforderung unserer Kolonien?" which disputed the benefit colonies in Africa would bring for Germany.[56] Darré noted the decision for the reclamation of the colonies or for *Ostraum*

(Eastern Space) was not a matter of consciousness or belief but something that was "determined solely by the external political ability of Germany's leadership." Darré explained there were two possibilities why the actual question "reclamation of colonies or the *Ostraum*" was being asked; these possibilities were either the extraction of raw materials or for the housing of the German population surplus. According to Darré, the issue of raw material supply was a thoughtlessly regurgitated argument and not a well-thought-out and justified claim. He concluded that Cameroon would possibly be the only viable option for reclamation; however, it could only take a maximum of three million Germans.[57]

Despite his reluctance for traditional overseas settlement, Darré appeared to recognize the similarities between German expansion in Poland and earlier European colonial patterns. In October 1939, Darré, concerned that Hitler had allocated resettling the ethnic Germans to Himmler and the RKFDV instead of his ministry, wrote to Lammers.[58] Additionally, he sent Lammers a book on the history of Anglo-Irish relations along with a warning that should the Polish settlement be carried out without regard to creating land laws, then Germany risked making similar mistakes with Poland as England had made with the historically rebellious Ireland.[59] Darré clearly noticed the similarities in skills needed by overseas colonial pioneers and by Germans who were to be sent to the East. In 1933, he attempted to convert the colonial school at Witzenhausen to an *Ostsiedler* (Eastern Settler) school, but his efforts were thwarted by the then Reich Minister of the Interior Wilhelm Frick.[60]

Despite his colonial education, Darré was against German expansion in Africa and argued for Eastern expansion. Conversely, other individuals who had been involved with German overseas colonialism began to see the German expansion into Poland as complimentary to the future reclamation of the African colonies. For example, Epp began to alter his ideas on African colonialism to make them compatible with the German resettlement in Poland and Eastern Europe and in turn, to help preserve the issue of the former German overseas colonies at a time when political support for the movement was dwindling. As a colonial celebrity, Epp helped to preserve the memory of German colonialism in the interwar period and during the Nazi regime, despite being unable to inspire any action. His ideas regarding the benefits of overseas colonies, like those of many other overseas colonial enthusiasts, reflected an awareness of the perceived problems (for example, the supposed urgent need for space to save the German people) and also an attempt at framing the African colonies as the solution.[61] Despite being ultimately unsuccessful in his goal of encouraging a German reclamation of colonies in Africa, Epp's rhetoric can still be viewed in terms of how he, like others in the regime, adapted his views to suit the contemporary situation in the Third Reich.[62]

Epp skilfully utilized Nazi keywords such as *Raumpolitik* and *Lebensraum* and attempted to merge National Socialist ideology with conservative imperialist aspirations.[63] In a speech in Düsseldorf in 1935, Epp mentioned that German expansion into Eastern Europe was impossible given the number of people who already lived there. Epp had previously expressed this opinion in a 1928 speech where he also noted that Eastern expansion was not a viable policy in comparison with an overseas colonial policy "because it is based on historical phenomena whose bases no longer exist."[64] Thus, he implied that the Eastern expansion was an outdated model of German expansion. However, by 1933, Epp already appeared to begin to soften his objection to the East. In a speech in Leipzig, he proclaimed that the overseas colonial empire would be a supplement (*Ergänzung*) to the great questions, which would be solved in the East.[65] With the outbreak of the war and the German progression eastwards, organizations and various business enterprises that originally had an interest in the African colonies began to increasingly focus their activities on Eastern Europe. In a letter Epp wrote to the director of the *Gruppe Deutscher Kolonialwirtschaftlicher Unternehmungen* (Colonial Economic Enterprises Group) Kurt Weigelt in November 1941, he took a step further in his supposed support for German settlement in Eastern Europe by not only encouraging colonial enthusiasts to go East but also by pointing out the service in the East did not mean a departure from the "real tasks." Instead, it presented a possibility to gain experience.[66] Epp further guaranteed, "Anyone who proves himself here [in the East], can be assured of being considered first for the future colonial assignment."[67]

Karsten Linne argues that the reason why obtaining overseas colonies was never made a concrete goal in Nazi policy was first, due to Hitler's preoccupation with eastern *Lebensraum*, and secondly, due to Epp's ambivalent position. Epp failed to integrate himself into Hitler's inner circle, despite having known him for years, and rarely succeeded in presenting his arguments and ideas directly to Hitler.[68] By the 1940s, Epp was already in his seventies, and despite his position as *Reichsstatthalter* of Bavaria and leader of the KPA and RKB, he was not in as active a position as the younger SS members of the RKFDV or RSHA planning departments were.[69] Epp's tactic of moving from opposing eastward expansion to then framing it as a way for overseas colonialists to gain experience was likely to be purely in response to the changing circumstances of Nazi Germany as opposed to being genuine support for the Eastern settlement policies. Nonetheless, Epp's understanding of how the settlement in Eastern Europe could compliment future German colonies in Africa is significant in demonstrating the similarities that a major advocate for overseas colonialism was able to draw between traditional colonial expansion and Nazi Germany's eastern expansion.

Like Epp, the *Koloniale Frauenschule* in Rendsburg also began to embrace the similarities between the German task in Africa and the German task in Poland to keep the institution relevant. The director of the *Koloniale Frauenschule*, Karl Körner, recognized an early opportunity for adding another dimension to his colonial school's training program in light of the German conquest of Poland. From 1939 onwards, the European East was described, along with the former African colonies, as colonial a territory in the school's promotional material. In 1940, *Ostfragen* (Questions of the East) were added to the school curriculum, and in 1943, the Russian language was also included as a subject.[70] The addition of topics relevant to Eastern Europe potentially helped raise the school's popularity as in 1938, only fifty-eight new students had enrolled at Rendsburg. In 1941, 122 students had enrolled and this increased to 201 in 1943. A total of 199 new students enrolled in 1944 making the total enrollment 1082. Similarly, the number of permanent teaching staff increased from five in 1934 to ten in 1942.[71]

Hulda Rautenberg and Mechtild Rommel highlight in their study of the *Koloniale Frauenschule* that with the outbreak of the war in 1939, the connection with the overseas was broken and, as a result, from 1939 graduates of the school took part in the *Osteinsatz* program.[72] Although no definitive list has been discovered of exactly where the students and graduates were sent, graduates are mentioned in reports about Złoty Potok, a town then located within the General Government.[73] Graduates were also reported to be working with the SS in the Ukraine, where they were employed as "*Landfrauen*" (peasant or farming women) with several small farms under their control. The graduates supposedly attended a special three-month training course to prepare them for going east.[74] Similarly, a former agricultural science teacher from the school was assigned to the Lublin district in the General Government at the end of 1942 to create and lead a school for village advisors.[75] In December 1940, a small piece published in the *Hamburger Anzeiger* newspaper reported that a lecturer from the BDM gave a lecture at the *Koloniale Frauenschule* on the subject of testing themselves and their skills in the Wartheland. In addition to speaking about the tasks in the "new German East," the lecturer Ilke H., told the students they could test their training during holiday assignments in the East or after their graduation. She showed the students pictures of herself and her many BDM colleagues in Toruń (Thorn) in the Wartheland where they were helping the resettlers.[76] The 1944 school prospectus described the former students' current positions as "custodians [of the Germanness of villagers], leaders or co-workers in the 'Mother and Child' aid agencies, as village custodians, [as workers on] the land administered by the SS, etc."[77] This information, coupled with the BDM lecturer's visit to the school in 1940, demonstrates that the students of the *Koloniale Frauenschule* were most likely designated similar or identical tasks to the female settlement advisors in the Wartheland and Danzig-West Prussia. One of Himmler's staff told Körner that Himmler approved of the "achievements of the Rendsburg girls in service in the East." Similarly, another member of his staff noted that Himmler had "the most favourable experiences" with Rendsburg graduates on estates in the East that were under the administration of the *SS Wirtschafts-und Verwaltungshauptamt* (SS Main Economic and Administrative Office).[78] It is likely the case that the former students worked as settlement advisors, but because their training was so varied it is also likely they could have been employed in a multitude of positions in the East.[79]

The *Koloniale Frauenschule* was easily able to transition from supporting Germany's past and future colonial endeavors in Africa to that of supporting Germany's new territorial expansion into Poland and further east. The gap between Germany's colonial aims in Africa and its expansionary aims in Poland did not appear to be a big one for the director of the school and the students. As the BDM also seemed to be specifically attempting to recruit girls from the *Koloniale Frauenschule*, it also demonstrates that the BDM institution had recognized the similarities between the colonial training and the skills needed for helping the Germanization of the *Reichsgaue*. Although the Nazi official colonial planning ended with the KPA's dissolution in 1943, the *Koloniale Frauenschule* remained open until 1945. Despite the school's change in geographical focus, interestingly, the school name did not change and the term "colonial" remained. Given that the term "colony" was generally intended to signify overseas colonies in Nazi parlance, the *Koloniale Frauenschule* appears to be unique in its use of the term "colonial" while simultaneously training Germans to go to Eastern Europe.

Similar to Epp who embodied an older tradition of German overseas colonial expansion while also attempting to appeal to the Nazi regime, the school simultaneously represented a preservation of overseas colonialism territories and an embracing of the new Nazi continental colonial goals. Correspondingly, the examples of graduates who went to the East demonstrate not only the practical similarities in the civilian maintenance of colonies between Africa and Poland, but also how women's colonial training and their predicted roles in the African colonies could seamlessly be adapted to match that of the skills necessary for German eastern expansion. For the overseas colonial enthusiasts who felt their position was under threat, the two geographical areas of German expansion could be intrinsically linked and even supplement each other.

Overlaps of Colonial Discourses

The colonial enthusiasts attempted to merge German colonialism in Africa and German settlement in Eastern Europe, and the *Koloniale Frauenschule* made progress in converting their curriculum to reflect this. However, the argument that the two geographical locations were different remained. Despite this difference and Nazi Germany's inaction in reclaiming the African colonies, elements related to the ongoing treatment of ethnic Germans, inclusionary and exclusionary population policies, and the attempts to transform infrastructure and landscapes were similar to traditional colonial contexts. Historians have previously attempted to demonstrate direct or indirect continuities from the *Kaiserreich* to the Third Reich and have used metaphors that describe the *Kaiserreich* as a "reservoir of knowledge" or suggest the existence of a theoretical "colonial archive," which was used by Nazi Germany.[80] However, such metaphors seem to imply there was a conscious effort on the part of the Nazi organizations, such as the SS or RSHA, in recalling and researching the previous German colonial experience and then choosing and drawing out the best methods or ideology from the variety held in the reservoir. Ideas and discourses certainly did crossover from a common European-wide understanding of colonialism and in turn, from the *Kaiserreich*; however, I argue that they were general colonial justifications, and, as such, a definitive continuation or transfer does not need to be demonstrated to understand the Nazi expansion in Poland as a colonial endeavor.

Discourses concerning German overseas expansion were created during the *Kaiserreich*, radicalized after the Treaty of Versailles and then remodeled or re-promoted by colonial enthusiasts during the Nazi regime to offer solutions to contemporary German problems. These discursive tropes and concepts, which surfaced in books, magazines, and speeches were the same as those utilized by those promoting Germany's eastern expansion. Akin to the desire for overseas territory, the German projection of expansionary desires onto Polish and Eastern European territory did not end in 1919. Nazi Germany, and indeed Hitler, did not abandon the prior history of German settlement in Poland or the colonial-style imagining and othering of the territory and people. Instead, National Socialists retained such colonial discourses and fortified their ideology with them. Although I will not explore colonial discourses related to race or those that may have influences on or links to the wider policies that ultimately informed the planning of the Holocaust, in his in-depth study on the development of colonial discourses related to Eastern Europe during the *Kaiserreich*, Christoph Kienemann argues that the influence of colonial discourse should be considered when researching the causes of the Holocaust. For Kienemann, two important aspects are worth noting concerning the topic. Firstly, Nazi Germany drew on the most radical aspects of racist colonial discourse, particularly about the biological racist principles that strengthened colonial discourses about Eastern Europe after 1900. Secondly, the German "inferiority complex" relating to Germany's standing as a global power, which was developed before 1914, was retained within Hitler's ideology.[81]

As Chapter 1 has addressed, discourses surrounding the benefits of German expansion had been circulating in Germany from the beginning of the *Kaiserreich* and had been strengthened and radicalized during the interwar period. Discourses, spread by colonial enthusiasts or by *Ostforscher* academics during the Third Reich, were further replicated in publically accessible magazines, newspapers, films, and books. In the case of *Ostforschung*, academics combined ethnic studies, population analysis, geography, and history to fuel the argument for Germany's reclamation of territories in Poland. Although their studies were purely related to continental expansion, the discourses elucidated in their writing overlapped with many of the discursive concepts used by the colonial enthusiasts produced at the same time. Both groups promoted romanticized versions of historical German interactions with the territories, plans for the future, and justifications for action. Undoubtedly, it is difficult to prove the direct influence of specific discourses on individuals or particular Nazi policies. However, the discourses circulating throughout the Third Reich in various texts, often disseminated by "experts," informed and facilitated public, political, and institutional knowledge and opinions regarding the justifications for German expansion. As such, much of the knowledge stemming from such discourses was not something new to civilian observers. Rather, it reinforced long-standing, identifiable tropes and justifications regarding Poland, the former overseas colonies, and Germany's ongoing problems.

One of the key discursive overlaps between supporters of Eastern expansion and colonial enthusiasts during the Third Reich was the topic of space, or rather, Germany's supposed lack of space. Space or *Lebensraum* was an essential concept in the philosophy of National Socialism and one of the driving forces behind the German occupation of Poland from 1939. However, the combination of arguments for the acquisition of space and the arguments for regaining African colonies during the interwar years and the Nazi regime were extremely common. Similar to discussions of the need for space in the East, colonial enthusiasts related the acquisition of space in Africa to the German nation's survival. For example, Epp highlighted this supposedly desperate need for *Lebensraum* in the promotional publication *Deutschland braucht Kolonien* (Germany needs Colonies), which accompanied the colonial exhibition held by the RKB in Hamburg in 1936. The publication quoted Epp as saying that "the German people need land, and we demand land for our starving people."[82] Similarly, in 1938, he described the return of the colonies as a "vital question [*Lebensfrage*] for the German nation" and implored the reader to "join the colonial fight and become a RKB member."[83] Schnee also tied the 1934 Colonial Exhibition to this crucial element of Nazi ideology: "We need to be clear: without colonies, poverty and deprivation. With colonies, work and bread!"⁸⁴ Correspondingly, Adolf Friedrich, the Duke of Mecklenburg, was quoted in the pamphlet as saying that "colonial possessions are the most visible expression of the will to live (*Lebenswille*) of a people."⁸⁵

The quotes connected the colonial exhibition, and what it was promoting, to the current issue of the need for territory. The idea that Germany needed more space for its population had already been present in public discussions since the *Kaiserreich*, but after the territorial loss because of the Treaty of Versailles, it became a subject that appeared to be increasingly more urgent. The question of space was furthered raised in the pamphlet *Deutschland braucht Kolonien*. The pamphlet included an extract from *Volk ohne Raum* and had a comparison table, titled "Der Deutsche hat am wenigsten Lebensraum!" (The German has the least living space of all!), which listed the size ratio of colonies to that of the European empires. It recorded that in 1914 England's colonies were 105 times as big as England, Belgium's colonies were eighty times the size of Belgium, France's colonies were twenty-two times the size of France, and Germany's colonies were five and a half times the size of Germany.⁸⁶ In Paul Leßner's publication, *Was müssen wir von unseren Kolonien wissen?* (What do we need to know about our colonies?), a graph visually illustrated the unfair distribution of *Lebensraum* in 1938 using the British Empire, France, Belgium, Portugal, Holland, and Germany as comparative examples.⁸⁷

The third volume of *Zeitfragen deutscher Kultur* was written by Heinrich Schnee and dedicated to the topic "Deutschlands koloniale Forderung" (Germany's Colonial Claim). Schnee argued that colonies were necessary for the minerals and raw materials that were unavailable in Germany, such as rice, corn, bananas, cocoa, coffee, tea, and spices. He also noted the former colonies in South West Africa, German East Africa, and the interior of Cameroon "offered space for a substantial number of German citizens," and the settlement in suitable colonies was significant for the preservation of the *Deutschtum* (Germanness) of German emigrants.⁸⁸ In addition to economics, Schnee also linked the need for colonies to being essential for the German people's development, especially the youth. He noted that activities in the colonies expanded one's horizons, strengthened their will, and developed their character. He highlighted that this not only effected the Germans who went abroad, but was also beneficial for the German nation as a whole.⁸⁹ The book, *Wer will in die Kolonien?* (Who wants to go to the colonies?), provided guidance for those who wanted to move to the former colonies and highlighted the historical and political background of German overseas colonialism. Like Schnee, the author Adolf von Duisburg, head of language and cultural studies at the Witzenhausen colonial school, highlighted the notion of German's lack of space and its link to Germany's economic distress.⁹⁰

Comparable to the colonial enthusiasts of the interwar years and early years of the Nazi regime, the *Ostforschung* academics regularly promoted the belief that Germany's territory was too small to sustain its growing population. As Ingo Haar argued, by 1937 the *Ostforschung* academics had already developed a "new order" model of Poland, which would be achieved by organizing Polish territory using population policy. This "new order" would see Poland denied national sovereignty and becoming a territory for German ethnic development. Polish Jews would be rendered stateless and deported.⁹¹ The *Ostforscher* Hermann Aubin noted that despite a fall in Polish migration to the West, it should be kept in mind that Poland still had "an abundance for its population."[92] Akin to publications by overseas colonial enthusiasts *Ostforschung* academics also used the tactic of including measurements of territories to demonstrate exactly how little *Lebensraum* Germany had and where it would be potentially available.[93] On the final page of *Der Deutsche Osten*, Arnold Hillen Ziegfeld proclaimed, "The people and the space in the German East are, once more, goals which must be fought for."[94] Ziegfeld thus linked the acquisition of eastern European space to the plight of the German people living there. Otto Fitzner, an engineer and economist, provided the population numbers per territory figures in his contribution to the book *Breslau und Deutscher Osten* where he demonstrated that the further east one went, the more land space available to them. He argued that in West Germany there were 209 inhabitants per square kilometer, in Central Germany there were 134 inhabitants, and in East Germany there were ninety-three inhabitants.[95]

The argument for the abundance of space in Poland and Eastern Europe linked seamlessly with the historical perceptions regarding the territories' primitive nature. It was argued that this space's only useful purpose would be as *Lebensraum* for the culturally and racially superior German neighbor.[96] Eduard Mühle has argued that the *Ostforschung* academics were purposely vague in their geographical specificity when referring to "the East." Although occasionally they specifically referred to Poland, often they used general terminology such as "East," "Eastern lands," and "Eastern space," thus leaving room for discussion about how far into Eastern Europe Nazi Germany could spread.[97] In October 1933, Aubin wrote a letter to Hitler and hailed him as the "re-newer of our people in the joyful certainty that there will be German what is German without boundaries and limits." The notion of the space that Germany required was closely linked with the supposedly endless possibilities of *Lebensraum* in the East in the eyes of the *Ostforschung* academics.[98] Aubin argued that the German movement into their neighbors' *Lebensraum* would crucially benefit Germany because the ability to truly understand questions regarding the Eastern movement would only be gained while occupying this space.[99] Thus, Aubin attempted to justify German expansion given that it would supposedly provide answers to historical and current queries regarding German eastern migration.

Another theme the colonial enthusiasts regularly discussed was the notion of a worthwhile "German task" in the African colonies. In a speech by Epp on December 6, 1937, which was published in the pamphlet *Der Deutsche Standpunkt in der Kolonialfrage* (The German Standpoint in the Colonial Question), he highlighted that the colonies and the space were needed to give the German youth "the opportunity to expand [their] horizons" and by sending the youth out, they would later bring their experience and skills back to the German people.[100] For colonial enthusiasts, *Lebensraum* was also essential for the German people's cultural advancement. Space would allow for Germans, particularly the youth, to embark on an adventure that would result in the widening of their horizons and eventually benefit those who had stayed behind in Germany, once they brought their knowledge and skills back. Germanness was not only located in Germany; instead, German culture, morals, and people could also be cultivated abroad.

Women's contribution to the German task was equally recognized by those promoting the ethnic German resettlement and by colonial enthusiasts. Both groups acknowledged that women were fundamental members of the population who would maintain and strengthen households and family bonds in the context of overseas and continental colonialism. These theories reflected the Nazi ideal of the romantic and traditional image of German women as caregivers, childbearers, and heads of household duties, but also as teachers and nurses. This promoted image was relevant regardless of whether it was perpetuated in German colonies in Africa or in annexed Poland.[101] Colonial literature demonstrated that women were not only needed in terms of being "teachers, kindergarten nurses and household help" but they were also important as being "the conservative element in human life." According to Duisburg, even in foreign environments, it was in a woman's nature to persevere.[102] The presence of women in the colonies was seen as so important that in the guidelines of *kolonialpolitische Ausbildung* (colonial politics apprenticeship), which were issued in 1939, it was stated that the wives of any married students must commit to an evaluation of their suitability for tropical climates and a four-week tropical hygiene course.[103]

In addition to theoretical and practical contributions, like what young women learnt in the colonial school in Rendsburg, for example, the colonial enthusiasts claimed that women had a specific mission in the colonies, which had a deeper impact and meaning for Germany as a whole. As the *Koloniales Taschenbuch* from 1941 highlighted, German honor could supposedly be brought "before the world, before the German people and before the coming generations of Germans" with German women's constructive work in the colonies.[104] Akin to the women of the BDM training for their *Osteinsatz* or helping resettled ethnic Germans in annexed Poland, women's roles in the planned African colonies would also strongly reflect the notion of a self-perceived German civilizing mission. Both the fantasy of overseas colonies and the reality of German eastern expansion reflected the notion of women having an immediate, specific, and important place in the newly acquired territories.

The *Ostforschung* academics' work also utilized and attempted to strengthen the notion of a German task, albeit in the East. This idea gave further legitimacy to a specifically German involvement in Poland and Eastern Europe. Max Hildebert Boehm linked the German task to longevity when he noted in his essay "Der Deutsche Osten und das Reich" that a Germandom that was "mission-conscious" could not acknowledge anything else as openly and as frankly as the thousand-year task that Germany would have in the East.[105] In the same collection of essays, Ziegfeld described how "the German East rises before Germany as a task which steels the will of the nation and through which the new German man will mature and reach perfection."[106] Similarly, in the foreword of his book, *Krisis und Aufbau in Osteuropa* (Crisis and Development in Eastern Europe), Albert Brackmann, the head of the *Publikationsstelle* (Publications Office, PuSte), noted that the German task in Eastern Europe was to be regarded not only as an ethnic responsibility but also a "general cultural obligation." He went on to mention that other Western democracies should know that Germany had honestly and unquestionably acquired its rightful task in Eastern Europe.[107] Later in the book, he demonstrated that Germany's historical relationship with Poland could also be understood as a German task based on previous

German work in Poland. The book included sections titled "The Decline of Poland" and "German Development Work in the East during the Statelessness of Poland."[108] By including the word "*Krisis*" in the book's title and by describing the decline of the Polish state and the German "development" there, Brackmann was alluding to a very common European colonial form of justification for action within the framework of a specifically "German task."

Fitzner began his chapter "Die Kommenden Aufgaben der Wirtschaft im Osten" (The Upcoming Tasks of the Economy in the East) by mentioning that just as centuries ago "our German ancestors filled the living space [*Lebensraum*] we call the German East, it is today the task for us to reinforce." Fitzner argued that it was necessary to fill the Eastern space [*Ostraum*] with German people. However, it should not just be filled with peasants but also people of agriculture and industry.[109] Hans Rothfels also pointed to a "German task," which was linked to the historic relations between the two countries. He concluded his essay in *Deutschland und Polen* by stating the duty for carrying out "pacification and establishing of order" should lie "on the shoulders of those people who have for centuries been most intimately and extensively bound up with the whole current of life of the East."[110]

Rothfels was, like Brackmann and Fitzner, presenting a mission in Poland and the East that should be taken on by the German people because of Germany's prior involvement there. Furthermore, the authors' beliefs in the superiority of Germany meant, by virtue of being German, they were the most suitable people for the task. This was parallel to the overseas colonialists who also expressed a similar sentiment. The discourses surrounding the importance of the German task in the East were not just limited to patriotic propaganda. Rather, they also shed light on the belief that the German people were inherently better than those in the territories where these tasks would be carried out. As Ingo Haar has noted concerning *Ostforschung*, the concept of the *Volk* as a factor within the fulfilment of a German "mission in the East" fed on resentment against non-Germans.[111] This mindset, which can be compared to colonial contexts, was neither limited to the *Ostforschung* academics nor the colonial enthusiasts. It could be observed in the treatment of the Polish population, and occasionally the newly Germanized ethnic Germans, by Reich Germans in the resettlement areas of the Wartheland and Danzig-West Prussia.[112]

A significant part of the German belief in the need for the reclamation of the African colonies was that Germans abroad apparently needed help after being stranded in Africa because of the Treaty of Versailles. The promotional brochure for the RKB, released in 1937 and titled *Reichskolonialbund - Deutschland, deine Kolonien*, shed light on how "even today, thousands of Germans are fighting to persevere their language and their kind" and "their struggle for Germandom, which they fight for at the outpost of Nazi Germany, is therefore of particular importance."[113] The propaganda pamphlet about ethnic Germans resettlers, *Der Führer hat uns gerufen* (The Führer called us, also mentioned in Chapter 2), which was released in 1940 by the VoMi, conveyed an almost identical sentiment. The pamphlet noted "these men and women had to struggle more for their Germanness than any German in the Reich."[114] Both the RKB brochure and the VoMi pamphlet aimed at depicting the Germans abroad as the citizens who were making true sacrifices for Germany. The messages attempted to evoke both pride in this German strength and compassion for their plight by using a particularly emotional, patriotic, and personable narrative to appeal to the reader.

Akin to the ethnic Germans coming to Poland who were occasionally portrayed as being "true" Germans in terms of their physical appearance, their language, and their culture, the Germans in former German colonies in Africa were depicted in the same way. As Willeke Sandler points out these German settlers "represented an idealized *Volksgemeinschaft* of racially-aware Germans."[115] This is perhaps best seen in photographs of the Germans living in the former colonies, which were taken during the 1930s and then used and reused in various publications released during the war. For example, *Das neue Volksbuch der Kolonien* (The New Folk Book of the Colonies) includes a photograph of two youths, one male, and one female. They are fair-haired and the caption notes they are third-generation Germans in South-West Africa. Although the photo is black and white so the colors are not visible, the male youth's uniform is identifiable as that of the *Deutsche Pfadfindern von Südwestafrika* (German Scouts of South West Africa). He wears a khaki uniform shirt, neckerchief, and grey felt slouch hat with a side fold, and a black, white, and red cockade (the colors of the *Kaiserreich* flag). The female also wears a scout's white shirt, identifiable by the hawthorn emblem of the South West African branch, and a neckerchief—similar to the BDM uniform. Both youths solemnly gaze into the distance while the caption underneath describes how the third-generation Germans in "the South West" are "German to the core and healthy."[116] Almost as inconsistent as the messaging in the photographs of ethnic Germans resettlers, the German scout association, including the group in former German South West Africa, had been banned by Nazi Germany since 1939. As such, the publication from 1941 was actually depicting members of an officially defunct association while attempting to link them with German society and culture.[117]

In another photo in the same book, German children sit in a circle around a fair-haired young boy. Perched on a rock beside him, lies a framed photograph of the boy with Hitler. The caption under the photo reveals the boy was "the pride of the school in Windhoek" as he had "sat upon the knee of the Führer."[118] The aforementioned RKB brochure also illustrated the supposed continuing Germanness of those in the former colonies by featuring pictures such as a swastika flag hanging outside the Lwandai-Mlalo German school in East Africa.[119] Literature produced to win support for German expansion into Africa relied on similar tactics to those that promoted the resettlement of ethnic Germans in annexed Poland. Germans abroad were portrayed as loyal to their homeland and Hitler. Despite living under foreign control for years, they managed to preserve their German values and physical characteristics. By portraying the Germans in Africa in such a way, colonial enthusiasts attempted to foster feelings of empathy in Germany, just like the VoMi and other institutions endeavored to do with photographs and sketches of the arriving ethnic German resettlers.

Like the colonial enthusiasts, the *Ostforschung* academics raised the issue of the struggles of ethnic Germans in Poland and Eastern Europe and promoted the idea of the Reich's duty to protect them.[120] In his contribution to the book of collected essays *Deutsche Ostforschung: Ergebnisse und Aufgaben seit dem ersten Weltkrieg* (German *Ostforschung*: Results and Tasks since the First World War), Erich Keyser described how large communities of German people were overtaken and soon the realization came about that "the expulsion and oppression of the Germans in the countries of the East would not only bring about a considerable cultural decline, but also the potential decline of the traditional political and social order."[121] Keyser specified that there is no other topic more important for the German population in the East, whether native or newly resettled there, "than the preservation and strengthening of their national communities." On the same page, Keyser ended his chapter with the remark that the grand hour for "*Volksforschung*" has begun and questioned whether the successors of the last twenty years of research are worthy of the task.[122]

In his publication *Krisis und Aufbau in Osteuropa*, Brackmann also alluded to the safety of ethnic Germans. He argued that it became clear overnight to the Germans that millions of Germans would now be living outside of the Reich borders, and these were the people "who had been longing for a close connection with Germany to avoid their perishing in foreign territory." He also noted:

> The main task for all … was to strengthen the Germandom (*Deutschtum*) of these splintered Germans until the great day would come when they could be accepted again as citizens into the realm, to which they belonged according to their blood and their history.[123]

Brackmann appeared not only to be alluding to the potential danger of the ethnic Germans' situation, he attempted to evoke feelings of sympathy in the reader by mentioning that ethnic Germans were the very people who desperately wanted to be connected with Germany. However, by a cruel fate, they ended up stranded outside Germany's borders. In a similar way to colonial enthusiasts' interest in Germans living in the former German colonies and the authors of propaganda pamphlets for the resettlement, Brackmann appeared to be promoting ethnic Germans as suitable citizens of the Reich who deserved to be helped. As if to further strengthen this point, Brackmann included a quote from *Mein Kampf*: "Common blood belongs in a common Reich."[124]

Similar to the colonial enthusiasts' desire to demonstrate that the Germans living abroad were still racially and culturally German, in his contribution to *Der Deutsche Osten*, Karl Thalheim argued that far in the East lay German people's land with residential areas of German ethnic groups and "splinters" of German people. Thalheim went so far as to note that these ethnic Germans still had their native dialects just as their Palatine, Swabian, and Silesian ancestors did.[125] Similarly, in his essay "Danzig," Erich Lindow noted the Germans in Danzig hold watch for Germany and cling to German East Prussia. Lindow tied this to irredentist claims on the territory by mentioning that in Danzig "German is the city and its culture, German is the spirit and German is the feeling of its citizens."[126]

The colonial enthusiasts not only saw the regaining of African colonies as a charitable mission for helping Germans abroad; they also saw it as a way of helping the native population of the former colonies by preserving Germany's supposed loyalty and reputation and by providing practical help. In the book *Kolonien oder Nicht?*, the author argued that there was not only "a duty of honor towards the natives of our [former] colonies" but also a responsibility to be grateful to those who died while fighting for a colonial Germany. He noted, "Their volition, their will was exclusively Germany, a strong colonial Germany."[127] Employing propaganda commonly used for justifying European expansion, Schnee remarked in his contribution to *Zeitfragen deutscher Kultur* that the natives would benefit from the medical work of German doctors and bacteriologists as the rate of illness and epidemics in the native population has increased since decolonization.[128] Other publications promoted the theory that the native population wanted the Germans to return. The book *Wann kommen die deutschen endlich wieder?* (When will the Germans finally return?) by Senta Dinglreiter was named with such a theory in mind. It describes the author's travel through Africa with a heavy focus on the plight of Africans who had once been under German rule. Dinglreiter elaborated on her encounters with local people and mentioned meeting an old man in tribal dress who approached her. Upon hearing she was German his "eyes lit up" and he asked her "when will the Germans finally return?" She replied, "God only knows." Dinglreiter reported she wished she could give him better information. She also noted that throughout her travels, many other Africans asked her the same question and she was proud of how the German character and work in the past were being recognized.[129]

Although the Nazi regime did not profess to embark on a developmental mission to help the majority of the Polish population, the notion of a supposed German cultural mission in the East was also prevalent in the works of *Ostforschung* academics. The particular German mission often related to bringing culture to Poland, which was depicted as being the opposite of Germany; uncultured, primitive, and unable to have a politically coherent state.[130] For the *Ostforschung* community, German cultural and political superiority over Polishness could certainly not be doubted.[131] Given this supposed superiority, the notion of intervention in Poland to bring culture and civilization, resembling how Germany had apparently done so in the past, was strengthened. Similarly, by professing how Germany could transform Poland, the *Ostforscher* were, in turn, self-promoting Germany's culture. In the book, *Deutschland und Polen—Beiträge zu ihren geschichtlichen Beziehungen* (Germany and Poland—Contributions regarding their Historical Relations), Rothfels' chapter, "Das Problem des Nationalismus im Osten" (The Problem of Nationalism in the East), explored the threat of nationalism in Eastern Europe given Germany's geographical position and borders. In the chapter, he noted that only a new reorganization, which could come about at a certain level of cultural achievement, could preserve the eastern space from the chaos that lurked within it.[132] Additionally, like the settlement planners later involved in the resettlement of ethnic German, the *Ostforschung* works also referenced the *Aufbau* of Eastern Europe. In the opening foreword of the fourth volume of *Raumforschung und Raumordnung* (Spatial Research and Spatial Planning) in 1940, the *Oberpräsident* of the province of Saxony, Curt von Ulrich, noted "the new integrated territories of the East must be reconstructed in terms of population, economic and cultural aspects."[133]

Although the African colonies had not been German to begin with (as is the nature of colonialism) and there was not an established historical migration or intracultural relationship between Germany and the territories, like in Poland for example, the authors of colonial literature during the Nazi regime still firmly portrayed the land as being inherently German and thus promoted romanticized irredentist claims on the territory. It appears the overall concept of prior German cultural or developmental efforts in the African territories elucidated through propaganda within literature and speeches ultimately contributed to the irredentist theories. The idea that the African colonies were legally obtained by Germany seemed to also intensify the desire for reclamation. Epp alluded to this fact in his speech on December 6, 1937, when he noted the colonies were "acquired by legal and peaceful means" and "with German thoroughness," they created the premises for development.[134] Similarly, several publications referred to the idea that the colonies had been stolen or robbed from Germany. For example, in the book *Wann kommen die deutschen endlich wieder?* the author stated one of her reasons for going to Africa was that she wanted to "see our stolen colonies."[135] The seventh issue in the booklet series *Deutsches Ringen um die kolonialen Raum* (German Struggle for Colonial Space) named "Der Kampf gegen die koloniale Schuldlüge" (The fight against the Colonial Guilt Lie) featured a foreword by the author Ernst Gerhard Jacob, which also referred to "the outrageous robbery of our colonial possessions."[136] The booklet stated it was avoiding the term "former German colonies" and instead would only refer to them as "German colonies" because Germany was "the rightful owner."[137]

Publications such as *Unvergessenes deutsches Land* (Unforgotten German Land) also promoted the image that the former colonies in Africa had remained intrinsically German. The book's opening line poetically described that "far in the South, in the dark continent and further over the unending expanses of ocean water, lies a German land."[138] The book featured numerous ethnographic pictures of indigenous Africans, farming activities, and houses, alongside pictures of German schoolchildren, German-style houses, administrative buildings, and infrastructure. The back cover featured a picture of a vast, rocky mountain, a sprawling field, and, in the foreground, a wooden cross, and gravestone. The grave is that of Reiter Richard Kramars who, according to the gravestone, was born in 1869 in Zabelkau (present-day Zabełków, Poland) and died in January 1894.[139] This final picture of the book seems to poignantly hint at the idea that Germans were deeply connected with Africa, not only in life but also in death.

Comparably, the *Ostforschung* academics also used historical German settlement, albeit much older than the *Kaiserreich*'s settlement, to fortify romanticized irredentist claims on Polish territory. In a speech to the German occupation forces in Kraków on the occasion of the opening of the new *Institut für deutsche Ostarbeit* (Institute for German Labor), Aubin illustrated how Germans had culturally shaped the Eastern European population since medieval times. He described a historical timeline of "upholders of German *Geist* in the East" such as Christian priests, Reformation preachers, and teachers of natural sciences. Mühle suggests that the members of the occupation forces in Kraków listening to this speech could have easily perceived themselves as a contemporary addition to this historical list.[140] Often the historical analysis heavily promoted Germany's cultural or civilizing influence on Eastern Europe and it coupled this with irredentist claims. Brackman noted that no other nation had come into as close contact with Poland as the Germans had and highlighted there was still evidence of this closeness. For example, Brackmann described, if one was to go through Warsaw and Kraków, Warsaw's Old Town appeared to be like a medieval German city such as Augsburg or Nuremberg with its winding streets, ancient market square, and tall houses that reminded one of their German builders.[141] The book continually stressed that the German people were the only culture bringers (*Kulturträger*) in the East and they both protected Western culture and introduced it into uncultured countries.

Heinrich Felix Schmid contributed a chapter titled "Das Deutsche Recht in Polen" (German Law in Poland) to the book *Deutschland und Polen*. He pointed out that the German medieval settlers brought their culture with them to Poland and these "German cultural values" impacted both Polish rural and urban life. Schmid described how Germans contributed to the construction of farms, field divisions, and food cultivation. In the towns, the city walls, houses, churches, schools, and market squares were strongly influenced by the Germans. Schmid also argues that the Polish language was shaped by German and "still today it contains in its vocabulary a vital picture of its power and richness."[142]

In another publication, Aubin stated this German colonization of the East during the Middle Ages could be recognized as one of the greatest achievements of the Germans. He explained that one could consider the national event as having doubled the *Lebensraum* of the German people or take it into account as a cultural event that had increased the German population, brought areas of Eastern Europe closer to Western culture, and, at the same time, elevated these areas to a much higher level.[143] Likewise, in the foreword of the published collection of *Ostforschung* essays, *Der Deutsche Osten*, the editors noted that "many of the greatest and lasting achievements which the German people have in their history are closely connected with the German East" and German life in the Middle Ages "found its most meaningful expression in the colonization of the German East."[144]

By continually mentioning the German historical achievements and linking them to feats of settlement and expansion, the *Ostforscher* simultaneously encouraged recognition of German influence in Eastern Europe and justified a repetition of these achievements. In a way that revealed not only colonial but also irredentist goals, this historical research of German settlement was also a way of legitimizing German involvement in the East. In a letter to the publishing house *Volk und Reich*, Aubin stated that the German colonization was a great cultural achievement in Europe and was the first legal title on which the claims on the German East were based. He stipulated this achievement should be fully elaborated (presumably in the planned publication he was discussing in the letter) as it must become common knowledge to the German people.[145]

The rhetoric and ideology of the *Afrikabücher* and the colonial enthusiasts may not have been consciously used by leading Nazi figures or policymakers as it related to Africa, which, after the outbreak of the Second World War, was labelled as German colonial territory of the past and not suitable for mass settlement. However, elements of *Ostforschung* were used in varying capacities by institutions during the invasion and occupation of Poland.[146] Comparable to the colonial enthusiasts who idealized the *Kaiserreich* and the German colonies in Africa, the *Ostforschung* research romanticized German involvement in Eastern Europe and used this as proof of Germany's destiny there. While *Ostforschung* academics conceived of Eastern Europe as the area most suitable for this great "German task" and the subject of irredentist romanticism due to Germany's historical involvement there, the German colonial enthusiasts perceived the former German African colonies in the same way. Both the *Ostforschung* academics and the colonial enthusiasts formed irredentist territorial claims that were based not only on previous German ownership of the territory but also glorified previous German contributions to the population, culture, and infrastructure of the territories.

Although the colonial enthusiasts did not have the power of numerous state-supported academic research institutions behind them, they also saw the solution to Germany's population problems as being the reclamation of former German territory through settlement. The perception of Poland as primitive and uncultured, as discussed by the *Ostforschung* academics, was verified by German soldiers and Nazi institutions involved in the initial expansion of German rule into Poland. Hence, the *Ostforschung* academics, who were already researching the apparent benefits of colonial expansion, settlement, culture bringing, and German rule in Poland and Eastern Europe, were then further called upon to provide expert advice on the racial policies in the new *Reichsgaue*.[147]

Conclusion

In practical terms, the reality of Eastern European space and settlement ultimately surpassed the fantasy of regaining African colonies. Once the Germans invaded Poland in 1939, the tradition of colonial involvement in Africa existed in competition with the tradition of German fantasies regarding the *Drang nach Osten* (Push/Drive toward the East). The quick conquest and occupation of Poland, the progress of the war in Eastern Europe, and the prior decision that the overseas colonies would not be suitable for mass settlement meant the colonial enthusiasts would be condemned to fight a losing battle and ultimately, they were unable to realize their plans. Despite this, the official Nazi colonial organizations operated until 1943 and were not disbanded until the war necessitated it. Colonial enthusiasts continued their planning from the loss of the colonies in 1919, through the interwar years and into the Third Reich. Africa remained an important location for the projection of not only spatial and economic fantasies but also fantasies related to "civilizing" the native populations of the continent.[148] Although the overseas colonial tradition had been surpassed and almost replaced by the realization of goals and the future planning for eastern expansion from 1939, it managed to cling to existence and keep the idea of overseas colonial reclamation as a political issue for almost the entire duration of the Third Reich.

Despite the divisions that existed between those who promoted overseas colonialism and those who promoted European expansion, colonial enthusiasts strived to make their goals relevant to Germany's contemporary situation and thus, drew on the practical similarities between German action in Eastern Europe and in Africa. While Epp recommended the East as an apt training opportunity for future colonialists, the *Koloniale Frauenschule* began to engage with such opportunities. By recognizing the parallels between colonial training and supposed developmental and settlement missions in Africa and the German efforts in Eastern Europe, the colonial enthusiasts demonstrated the manipulability of colonial preparation and its application in real-life scenarios.

Similarly, the discursive overlaps that existed between literature that discussed German expansion in Africa and that which discussed German expansion in Eastern Europe demonstrated elements of comparability between the two mindsets. The *Ostforschung* academics did not bridge a continuity or knowledge gap from Nazi spatial goals in Africa and spatial goals in Eastern Europe as, from the beginning, their research specifically promoted Eastern Europe as the ideal space for German settlement and not the former African colonies. Nonetheless, the similarity of the theories produced by the *Ostforschung* academics to that of the colonial enthusiasts, and vice versa, is significant. Much of the *Ostforschung*s research would ultimately contribute toward the "science" that informed and supported policies regarding the racial classification and resettlement of ethnic Germans and the racial classification of Jews and Poles.

A clear difference between the colonial enthusiasts and the *Ostforschung* academics was that the academics were largely successful in using their positions as professionals and experts in the subjects of history, economics, geography, and population demographics to legitimize their points. As members of the newly significant Eastern Europe-orientated field, their opinions and research were trusted to such an extent that *Ostforschung* research concerning geography, population statistics, history, and ethnology was applied in Poland and further east. One reason why *Ostforschung* was such a success was because it was, in a way, a self-fulfilling discipline. The *Ostforschung* academics skillfully described contemporary problems in Germany while also prescribing solutions. Unlike the goal destination of the colonial enthusiasts, the goal destination of many of the *Ostforschung* academics was invaded, conquered, and occupied by Germany.

As highlighted in this chapter, the discourses related to the reclamation of the African colonies referred exclusively to plans that would not materialize and as such, the discourses never had an impact on actual colonial policy. This variant of discourses relied heavily on an idealized interpretation of the past and hopeful projections into the future. Although they did not manifest into reality, the discourses related to German expansion in Africa and how they coincided with discourses regarding expansion into Poland and further East can still be useful within the context of the debate on the potential similarities between colonialism and the Third Reich's expansion into Poland. Undisputedly, the quoted texts are examples of propaganda that were used in support of a German expansionary mission. The texts, especially those relating to the native population in the former colonies and those relating to ethnic German resettlers, largely utilized humanitarian principles to hide national and individual interests or gain. Nevertheless, this was a common tactic by colonial powers and thus aligns with traditional patterns of colonial rhetoric.

The overlaps between the two groups of discourses can be identified within the context of the justifications for the Nazi resettlement of ethnic Germans in Poland. By using elements from the resettlement of ethnic Germans as an example, the exact location of discourses related to German expansion in Africa within the Third Reich can be identified. The Nazi regime placed overseas colonialism at a lower priority than eastern expansion; however, it is apparent that both groups of discourses were based on proposing parallel solutions to parallel problems. Although the groups can be understood as developing separately (albeit simultaneously), the areas of the two groups' overlaps can be seen in the Third Reich through their rhetorical and occasionally practical expression during the resettlement of ethnic Germans in Poland. Hence, it can be argued that links did not exist *from* the *Kaiserreich*'s expansion in Africa to Nazi Germany's expansion into Poland. Rather, the links existed *between* the two groups of discourses during the Third Reich. Additionally, the discourse related to Poland and Eastern Europe can be understood as relying on easily identifiable universal discourses, which could be applied to both overseas and continental colonialism. These colonial discourses of conquest, expansion, settlement, and developmental missions, alongside the policies of inclusion and exclusion, were not a German or Nazi peculiarity but a standard part of European colonialism.

Conclusion

In 1942, the authors of the Polish Research Centre's pamphlet on the German policies in Poland already called out the complications of inclusion and exclusion for ruling territory. They noted that "Himmler's policy of transfer of population and Germanisation simply produces chaos. It creates nothing. It lays bare the gulf existing between people of the same race, breeds hatred and destroys European culture in Polish territories."[1] The integration of the *Reichsgaue* Wartheland and Danzig-West Prussia and the population groups who lived or resettled there into Germany and German society, alongside the disintegration of Poland, its society, language, culture, and people, were not straightforward processes. Ultimately, Nazi Germany's attempt at destroying Poland and making the *Reichsgaue* and their populations German failed given the German defeat in 1945. Even if Nazi Germany had somehow won the Second World War, the exact outlook for Poland and the various population groups is unclear. Perhaps Nazi Germany would have succeeded in annihilating all Polish Jews; however, how would the German societal structures have looked ten, fifty, or one hundred years into the future? The GPO planned the complete Germanization of the territory and the population after the war, but as historical cases from colonized territories have shown, a completely racially or ethnically homogenous society was most probably unachievable. Academic and non-academic discussions on Nazi Germany and its expansion often assume that society during the Third Reich functioned strictly along the lines of the racial state in accordance with National Socialist ideology and fantasies of racial order.[2] Conversely, as this book shows in relation to Nazi population policies in annexed Poland, the realities of attempting to reorder a multiethnic society were extremely complex, and it was the attempts to instill racial hierarchies that often amplified differences as opposed to wiping them out. As Frederick Cooper has pointed out regarding empires, they were constantly faced with the challenges of inclusion and exclusion: empires "reproduced rather than absorbed cultural distinction."[3] Nazi Germany was no different. Although it is not seen by historians as an official empire, as Cooper notes, it was a "would be empire."[4] This book has demonstrated that, if it had the time to establish itself as an imperial power, Nazi Germany would not have faced any fewer challenges than other empires when it came to ruling societies that were naturally heterogeneous by applying artificial segregating criteria aimed at ethnic homogeneity.

This book has explored the annexation of Poland and Nazi Germany's attempts to transform society and territory from the viewpoint of colonialism and its inherent complexities. There was no direct, solely German continuity from the *Kaiserreich* to the Third Reich in terms of practical methods or individuals, which made Nazi Germany's expansion and rule in Poland colonial. Similarly, Nazi ideologists, planners, or policymakers were not necessarily consciously sifting through ideas and drawing on policies and methods from a global "colonial archive."[5] The Nazi form of rule in Poland resembled wider colonial situations because universal colonial patterns of domination such as settlement, assimilation, separation, and violence were fundamental parts of Nazi Germany's arsenal for achieving its expansionary, inclusionary, and exclusionary goals. Nevertheless, the prehistory of Nazi Germany was important because it was during the *Kaiserreich* when Germany, with both the political and public spheres, first experienced owning an empire and ruling overseas colonies. The First World War resulted in what was seen as a devastating loss of territory for the German people; for a nation that had already displayed an obsession with space as a means of securing the future of the population, such a loss was particularly harsh. The continuation of colonial culture and memories and the obsession with gaining and reclaiming territory was preserved in the interwar period and thus, fed into the National Socialist war aims. Similarly, the long-standing promotion of Poland as the most suitable territory for future expansion and ideology regarding the primitiveness of Germany's neighbors, coupled with thousands of ethnic Germans "stranded" there meant the National Socialists' expansionist gaze could first be cast just over the border.

Despite Nazi Germany's expansion to the east, as this book has shown, German colonial enthusiasts did take their task of planning the reclamation of former German colonies in Africa seriously. Overseas colonialism in the Third Reich was mostly obscured by the immediacy of war aims in Eastern Europe; however, unlike what much of the secondary literature on comparisons between colonialism and Nazi Germany's eastern expansion seems to assume, Nazi Germany's fantasy of overseas colonialism did not disappear. This book has utilized an investigation of the discourses related to overseas colonialism and has highlighted that colonial enthusiasts attempted to address the same problems as the *Ostforschung* academics, albeit with different geographical solutions. The two groups were fundamentally separate, but they operated under similar expansionist and irredentist fantasies. By using the later resettlement of ethnic Germans as a context to investigate texts produced by the colonialists and the *Ostforschung* academics, the exact location of discursive overlaps between the two groups can be identified. In addition to showing the similarity between traditional colonial expansion and the planned eastern, continental expansion, the analysis of texts by both groups highlights rhetoric and justifications used within easily identifiable standard colonial discourses. As such, this book shows, regardless of its future location, Nazi Germany's expansion was often rhetorically translated into the legitimizing language of European colonial expansion and rule of foreign territories.

The focus of the comparative debate on Nazi Germany and colonialism has largely revolved around the issue of the Holocaust and violence. Historians have argued that Nazi Germany's lack of humanitarian pretenses or a developmental mission constitutes a break from traditional colonial conquests, which often were justified by the notion of civilizing missions. Conversely, by using an investigation of inclusionary policies, which has rarely been examined within the comparative debate, this book has demonstrated Germans did utilize a self-conceived developmental mission toward ethnic Germans and the transformation of the Polish territory to justify their actions in the *Reichsgaue*. Like in colonial contexts, however, Nazi Germany's fantasy of humanitarian interventions for ethnic Germans in Poland was entirely self-serving. The main goal was racial and cultural assimilation. This mission linked heavily with the notion of a particular "German task" in the East, a task that supposedly had both historical roots and a massive significance for the future. Additionally, this book has explored how women were particularly important to the German work in the East and their gendered work was assigned a specific significance. As teachers, nurses, and settlement advisors, they infiltrated the public and private lives of the ethnic Germans to help transform them into suitable Germans and blurred the boundaries between politics, ideology, and the domestic sphere.

The self-conceived developmental mission and the significant involvement of women in carrying it out were parallel to many colonial contexts. Although the Germans did not aim to help the majority of the Polish population, this book has demonstrated that through the interactions with ethnic German resettlers, societal divides, and paternalistic attitudes common to colonizer versus colonized situations did develop in annexed Poland. Additionally, by viewing the resettlement and Germanization of ethnic Germans through a colonial lens, this study has highlighted a fact often overlooked in secondary literature. Despite what Nazi ethnic "experts" claimed, ethnic Germans who had been born and were living in Poland before the outbreak of the war were officially part of the Polish population since they had not been born within the borders of Germany. Although German propaganda attempted to frame them as ethnically or culturally German, this was not always the case, and many ethnic Germans, particularly those born in Poland, were native to the territory. As such, comparisons between ethnic Germans living and working in Poland and examples of colonized populations are not illogical. Such comparisons further highlight the complex position of the ethnic Germans while also demonstrating that their treatment and the attempts to assimilate them were not unique to Nazi Germany. Rather, such inclusionary policies and the resulting complexities reflect colonial models.

As this book has highlighted, Nazi Germany relied on assimilating people into German society, as much as it relied on excluding people. Akin to certain colonial cases, criteria for being recognized as German did not always center on racial descent. Rather, German authorities also factored culture, language, and political loyalty into many assessments.[6] Ethnic Germans, both the resettlers and Polish ethnic Germans, and certain Poles and foreigners were permitted to assimilate into Nazi Germany provided they met the criteria. This process was not easy, and both individuals and German authorities were faced with many difficulties that stemmed from the ordering of society along racial lines, in other words, along the basis of superior versus inferior. Similar to colonial assimilation, the divisions that occupying powers attempted to enforce could act as unifying to one particular group while working in contradiction to the unity of society as a whole. Inclusion, and assimilation, aimed to remove or limit differences, but by pursuing a policy of inclusion within a society run along the dividing lines of racial ideology, differences were further exacerbated.

In addition to inclusionary policies, the Nazi regime in Poland also employed a range of exclusionary policies to create and manage societal hierarchies. To do so, German authorities used methods such as the legal subjugation, segregation, and removal of Jewish and non-Jewish Poles. As the increasing need to provide a decisive exclusionary solution in the *Reichsgaue* intensified, the systematic murder of Jewish Poles, and Sinti and Roma began at Chełmno. Undoubtedly, the case of Nazi Germany's exclusion from Poland was, in its entirety, a particular example of the extreme racial reordering of society. However, it was just that—one particular example out of many historical cases of radical exclusion. As this book has highlighted, the methods used to achieve the exclusion were similar to colonial situations where occupying powers also aimed for a transformation of the population. Additionally, such transformations were, as was the case in annexed Poland, riddled with problems and contradictions.

The use of particular killing methods, such as gas vans and gas chambers, in extermination sites such as Chełmno and Auschwitz have, to an extent, shaped perceptions of the Holocaust's uniqueness given the industrial-style nature of the murder. However, as this book and other historians have pointed out, many Jews were victims of face-to-face killing and half of all Jews who died during the war did not die in gas chambers.[7] As such, many killing methods used against the Jews, and other population groups in annexed Poland, were the same as those used to kill indigenous populations in colonial contexts. Similarly, the invention of new murder methods specifically for use against a particular population group was not specific to the Holocaust, it was also a tactic in colonial warfare.[8] The ultimate removal of population groups by murdering them with direct methods, like shooting, and indirect methods characterized by an apathetic approach to the victims, such as through starvation, were crucial parts of Nazi Germany's rule. Direct and indirect murder methods, with the goal of permanent removal, were also present in cases of settler colonial rule. Unlike other forms of colonialism, settler colonialism did not rely on indigenous populations for labor. It functioned by removing the supposed threat to settler society by deportation, assimilation, or murder. By applying examples of Lorenzo Veracini's settler colonial removal strategies to Nazi Germany's population reordering in annexed Poland, this book has shown that akin to the settler colonial model, Nazi Germany utilized inclusion and exclusion in an attempt to efface difference.[9] In a somewhat contradictory way, in both settler colonial cases and the case of Nazi Germany, the occupier first identified and created difference based on supposed racial categories and the criteria of belonging to ultimately allow or legitimize the later removal of those categorized as different.

Although the exclusionary methods that facilitated and contributed to the Holocaust were similar to colonial and settler colonial exclusionary methods, the Holocaust was not "just" a colonial genocide.[10] Nazi Germany aimed at the annihilation of all Jews, both inside and outside German borders; they did not limit the target group of their extermination to the conquered foreign territory as was the case in settler colonialism. However, as this book has shown, the Holocaust can still be integrated into patterns of colonial and settler colonial rule and violence based on the comparable ways in which

Nazi Germany expanded its territory, ruled, settled, and transformed Poland and included and excluded the native Polish population. Akin to colonial contexts, racism was enshrined into laws and society by Nazi Germany and this, in turn, facilitated the settlement, control, and transformation of the annexed territory, just as it facilitated the Holocaust.

Intersecting Third Reich and Colonial Histories

By examining Nazi Germany's inclusion and exclusion, its transformation of Polish territory and its legitimization of the German presence there from a comparative standpoint which utilizes studies and histories of colonialism, scholars can gain a variety of new perspectives for the study of the Third Reich. As I have argued, such a comparative approach highlights Nazi Germany's self-perceived developmental mission in annexed Poland. Far from being devoid of common colonial humanitarian justifications for expansion, Germans used the case of ethnic Germans and their supposed need for guidance to legitimize their work in Poland. Some Germans appeared to genuinely believe in the benefits they were bringing with them, even if this was aimed at ethnic Germans as opposed to the majority of the Polish population. Like colonial contexts, such developmental missions were often propaganda for expansion and destructive policies aimed at the indigenous population; however, it is interesting to see how the propaganda related to Poland, perhaps unintentionally, reflected colonial missions. Additionally, whether intentionally or not, individual Germans perceived and portrayed their actions in ways that aligned with identifiable colonial justifications.

The intersection of the history of the Third Reich and colonial studies demonstrates the extent to which racial categories were a construct that often had little basis, or little success, in reality. I have highlighted how certain difficulties occurred, for example, in the treatment of ethnic German resettlers, the assimilation processes of the DVL, and interactions between Germans and Poles. As colonial scholars have shown, life within societies ordered along ethnic or racial hierarchies was not as simple as strict racial categorization and physical division. Hierarchies not only existed between the colonizer and the colonized but also between the colonizers. Social intermixing between members of different groups resulted in the blurring of colonial divides and it was made all the more complex by the inherently artificial nature of the divides to begin with. As Ann Laura Stoler has argued, "colonial regimes were not hegemonic institutions but uneven, imperfect, and even indifferent knowledge-acquiring machines." As previously quoted in Chapter 4 of this book, Stoler goes on to note how these regimes were "taxonomic states" and their "administrations were charged with defining and interpreting racial membership, requirements for citizenship, acts of political subversion, and, not least, determining what intimate practices and what sorts of persons confirmed or threatened European notions of morality."[11] If we apply this to Nazi Germany, especially within annexed Poland, it can be considered just as taxonomic and thus facing similar challenges as colonial states. As such, studies of colonial societal hierarchies bring new perspectives to the analysis of Nazi Germany's obsession and struggle with classifying human beings.

The Holocaust was not a colonial genocide as, at its core; Nazi Germany's anti-Semitism saw all European Jews, not just German or Polish ones, as a threat. However, as this book's comparative investigation has demonstrated, Nazi Germany's identification and creation of a pseudoscientific racial category, being Jewish, which linked with the claim of superiority versus supposed inferiority was not unique. Such categorization was not unusual in colonial contexts. As white skin was seen as superior to black skin, phenotypes were thus constructed as indications of different "races." However, the artificial nature of such racial categorization is perhaps best seen in examples like those discussed in Chapter 2 and Chapter 4 where, similar to Nazi Germany's treatment of European Jews, skin color was disregarded. For example, the colonization of Ireland and the historical perception of Irish people as being "non-white" whites or in German South West Africa where an individual's skin color did not determine their racial categorization, rather their ancestry did.

Comparisons allow historians to assess which elements are comparable or fit particular patterns and which do not. The identification of a population group's specific collective characteristic, whether national, ethnic, religious, political, or otherwise, the use of that characteristic to distinguish or "other" the group, and the attribution of danger to that characteristic were not unusual processes when compared to colonial and imperial regimes.[12] In Nazi Germany's case, anti-Semitism was not therefore unusual insofar as it was a version of this stereotypical characteristic or threat identification tactic. However, what was specific about anti-Semitism in contrast to colonial or imperial racism, for example, was that for Nazi Germany, Jews were a global threat, not one within a single geographic territory.[13] The borderless nature of anti-Semitism thus meant Nazi Germany could also justify violence against its own Jewish citizens. Comparative analysis allows us to both highlight these particularities while also demonstrating that anti-Semitism was specific in so far as it was a particular facet of Nazi genocide, but it was in itself not unique or incomparable in that other genocides also had specific driving forces that they did not share with others.

Concluding Remarks

As detailed above, approaching different elements of the Nazi regime from other scholarly perspectives can be beneficial for deepening the analysis of Nazi Germany's expansion, rule, population management, and violence. Integrating the history of Nazi Germany and the Holocaust into wider analytical frameworks can also benefit how scholars and the public approach colonialism and imperialism in today's world. The Holocaust and Nazi Germany have been thoroughly explored in Germany and Europe, both inside and outside the academic sphere. Germany's Nazi past forms the subject basis of numerous exhibitions, museums, documentaries, public discussions, books, memorials, university courses, and school classes. The open, public memorialization of the Holocaust and the engagement with the history of the Third Reich and its crimes, particularly in Germany, show that nations can recognize and teach the dark episodes of their history. They can recognize where political systems went wrong, where a state can turn on itself, turn against its own citizens or turn outwards against others. Just as the Nazi crimes are critically engaged with, so too can the aspects of Europe's colonial past. The skills for critical historical assessment are present in the public and political spheres; it is now time to begin to apply them to a wider range of historical topics.

This is not to say one topic should be treated as a higher priority than the other or by linking the Holocaust and colonial violence that colonial crimes may seem more significant. Rather, I argue that an integrative approach will allow for a more comprehensive understanding of how states and societies were formed through acquisition or loss, subjugation or resistance, and perpetrating violence or falling victim to it. National histories, which still impact national identities, collective memories, political systems, and societies today, have been shaped by historical experiences of being the occupier or the occupied, or occasionally by being both.[14] As Michael Rothberg argues, memory is not a zero-sum game; consequently, national histories can borrow and intertwine with one another and can reflect on the patterns inherent to taking land, livelihoods, and freedom away from others.[15] This book and other works by historians who embrace an integrative approach do not aim to promote less of a Holocaust focus within the academic or public sphere. Instead, they contribute to highlighting the need for a nuanced treatment of national histories that incorporates specificities, as well as the recognition of the broader European phenomenon of violence.

Within this book, I have shown how analyzing comparisons between colonialism and arguably the definitional point of the Nazi regime, the Holocaust, does not have to directly focus on it. Comparative analysis can be applied to a wide range of topics that historians already explore in studies of Nazi Germany. For example, subjects such as resistance and collaboration, childhood experiences, perpetrator motivations, photography, the role of the state or the military, and institutional, religious, and societal complicity can all be approached from a nuanced comparative perspective which recognizes specificity but also mutual elements. As Charles Marlow, the main character in Joseph Conrad's *Heart of Darkness*, said "the conquest of the earth ... is not a pretty thing when you look into it too much."[16] This sentiment can be applied to colonialism and imperialism but equally to Nazi Germany. Comparing these conquests, acknowledging the patterns and the particulars, and investigating the aims and the complexities are key factors for understanding expansion, domination, and violence, both inside and outside of Europe.

Notes

Introduction

1. Polish Research Centre London, ed., *German Failures in Poland: Natural Obstacles to Nazi Population Policy* (London: Cornwall Press, 1942), 6. The Polish Research Centre was an agency of the Polish Government-in-Exile in London.
2. Ibid., 11.
3. Ibid.
4. Ibid., 12, 23.
5. Ibid., 14.
6. Raphael Lemkin, *Axis Rule in Occupied Europe: Laws of Occupation, Analysis of Government, Proposals for Redress* (Clark: Lawbook Exchange, 2008), 79.
7. See, for example, A. Dirk Moses, "Raphael Lemkin, Culture, and the Concept of Genocide," in *The Oxford Handbook of Genocide Studies*, ed. Donald Bloxham and A. Dirk Moses (Oxford: Oxford University Press, 2010), 19–41.
8. Aimé Césaire, *Discours sur le colonialisme* (Paris: Présence Africaine, 1955), 13. This echoed a similar argument made by W. E. B. Du Bois. See, W. E. B. Du Bois, *The World and Africa: An Inquiry into the Part Which Africa Has Played in World History* (New York: Viking, 1947), 15.
9. Hannah Arendt, *The Origins of Totalitarianism*, 4th ed. (New York: Harcourt, 1973). See also Jean-Paul Sarte, "Preface," in Frantz Fanon, *The Wretched of the Earth*, trans. Constance Farrington (New York: Grove Press, 1963). The book was originally published in French as *Les Damnés de la terre* (Paris: François Maspero, 1961).
10. For a further study on the fantasy of Nazism, and the attempts to create a "utopia," see Christian Ingrao, *The Promise of The East: Nazi Hopes and Genocide, 1939–43*, trans. Andrew Brown (Cambridge: Polity Press, 2019).
11. For in-depth studies on aspects of the resettlement see, Stephan Döring, *Die Umsiedlung der Wolhyniendeutschen in den Jahren 1939 bis 1940* (Frankfurt am Main: Peter Lang, 2001); Markus Leniger, *Nationalsozialistische "Volkstumsarbeit" und Umsiedlungspolitik 1933–1945: Von der Minderheitenbetreuung zur Siedlerauslese* (Berlin: Frank & Timme, 2006).
12. On the topic of the institutions that supported the resettlement, see for example, Robert L. Koehl, *RKFDV: German Resettlement and Population Policy, 1939–1945: A History of the Reich Commission for the Strengthening of Germandom* (Cambridge, MA: Harvard University Press, 1957); Valdis O. Lumans, *Himmler's Auxiliaries: The Volksdeutsche Mittelstelle and the German National Minorities of Europe, 1933–1945* (Chapel Hill: University of North Carolina Press, 1993).
13. Elizabeth Harvey, *Women and the Nazi East: Agents and Witnesses of Germanization* (New Haven: Yale University Press, 2003).
14. Andreas Strippel, *NS-Volkstumspolitik und die Neuordnung Europas: rassenpolitische Selektion der Einwandererzentralstelle des Chefs der Sicherheitspolizei und des SD 1939–1945* (Paderborn: Ferdinand Schöningh, 2011); see also, Michael G. Esch,

"Gesunde Verhältnisse." Deutsche und polnische Bevölkerungspolitik in Ostmitteleuropa 1939–1950 (Marburg: Verlag Herder-Institut, 1998).
15. Isabel Heinemann, Rasse, Siedlung, deutsches Blut: Das Rasse- und Siedlungshauptamt der SS und die rassenpolitische Neuordnung Europas (Göttingen: Wallstein Verlag, 2003).
16. Gerhard Wolf, Ideologie und Herrschaftsrationalität: Nationalsozialistische Germanisierungspolitik in Polen (Hamburg: Hamburger Edition, 2012), 467.
17. An exception to this would be Bradley J. Nichols's PhD thesis; however, he focuses on the Wiedereindeutschungsverfahren (WED) and not on ethnic Germans as this study will do. See Bradley J. Nichols, "The Hunt for Lost Blood: Nazi Germanization Policy in Occupied Europe" (PhD Diss., University of Tennessee, 2016).
18. For more on "civilizing missions," see, for example, Boris Barth and Jürgen Osterhammel (eds.), Zivilisierungsmissionen. Imperiale Weltverbesserung seit dem 18. Jahrhundert (Konstanz: UVK Verlagsgesellschaft, 2005).
19. See Diemut Majer's comprehensive study on the judicial treatment of non-Germans in the annexed Poland, Diemut Majer, Fremdvölkische im Dritten Reich. Ein Beitrag zur nationalsozialistischen Rechtssetzung und Rechtspraxis in Verwaltung und Justiz unter besonderer Berücksichtigung der eingegliederten Ostgebiete und des Generalgouvernements (Munich: Oldenbourg, 1993).
20. For studies on the perpetration of violence and murder against the Jews, see, for example, Michael Alberti, Die Verfolgung und Vernichtung der Juden im Reichsgau Wartheland 1939–1945 (Wiesbaden: Harrassowitz Verlag, 2006); Ingo Loose, "Wartheland," in The Greater German Reich and the Jews: Nazi Persecution Policies in the Annexed Territories, 1939–1945, ed. Wolf Gruner and Jörg Osterloh, trans. Bernard Heise (New York: Berghahn Books, 2015), 189–218; for a comprehensive primary source collection on the annexed territories, see, Ingo Loose et al., eds., Die Verfolgung und Ermordung der europäischen Juden durch das nationalsozialistische Deutschland, 1933–1945: Band 10, Polen: Eingegliederte Gebiete August 1941–1945 (Berlin: De Gruyter, 2020).
21. Jürgen Zimmerer, "The First Genocide of the Twentieth Century: The German War of Destruction in South West Africa (1904–1908) and the Global History of Genocide," in Lessons and Legacies VIII: From Generation to Generation, ed. Doris L. Bergen (Evanston: Northwestern University Press, 2008), 36, 56. Most of Zimmerer's articles have been compiled in the book Jürgen Zimmerer, Von Windhuk nach Auschwitz? Beiträge zum Verhältnis von Kolonialismus und Holocaust (Münster: LIT, 2011). For an earlier argument, see Helmut Bley, Kolonialherrschaft und Sozialstruktur in Deutsch-Südwestafrika 1894–1914 (Hamburg: Leibniz Verlag, 1968). Benjamin Madley has also argued for the thesis of direct continuity or the influence of the Kaiserreich. See, Benjamin Madley, "From Africa to Auschwitz: How German South West Africa Incubated Ideas and Methods Adopted and Developed by the Nazis in Eastern Europe," European History Quarterly 35, no. 3 (2005): 429–62.
22. For example, see the chapter Zimmerer, "Holocaust und Kolonialismus: Beitrag zu einer Archäologie des genozidalen Gedankens," in Von Windhuk nach Auschwitz?, 170.
23. For criticisms of the continuity thesis see, for example, Birthe Kundrus, "From the Herero to the Holocaust? Some Remarks on the Current Debate," Africa Spectrum, 40 (2005): 299–308; Sybille Steinbacher, "Sonderweg, Kolonialismus, Genozide: Der Holocaust im Spannungsfeld von Kontinuitäten und Diskontinuitäten der deutschen Geschichte," in Der Holocaust: Ergebnisse und neue Fragen der Forschung, ed. Frank

Bajohr and Andrea Löw (Frankfurt am Main: S. Fischer Verlag Gmbh, 2015), 83–101; Robert Gerwarth and Stephan Malinowski, "Hannah Arendt's Ghosts: Reflections on the Disputable Path from Windhoek to Auschwitz," *Central European History* 42, no. 2 (2009): 279–300.
24. Dirk van Laak, *Imperiale Infrastruktur: Deutsche Planungen für die Erschließung Afrikas 1880–1960* (Paderborn: Ferdinand Schöningh Verlag, 2004).
25. Susanne Zantop, *Colonial Fantasies: Conquest, Family, and Nation in Precolonial Germany, 1770–1870* (Durham: Duke University Press, 1997).
26. Birthe Kundrus, ed., *Phantasiereiche: Zur Kulturgeschichte des deutschen Kolonialismus* (Frankfurt am Main: Campus Verlag, 2003).
27. See, for example, Sebastian Conrad, *Globalisation and the Nation in Imperial Germany*, trans. Sorcha O'Hagan (Cambridge: Cambridge University Press, 2010); Matthew P. Fitzpatrick, *Purging the Empire: Mass Expulsions in Germany, 1871–1914* (Oxford: Oxford University Press, 2015).
28. Christoph Kienemann, *Der koloniale Blick gen Osten: Osteuropa im Diskurs des Deutschen Kaiserreiches von 1871* (Paderborn: Ferdinand Schöningh 2018).
29. Michael Burleigh, *Germany Turns Eastwards: A Study of Ostforschung in the Third Reich* (London: Pan Macmillan, 2002).
30. Ingo Haar, *Historiker im Nationalsozialismus: Deutsche Geschichtswissenschaft und der 'Volkstumskampf' im Osten* (Göttingen: Vandenhoeck und Ruprecht, 2000); Götz Aly and Susanne Heim, *Architects of Annihilation: Auschwitz and the Logic of Destruction*, trans. Allan Blunden (London: Phoenix, 2003). See also Haar's and other contributions to *German Scholars and Ethnic Cleansing, 1920–1945*, ed. Ingo Haar and Michael Fahlbusch (New York: Berghahn Books, 2005).
31. Klaus Hildebrand's book on colonial politics in the Third Reich is an exception. Klaus Hildebrand, *Vom Reich zum Weltreich. Hitler, NSDAP und koloniale Frage 1919–1945* (Munich: W. Fink, 1969).
32. Karsten Linne, *Deutschland jenseits des Äquators? Die NS-Kolonialplanungen für Afrika* (Berlin: Ch. Links Verlag, 2008).
33. Willeke Sandler, *Empire in the Heimat: Colonialism and Public Culture in the Third Reich* (New York: Oxford University Press, 2018).
34. On the origins of the theory of "uniqueness," see publications such as Gavriel D. Rosenfeld, "The Politics of Uniqueness: Reflections on the Recent Polemical Turn in Holocaust and Genocide Scholarship," *Holocaust and Genocide Studies* 13, no. 1 (Spring 1999): 28–61 and Andrea Löw, "Ein Verbrechen, dessen Grauen mit nichts zu vergleichen ist: Die Ursprünge der Debatte über die Singularität des Holocaust," in *Holocaust und Völkermorde: Die Reichweite des Vergleichs*, ed. Sybille Steinbacher (Frankfurt am Main: Campus, 2012), 125–43.
35. The *Historikerstreit* began in 1986 and largely played out in German mainstream media. Scholars such as Ernst Nolte and Jürgen Habermas argued about topics such as whether the Holocaust could be considered as uniquely evil and if Germany followed a special path (*Sonderweg*) to the Holocaust. See, for example, Ernst Nolte, "Vergangenheit, die nicht vergehen will. Eine Rede, die geschrieben, aber nicht gehalten werden konnte," *Frankfurter Allgemeine Zeitung*, June 6, 1986.
36. On the status of the debate some years ago, see Thomas Kühne, "Colonialism and the Holocaust: Continuities, Causations, and Complexities," *Journal of Genocide Research* 15, no. 3 (2013): 339–62; Matthew Fitzpatrick, "The Pre-History of the Holocaust? The Sonderweg and Historikerstreit Debates and the Abject Colonial Past," *Central European History* 41, no. 3 (2008): 477–503.

37. A. Dirk Moses, "The Holocaust and Genocide," in *The Historiography of the Holocaust*, ed. Dan Stone (New York: Palgrave Macmillan, 2004), 548; Donald Bloxham, *The Final Solution: A Genocide* (Oxford: Oxford University Press, 2009), 1. For further discussion, see also Moses, "Conceptual blockages and definitional dilemmas in the 'racial century': Genocides of indigenous peoples and the Holocaust," *Patterns of Prejudice* 36, no. 4 (2002): 7–36.
38. Dan Stone, *Histories of the Holocaust* (Oxford: Oxford University Press, 2010), 8.
39. Ibid., 243.
40. A. Dirk Moses, *The Problems of Genocide: Permanent Security and the Language of Transgression* (Cambridge: Cambridge University Press, 2021); on his earlier argument on the Holocaust and subaltern genocide, see also A. Dirk Moses, "Empire, Colony, Genocide: Keynotes and the Philosophy of History," in *Empire, Colony, Genocide: Conquest, Occupation, and Subaltern Resistance in World History*, ed. A. Dirk Moses (New York: Berghahn Books, 2008), 3–54.
41. Pascal Grosse, "What does German Colonialism Have to Do with National Socialism? A Conceptual Framework," in *Germany's Colonial Pasts*, ed. Eric Ames, Marcia Klotz and Lora Wildenthal (Lincoln: University of Nebraska Press), 128–9; see also Grosse, *Kolonialismus, Eugenik und bürgerliche Gesellschaft in Deutschland: 1850–1918* (Frankfurt a. M.: Campus, 2000).
42. Mark Mazower, *Hitler's Empire: How the Nazis Ruled Europe* (New York: Penguin Press, 2008), 2.
43. Ibid., 12.
44. Shelley Baranowski, *Nazi Empire: German Colonialism and Imperialism from Bismarck to Hitler* (Cambridge: Cambridge University Press, 2011); Baranowski, "Nazi Colonialism and the Holocaust," *Dapim–Studies on the Holocaust* 27, no. 1 (2013): 59.
45. Roberta Pergher and Mark Roseman, "The Holocaust–An Imperial Genocide?," *Dapim–Studies on the Holocaust* 27, no. 1 (2013): 43, 48.
46. Gerwarth and Malinowski, "Hannah Arendt's Ghosts," 285, 293.
47. Michael Rothberg, *Multidirectional Memory: Remembering the Holocaust in the Age of Decolonization* (Stanford: Stanford University Press, 2009), 3. Emphasis in original.
48. Rebecca Jinks, *Representing Genocide: The Holocaust as Paradigm?* (London: Bloomsbury Academic, 2016).
49. Kitty Millet, *The Victims of Slavery, Colonization and the Holocaust: A Comparative History of Persecution* (London: Bloomsbury Academic, 2017); Edward Kissi, *Africans and the Holocaust: Perceptions and Responses of Colonised and Sovereign Peoples* (London: Routledge, 2020).
50. Roni Mikel-Arieli, *Remembering the Holocaust in a Racial State: Holocaust Memory in South Africa from Apartheid to Democracy (1948–1994)* (Oldenbourg: De Gruyter, 2022).
51. Michelle Gordon and Rachel O'Sullivan, eds., *Colonial Paradigms of Violence: Comparative Analysis of the Holocaust, Genocide, and Mass Killing* (Göttingen: Wallstein Verlag, 2022).
52. The debate began after Mbembe was invited to speak at the Ruhrtriennale. The most notable accusations were made by Felix Klein, the German government anti-Semitism Commissioner. For more on these discussions, see for example, the contributions to the *Journal of Genocide Research* Forum: "The Achille Mbembe Controversy and the German Debate About Antisemitism, Israel, and the Holocaust," *Journal of Genocide Research* 23, no. 3 (2021): 371–435.

53. A. Dirk Moses, "The German Catechism," *Geschichte der Gegenwart*, https://geschichtedergegenwart.ch/the-german-catechism/, accessed August 9, 2021.
54. Saul Friedländer, "Ein fundamentales Verbrechen," *Die Zeit* (July 7, 2021); Götz Aly, "Es gibt nichts, das deckungsgleich mit dem Holocaust wäre," interview with Deutschlandfunk Kultur (July 13, 2021), https://www.deutschlandfunkkultur.de/goetz-aly-es-gibt-nichts-das-deckungsgleich-mit-dem-100.html, accessed October 6, 2022; see also Dan Diner, "Epistemics of the holocaust considering the question of 'why?' And of 'how?,'" *Naharaim—Zeitschrift Für Deutsch-Jüdische Literatur Und Kulturgeschichte* 1, no. 2 (2008): 195–213.
55. Steffen Klävers, *Decolonizing Auschwitz?: Komparativ-postkoloniale Ansätze in Der Holocaustforschung* (Berlin: de Gruyter, 2019), 202. "Redemptive" anti-Semitism refers to Saul Friedländer's thesis. See Saul Friedländer, *Nazi Germany and the Jews: The Years of Persecution, 1933–1939* (New York: HarperCollins, 1997).
56. Frank Bajohr and Rachel O'Sullivan, "Holocaust, Kolonialismus und NS-Imperialismus: Wissenschaftliche Forschung im Schatten einer polemischen Debatte," *Vierteljahrshefte für Zeitgeschichte* 70, no. 1 (2022): 191–202.
57. Michael Wildt, "Was heißt: Singularität des Holocaust?," *Zeithistorische Forschungen/Studies in Contemporary History* 19 (2022): 146.
58. On such criticisms, see, for example, Kühne, "Colonialism and the Holocaust"; Gerwarth and Malinowski, "Hannah Arendt's Ghosts."
59. For more on the importance of the topic of colonial violence as an independant field of study, see Michelle Gordon and Rachel O'Sullivan, "Introduction: Colonial Paradigms of Violence," in *Colonial Paradigms of Violence*, ed. Gordon and O'Sullivan, 18–19.
60. Work by scholars such as Ann Laura Stoler provide innovative new viewpoints on how historians can approach Nazi Germany's societal hierarchies in Poland. See, for example, Ann Laura Stoler, "Rethinking Colonial Categories: European Communities and the Boundaries of Rule," *Comparative Studies in Society and History* 31, no. 1 (1989): 134–61.
61. For example, Wendy Lower focused on Ukraine as a potential imperial territory, while Jadwiga Biskupska has applied the settler colonial model to the Zamość region in the General Government. See Wendy Lower, *Nazi Empire-Building and the Holocaust in Ukraine* (Chapel Hill: University of North Carolina Press, 2007); Jadwiga Biskupska, "Zamość Experiments: SS Settler Colonialism and Violence in Eastern Poland," in *Colonial Paradigms of Violence*, ed. Gordon and O'Sullivan, 161–84.
62. For more discussion on the definition of colonialism, see Jürgen Osterhammel, *Colonialism: A Theoretical Overview* (Princeton: Markus Wiener Publishers, 1997).
63. In contrast, other parts of Poland, such as the General Government, were ruled in ways that were more similar to an imperial administrative system.
64. See, for example, Lorenzo Veracini, *Settler Colonialism: A Theoretical Overview* (London: Palgrave Macmillan, 2010).
65. On the concept of "the East" and *Ostforschung*, see Eduard Mühle, "The Mental Map of German *Ostforschung*," in *Germany and the European East in the Twentieth Century*, ed. Eduard Mühle (Oxford: Berg, 2003), 117; on the mystification of the East see Ingrao, *The Promise of The East*.
66. On the "othering" of Eastern European spaces, particularly in Holocaust Studies, see Aleksandra Szczepan, "Terra Incognita? Othering East-Central Europe in Holocaust Studies," in *Colonial Paradigms of Violence*, ed. Gordon and O'Sullivan, 185–214.

67. See, for example, Doris L. Bergen, "The Nazi Concept of 'Volksdeutsche' and the Exacerbation of Anti-Semitism in Eastern Europe, 1939–45," *Journal of Contemporary History* 29, no. 4 (1994): 569–82.
68. For example, Robert L. Koehl, *RKFDV: German Resettlement and Population Policy, 1939–1945: A History of the Reich Commission for the Strengthening of Germandom* (Cambridge, MA: Harvard University Press, 1957); Lumans, *Himmler's Auxiliaries*. Some more recent publications are currently only available in German, for example, Alexa Stiller, *Völkische Politik: Praktiken der Exklusion und Inklusion in polnischen, französischen und slowenischen Annexionsgebieten 1939–1945* (Göttingen: Wallstein Verlag, Forthcoming 2022); Leniger, *Nationalsozialistische "Volkstumsarbeit" und Umsiedlungspolitik 1933–1945*.
69. An exception to this would be the Elizabeth Harvey's important work. Harvey does allude to colonial civilizing missions and mindsets in relation to the resettlement; however, differing from this book, Harvey refers to colonialism generally and does not use specific examples. See Harvey, *Women and the Nazi East*.
70. Edward. Said, *Orientalism* (London: Routledge & Kegan Paul, 1978), 10.
71. Bill Ashcroft, Gareth Griffiths, and Helen Tiffin, eds. *Post-Colonial Studies: The Key Concepts*, 2nd ed. (London: Routledge, 2000), 37.

1 "A Bigger Germany, It Shall Be!": Germany's Colonial Past in Africa and Poland

The quote in the chapter title is taken from "Besiedlung im Inlande und in den Kolonien. Ein Vorwort zur Kolonialnummer," *Archiv für innere Kolonisation* 4, no. 5 (1912): 147.
1. Bundesarchiv Berlin-Lichterfelde (BArch) R8023/74, 63: Jubiläumstagung zum 50-jährigen Bestehen der Deutschen Kolonialgesellschaft am October 10, 1932 in Berlin. Letter from Bildhauer Möbus to the DKG Abteilung Frankfurt (January 8, 1932).
2. BArch R8023/74, 54. Letter from Ludwig Pieper, Gauverband Niederrhein Westfalen der DKG to the DKG Berlin (May 5, 1932).
3. L. H. Gann and Peter Duignan, *The Rulers of German Africa, 1884–1914* (Stanford: Stanford University Press, 1977), x.
4. Otto von Bismarck, born in the Prussian province of Saxony, was the German chancellor from March 21, 1871 till March 20, 1890.
5. Rohlfs was the first European to cross Africa from Tripoli to Lagos.
6. For example, Gerhard Rohlfs, *Land und Volk in Afrika: Berichte aus den Jahren 1865–1870* (Bremen: J. Kühtmann Verlagshandlung, 1870); Carl Claus von der Decken, *Reisen in Ost-Afrika in den Jahren 1859 bis 1865*, Heft 1 (Leipzig and Heidelberg: Winter'sche Verlagshandlung, 1869).
7. For an overview of the debate on whether Christian missionaries can be considered as predecessors of colonial rule with focus on the German colonies, see Ulrich van der Heyden, "Christian Missionary Societies in the German Colonies, 1884–85–1914/15," in *German Colonialism: Race, the Holocaust and Postwar Germany*, ed. Volker Langbehn and Mohammad Salma (New York: Columbia University Press, 2011), 215–53.
8. Sean Andrew Wempe, *Revenants of the German Empire: Colonial Germans, Imperialism, and the League of Nations* (Oxford: Oxford University Press, 2019), 143.

9. Jeremy Best, "Godly, International, and Independent: German Protestant Missionary Loyalties before World War I," *Central European History* 47, no. 3 (September 2014): 586.
10. Sebastian Conrad, *German Colonialism: A Short Introduction*, trans. Sorcha O'Hagan (Cambridge: Cambridge University Press, 2012), 25.
11. Horst Gründer, *Geschichte der deutschen Kolonien*, 7th ed. (Paderborn: Verlag Ferdinand Schöningh, 2018), 89.
12. Susanne Zantop, *Colonial Fantasies: Conquest, Family, and Nation in Precolonial Germany, 1770–1870* (London: Duke University Press, 1997), 6. For more on German colonial fantasies, see also Sara Friedrichsmeyer, Sara Lennox, and Susanne Zantop, eds., *The Imperialist Imagination: German Colonialism and Its Legacy* (Ann Arbor: University of Michigan Press, 1998); Birthe Kundrus, ed., *Phantasiereiche. Zur Kulturgeschichte des deutschen Kolonialismus* (Frankfurt: Campus, 2003).
13. Nicole Grewling, "Blood Brothers? Indians and the Construction of a German Colonial Self in Friedrich Gerstäcker's Fiction," *Arkansas Historical Quarterly* 73, no. 1 (Spring 2014): 90, 93.
14. Gründungsmanifest der Gesellschaft für Deutsche Kolonisation (March 28, 1885). German History in Documents and Images, http://ghdi.ghi-dc.org/docpage.cfm?doc page_id=1045, accessed April 1, 2020.
15. Edgar Hartwig, "Deutsche Kolonialgesellschaft (DKG) 1887–1936," in *Lexikon zur Parteiengeschichte 1789–1945. Die bürgerlichen und kleinbürgerlichen Parteien und Verbände in Deutschland*, vol. 1, ed. Dieter Fricke, Werner Fritsch, Herber Gottwald, Siegfried Schmidt, and Manfred Weißbecker (Leipzig: VEB Bibliographisches Institut, 1985), 726.
16. *Jahresbericht der Deutschen Kolonialgesellschaft 1897* (Berlin: Karl Heymanns Verlag, 1897), 44.
17. BArch R1001/6726m, 2: Verschiedene Gesellschaften und Vereine 1890–1937. Gustav Nachtigal (1834–85) was a German explorer and German commissioner for West Africa.
18. Sebastian Conrad, *German Colonialism*, 21. For discussions on how imperial discourse and the desire for empire interacted with the agenda of Germany's liberals before 1884, see Matthew P. Fitzpatrick, *Liberal Imperialism in Germany: Expansionism and Nationalism, 1848–1884* (New York: Berghahn, 2008).
19. Holger H. Herwig, *"Luxury" Fleet: The Imperial German Navy 1888–1918* (New York: Routledge, 1980), 107.
20. Gann and Duignan, *The Rulers of German Africa*, 149.
21. Wilhelm Gronauer, "Gesundheitszustand und Krankheiten der Eingeborenen. Ernährung. Bekleidung. Ärztlicher Kontrolle. Ärztlicher Bericht," in *Deutschland und seine Kolonien im Jahre 1896*, ed. Gustav Meinke (Berlin: Verlag von Dietrich Reimer, 1897), 43.
22. BArch R1001/6339, 97: Ausstellungen. Allgemeines.
23. Keith Holston, "A Measure of the Nation: Politics, Colonial Enthusiasm and Education in Germany, 1896–1933" (PhD diss., University of Pennsylvania, 1996), 23.
24. Ibid., 24.
25. David Ciarlo, *Advertising Empire: Race and Visual Culture in Imperial Germany* (Cambridge, MA: Harvard University Press, 2011), 266–71.
26. Ibid., 306.
27. Jeff Bowersox, *Raising Germans in the Age of Empire: Youth and Colonial Culture, 1871–1914* (Oxford: Oxford University Press, 2013), 55.
28. Holston, "A Measure of the Nation," 30.

29. Bowersox, *Raising Germans in the Age of Empire*, 104.
30. Paul Thiele, "Deutsche Kolonialschule zu Witzenhausen a. d. Werra," *Der Tropenpflanzer: Zeitschrift für Tropische Landwirtschaft* 3 (January 1899), 7. The *Kolonialschule* will be discussed in more depth in Chapter 5.
31. Bowersox, *Raising Germans in the Age of Empire*, 45.
32. Ibid., 43. Bowersox notes that the game was created by Gustav Weise, Stuttgart c.1905.
33. Karl May (1842–1912) was the creator of the popular protagonists Winnetou and Old Shatterhand who appeared both in May's books and in later German cinematic adaptations in the 1960s.
34. Hermann von Wissman (1853–1905) was an explorer and governor of German East Africa from 1895.
35. Jeff Bowersox, "Boy's and Girl's Own Empires: Gender and the Uses of the Colonial World in *Kaiserreich* Youth Magazines," in *German Colonialism and National Identity*, ed. Michael Perraudin and Jürgen Zimmerer (New York: Routledge, 2011), 59.
36. Union of South Africa, *Report on the Natives of South West Africa and their Treatment by Germany* (London: HMSO, 1918). An annotated version of the report was also published in 2003. See Jeremy Silvester and Jan-Bart Gewald, eds., *Words Cannot Be Found: German Colonial Rule in Namibia: An Annotated Reprint of the 1918 Blue Book* (Leiden: Brill, 2003).
37. Wempe, *Revenants of the German Empire*, 37.
38. Hans Poeschel, *Die Kolonialfrage im Frieden von Versailles. Dokumente zu ihrer Behandlung* (Berlin: E. S. Mittler & Sohn, 1920), 15 quoted in Dirk van Laak, "Ist je ein Reich, das es nicht gab, so gut verwaltet worden?" Der imaginäre Ausbau der imperialen Infrastruktur in Deutschland nach 1918," in *Phantasiereiche*, 74.
39. Geoff Eley, "Empire by Land or Sea? Germany's Colonial Imaginary, 1840–1945," in *German Colonialism in a Global Age*, ed. Bradley Naranch and Geoff Eley (London: Duke University Press, 2014), 20.
40. Conrad, *German Colonialism*, 187. For a study on other genres of German literature and the reaction to the loss of colonies during the Weimar Republic, see Jared Poley, *Decolonization in Germany: Weimar Narratives of Colonial Loss and Foreign Occupation* (Oxford: Peter Lang, 2005).
41. Lora Wildenthal, *German Women for Empire, 1884–1945* (Durham: Duke University Press, 2001), 54.
42. Friederike Eigler, "Engendering German Nationalism: Gender and Race in Frieda von Bülows Colonial Writings," in *The Imperialist Imagination: German Colonialism and Its Legacy*, ed. Sara Friedrichsmeyer, Sara Lennox, and Susanne Zantop (Ann Arbor: University of Michigan Press, 1998), 74, 85. The book was first published in Dresden in 1899.
43. Britta Schilling, *Postcolonial Germany: Memories of Empire in a Decolonised Nation* (Oxford: Oxford University Press, 2014), 21. Paul von Lettow-Vorbeck was the commander of the German Army during the campaign in East Africa.
44. Francis L. Carsten, "Volk ohne Raum: A Note on Hans Grimm," *Journal of Contemporary History* 2, no. 2 (1967): 221.
45. Schilling, *Postcolonial Germany*, 40.
46. Wempe, *Revenants of the German Empire*, 41.
47. "Kolonial-und Schifffahrtstag der Kultur- und Sport Woche," *Hamburger Anzeiger* (August 18, 1921), 3.
48. Deimling had also been in command of forces at such First World War battles as the First Battle of Ypres and the Battle of the Somme. *Schutztruppe* were the colonial

troops in the African territories of the German colonial empire comprising of both European and indigenous soldiers.
49. "Vortrag von General von Deimling," *Freiburger Zeitung* (January 20, 1923), 2. http://www.freiburg-postkolonial.de/Seiten/presse.htm, accessed March 23, 2017.
50. In addition to others, Paul von Lettow-Vorbeck also gave numerous lectures.
51. For an interesting discussion on this topic see Joachim Zeller, "Decolonization of the Public Space? (Post)colonial Culture of Remembrance in Germany," in *Hybrid Cultures, Nervous States: Britain and Germany in a (Post)Colonial World*, ed. Ulrike Lindner, Maren Möhring, Mark Stein, and Silke Stroh (Amsterdam: Rodophi, 2010), 65–89.
52. Some of these street names have been changed due to public protest; however, some still exist to this day. For example, in the Wedding district of Berlin which includes such street names as: Kameruner Straße and Windhuker Straße. Similarly, the *Kolonialviertel* which was formed in June 1933 in the Trudering area of Munich includes such streets as Samoa Straße and Kameruner Straße. See Alexander Honold, "Afrikanisches Viertel: Straßennamen als kolonialer Gedächtnisraum," in *Phantasiereiche: Zur Kulturgeschichte des deutschen Kolonialismus*, ed. Birthe Kundrus (Frankfurt: Campus Verlag, 2003), 305–21.
53. Stadtplan von Litzmannstadt (1942). Sächsische Landesbibliothek- Staats- und Universitätsbibliothek, Dresden, http://www.deutschefotothek.de/documents/obj/90066471/df_dk_0009664, accessed April 9, 2020.
54. Stadtplan von Posen (1939). Sächsische Landesbibliothek- Staats- und Universitätsbibliothek, Dresden, http://www.deutschefotothek.de/documents/obj/90061895/df_dk_0011894, accessed April 9, 2020.
55. Winfried Speitkamp, "Kolonialdenkmäler," in *Kein Platz an der Sonne: Erinnerungsorte der deutschen Kolonialgeschichte*, ed. Jürgen Zimmerer (Frankfurt: Campus Verlag, 2013), 409.
56. The monument was controversial and was torn down, after several attempts, by university students in 1968.
57. The *Kolonial-Ehrenmal* elephant was redesignated in 1990 as an anti-colonial monument. For more information on the toppling of the Wissmann monument, see Ingo Cornils, "Denkmalsturz: The German Student Movement and German Colonialism," in *German Colonialism and National Identity*, ed. Michael Perraudin and Jürgen Zimmerer (New York: Routledge, 2011), 197–212.
58. Speitkamp, "Kolonialdenkmäler," 413.
59. BArch R1001/6914, 96: Errichtung von Kolonialkriegsdenkmälern in Deutschland. "Einladung Herr Geheimrat von Abteilung Bremen der Deutschen Kolonialgesellschaft" (June 10, 1932).
60. BArch R1001/6914, 95: "Deutsches Kolonial-Ehrenmal in Bremen, Einweihungsfeier am 6. Juli 1932."
61. "Tanga-Feier," *Freiburger Zeitung* (November 5, 1926), 4. http://www.freiburg-postkolonial.de/Seiten/presse.htm, accessed March 24, 2017.
62. "Tangagedenkfeier der Kolonialdeutschen," *Freiburger Zeitung* (November 8, 1926), 2. http://www.freiburg-postkolonial.de/Seiten/presse.htm, accessed March 23, 2017.
63. The Askaris were the native Africans who fought for *Schutztruppe*, the colonial forces of the German Army.
64. For more on women's colonial activism during the *Kaiserreich*, see Wildenthal, *German Women for Empire*. See also Birthe Kundrus, "Weiblicher Kulturimperialismus: Die

imperialistischen Frauenverbände des Kaiserreichs," in *Das Kaiserreich transnational. Deutschland in der Welt 1871–1914*, ed. Sebastian Conrad und Jürgen Osterhammel (Göttingen: Vandenhoeck & Ruprecht, 2004), 213–35.
65. Britta Schilling, "Deutsche Frauen! Euch und euer Kinder geht es an! Deutsche Frauen als Aktivistinnen für die koloniale Idee," in *Frauen in den deutschen Kolonien*, ed. Marianne Bechhaus-Gerst and Mechthild Leutner (Berlin: C. H. Links Verlag, 2009), 77.
66. "Kolonialfest 1927," *Altonaer Nachrichten* (January 26, 1927), 6.
67. "Auf der Höhe der Festsaison," *Hamburgischer Correspondent* (February 2, 1930), 17.
68. See, for example, Wolfgang Fuhrmann, *Imperial Projections: Screening the German Colonies* (London: Berghahn, 2015).
69. Etienne François and Hagen Schulze, *Deutsche Erinnerungsorte*, vol. 1 (Munich: Verlag C. H. Beck, 2001), 13 quoted in Jürgen Zimmerer, "Kolonialismus und kollektive Identität," in *Kein Platz an der Sonne*, 11.
70. Wempe, *Revenants of the German Empire*, 72–3.
71. Vejas Gabriel Liulevicius, *The German Myth of the East: 1800 to the Present* (Oxford: Oxford University Press, 2009), 24–5.
72. After the brief creation of the Kingdom of Poland by the German and Austro-Hungarian Empires between 1917 and 1918, the Second Polish Republic emerged as an independent state as a result of the 1919 Paris Peace Conference.
73. *Kulturkampf* was the "struggle" of the German state against the Roman Catholic Church in order to bring the Church under the control of the state. The policy, which gained momentum from 1871, brought with it such measures as the Pulpit Law which banned priests from including any political topics in their sermons, the banning of the Jesuit order in 1872 and the May Laws (*Maigesetze*, 1873–5) which included a provision for the state to supervise the training and also the appointment of clergy.
74. Sebastian Conrad, *Globalisation and the Nation in Imperial Germany*, trans. Sorcha O'Hagan (Cambridge: Cambridge University Press, 2010), 148.
75. Otto Pflanze, *Bismarck and the Development of Germany, Volume III: The Period of Fortification, 1880–1898* (Princeton: Princeton University Press, 1990), 203.
76. Conrad, *Globalisation and the Nation in Imperial Germany*, 148.
77. Kristin Kopp, *Germany's Wild East: Constructing Poland as Colonial Space* (Ann Arbor: University of Michigan Press, 2012), 67.
78. This was also one of the reasons behind encouraging the settlement of the African colonies which was promoted at this time.
79. Scott M. Eddie, "The Prussian Settlement Commission and its Activities in the Land Market, 1886–1918," in *Germans, Poland, and Colonial Expansion to the East: 1850 Through the Present*, ed. Robert L. Nelson (Basingstoke: Palgrave Macmillan, 2009), 41. Nelson estimates the number of individuals to be settled was about 150,000.
80. Conrad, *Globalisation and the Nation in Imperial Germany*, 177.
81. Eddie, "The Prussian Settlement Commission," 56–7.
82. Elizabeth A. Drummond, "From 'verloren gehen' to 'verloren bleiben': Changing German Discourses on Nation and Nationalism in Poznania," in *The Germans and the East*, ed. Charles W. Ingrao and Franz A. J. Szabo (West Lafayette: Purdue University Press, 2008), 227. Drummond selects these characteristics as being common in such texts as *Die Ostmark* and the *Alldeutsche Blätter*, publications of the Deutsche Ostmarkenverein (the German Eastern Marches Society) and the *Alldeutscher Verband* (Pan-German League), respectively.

83. Matthew P. Fitzpatrick, *Purging the Empire: Mass Expulsions in Germany, 1871–1914* (Oxford: Oxford University Press, 2015), 96.
84. Conrad, *Globalisation and the Nation in Imperial Germany*, 180.
85. David Blackbourn, "Das Kaiserreich transnational. Eine Skizze," in *Das Kaiserreich transnational. Deutschland in der Welt 1871–1914*, ed. Sebastian Conrad und Jürgen Osterhammel (Göttingen: Vandenhoeck & Ruprecht, 2004), 323.
86. Uwe-K. Ketelsen, "Der koloniale Diskurs und die Öffnung des europäischen Ostens im deutschen Roman," in *Kolonialismus: Kolonialdiskurs und Genozid*, ed. Mihran Dabag, Horst Gründer, and Uwe-K. Ketelsen (München: Wilhelm Fink Verlag, 2004), 80.
87. Kristin Kopp, "Contesting Borders: German Colonial Discourse and the Polish Eastern Territories" (PhD Diss., University of California, Berkeley, 2001), 19. See also Kopp, *Germany's Wild East* and Izabela Surynt, *Das "ferne," "unheimliche" Land: Gustav Freytags Polen* (Dresden: Thelem, 2004).
88. Mark Tilse, *Transnationalism in the Prussian East: From National Conflict to Synthesis, 1871–1914* (Basingstoke: Palgrave Macmillan, 2011), 116.
89. Izabela Surynt, "Postcolonial Studies and the 'Second World': Twentieth-Century German Nationalist-Colonial Constructs," *Werkwinkel* 3, no. 1 (2008): 77.
90. Kopp, "Contesting Borders," 22.
91. Christoph Kienemann, *Der koloniale Blick gen Osten: Osteuropa im Diskurs des Deutschen Kaiserreiches von 1871* (Paderborn: Ferdinand Schöningh, 2018), 233.
92. Edward Said, *Orientalism* (New York: Vintage Books, 1978), 94. Emphasis in the original.
93. Ibid., 95.
94. Robert L. Nelson, "The Archive for Inner Colonisation, The German East, and World War I," in *Germans, Poland, and Colonial Expansion to the East: 1850 Through the Present*, ed. Robert L. Nelson (Basingstoke: Palgrave Macmillan, 2009), 65.
95. Irene Stoehr, "Von Max Sering zu Konrad Meyer - ein machtergreifender' Generationswechsel in der Agrar- und Siedlungswissenschaft," in *Autarkie und Ostexpansion: Pflanzenzucht und Agrarforschung im Nationalsozialismus*, ed. Susanne Heim (Göttingen: Wallstein Verlag, 2002), 74.
96. Max Sering, *Die innere Kolonisation im östlichen Deutschland* (Leipzig: Duncker and Humbolt, 1893), 280.
97. Nelson, "The Archive for Inner Colonisation," 74.
98. For further discussion on Rohrbach and his potential colonial influence in Germany, see Mark T. Kettler, "What Did Paul Rohrbach Actually Learn in Africa? The Influence of Colonial Experience on a Publicist's Imperial Fantasies in Eastern Europe," *German History* 38, no. 2 (2020): 240–62.
99. Paul Rohrbach, "Siedlungsbestrebungen in unseren afrikanischen Kolonien," *Archiv für innere Kolonisation* 3, no. 3 (1910): 86.
100. "Besiedlung im Inlande und in den Kolonien. Ein Vorwort zur Kolonialnummer," *Archiv für innere Kolonisation* 4, no. 5 (1912): 147.
101. Nelson, "The Archive for Inner Colonisation," 82–5.
102. *Ober Ost* was the abbreviation for *Oberbefehlshaber der gesamten Deutschen Streitkräfte im Osten* (Supreme Commander of All German Forces in the East) which was both a military post and used to describe the German-occupied territory on the Eastern front. Stephan Lehnstaedt has written about occupation policy in the *Generalgouvernement Warschau* and has compared and contrasted this with the *Militärgeneralgouvernement Lublin* and the Nazi General Government between 1939

and 1945. Lehnstaedt argues none of the three should be considered to be colonial. See Lehnstaedt, *Imperiale Polenpolitik in den Weltkriegen. Eine vergleichende Studie zu den Mittelmächten und zu NS-Deutschland* (Osnabrück: Fibre Verlag, 2017).
103. Vejas Gabriel Liulevicius, *War Land on the Eastern Front: Culture, National Identity, and German Occupation in World War I* (Cambridge: Cambridge University Press, 2000), 95.
104. Nelson, "The Archive for Inner Colonisation," 83.
105. For more information, see Stoehr, "Von Max Sering zu Konrad Meyer," 57–91. Konrad Meyer (occasionally also named as Meyer-Hetling) was appointed by Heinrich Himmler as the head of the RKFDV planning department. He was one of the main figures in charge of the creation of the *General Plan Ost* (GPO). This will be further discussed in Chapters 3 and 4.
106. Other radical nationalist groups also existed at the time. For example, the *Deutscher Ostmarkenverein* (German Eastern Marches Society) was founded in 1894. It aimed to promote the Germanization of Poles living in Prussia and to destroy Polish national identity in the German eastern provinces.
107. As mentioned at the beginning of this chapter, the *Gesellschaft für Deutsche Kolonisation* merged with the *Deutscher Kolonialverein* (German Colonial Association) in 1887 to form the *Deutsche Kolonialgesellschaft* (German Colonial Society, DKG).
108. Hasse was also a member of the *Reichstag* and represented the *Nationalliberale Partei* (National Liberal Party) from 1893 to 1903.
109. Dennis Sweeney, "Pan-German Conceptions of Colonial Empire," in *German Colonialism in a Global Age*, ed. Bradley Naranch and Geoff Eley (London: Duke University Press, 2014), 268.
110. Alfred Kruck, *Die Geschichte des Alldeutschen Verbandes 1890–1939* (Wiesbaden: Steiner, 1954), 10.
111. Daniel Frymann [Heinrich Claß], *Wenn ich der Kaiser wär'. Politische Wahrheiten und Notwendigkeiten* (Leipzig: Dieterich'schen Verlagsbuchhandlung, 1913), 135.
112. Conrad, *Globalisation and the Nation in Imperial Germany*, 177.
113. Baranowski, *Nazi Empire*, 44–5.
114. "Die Polenfrage im Reichstag," *Alldeutsche Blätter* (February 16, 1901), 78–9 and F. von Loewenthal, "Die Zukunft des Deutschtums in den Baltischen Provinzen," *Alldeutsche Blätter* (March 3, 1901), 103–6.
115. Woodruff D. Smith, *The Ideological Origins of Nazi Imperialism* (New York: Oxford University Press, 1986), 100–1. For further explanation of the Pan-German League's conceptualization of Lebensraum, see Woodruff, *The Ideological Origins of Nazi Imperialism*, 94–111.
116. Frymann [Claß], *Wenn ich der Kaiser wär'*,186.
117. Frymann [Claß], *Wenn ich der Kaiser wär'*, 91–2.
118. For more information on the League's conceptualization of the threats to Germany see Roger Chickering, *We Men Who Feel Most German: A Cultural Study of the Pan-German League, 1886–1914* (Boston: Allen & Unwin, 1984).
119. Sylvia Jaworska, "Anti-Slavic Imagery in German Radical Nationalist Discourse at the Turn of the Twentieth Century: A Prelude to Nazi Ideology?," *Patterns of Prejudice* 45, no. 5 (2011): 445, 448–9, 451.
120. This technique was not far removed from cases of colonial "othering" in conquered territories.

121. Dennis Sweeney, "Race, Capitalism and Empire" The Alldeutscher Verband and German Imperialism" (paper presented at the Annual Meeting of the German Studies Association, Pittsburgh, PA, September 29, 2006) quoted in Baranowski, *Nazi Empire*, 71.
122. Gerd Hardach, *The First World War, 1914–1918* (Berkeley: University of California Press, 1981), 228.
123. Woodruff, *The Ideological Origins of Nazi Imperialism*, 108–9.
124. Felicity Rash, *German Images of the Self and the Other: Nationalist, Colonialist and Anti-Semitic Discourse, 1871–1918* (Basingstoke: Palgrave Macmillan, 2012), 63–4.
125. Sebastian Conrad, "Internal Colonialism in Germany; Culture Wars, Germanification of the Soil, and the Global Market Imaginary," in *German Colonialism in a Global Age*, ed. Bradley Naranch and Geoff Eley (London: Duke University Press, 2014), 260–1.
126. Peter Walkenhorst, *Nation-Volk-Rasse: Radikaler Nationalismus im Deutschen Kaiserreich 1890–1914* (Göttingen: Vandenhoeck & Ruprecht, 2007), 341.
127. Rainer Hering, *Konstruierte Nation: Der Alldeutsche Verband 1890 bis 1939* (Hamburg: Christians, 2003), 12, 15. Anderson's theory of "imagined community" describes the nation as a socially constructed community which is created by those who believe they are part of that community. See Benedict Anderson, *Imagined Communities: Reflections on the Origin and Spread of Nationalism* (London: Verso, 1991).
128. Jaworska, "Anti-Slavic imagery in German radical nationalist discourse," 451.
129. The term "cognitive weapons" is used by Chickering. See Chickering, *We Men Who Feel Most German*, 9.

2 "Our Children Will Have It Better Than We Do!": Societal Stratification and Assimilation in Poland

Parts of this chapter are derived from the article Rachel O'Sullivan, "Integration and Division: Nazi Germany and the 'Colonial Other' in Annexed Poland," *Journal of Genocide Research* 22, no. 4 (2020): 437–58. I would like to thank the anonymous reviewers and the journal editors for feedback on initial drafts of the article; Bundesarchiv Berlin (BArch) R49/3084, 62: Lage und Stimmung der Umsiedler im Reichsgau Danzig-Westpreußen. Tätigkeitsberichte von Ansiedlerbetreuerinnen, „Aufbruch zu neuer Heimat' von Irmgard von Maltzahn (October 28, 1940). The attribution of this quote to an ethnic German resettler cannot be verified as it is included in activity reports written by female settlement advisors who may have been recording actual events, but who also may have added embellishment for propaganda purposes. Regardless, the quote captures the Nazi regime's fantasy of a safer and better future for the resettled ethnic Germans.

1. Otto Engelhardt-Kyffhäuser, *Der große Treck: Die Heimkehr der deutschen Bauern aus Galizien und Wolhynien. Führer durch die Ausstellung Im Haus der Kunst* (Berlin: Thormann & Goetsch, 1940), 8, 12.
2. Claudia Molnar, *Von der bürgerlichen Villa zur NS-Kunsthalle: Die Berliner Hardenbergstraße 21–23* (Norderstadt: BoD Books on Demand, 2018), 45–6. For more information on Engelhardt-Kyffhäuser, see Wilhelm Fielitz, *Das Stereotyp des Wolhyniendeutschen Umsiedlers. Popularisierungen zwischen Sprachinselforschung und Nationalsozialistischer Propaganda* (Marburg: N. G. Elwert Verlag, 2000).

For more on the emotional and political weight attached to the myth of the "trek" and the exhibiton, see Christian Ingrao, *The Promise of The East: Nazi Hopes and Genocide, 1939–43*, trans. Andrew Brown (Cambridge: Polity Press, 2019), 78–9.
3. BArch R49/20 Bd. 1 1939–1942, 1: Reden führender Personen über die Umsiedlungsaktion, 1939–42. Speech by *SS-Obergruppenführer* Ulrich Greifelt (at the time he was an SS-Brigadeführer) on behalf of the RKFDV in Berlin (December 13, 1939).
4. BArch R 49/12, 1: Befehle und Rundschreiben des RKFV (Erlasse und Verordnungen sowie Besprechungsvermerke über Fragen der Umsiedlung 1939–1942), "Erlass des Führers und Reichkanzlers zur Festigung deutschen Volkstums. Vom 7 Oktober 1939."
5. Robert L. Koehl, *RKFDV: German Resettlement and Population Policy, 1939–1945: A History of the Reich Commission for the Strengthening of Germandom* (Cambridge, MA: Harvard University Press, 1957), 56.
6. Michael G. Esch, *"Gesunde Verhältnisse." Deutsche und polnische Bevölkerungspolitik in Ostmitteleuropa 1939–1950* (Marburg: Verlag Herder-Institut, 1998), 409.
7. Richards Olafs Plavnieks, "Wall of Blood": The Baltic German Case Study in National Socialist Wartime Population Policy, 1939–1945" (MA Diss., University of North Carolina, 2008), 43–5. This dissertation provides a good statistical overview and analysis of the Baltic German resettlement.
8. Götz Aly, *Final Solution: Nazi Population Policy and Murder of the European Jews* (London: Arnold, 1999), 35–7. See also, Valdis O. Lumans, *Himmler's Auxiliaries: The Volksdeutsche Mittelstelle and the German National Minorities of Europe, 1933–1945* (Chapel Hill: University of North Carolina Press, 1993), 165.
9. Albert Forster (1902–1952) was appointed the *Gauleiter* and *Reichsstatthalter* of Danzig-West Prussia in October 1939 having previously been *Gauleiter* of the Free City of Danzig since 1930.
10. Koehl, *RKFDV: German Resettlement and Population Policy*, 63.
11. BArch R59/229, 3: Arbeits- und Tatigkeitberichte. "Tätigkeitsbericht der Volksdeutschen Mittelstelle Einsatzstab Lodsch im Rahmen der Umsiedlung der Volksdeutschen aus Wolhynien, Galizien und dem Narewdistrikt."
12. Lumans, *Himmler's Auxiliaries*, 173.
13. Doris L. Bergen, "The Nazi Concept of 'Volksdeutsche' and the Exacerbation of Anti-Semitism in Eastern Europe, 1939–45," *Journal of Contemporary History* 29, no. 4 (1994): 569. For a thorough discussion on the meaning of the term "*Volksdeutsche*" and how it was often altered, see Bergen.
14. BArch R 49/3082, 40: Umsiedlerbetreuung. Zeitungsausschnittsammlung der Gaufrauenschaftsleitung Danzig-Langfuhr der NS-Frauenschaft Danzig (Fotokopien). "Merkblatt über wichtigste volkspolitische Begriffe" (undated).
15. Alexa Stiller, "On the Margins of Volksgemeinschaft: Criteria for Belonging to the Volk within the Nazi Germanization Policy in the Annexed Territories, 1939–1945," in *Heimat, Region, and Empire: Spatial Identities under National Socialism*, ed. Claus-Christian W. Szejnmann and Maiken Umbach (New York: Palgrave Macmillan, 2012), 238.
16. Ibid., 238. This proof was not a necessity as their application could still be approved by a member of the VoMi and a representative member of their community.
17. Pertti Ahonen, Jerzy Kochanowski, Gustavo Corni, Tamás Stark, Rainer Schulze, and Barbara Stelzl-Marx, *People on the Move: Forced Population Movements in Europe in the Second World War and its Aftermaths* (Oxford: Berg, 2008), 112.

18. Andreas Strippel, "Race, Regional Identity and *Volksgemeinschaft*: Naturalization of Ethnic German Resettlers in the Second World War by the *Einwandererzentralstelle*/Central Immigration Office of the SS," in *Heimat, Region, and Empire*, 187.
19. Isabel Heinemann, *Rasse, Siedlung, deutsches Blut: Das Rasse- und Siedlungshauptamt der SS und die rassenpolitische Neuordnung Europas* (Göttingen: Wallstein Verlag, 2003), 243. See also, Maria Fiebrandt, *Auslese für die Siedlergesellschaft. Die Einbeziehung Volksdeutscher in die NS-Erbgesundheitspolitik im Kontext der Umsiedlungen 1939–1945* (Göttingen: Vandenhoeck & Ruprecht, 2014).
20. Andreas Strippel, *NS-Volkstumspolitik und die Neuordnung Europas: rassenpolitische Selektion der Einwandererzentralstelle des Chefs der Sicherheitspolizei und des SD 1939–1945* (Paderborn: Ferdinand Schöningh, 2011), 105. For more in-depth information on each of the screening stages, see Strippel.
21. Ibid., 107.
22. Ibid., 113.
23. Heinemann, *Rasse, Siedlung, deutsches Blut*, 244–5.
24. Strippel, *NS-Volkstumspolitik und die Neuordnung Europas*, 118.
25. BArch R69/281, 1, 3: Volksdeutsche aus Wolhynien und Galizien. "Richtlinien für die Feststellung der Volkszugehörigkeit der Volksdeutschen aus Wolhynien und Galizien" (December 13, 1939), "Richtlinien für die Einbürgerung von Volksdeutschen aus Wolhynien und Galizien" (December 12, 1939).
26. Markus Leniger, *Nationalsozialistische "Volkstumsarbeit" und Umsiedlungspolitik 1933–1945: Von der Minderheitenbetreuung zur Siedlerauslese* (Berlin: Frank & Timme, 2006), 213.
27. Strippel, *NS-Volkstumspolitik und die Neuordnung Europas*, 126. Lumans, *Himmler's Auxiliaries*, 191.
28. Alexa Stiller, "Völkischer Kapitalismus: Theoretische Überlegungen anhand des empirischen Beispiels der Deutschen Umsiedlungs-Treuhandgesellschaft 1939–1945," *Zeitschrift für Geschichtswissenschaft* 66, no. 6 (2018): 510.
29. Lumans, *Himmler's Auxiliaries*, 188.
30. Leniger, *Nationalsozialistische "Volkstumsarbeit" und Umsiedlungspolitik 1933–1945*, 98.
31. Ibid., 119.
32. Arthur Greiser (1897–1947) was appointed *Gauleiter* of the then named *Reichsgau* Posen in October 1939 and *Reichsstatthalter* in November 1939. He was born in Prussia and joined the National Socialist Party and SA in 1929.
33. Archiwum Państwowe w Poznaniu (APP) 53/2202 (Microfilm 0–61044), 206–8: Umsiedlerkreisfürsorge (January 12, 1942).
34. Daniel Mühlenfeld, "Reich Propaganda Offices and Political Mentoring of Ethnic German Resettlers," in *Heimat, Region, and Empire*, 200–1.
35. Lumans, *Himmler's Auxiliaries*, 194.
36. Ibid., 192.
37. APP 53/2202 (Microfilm 0–61044), 8–10, 16: Umsiedlerkreisfürsorge (September 9, 1940).
38. Gaëlle Fisher, "From Model to Warning: Narratives of Resettlement 'Home to the Reich' after World War II," in *German-Balkan Entangled Histories in the Twentieth Century*, ed. Mirna Zakić and Christopher A. Molnar (Pittsburgh: University of Pittsburgh Press, 2020), 188, 200–1.
39. Catherine Epstein, "Germanization in the Warthegau: Germans, Jews and Poles and the Making of a 'German' Gau," in *Heimat, Region, and Empire*, 106.

40. Elizabeth Harvey, *Women and the Nazi East: Agents and Witnesses of Germanization* (New Haven: Yale University Press, 2003), 157.
41. Jana Elena Bosse, "Siebzig Jahre nach der Umsiedlung—deutschbaltische Zeitzeugen erinnern sich," in *Umgesiedelt—Vertrieben: Deutschbalten und Polen 1939-1945 im Warthegau*, ed. Eckhart Neander and Andrzej Sakson (Marburg: Verlag Herder-Institut, 2010), 32-3.
42. Hans Krieg, ed., *Baltenbriefe zur Rückkehr ins Reich* (Berlin: Nibelungen-Verlag, 1940), 36.
43. Bosse, "Siebzig Jahre nach der Umsiedlung," 33.
44. BArch R49/3057, 93-4: Generalbericht vom studentischen Osteinsatz im Warthegau und Oberschlesien von der Einsatzleitung Ost der Reichsstudentenführung, 1940-1. "Arbeitsanweisung für die Hausbesuche."
45. Harvey, *Women and the Nazi East*, 160-1.
46. BArch R49/3082, 35: "Heimat bereiten—Aufgabe der Frau" von Irmgard von Maltzahn in *Der Gauring: Mitteilungsblatt des Gauringes Danzig-Westpreußen der NSDAP* (1942).
47. BArch R49/3082, 36: "Wie unsern Müttern geholfen wird" in *Der Gauring* (1942).
48. Harvey, *Women and the Nazi East*, 195.
49. Diemut Majer, *"Non-Germans" under the Third Reich: The Nazi Judicial and Administrative System in Germany and Occupied Eastern Europe, with Special Regard to Occupied Poland, 1939-1945*, trans. Peter Thomas Hill, Edward Vance Humphrey, and Brian Levin (Lubbock: Texas Tech University Press, 2013), 224-5. See Chapter 4 for further discussion on Polish schools.
50. BArch R49/3057, 94: "Arbeitsanweisung für die Hausbesuche."
51. BArch R49/3057, 46: "Lehrereinsatz als Hilfe der Ansiedlung der Wolhynien-und Galiziendeutschen im östlichen Warthegau."
52. BArch R49/3057, 54: "Auszug aus dem Tagesbuch eines eingesetzten Studenten."
53. David Furber and Wendy Lower, "Colonialism and Genocide in Nazi-occupied Poland and Ukraine," in *Empire, Colony, Genocide: Conquest, Occupation, and Subaltern Resistance in World History*, ed. A. Dirk Moses (New York: Berghahn Books, 2008), 372-402.
54. Elizabeth Harvey's publications on women in Poland are an exception to this, as she does allude to colonial civilizing missions and mindsets in relation to the resettlement; however, Harvey refers to colonialism generally and does not use specific comparisons. See Harvey, *Women and the Nazi East*. See also Elizabeth Harvey, "Management and Manipulation: Nazi Settlement Planners and Ethnic German Settlers in Occupied Poland," in *Settler Colonialism in the Twentieth Century: Projects, Practices, Legacies*, ed. Caroline Elkins and Susan Pedersen (New York: Routledge, 2015), 95-112.
55. French Indochina (1887-1954) was a grouping of French colonial territories in Southeast Asia which included Cambodia, Laos and parts of Vietnam.
56. Gaston Valran, "L'éducation coloniale des jeunes filles," *Bulletin de l'Oeuvre coloniale des femmes françaises*, 207 (November 1906) quoted in Marie-Paule Ha, in *French Women and the Empire: The Case of Indochina* (Oxford: Oxford University Press, 2014), 73. On German women's work in the colonies, see Lora Wildenthal, *German Women for Empire, 1884-1945* (Durham: Duke University Press, 2001).
57. Ha, *French Women and the Empire*, 74.
58. Jessica M. Howell, "Nurse going native: Language and identity in letters from Africa and the British West Indies," *Journal of Commonwealth Literature* 51, no. 1 (2016): 166.

59. Roy MacLeod, "Preface," in *Disease, Medicine, and Empire: Perspectives on Western Medicine and the Experience of European Expansion*, ed. Roy MacLeod and Milton Lewis (London: Routledge, 1988), x.
60. Nancy R. Reagin, *Sweeping the German Nation: Domesticity and National Identity in Germany, 1870–1945* (Cambridge: Cambridge University Press), 219.
61. Penny Russell, "'Unhomely moments': Civilising domestic worlds in colonial Australia," *History of the Family* 14, no. 4 (2009): 328.
62. Reagin, *Sweeping the German Nation*, 223.
63. Rebecca Swartz, *Education and Empire: Children, Race and Humanitarianism in the British Settler Colonies, 1833–1880* (London: Palgrave Macmillan, 2019), 4.
64. Tom Walsh, "The National System of Education, 1831–2000," in *Essays in the History of Irish Education*, ed. Brendan Walsh (London: Palgrave Macmillan, 2016), 8.
65. Eugen Weber, *Peasants into Frenchmen: The Modernization of Rural France, 1870–1914* (Stanford: Stanford University Press, 1976), 486.
66. Hans Henning Hahn and Eva Hahn, *Die Vertreibung im deutschen Erinnern: Legenden, Mythos, Geschichte* (Paderborn: Verlag Ferdinand Schöningh GmbH, 2010), 188.
67. Fielitz, *Das Stereotyp des Wolhyniendeutschen Umsiedlers*, 363–5.
68. Helmut Sommer, *Völkerwanderung im 20. Jahrhundert: Die große Heimkehr der Volksdeutschen ins Reich* (Berlin: Wilhelm Limpert-Verlag, 1940). Sommer's book also featured sketches by Engelhardt-Kyffhäuser.
69. For more information specifically on the Volhynian ethnic Germans see Stephan Döring, *Die Umsiedlung der Wolhyniendeutschen in den Jahren 1939 bis 1940* (Frankfurt am Main: Peter Lang, 2001).
70. *Der Führer hat uns gerufen* (Berlin-Luck: VoMi-Berlin, Deutsches Kommando für die Umsiedlung der Deutschen aus Galizien, Wolhynien und Bialystok, 1940), 13. Rainer Schulze also mentions this type of propaganda and discusses the myth of "travelling home to the Reich" alongside the experiences of individuals. See Rainer Schulze, "Der Führer ruft! Zur Rückholung der Volksdeutschen aus dem Osten," in *Die Volksdeutschen in Polen Frankreich Ungarn und der Tschechoslowakei*, ed. Jerzy Kochanowski and Maike Sach (Osnabrück: Fibre, 2006), 188–96.
71. *Der Führer hat uns gerufen*, 16. Here I am translating "*Deutschtum*" as "Germanness" but it also signifies German culture, nationhood, and tradition.
72. Hellmut Sommer, *135,000 gewannen das Vaterland* (Berlin: Nibelungen Verlag, 1940), 9.
73. Sommer, *135,000 gewannen das Vaterland*, 15.
74. Fielitz's study provides an in-depth analysis of the Volhynian Germans and the stereotypes that National Socialist propaganda formed. See Fielitz, *Das Stereotyp des Wolhyniendeutschen Umsiedlers*.
75. Greta Weltzien, "Auf dem Weg zu neuen Aeckern," *Hamburger Anzeiger* (March 3, 1941): 9.
76. Andreas Pampuch, "Dös hab i net gewußt!" in *Heimkehr der Bessarabiendeutschen*, ed. Andreas Pampuch (Breslau: Schlesien-Verlag, 1941), 118–19.
77. Sommer, *135,000 gewannen das Vaterland*, 42.
78. Otto Engelhardt-Kyffhäuser, "Aus meinem Tagebuch," in *Das Buch vom großen Treck*, ed. Otto Engelhardt-Kyffhäuser (Berlin: Verlag Grenze und Ausland GmbH, 1940), 31.
79. Sommer, *135,000 gewannen das Vaterland*, 43.

80. Werner Lorenz, ed., *Der Zug der Volksdeutschen aus Bessarabien und dem Nord-Buchenland* (Berlin: Volk und Reich Verlag GmbH, 1942), 24–5.
81. Elizabeth Harvey, "Documenting *Heimkehr*: Photography, Displacement and 'Homecoming' in the Nazi Resettlement of the Ethnic Germans, 1939–1940," in *The Ethics of Seeing: Photography and Twentieth-Century German History*, ed. Jennifer Evans, Paul Betts, and Stefan-Ludwig Hoffmann (New York: Berghahn Books, 2018), 92.
82. Kristin Kopp has previously described how Poles and Poland were perceived in colonial terms by Germany in her literature analysis. See Kristin Kopp, *Germany's Wild East: Constructing Poland as Colonial Space* (Ann Arbor: University of Michigan Press, 2012).
83. USHMM Steven Spielberg Film and Video Archive, Claude Lanzmann Shoah Collection, Film ID: 3352–3354, Interview with Martha Michelsohn, German interview transcript, 3- http://www.ushmm.org/online/film/display/detail.php?file_num=5134, accessed February 12, 2016. For simplified reference purposes, I quote and reference from the interview transcript.
84. Ibid., 43.
85. Harvey, *Women and the Nazi East*, 159.
86. BArch R49/3084, 10: "Tätigkeitsberichte der Ansiedlerbetreuerinnen aus Thorn" (January 31, 1942).
87. BArch R49/3084, 3–4: "Tätigkeitsberichte der Ansiedlerbetreuerinnen" (September 1, 1943).
88. Harvey, *Women and the Nazi East*, 160.
89. Andrzej Sakson, "Polnische Zeitzeugen berichten," in *Umgesiedelt—Vertrieben: Deutschbalten und Polen 1939–1945 im Warthegau*, ed. Eckhart Neander and Andrzej Sakson (Marburg: Verlag Herder-Institut, 2010), 27.
90. Geoffrey Hughes, *An Encyclopaedia of Swearing: The Social History of Oaths, Profanity, Foul Language and Ethnic Slurs in the English-Speaking World* (London: M. E. Sharpe, 2006), 241–3. During the *Kaiserreich*, the term "Hottentot" was used to refer to the people of the Nama tribe who inhabited German South West Africa.
91. *Reichsbund der Kinderreichen* membership was open to those with at least four children.
92. Archivum Instytut Zachodni Poznań (AIZ) Dok.I-586, 1–2: Nastrój Volksdeutschów w stosunku do Reichsdeutschów w marcu 1940 w powiecie bydgoskim. "Bericht betr. Stimmung der Volksdeutschen" (March 12, 1940). Letter unsigned.
93. AIZ Dok.I-32, 2: Niedostateczne opanowanie języka niemieckiego przez zatrudnionych na poczcie dzieci Volksdeutschów. Letter from Fritz Richter to the *Reichsstatthalter* Abteilung 3 (August 9, 1940).
94. AIZ Dok.I-32, 2.
95. AIZ Dok.I-32, 3.
96. BArch R49/3057, 107: "Eine Jenaer ANSt.- Kameradin über ihre Arbeit im Kindergarten der Kreishauptstadt Gostynin."
97. Harvey, *Women and the Nazi East*, 160.
98. Ibid., 161.
99. C. Baeskow and H. Schrader, "Als NSV.-Schwestern bei der Umsiedlung der Bessarabiendeutschen," in *Heimkehr der Bessarabiendeutschen*, 212.
100. Harvey, "Documenting *Heimkehr*," 89, 93–4.
101. For example, similar pictures can also be seen in Lorenz, ed., *Der Zug der Volksdeutschen*.

102. Miriam Y. Arani, "Photojournalism as a means of deception in Nazi-occupied Poland, 1939–45," in *Visual Histories of Occupation: A Transcultural Dialogue*, ed. Jeremy E. Taylor (London: Bloomsbury Academic, 2021), 169.
103. Harvey, "Documenting *Heimkehr*," 90.
104. Swartz, *Education and Empire*, 12.
105. William B. Cohen, "The Colonised as Child: British and French Colonial Rule," *African Historical Studies* 3, no. 2 (1970): 427.
106. Raymond Suttner, "Masculinities in the ANC-led liberation movement," in *From Boys to Men: Social Constructions of Masculinity in Contemporary Society*, ed. Tamara Shefer, K. Ratele, and A. Strebel (Lansdowne: UCT Press, 2007), 197.
107. See David Ciarlo, *Advertising Empire: Race and Visual Culture in Imperial Germany* (Cambridge, MA: Harvard University Press, 2011).
108. Fielitz, *Das Stereotyp des Wolhyniendeutschen Umsiedlers*, 148–50.
109. APP 53/68, 54: Weltanschauliche Erziehung der Ordnungspolizei.
110. Archiwum Państwowe w Gdańsku (APG) 10/4498, 29: Korespondencja. Report on student assignments in Kelpin from August 5 till September 25, 1942.
111. APG 10/265/4498, 19: Letter to the *Höherer SS- und Polizeiführer* Gottenhafen on observations of the Bessarabian Germans (December 4, 1942).
112. Winson Chu, *The German Minority in Interwar Poland* (Cambridge: Cambridge University Press, 2012), 265–70.
113. The death toll was vastly inflated by the German Propaganda Ministry at the beginning of the war.
114. "Eine baltendeutsche Umsiedlerin gibt am 19. März 1940 ihre Meinung über die Lodzer Volksdeutschen kund," in *Lodz im Zweiten Weltkrieg: Deutsche Selbstzeugnisse über Alltag, Lebenswelten und NS-Germanisierungspolitik in einer multiethnischen Stadt*, ed. Hans-Jürgen Bömelburg and Marlene Klatt (Ösnabrück: fibre Verlag, 2015), 178.
115. Institut für Zeitgeschichte Archiv, Munich (IfZ), MA 225/1, 9154: NS-Frauenschaft/ Gau Wartheland: Betreuung der volksdeutschen Umsiedler, 1940–1942, "Monatsbericht Kreis Wielun Februar 1942."
116. Alexa Stiller, "Ethnic Germans," in *A Companion to Nazi Germany*, ed. Shelley Baranowski, Armin Nolzen, and Claus-Christian W. Szejnmann (Oxford: Wiley Blackwell, 2018), 541.
117. Ann Laura Stoler, "Rethinking Colonial Categories: European Communities and the Boundaries of Rule," *Comparative Studies in Society and History* 31, no. 1 (1989): 146, 137.
118. Dörte Lerp, *Imperiale Grenzräume: Bevölkerungspolitiken in Deutsch-Südwestafrika und den östlichen Provinzen Preußens 1884–1914* (Frankfurt a. Main: Campus, 2016), 182. See also Robbie Aitken, *Exclusion and Inclusion: Gradations of Whiteness and Socio-Economic Engineering in German Southwest Africa, 1884–1914* (Oxford: Perter Land, 2007).
119. Lerp, *Imperiale Grenzräume*, 183–4.
120. Aitken, *Exclusion and Inclusion*, 86–7.
121. Gerhard Wolf, "Negotiating Germanness: National Socialist Germanization policy in the Wartheland," *Journal of Genocide Research* 19, no. 2 (2017): 220.
122. Alexa Stiller, "On the Margins of *Volksgemeinschaft*: Criteria for Belonging to the Volk within the Nazi Germanization Policy in the Annexed Territories, 1939–1945," in *Heimat, Region, and Empire: Spatial Identities under National Socialism*,

ed. Claus-Christian W. Szejnmann and Maiken Umbach (New York: Palgrave Macmillan, 2012), 243.
123. See Bradley J. Nichols, "The Hunt for Lost Blood: Nazi Germanization Policy in Occupied Europe" (PhD Diss., University of Tennessee, 2016), 217–19.
124. Gerhard Wolf, *Ideologie und Herrschaftsrationalität: Nationalsozialistische Germanisierungspolitik in Polen* (Hamburg: Hamburger Edition, 2012), 14.
125. Diemut Majer, *Fremdvölkische im Dritten Reich. Ein Beitrag zur nationalsozialistischen Rechtssetzung und Rechtspraxis in Verwaltung und Justiz unter besonderer Berücksichtigung der eingegliederten Ostgebiete und des Generalgouvernements* (Munich: Oldenbourg, 1993), 241–2.
126. Wolf, *Ideologie und Herrschaftsrationalität*, 461.
127. "Ein volksdeutscher Lehrer wehrt sich am 12. November 1941 gegen seine Einstufung in die grüne Volksliste," in *Lodz im Zweiten* Weltkrieg, 252–3. See Wolf, *Ideologie und Herrschaftsrationalität* for more discussion on applicants attempting to appeal DVL decisions.
128. AIZ Dok.I-616, 5, 7–8: Sprawozdanie o nastroju i postawie ludności polskiej i "eindeutschowanej" na Pomorzu. Report on the mood and attitude of Poles and *Eingedeutsche*, Sopot (Zoppot) (April 10, 1944).
129. "Deutschstämmige in Pabianice lehnen die Aufnahme in die Deutsche Volksliste ab," in *Lodz im Zweiten Weltkrieg*, 254–5.
130. APP 53/2188, 93: Arbeitstagung für Volkspflege. Öffentliche Fürsorge. Fürsorge beim Einsatz von eindeutschungsfähigen Polen: Der Reichsminister des Inneren (December 23, 1940).
131. Bradley J. Nichols, "The Re-Germanization Procedure: A Domestic Model for Nazi Empire-Building," *German Historical Institute Bulletin* (2018): 74, 77.
132. Ibid., 76.
133. Nichols, "The Hunt for Lost Blood," 279.
134. Wolf, *Ideologie und Herrschaftsrationalität*, 461, 467.
135. See such studies as Alexander Keese, *Living with Ambiguity: Integrating an African Elite in French and Portuguese Africa, 1930–61* (Stuttgart: Franz Steiner Verlag, 2007).
136. Paul R. Bartrop, "The Holocaust, the Aborigines, and the bureaucracy of destruction: An Australian dimension of genocide," *Journal of Genocide Research* 3, no. 1 (2001): 84–5.
137. Devin O. Pendas, "Racial States in Comparative Perspective," in *Beyond the Racial State: Rethinking Nazi Germany: Rethinking Nazi Germany*, ed. Devin O. Pendas, Mark Roseman, and Richard F. Wetzell (Cambridge: Cambridge University Press, 2017), 118.
138. On the complexitiy and the resulting flexibility of the DVL categories in various situations, see, Wolf, *Ideologie und Herrschaftsrationalität*.
139. Alan Knight, *Mexico: Volume 2, The Colonial Era* (Cambridge: Cambridge University Press, 2002), 110–11. See also, *Imperial Subjects: Race and Identity in Colonial Latin America*, ed. Matthew D. O'Hara and Andrew B. Fisher (London: Duke University Press, 2009).
140. Christopher Joon-Hai Lee, "The 'Native' Undefined: Colonial Categories, Anglo-African Status and the Politics of Kinship in British Central Africa, 1929–38," *Journal of African History* 46, no. 3 (2005): 471.
141. See the cases mentioned by Lora Wildenthal, "Race, Gender, and Citizenship in the German Colonial Empire," in *Tensions of Empire: Colonial Cultures in a Bourgeois*

World, ed. Frederick Cooper and Ann Laura Stoler (Berkeley: University of California Press, 1997), 273–8.
142. Aitken, *Exclusion and Inclusion*, 144.
143. Thomas Kühne, "Colonialism and the Holocaust: Continuities, Causations, and Complexities," *Journal of Genocide Research* 15, no. 3 (2013): 345.
144. Robert Gerwarth and Stephan Malinowski, "Hannah Arendt''s Ghosts: Reflections on the Disputable Path from Windhoek to Auschwitz," *Central European History* 42, no. 2 (2009): 293.
145. The "Colonial Other" can be defined as those who were not members of the colonial or imperial power's population and who began to be perceived as culturally or racially distinct. Often the act of "othering," or conceptualizing a distinct opposite or opposing group to that of the colonizer, facilitated or legitimized colonial policies such as violence or civilizing missions.
146. Russell, "Unhomely Moments," 332.
147. Jürgen Osterhammel, *Colonialism: A Theoretical Overview* (Princeton: Markus Wiener Publishers, 1997), 4.
148. For a discussion of the complexities, see for example, Bogdan Stefanescu, *Postcommunism/Postcolonialism: Siblings of Subalternity* (Bucharest: Editura Universitatii din Bucuresti, 2013), 53–8.

3 A German Task: The Reich German Mission

1. "Offene Stellen," *Litzmannstädter Zeitung* (April 12, 1942), 10. Hermannsbad (Ciechocinek) was in the *Regierungsbezirk* Hohensalza near the border with the *Reichsgau* Danzig-West Prussia.
2. "White Man's Burden" refers to the well-known poem by Rudyard Kipling. Kipling, "The White Man's Burden," *McClure's Magazine* XII, no. 4 (February, 1899). The poem is now widely available online.
3. Quote by Albert Forster, Marienburg (May 19, 1940) in Wolfgang Diewerge, *Der neue Reichsgau Danzig-Westpreußen* (Berlin: Junker und Dünnhaupt Verlag, 1940), 25.
4. Niels Gutschow, *Ordnungswahn: Architekten planen im „eingedeutschten Osten' 1939–1945* (Basel: Birkhäuser, 2001), 64. The role of architects and planners within the Third Reich is more fully discussed in Gutschow. See also Winfried Nerdinger (ed.), *Architektur und Verbrechen: Die Rolle von Architekten im Nationalsozialismus* (Göttingen: Wallstein Verlag, 2014).
5. Joshua Hagen and Robert C. Ostergren, *Building Nazi Germany: Place, Space, Architecture, and Ideology* (London: Rowman & Littlefield, 2020), 199.
6. As discussed in Chapter 1, *Neues Bauerntum* had initially been the journal of the *Archiv für innere Kolonisation* (published under the same name) but from 1934 it changed name to *Neues Bauerntum*. From 1933, Konrad Meyer, the leader of the RKFDV planning department, was the editor of the journal alongside Richard Walther Darré.
7. BArch R49/157, 33: Planungsgrundlagen für den Aufbau der Ostgebiete. Bericht der Planungshauptabteilung des RKFV. "Der Stand der Raumordnungsplanung für die eingegliederten Ostgebiete" von Oberbaurat J. Umlauf (beim RKFDV) in *Neues Bauerntum*, Sonderdruck aus Heft 8 (1942).

8. BArch R49/157, 33, 38: "Der Stand der Raumordnungsplanung für die eingegliederten Ostgebiete."
9. BArch R49/157, 24: "Der Deutsche Baumeister" in *Zeitschrift der Fachgruppe Bauwesen e.v.* im NS-Bund Deutscher Technik und Mitteilungen des Generalbevollmächtigen für die Regelung der Bauwirtschaft Querschnitt durch den ländlichen Aufbau des Ostens von Herbert Frank (Hauptabteilung Planung und Boden beim RKFDV, Stabshauptamt) (1941).
10. Archiwum Państwowe w Poznaniu (APP) 53/299/0/7.1/2824 (Microfilm: O-61666), 10: Protokoły zebrań zespołu "Baugestaltung und Baupflege im Reichsgau Wartheland." Directive from Greiser (September 9, 1940).
11. Czesław Madajczyk, *Die Okkupationspolitik Nazideutschlands in Polen 1939–1945* (Cologne: Pahl-Rugenstein Verlag GmbH, 1988), 333. Madajczyk fully describes the robbery and destruction of cultural artifacts and art in the General Government in his publication.
12. Catherine Epstein, *Model Nazi: Arthur Greiser and the Occupation of Western Poland* (Oxford: Oxford University Press, 2010), 242–3.
13. APP 53/2609 (Microfilm: O-61451), 5: Kaiser-Friedrich-Museum-Landesmuseum des Reichsgaus Wartheland-in Posen. Letter from Dr Rühle to the *Reichsstatthalter* (March 13, 1940).
14. APP 53/3383 (Microfilm: O-62225): Sprawozdania i korespondencja w sprawie rejestracji dzieł sztuki na terenie Kraju Warty. Reports and correspondence regarding the registration of works of art in the Wartheland from 1941 till 1944.
15. APP 53/2609, 39: Kaiser-Friedrich-Museum-Landesmuseum des Reichsgaus Wartheland-in Posen. Letter from Dr Rühle to the *Reichsstatthalter* (October 27, 1941).
16. Archivum Instytut Zachodni Poznań (AIZ) Dok. I-27, 21: Różne afisze niemieckie z czasów okupacji dot. Poznańia i ziem wcielonych do Rzeszy. "Ausstellung im Kaiser-Friederich-Museum, Kampf und Aufbau im Wartheland."
17. APP 53/2379 (Microfilm O-61221), 32: Besichtigung deutscher Schulen durch auswärtige Besucher. Schulstreik 1906–1909- Ausstellung "Kampf und Aufbau im Wartheland." Letter from Kurt Schmalz (January 19, 1943).
18. Franz Josef Gangelmayer, "Das Parteiarchivwesen der NSDAP Rekonstruktionsversuch des Gauarchivs der NSDAP-Wien" (PhD diss., Universität Wien, 2010), 165.
19. P. Haß, "Mit 21200 Planwagen in die neue Ostheimat," *Litzmännstadter Zeitung* (March 13, 1943), 5.
20. BArch R49/2355, 1–2: Presseberichte zur Umsiedlung Volksdeutscher. "Pressematerial zur Ausstellung" von RKFDV Pressestelle; regarding the other exhibitions see Epstein, *Model Nazi*, 248.
21. "Deutscher Geist und deutsche Kultur formen den Ostraum," *Litzmannstädter Zeitung* (March 9, 1941), 3.
22. Fritz Gissibl, ed., *Der Osten des Warthelands* (Stuttgart: Stähle & Friedel, 1941), 298–300. The cover of the book notes the exhibition took place at König-Heinrich-Straße 33 in Litzmannstadt and Fritz Gissibl from the Reich Propaganda Office was responsible for it.
23. Arthur Greiser quoted in Gissibl, ed., *Der Osten des Warthelands*, 3.
24. Elizabeth Harvey, *Women and the Nazi East: Agents and Witnesses of Germanization* (New Haven & London: Yale University Press, 2003), 125–9.

25. APP 53/2817 (Microfilm: O-61659), 116: Wirtschaft des Warthelandes in den Zeitschriften. Newspaper cutting from the *Völkischer Beobachter* (December, 8 1942).
26. APP 53/2817 (Microfilm: O-61659), 116: Wirtschaft des Warthelandes in den Zeitschriften. Newspaper cutting from the *Völkischer Beobachter* (December, 8 1942).
27. BArch R49/117, 5: Ansiedlung von Wolhynien- und Galiziendeutschen im Regierungsbezirk Zichenau. "Ansiedlung von Volksdeutschen in Südostpreußen" (April 11, 1940).
28. BArch R49/2355, 9, 12: "Pflege und Verbesserung des Ortsbildes im deutschen Osten von Werner Lindner." Lindner was a Party member who was editor of the magazine *Heimatleben*.
29. "Ein volksdeutscher Lehrer aus Lodz bittet am 11. März um eine Beschinigung über seine deutsche Gesinnung während der Zwischenkriegszeit," in *Lodz im Zweiten Weltkrieg: Deutsche Selbstzeugnisse über Alltag, Lebenswelten und NS-Germanisierungspolitik in einer multiethnischen Stadt*, ed. Hans-Jürgen Bömelburg and Marlene Klatt (Ösnabrück: fibre Verlag, 2015), 97.
30. The *Generalplan Ost* (General Plan East, GPO) will be discussed in detail in Chapter 4.
31. BArch R49/157a, 34: Generalplan Ost. Rechtliche, wirtschaftliche und räumliche Grundlagen des Ostaufbaus von Prof. Dr Konrad Meyer.
32. Alan E. Steinweis, "Eastern Europe and the notion of the 'frontier' in Germany to 1945," *Yearbook of European Studies* 13 (1999): 63–4.
33. APP 53/1158 (Microfilm 0–60010), 1: Reichsstatthalter-Posen. "Schaffung Deutscher Häuser im Warthegau." Letter from August Jäger, Deputy *Reichsstatthalter* (April 9, 1940).
34. APP 53/1158, 3: "Schaffung Deutscher Häuser im Warthegau."
35. Mrinalini Sinha, "Britishness, Clubbability, and the Colonial Public Sphere: The Genealogy of an Imperial Institution in Colonial India," *Journal of British Studies* 40, no. 4 (2001), 489.
36. David Furber, "Going East: Colonialism and German Life in Nazi-Occupied Poland" (PhD Diss., University of New York, 2003), 287–90.
37. Stephan Lehnstaedt, "Deutsche in Warschau: Das Alltagsleben der Besatzer 1939–1944," in *Gewalt und Alltag im besetzten Polen, 1939–1945*, ed. Jochen Böhler and Stephan Lehnstaedt (Osnabrück: Fibre Verlag, 2012), 210.
38. Itohan Osayimwese, "Demystifying Colonial Settlement: Building Handbooks for Settlers, 1904–1930," in *German Colonialism, Visual Culture, and Modern Memory*, ed. Volker Langbehn (Oxon: Routledge, 2010), 124–47, see 141.
39. Jillian Barteaux, "Urban Planning as Colonial Marketing Strategy for the Swan River Settlement, Western Australia," *Australasian Historical Archaeology* 34 (2016): 23.
40. Ibid., 22–31.
41. Ibid., 29.
42. Stadtplan von Bromberg (1941). Landkartenarchiv, https://landkartenarchiv.de/vol lbild_stadtplansammlung.php?q=stadtplan_bromberg_25T_1941, accessed October 26, 2019.
43. Stadtplan von Posen (1939). Sächsische Landesbibliothek-Staats-und Universitätsbibliothek, Dresden, http://www.deutschefotothek.de/documents/obj/90061895/df_dk_0011894, accessed October 26, 2019.

44. Stadtplan von Litzmannstadt (1942). Sächsische Landesbibliothek-Staats-und Universitätsbibliothek, Dresden, http://www.deutschefotothek.de/documents/obj/90066471/df_dk_0009664, accessed October 26, 2019.
45. Kahina Amal Djiar, "Locating Architecture, Post-Colonialism and Culture: Contextualisation in Algiers," *Journal of Architecture* 14, no. 2 (2009): 169. On this topic, see also Zeynep Çelik, *Urban Forms and Colonial Confrontations: Algiers under French Rule* (Berkeley: University of California Press, 1997).
46. Sandip Hazareesingh, *The Colonial City and the Challenge of Modernity: Urban Hegemonies and Civic Contestations in Bombay City 1900–25* (Hyderabad: Orient Longman) 331, 341 quoted in Howard Spodek, "City Planning in India under British Rule," *Economic and Political Weekly* 48, no. 4 (2013): 57.
47. See, for example, Piers Brendon, *The Decline and Fall of the British Empire 1781–1997* (London: Vintage Books, 2008), 343–8.
48. For example, it was argued that the word "colony" would be associated with the British Empire and become synonymous with exploitation. See Sandler, "Colonizers Are Born, Not Made," 426.
49. Rudolf Walther, "Imperialismus," *Geschictliche Grundbegriffe* 3 (1982): 231 quoted in Birthe Kundrus, "Colonialism, Imperialism, National Socialism: How Imperial Was the Third Reich?," in *German Colonialism in a Global Age*, ed. Bradley Naranch and Geoff Eley (Durham: Duke University Press, 2014), 337.
50. Albert Brackmann and *Ostforschung* will be discussed more extensively in Chapter 5.
51. Brackmann quoted in Michael Burleigh, *Germany Turns Eastwards: A Study of Ostforschung in the Third Reich* (London: Pan Macmillan, 2002), 113.
52. Gutschow, *Ordnungswahn*, 204. Liedecke is also mentioned in Jürgen Zimmerer, "The Birth of the Ostland Out of the Spirit of Colonialism: A Postcolonial Perspective on the Nazi Policy of Conquest and Extermination," *Patterns of Prejudice* 39, no. 2 (2005): 197.
53. Hallbauer quoted in Gutschow, *Ordnungswahn*, 146.
54. BArch R49 Bild-0705/ Unknown Creator, "Karte.-Übersicht zur Herkunft deutschstämmiger Umsiedler im Wartheland" (ca. 1939/1941).
55. Instytut Pamięci Narodowej (IPN) Proces Artura Greiser: Sygn. GK 196/36, 20. Report on the status of the *Gendarmerie* by the commander of Gendarmerie for the *Regierungspräsident* in Litzmannstadt to the commander of the *Ordnungspolizei* (January 25, 1942).
56. Patrick Bernhard, "Borrowing from Mussolini: Nazi Germany's Colonial Aspirations in the Shadow of Italian Expansionism," *Journal of Imperial and Commonwealth History* 41, no. 4 (2013): 623–7.
57. Patrick Bernhard, "Hitler's Africa in the East: Italian Colonialism as a Model for German Planning in Eastern Europe," *Journal of Contemporary History* 51, no. 1 (2015): 21–6.
58. Ernst Wagemann, "Geh' nach dem Osten, junger Mann!," *Schlesische Tageszeitung* (December 30, 1941), 2. Also quoted in Furber, "Going East," 144.
59. Robert C. Williams, *Horace Greeley: Champion of American Freedom* (New York: New York University Press, 2006), 40–3. There is some debate over whether Greely was the one to coin the phrase; however, Williams notes Greely certainly did encourage Americans to move West from 1837 until his death. For more information, see Williams, as above.

60. *Kulturfilms* were normally screened before the main film in cinemas. Although they were educational documentary films based on a variety of topics, during the Third Reich, the films heavily reflected Nazi politics and ideology.
61. United States Holocaust Memorial Museum (USHMM) Steven Spielberg Video and Film Archive, Film ID: 2559 "Mädel verlassen die Stadt," http://www.ushmm.org/online/film/display/detail.php?file_num=521, accessed February 13, 2016. For a more in-depth discussion of the film and its portrayal of the German self-conceived developmental mission, see Rachel O'Sullivan, "The German Mission in Africa and Poland: Women, Expansion, and Colonial Training during the Third Reich," *Journal of Colonialism and Colonial History* 22, no. 2 (2021). muse.jhu.edu/article/801556.
62. USHMM Steven Spielberg Video and Film Archive, Film ID: 2628 "Ostlanddeutsches Land," http://www.ushmm.org/online/film/display/detail.php?file_num=3877, accessed February 13, 2016.
63. See, for example, BArch 12611-1, *Die Deutsche Wochenschau*, 534 / - / 49 / 1940 / - (Berlin: Universum Film AG, 1940).
64. BArch 22066-2, *Die Deutsche Wochenschau*, 528 / - / 43 / 1940 / - (Berlin: Universum Film AG, 1940).
65. BArch K 136099-1, *Die Deutsche Wochenschau*, 552 / - / 15 / 1941 / - (Berlin: Universum Film AG, 1941).
66. BArch K 152565-2, *Heimkehr*, Director: Gustav Ucicky (Berlin: Universum Film AG, 1941).
67. For an in-depth study, see Gerald Trimmel, *Heimkehr: Strategien eines nationalsozialistischen Films* (Vienna: W. Eichbauer Verlag, 1998).
68. The series was commissioned by the RKFDV.
69. Walter Geisler, *Deutscher! Der Osten ruft dich!* (Berlin: Volk und Reich Verlag, 1942), 11. Geisler was a geographer who was appointed as a professor in the *Reich*'s university in Poznań.
70. Ibid., 14.
71. Ibid., 94.
72. Georg Blohm, *Siedlung und Landwirtschaft im Reichsgau Danzig-Westpreußen* (Berlin: Deutsche Landbuchhaltung Sohnrey, 1941), 11.
73. Wilhelm Löbsack, *Albert Forster, Gauleiter und Reichsstatthalter im Reichsgau Danzig-Westpreußen* (Danzig: Danziger Verlags-Gesellschaft m.b.H [Paul Rosenburg], 1940), 70.
74. Diewerge, *Der neue Reichsgau Danzig-Westpreußen*, 53.
75. Konstantin Hierl quoted in Luise Essig, "Unsere Ziele für die Mädchen und Frauen des Landvolks," in *Landvolk im Werden: Material zum ländlichen Aufbau in den neuen Ostgebieten und zur Gestaltung des dörflichen Lebens*, ed. Konrad Meyer (Berlin: Deutsche Landbuchhandlung, 1941), 139.
76. Ibid.
77. This will be further discussed in Chapter 5.
78. BArch R49/3082, 34: "Die deutsche Frau in der Volkstumsarbeit" von F. Balcerek in *Der Gauring* (1942).
79. Adolf Kargel, "Das Litzmannstadt Gebiet ist germanische Urheimat," in *Der Osten des Warthelands*, ed. Fritz Gissibl (Stuttgart: Stähle & Friedel, 1941), 30.
80. Ludwig Wolff, "Der Volkstumskampf des Deutschtums im Osten des Warthelandes," in *Der Osten des Warthelands*, ed. Fritz Gissibl (Stuttgart: Stähle & Friedel, 1941), 176.

81. BArch R49/20, 30: R49/20 Bd. 1 1939–1942: Reden führender Personen über die Umsiedlungsaktion, 1939–1942. "Himmler über Siedlungsfragen Ep. Madrid, 22 Oktober 1940."
82. Stephanie Malia Hom, "Empires of Tourism: Travel and Rhetoric in Italian Colonial Libya and Albania, 1911–1943," *Journal of Tourism History* 4, no. 3 (2012): 286.
83. Ibid.
84. Furber, "Going East," 159.
85. Ibid., 166–7.
86. Ibid., 164, 166.
87. Götz Aly and Susanne Heim, *Architects of Annihilation: Auschwitz and the Logic of Destruction*, trans. Allan Blunden (London: Phoenix, 2003), 121.
88. Wendy Lower, *Hitler's Furies: German Women in the Nazi Killing Fields* (London: Chatto & Windus, 2013), 101.
89. "Der Reichsstatthalter im Reichsgau Wartheland - March 17, 1941," in *Wysiedlenia ludności polskiej na tzw. Ziemiach wcielonych do Rzeszy 1939–1945, vol. VIII of Documenta Occupationis*, ed. Czesław Łuczak (Poznań: Instytut Zachodni, 1969), 95–6.
90. "Ein Mitarbeiter der Stadtverwaltung Litzmannstadt beansprucht am 14. Dezember 1942 die Wohnung eines Polen - E. Minkes an den Oberbürgermeister," in *Lodz im Zweiten Weltkrieg*, 210–11.
91. Furber, "Going East," 160, 203–4. This study will not repeat all of Furber's numerous results; his thorough research has given insight into the "average" Reich Germans in specific areas of occupied Poland. For further information see Furber, "Going East," especially Chapter 4.
92. Lower, *Hitler's Furies*, 99.
93. Furber, "Going East," 149, 155.
94. "Offene Stellen," *Litzmannstädter Zeitung* (April 12, 1942), 10; "Offene Stellen," *Litzmannstädter Zeitung* (December 11, 1941), 8.
95. Strippel, *NS-Volkstumspolitik und die Neuordnung Europas*, 182–3.
96. Alexander Hohenstein [Franz Heinrich Bock], *Wartheländisches Tagebuch aus den Jahren 1941/1942* (Stuttgart: Deutsche Verlags-Anstalt, 1961), 157.
97. Ibid., 53.
98. Ibid., 166–7.
99. Ibid., 30, 106.
100. Ibid., 57.
101. USHMM, Film ID: 3352-3354 "Interview with Martha Michelsohn," 47–8. The German word "Weite" can also be translated as "vastness" or "expanse."
102. Martin Broszat, ed., *Kommandant in Auschwitz. Autobiographische Aufzeichnungen des Rudolf Höß* (Munich: DTV, 2000), 134 quoted in Elissa Mailänder Koslov, "Going East": Colonial Experiences and Practices of Violence among Female and Male Majdanek Camp Guards (1941–44)," *Journal of Genocide Research* 10, no. 4 (2008): 564. Mailänder Koslov's article gives a crucial insight into the perception of Poland as colonial land by the camp guards in Majdanek. On the lack of geographical knowledge regarding Poland, particularly the opening example of Adolf Eichmann, see also Aleksandra Szczepan, "Terra Incognita? Othering East-Central Europe in Holocaust Studies," in *Colonial Paradigms of Violence*, ed. Michelle Gordon and Rachel O'Sullivan (Göttingen: Wallstein, 2022), 185–7.
103. USHMM, Film ID: 3352-3354 "Interview with Martha Michelsohn," 3.

104. Aly and Heim, *Architects of Annihilation*, 118.
105. Harvey, *German Women and the Nazi East*, 111, 103, 105.
106. USHMM, Film ID: 3352–3354 "Interview with Martha Michelsohn," 48.
107. Lower, *Hitler's Furies*, 125. Thomas Kühne has also written about the contribution of women to violence. See Thomas Kühne, *Belonging and Genocide. Hitler's Community, 1918–1945* (New Haven: Yale University Press, 2010).
108. Lower, *Hitler's Furies*, 114–17.
109. Christian Ingrao, *The Promise of The East: Nazi Hopes and Genocide, 1939–43*, trans. Andrew Brown (Cambridge: Polity Press, 2019), 72.
110. Ulrike Lindner and Dörte Lerp, "Introduction: Gendered Imperial Formations," in *New Perspectives on the History of Gender and Empire; Comparative and Global Approaches*, ed. Ulrike Lindner and Dörte Lerp (London: Bloomsbury, 2018), 18. See also Lora Wildenthal, *German Women for Empire, 1884–1945* (Durham: Duke University Press, 2001).
111. Leonore Niessen-Deiters, *Die Deutsche Frau im Auslande und in den Schutzgebieten* (Berlin: Egon Fleischel, 1913), 7 quoted in Lora Wildenthal, *German Women for Empire*, 5–6.
112. For example, see Kühne, "Colonialism and the Holocaust" and Gerwarth and Malinowski, "Hannah Arendt's Ghosts."
113. Wiebke Lisner, "Midwifery and Racial Segregation in Occupied Western Poland, 1939–1945," *German History* 35, no. 1 (2017): 229.
114. BArch R49/3057, 108: "Eine Jenaer ANSt.- Kameradin über ihre Arbeit im Kindergarten der Kreishauptstadt Gostynin."
115. BArch R49/3084, 20: "Abschrift der Tätigkeitsberichte aus dem Kreise Zempelburg" (December 5, 1942).
116. Harvey, *German Women and the Nazi East*, 184.
117. Howell, "Nurse Going Native," 171.
118. The treatment of Jewish and non-Jewish Poles and the violence that Germany inflicted on them will be thoroughly investigated in the next chapter.
119. Elizabeth Harvey, "Management and Manipulation: Nazi Settlement Planners and Ethnic German Settlers in Occupied Poland," in *Settler Colonialism in the Twentieth Century: Projects, Practices, Legacies*, ed. Caroline Elkins, and Susan Pedersen (New York: Routledge, 2005), 95.
120. Craig Fortier and Edward Hon-Sing Wong, "The settler colonialism of social work and the social work of settler colonialism," *Settler Colonial Studies* 9, no. 4 (2019): 438–40.
121. Jürgen Osterhammel, *Colonialism: A Theoretical Overview*, trans. Shelley L. Frisch (Princeton: Markus Wiener Publications, 2002), 108–9. The three basic elements of colonial thought as described by Osterhammel are the construction of the inferior, the belief in mission and guardianship, and the utopia of an administration free of politics.
122. Penelope Edmonds and Anna Johnston, "Empire, Humanitarianism and Violence in the Colonies," *Journal of Colonialism and Colonial History* 17 (2016), https://muse.jhu.edu/article/613279, accessed December 16, 2019.
123. BArch R49/3057, 9: "Geschichtliche Entwicklung des studentischen Osteinsatzes" (1940).
124. Wildenthal, *German Women for Empire*, 131.

4 Effacing Difference and the Settler Colonial Model

1. More systematic, side-by-side comparisons have already been undertaken by historians such as Carroll P. Kakel, *The American West and the Nazi East: A Comparative and Interpretative Perspective* (New York: Palgrave Macmillan, 2011) and Benjamin Madley, "From Africa to Auschwitz: How German South West Africa Incubated Ideas and Methods Adopted and Developed by the Nazis in Eastern Europe," *European History Quarterly* 35, no. 3 (2005): 429–4.
2. Diemut Majer, *"Non-Germans" under the Third Reich: The Nazi Judicial and Administrative System in Germany and Occupied Eastern Europe, with Special Regard to Occupied Poland, 1939–1945*, trans. Peter Thomas Hill, Edward Vance Humphrey, and Brian Levin (Lubbock: Texas Tech University Press, 2013), 206–7.
3. The full name for the laws was *Verordnung über die Strafrechtspflege gegen Polen und Juden in den eingegliederten Ostgebieten*. See Dok. 46 (Verordnung über die Strafrechtspflege gegen Polen und Juden in den eingegliederten Ostgebieten vom 4. Dezember 1941), in *Die Verfolgung und Ermordung der europäischen Juden durch das nationalsozialistische Deutschland, 1933–1945: Band 10, Polen: Eingegliederte Gebiete August 1941–1945* (VEJ 10), ed. Ingo Loose (Berlin: De Gruyter, 2020), 203–6.
4. See, for example, Ingo Loose, "Die Enteignung der Juden im besetzten Polen 1939–1945," in *Vor der Vernichtung. Die staatliche Enteignung der Juden im Nationalsozialismus*, ed. Katharina Stengel (New York: Campus Verlag, 2007), 283–307.
5. The treatment of the Polish Jews will be discussed more thoroughly later in this chapter.
6. Majer, *"Non-Germans,"* 248. The death penalty for sexual relations between Germans and Poles was later verified by Himmler in an unpublished circular decree, see Majer, *"Non-Germans,"* 369. For a comparison between marriage policies in the *Warthegau* and the General Government, see Birthe Kundrus, "Regime der Differenz: Volkstumspolitische Inklusionen und Exklusionen im Warthegau und im Generalgouvernement 1939–1944," in *Volksgemeinschaft: Neue Forschungen zur Gesellschaft des Nationalsozialismus*, ed. Frank Bajohr and Michael Wildt (Frankfurt am Main: Fischer, 2009), 105–23. The marriage ban could be waived in individual cases once racial value had been assessed.
7. Instytut Pamięci Narodowej (IPN) Proces Artura Greisera: Sygn. GK 196/16, 14. Letter from the *Regierungspräsident* Viktor Böttcher to the Mayor of Posen and district authorities (January 9, 1942).
8. IPN Proces Artura Greiser: Sygn. GK 196/16, 21. *Reichsstatthalter* note (December 1942).
9. IPN Proces Artura Greisera: Sygn. GK 196/16, 22. *Reichsstatthalter* note (December 10, 1942).
10. Maren Röger, "The Sexual Policies and Sexual Realities of the German Occupiers in Poland in the Second World War," *Contemporary European History* 23, no. 1 (2014): 7, 12.
11. As was the nature of the DVL, this did not necessarily always mean that the Polish partner was of German descent (for example, those in the first category of the DVL).
12. Maren Röger, *Wartime Relations: Intimacy, Violence, and Prostitution in Occupied Poland, 1939–1945*, trans. Rachel Ward (Oxford: Oxford University Press, 2021), 134.
13. Archiwum Państwowe w Łodzi (APL) 39/31870, 26: Beurteilung wiedereizudeutscher Polen [*sic*]. Marriage application of Stephan H. and Wanda Z. (June 23, 1941).

14. APL 39/31870, 21. Sippenfragebogen Wanda Z.
15. APL 39/31870, 19: Letter from the *Amtsarzt* to *Sicherheitsdienst des Reichsführers SS* (July 12, 1941); APL 39/31870, 20: Letter from the *Amtsarzt* to *Standesamt* Bromberg (July 12, 1941).
16. APL 39/31870, 20: Letter from the *Amtsarzt* to *Standesamt* Bromberg (July 12, 1941).
17. APL 39/31870, 18: Letter from the *Standesamt* Bromberg to *Gesundheitsamt* Litzmannstadt (July 21, 1941).
18. Majer, *"Non-Germans,"* 252.
19. Archivum Instytut Zachodni Poznań (AIZ) Dok.I-424, 1–2: Korzystanie z publicznych środków lokomocji przez Polaków. *Reichsstatthalter* instructions to the *Regierungspräsidenten* in Posen, Hohensalza, and Litzmannstadt (June 15, 1940).
20. AIZ Dok.I-424, 2.
21. AIZ Dok.I-423, 1: Używanie rowerów przez Polaków w okręgu regencyjnym Poznań. Polizeiverordnung, *Regierungsbezirk* Posen (July 25, 1941).
22. Majer, *"Non-Germans,"* 207–8.
23. Czesław Łuczak, *Pod niemieckim jarzmem (Kraj Warty 1939–1945)* (Poznań: PSO, 1996), 195 quoted in Catherine Epstein, *Model Nazi. Arthur Greiser and the Occupation of Western Poland* (Oxford: Oxford University Press, 2010), 199; Majer, *"Non-Germans,"* 210.
24. AIZ Dok.I-9, 110: Położenie prawne Polaków w Kraju Warty. Letter to the *Polizeipräsident* Posen from Alexander von Woedtke (January 23, 1941).
25. AIZ Dok.I-9, 5: Letter from the *Oberbürgermeister* Gerhard Scheffler to the *Polizeipräsident* Posen (September 4, 1944).
26. AIZ Dok.I-200, 2: Traktowanie Polaków (także Żydów) - również sprawy wysiedlenia. Directive from Viktor Böttcher on road closure times for Poles (1943).
27. AIZ Dok.I-31, 3: Nakaz obowiązkowego noszenia oznak przez Niemców w "Kraju Warty." Undated letter to all departments of the authorities in the *Reichsgau* Wartheland from the *Reichsstatthalter*, signed by A. Jäger as *Reichsstatthalter* representative.
28. Epstein, *Model Nazi*, 199.
29. AIZ Dok.I-69, 2: Okólnik Greisera w sprawie używania języka polskiego przez Polaków. Circular from *Reichsstatthalter* Greiser to German authorities in the Warthegau (February 23, 1943).
30. AIZ Dok.I-69, 3: Circular from *Reichsstatthalter* Greiser to German authorities in the Warthegau (February 23, 1943).
31. AIZ Dok.I-12, 9: Szkolnictwo niemieckie dla Polaków w Kraju Warty. Letter from the *Schulrat des Stadt-und Landkreises Gnesen* to the *Arbeitsamt* in Gnesen (April 24, 1940).
32. AIZ Dok.I-12, 24: Letter from the *Reichsstatthalter* offices on the use of alphabet books in schools for Polish children (May 29, 1943).
33. AIZ Dok.I-12, 14: Letter from the *Regierungspräsident* Hohensalza (June 20, 1940).
34. Epstein, *Model Nazi*, 164. The *Reichssicherheitshauptamt* (Reich Security Main Office, RSHA) was headed by Himmler.
35. Gerhard Wolf, "The Wannsee Conference in 1942 and the National Socialist Living Space Dystopia," *Journal of Genocide Research* 17, no.2 (2015): 160.
36. Götz Aly, *"Endlösung:" Völkerverschiebung und der Mord an den europäischen Juden* (Frankfurt am Main: Fischer, 1995) 203 quoted in Epstein, *Model Nazi*, 168–9.
37. IPN Proces Artura Greiser: Sygn. GK 196/36, 93–4: Correspondance from *Der Reichsstatthalter Abteilung Arbeit* to the *Arbeitsämter im Warthegau* (January 10, 1940).

38. IPN Proces Artura Greiser: Sygn. GK 196/36, 100: Richtlinien für die ärtzliche Untersuchung der landwirtschaftlichen Arbeitskräfte aus den besetzen Gebieten des ehemaligen Polen.
39. AIZ Dok. I-120, 2–4: Wysiedlanie Polaków. Abschlussbericht über die Aussiedlungen im Rahmen der Ansetzung der Bessarabiendeutschen (3.Nahplan) vom 21.1.41 – 20.1.1942 im Reichsgau Wartheland. All the figures listed comes from this report.
40. "No.83: Dok. I-580. Fragment of a report by the Umwandererzentralstelle in the Reichsgau Wartheland 1943," in *Wysiedlenia ludności polskiej na tzw. Ziemiach wcielonych do Rzeszy 1939–1945, vol. VIII of Documenta Occupationis*, ed. Czesław Łuczak (Poznań: Instytut Zachodni, 1969), 114.
41. AIZ Dok. I-25, 1: Wysiedlanie Polaków z powiatu międzychodzkiego i osiedlanie Niemców. UWZ 1940 report from *Kreis* Birnbaum (October 1, 1940).
42. Dok.I-25, 2.
43. Ibid.
44. AIZ Dok.I-109, 7–8: Różne dokumenty w sprawie akcji wysiedleńczej wobec Polaków oraz odrębnego traktowania Polaków nadających się do zniemczenia. Guidelines for police authorities for the eviction of Polish farm owners (May 9, 1940).
45. AIZ Dok.I-109, 7–8.
46. United Nations War Crimes Commission, ed., "Case No. 74, Trial of Artur [sic] Greiser: Supreme National Tribunal of Poland, June 21–July 7, 1946," in *Law Reports of Trials of War Criminals*, vol. 13 (London: His Majesty's Stationary Office, 1949), 87.
47. APL 39/29181, 1:"Bildung eines Ghettos in der Stadt Lodsch" (December 10, 1939).
48. Epstein, *Model Nazi*, 169–70.
49. Götz Aly and Susanne Heim, *Architects of Annihilation: Auschwitz and the Logic of Destruction*, trans. Allan Blunden (London: Phoenix, 2003), 186–7.
50. Dieter Schenk, *Hitlers Mann in Danzig: Albert Forster und die NS-Verbrechen in Danzig-Westpreußen* (Bonn: J. H. W. Dietz, 2000), 217 quoted in Wolfgang Gippert, "Danzig-West Prussia," in *The Greater German Reich and the Jews: Nazi Persecution Policies in the Annexed Territories 1935–1945*, ed. Wolf Gruner and Jörg Osterloh, trans. Bernard Heise (New York: Berghahn Books, 2015), 167.
51. Gippert, "Danzig-West Prussia," 161–7.
52. The Łódź ghetto administration recorded death tolls based on gender, age and cause of death. For example the graphic representing of the death toll in the ghetto in May 1940: APL 39/741, 1: Graphische Aufstellung der Todesfälle für den Monat Mai 1940 in Litzmannstadt-Ghetto.
53. Dok. 186 (Tagebuch von Oskar Rosenfeld, Januar 8 bis Februar 12, 1943), *VEJ* 10, 535–6.
54. For in-depth research on the experiences Łódź ghetto inhabitants, see, for example, Andrea Löw, *Juden im Getto Litzmannstadt: Lebensbedingungen, Selbstwahrnehmung, Verhalten* (Göttingen: Wallstein Verlag, 2006).
55. Peter Klein, *Die "Ghettoverwaltung Litzmannstadt" 1940 bis 1944: Eine Dienststelle im Spannungsfeld von Kommunalbürokratie und staatlicher Verfolgungspolitik* (Hamburg: Hamburger Edition, 2009), 267.
56. Ibid., 268.
57. IPN BU 2586/200, 31: Zbiór akt z postępowań karnych dotyczących zbrodni nazistowskich. Reports on the sentencing of Nazi criminals in Hannover from September to November 1963.

58. Dominika Bopp, Sascha Feuchert, Andrea Löw, Jörg Riecke Markus Roth, and Elisabeth Turvold, eds. *Die Enzyklopädie des Gettos Lodz/Litzmannstadt* (Göttingen: Wallstein Verlag, 2020), 19.
59. Patrick Montague, *Chełmno and the Holocaust: The History of Hitler*'*s First Death Camp* (London: I. B Tauris, 2012), 16–18.
60. Ibid., 47.
61. IPN BU 2586/168, 13: The information is taken from files of criminal proceedings from July 5 to 23, 1965 in Bonn against members of the so-called *Vernichtungskommando* at Chełmno.
62. IPN BU 2586/168, 21.
63. Gordon J. Horwitz, *Ghettostadt: Łódź and the Making of a Nazi City* (Cambridge: University of Cambridge, 2008), 163.
64. Michael Alberti, *Die Verfolgung und Vernichtung der Juden im Reichsgau Wartheland 1939–1945* (Wiesbaden: Harrassowitz Verlag, 2006), 435.
65. Ibid., 442–3. See Alberti for an in-depth discussion on the background to the decision to also murder the western Jews.
66. United Nations War Crimes Commission, "Case No. 74, Trial of Artur [sic] Greiser," 95.
67. Alberti, *Die Verfolgung und Vernichtung der Juden*, 451.
68. IPN BU 2586/179, 8: Criminal proceedings against members of the crew of the Sztutowo concentration camp (KL Stutthof) held in Bochum (June 4, 1957).
69. IPN BU 2586/179, 10.
70. Dok. 259 (Protokoll der Aussage von Paja Pavlowskaja), *VEJ* 10, 707.
71. Nikolaus Wachsmann, *KL: Die Geschichte der nationalsozialistischen Konzentrationslager* (Munich: Siedler Verlag, 2016), 635.
72. Ibid., 636. For more in-depth studies of Stutthof, see, Danuta Drywa, *The Extermination of Jews in Stutthof Concentration Camp* (Gdańsk: Stutthof Museum in Sztutowo, 2004); Wolfgang Benz and Barbara Distel, ed., *Der Ort des Terrors. Geschichte der nationalsozialistischen Konzentrationslager: Natzweiler, Groß-Rosen, Stutthof*, vol. 6 (Munich: C. H.Beck, 2007).
73. IPN BU 2586/179, 20.
74. Wachsmann, *KL*, 728.
75. Peter Longerich, *Holocaust: The Nazi Persecution and Murder of the* Jews (Oxford: Oxford University Press, 2010), 144.
76. For more in-depth studies, see, for example, Klaus-Michael Mallmann, Jochen Böhler, and Jürgen Matthäus, eds., *Einsatzgruppen in Polen. Darstellung und Dokumentation* (Darmstadt: Wissenschaftliche Buchgesellschaft, 2008). On the *Intelligenzaktion*, see, Anna Meier, *Die Intelligenzaktion: Die Vernichtung der Polnischen Oberschicht Im Gau Danzig-Westpreußen* (Saarbrücken: VDM Verlag Dr. Müller, 2008).
77. Rolf-Dieter Müller, *Hitlers Ostkrieg und die deutsche Siedlungspolitik* (Frankfurt am Main: Fischer Taschenbuch Verlag GmbH, 1991), 89. One of Meyer's versions of the plan is discussed in Chapter 2.
78. For more information on the GPO, see, for example, Czesław Madajczyk, ed., *Vom Generalplan Ost zum Generalsiedlungsplan: Dokumente* (Munich: K. G. Saur, 1994); Czesław Madajczyk, "Generalplan Ost," *Polish Western Affairs* 3 (1962): 391–442; Mechtild Rössler and Sabine Schleiermacher, ed., *Der "Generalplan Ost": Hauptlinien der nationalsozialistischen Planungs- und Vernichtungspolitik* (Berlin: Akademie, 1993); Mark Mazower, *Hitler's Empire: Nazi Rule in Occupied Europe* (London: Allen

Lane, 2008), 204–11; Christian Ingrao, *The Promise of The East: Nazi Hopes and Genocide, 1939–43*, trans. Andrew Brown (Cambridge: Polity Press, 2019), 43–7.
79. Wetzel was a high-level official in the *Reichsministerium für die besetzten Ostgebiete*.
80. "Stellungnahme und Gedanken von Dr. Erhard Wetzel zum Generalplan Ost des Reichführers SS (27 April 1942)," in Madajczyk, *Vom Generalplan Ost zum Generalsiedlungsplan*, 53–4.
81. "Stellungnahme und Gedanken von Dr. Erhard Wetzel," in Madajczyk, *Vom Generalplan Ost zum Generalsiedlungsplan*, 61–2.
82. "Stellungnahme und Gedanken von Dr. Erhard Wetzel," in Madajczyk, *Vom Generalplan Ost zum Generalsiedlungsplan*, 63.
83. The tables and figures, which still exist from this plan are published in Madajczyk, *Vom Generalplan Ost zum Generalsiedlungsplan*, 235–55.
84. Madajczyk, *Vom Generalplan Ost zum Generalsiedlungsplan*, xiii.
85. Concubinage was the term used for cohabitation between European men and an indigenous woman outside of marriage.
86. On the banning of mixed marriages in Africa and the parallels to the Third Reich, see Madley, "From Africa to Auschwitz," 438–9 and Jürgen Zimmerer, "The Birth of the *Ostland* Out of the Spirit of Colonialism: A Postcolonial Perspective on the Nazi Policy of Conquest and Extermination," *Patterns of Prejudice* 39, no. 2 (2005): 104–5.
87. Emanuele Ertola, "The Italian fascist settler empire in Ethiopia, 1936–1941," in *The Routledge Handbook of the History of Settler Colonialism*, ed. Edward Cavanagh and Lorenzo Veracini (London: Routledge, 2017), 269.
88. Ann Laura Stoler, "Making Empire Respectable: The Politics of Race and Sexual Morality in 20th-Century Colonial Cultures," *American Ethnologist* 16, no. 4 (1989): 638.
89. Will Jackson, "Not Seeking Certain Proof: Interracial Sex and Archival Haze in High-Imperial Natal," in *Subverting Empire: Deviance and Disorder in the British Colonial World*, ed. Will Jackson and Emily J. Manktelow (London: Palgrave Macmillan, 2015), 185.
90. Stoler, "Making Empire Respectable," 652.
91. Röger, *Wartime Relations*.
92. See, for example, Frederick Cooper and Ann Laura Stoler's edited collection for further discussions on the blurring of colonial boundary lines Fredrick Cooper and Ann Laura Stoler, eds., *Tensions of Empire: Colonial Cultures in a Bourgeois World* (Berkeley: University of California Press, 1997).
93. Ertola, "The Italian Fascist Settler Empire," 269.
94. Devin O. Pendas, "Racial States in Comparative Perspective," in *Beyond the Racial State: Rethinking Nazi Germany: Rethinking Nazi Germany*, ed. Devin O. Pendas, Mark Roseman, and Richard F. Wetzell (Cambridge: Cambridge University Press, 2017), 131.
95. Ibid.
96. For further discussion, see Rebecca Swartz, *Education and Empire: Children, Race and Humanitarianism in the British Settler Colonies, 1833–1880* (London: Palgrave Macmillan, 2019).
97. Robert Foster, "Rations, Coexistence, and the Colonization of Aboriginal Labour in the South Australian Pastoral Industry, 1860–1911," *Aboriginal History* 24 (2000): 1.
98. Matteo Pretelli, "Education in the Italian Colonies during the Interwar Period," *Modern Italy* 16, no. 3 (2011): 279–80.

99. David Furber, "Going East: Colonialism and German Life in Nazi-Occupied Poland" (PhD diss., University of New York, 2003), 45–6. For a summary of some of the main points of his thesis, see Furber, "Near as Far in the Colonies: The Nazi Occupation of Poland," *International History Review* 26, no. 3 (2004): 541–79.
100. See, for example, David R. Roediger, "Whiteness and Race," in *The Oxford Handbook of American Immigration and Ethnicity*, ed. Ronald H. Bayor, 197–212 (Oxford: Oxford University Press, 2016); Noel Ignatiev, *How the Irish Became White* (New York: Routledge, 1995).
101. David A. Gerber and Alan M. Kraut, "Introduction: Becoming White: Irish Immigrants in the Nineteenth Century," in *American Immigration and Ethnicity*, ed. Geber and Kraut (Basingstoke: Palgrave Macmillan, 2005), 161.
102. As mentioned in relation to the DVL, in addition to skin color, even evidence of German descent was also not always sufficient for inclusion. The unreliability, and resulting lack of usage or inconsistent usage, of skin color as a "marker of difference" is also alluded to by Pendas. He has further applied this to the Holocaust and the impetus behind the annihilation of the Jews. He argues the lack of a visual difference meant the Jewish threat was perceived as a "parasitical, disguised intrusion into the heart of the German/Aryan people." Pendas, "Racial States in Comparative Perspective," 118–19, 137.
103. Kakel, *The American West and the Nazi East*, 158–61.
104. Colin Samson and Carlos Gigoux, *Indigenous Peoples and Colonialism: Global Perspectives* (Cambridge: Polity Press, 2017), 101, 103.
105. See Jürgen Zimmerer, *Von Windhuk nach Auschwitz? Beiträge zum Verhältnis von Kolonialismus und Holocaust* (Münster: LIT, 2011).
106. For more on the use of concentration camps during the Anglo-Boer War, see, for example, Elizabeth van Heyningen, *The Concentration Camps of the Anglo-Boer War: A Social History* (Johannesburg: Jacana Media, 2013). Interestingly, as Paul Moore has demonstrated, propaganda during the Nazi regime used criticisms of British concentration camps to stir up anti-British sentiment among the Germans and to promote their own use of camps, albeit with the view that the Nazi German camps were humane compared to the British ones. See Paul Moore, "'And What Concentration Camps Those Were!': Foreign Concentration Camps in Nazi Propaganda, 1933–9," *Journal of Contemporary History* 45, no. 3 (2010): 649–74.
107. Joachim Zeller, "Ombepera I koza- Die Kälte tötet mich," Zur Geschichte des Konzentrationslagers in Swakopmund," in *Völkermord in Deutsch-Südwestafrika: Der Kolonialkrieg (1904–1908) in Namibia und seine Folgen*, ed. Jürgen Zimmerer and Joachim Zeller (Berlin: Christoph Links Verlag GmbH, 2016), 66–7, 76.
108. Casper W. Erichsen, "Zwangsarbeit im Konzentrationslager auf der Haifischinsel," in *Völkermord in Deutsch-Südwestafrika*, 83.
109. Iain R. Smith & Andreas Stucki, "The Colonial Development of Concentration Camps (1868–1902)," *Journal of Imperial and Commonwealth History* 39, no. 3 (2011): 417, 418.
110. Jonas Kreienbaum, *A Sad Fiasco: Colonial Concentration Camps in Southern Africa, 1900–1908*, trans. Elizabeth Janik (New York: Berghahn Books, 2019), 228.
111. Kreienbaum, *A Sad Fiasco*, 231, 235, 242.
112. Isabel V. Hull, *Absolute Destruction: Military Culture and the Practices of War in Imperial Germany* (New York: Cornell University Press, 2005), 149.
113. See Madley, "From Africa to Auschwitz."

114. Given the number of deaths in Auschwitz-Birkenau, approximately 900,000 to one million people, it is not surprising that such dominance exists. However, it needs to be stressed that Auschwitz-Birkenau was only one part of a much larger campaign.
115. Madley, "From Africa to Auschwitz"; Zimmerer, *Von Windhuk nach Auschwitz*; Steffen Klävers, *Decolonizing Auschwitz?: Komparativ-postkoloniale Ansätze in Der Holocaustforschung* (Berlin: de Gruyter, 2019).
116. Frank Bajohr und Andrea Löw, "Tendenzen und Probleme der neueren Holocaust-Forschung: Eine Einführung," in *Der Holocaust: Ergebnisse und neue Fragen der Forschung*, ed. Frank Bajohr and Andrea Löw (Frankfurt am Main: S. Fischer Verlag GmbH, 2015), 14–16.
117. Christian Gerlach, *The Extermination of the European Jews* (Cambridge: Cambridge University Press, 2016), 119–22. On the *Einsatzgruppen* in the Soviet territiories, see, for example, Peter Klein, ed., *Die Einsatzgruppen in der besetzten Sowjetunion 1941/42. Die Tätigkeits- und Lageberichte des Chefs der Sicherheitspolizei und des SD* (Berlin: Wannsee-Haus, 1997); Andrej Angrick, *Besatzungspolitik und Massenmord: Die Einsatzgruppe D in der südlichen Sowjetunion 1941–1943* (Hamburg: Hamburger Edition, 2003).
118. Gerlach, *The Extermination of the European Jews*, 120, 122.
119. In relation to the General Government, see for example Jan Grabowski, *Hunt for the Jews: Betrayal and Murder in German-Occupied Poland* (Bloomington: Indiana University Press, 2013).
120. For example, the Spanish Army of Africa (*Ejército de África*) dropped toxic gas bombs containing such substances as phosgene, diphosgene, and mustard gas on civilian targets in Spanish Morocco during the Third Rif War (1921–1926). See for example, Rudibert Kunz and Rolf-Dieter Müller, *Giftgas gegen Abd el Krim: Deutschland, Spanien und der Gaskrieg in Spanisch- Marokko 1922–1927* (Freiburg: Verlag Rombach, 1990).
121. Historians such as Zimmerer have also alluded to this point in relation to colonial similarities. See, for example, Zimmerer, *Von Windhuk nach Auschwitz*, 194.
122. David Killingray, "Colonial Warfare in West Africa, 1870–1914," in *Imperialism and War: Essays on Colonial Wars in Asia and Africa*, ed. J. A. de Moor and H. L. Wesseling (Leiden: Brill, 1989) quoted in Michelle Gordon, "Colonial violence and Holocaust studies," *Holocaust Studies* 21, no. 4 (2015): 279. For further discussion, see also Alex J. Bellamy, "Mass Killing and the Politics of Legitimacy: Empire and the Ideology of Selective Extermination," *Australian Journal of Politics and History* 58, no. 2 (2012): 159–80.
123. Gordon, "Colonial violence and Holocaust studies," 281. On British imperial violence and arguments on how British racial "superiority" was used to rationalize the perpetration of extreme violence in colonies, see Michelle Gordon, *Extreme Violence and the "British Way": Colonial Warfare in Perak, Sierra Leone and Sudan* (London: Bloomsbury, 2020).
124. United Nations Convention on the Prevention and Punishment of the Crime of Genocide, Article II, https://www.un.org/en/genocideprevention/documents/atrocity-crimes/Doc.1_Convention%20on%20the%20Prevention%20and%20Punishment%20of%20the%20Crime%20of%20Genocide.pdf, accessed May 26, 2021.
125. Raphael Lemkin, *Axis Rule in Occupied Europe: Laws of Occupation, Analysis of Government, Proposals for Redress* (Clark: Lawbook Exchange, 2008), 79.
126. A. Dirk Moses, *The Problems of Genocide: Permanent Security and the Language of Transgression* (Cambridge: Cambridge University Press, 2021), 2, 17, 28.

127. Moses argues for using the broader term "permanent security" to describe the violence perpetrated against civilians by states attempting to make themselves invulnerable to threat. For more, see Moses's in-depth and thought-provoking publication *The Problems of Genocide*.
128. Roberta Pergher and Mark Roseman also make the point that Nazi Germany viewed the Jewish threat as a global one and not just one within Germany or its annexed territories. Additionally, they argue the Holocaust was the first "pan-imperial genocide" in that it was carried out throughout the entirety of the empire. Roberta Pergher and Mark Roseman, "The Holocaust—An Imperial Genocide?" *Dapim–Studies on the Holocaust* 27, no. 1 (2013): 42–9.
129. Isabel Heinemann, *Rasse, Siedlung, deutsches Blut: Das Rasse- und Siedlungshauptamt der SS und die rassenpolitische Neuordnung Europas* (Göttingen: Wallstein Verlag, 2003), 589.
130. See, for example, Alexa Stiller, "Germanisierung und Gewalt: Nationalsozialistische Politik in den annektierten Gebieten Polens, Frankreichs und Sloweniens, 1939–1945" (PhD diss., Historisches Institut Bern, 2014/2015).
131. AIZ Dok.I-25, 2.
132. Marek Orski, "Organisation und Ordnungsprinzipien des Lagers Stutthofs," in *Die nationalsozialistischen Konzentrationslager: Entwicklung und Struktur*, vol. 1, ed. Ulrich Herbert, Karin Orth and Christoph Dieckmann (Göttingen: Wallstein Verlag, 1998), 300.
133. Montague, *Chełmno and the Holocaust*, 165.
134. Alberti, *Die Verfolgung und Vernichtung der Juden*, 456. Hans Biebow was the head of the German Ghetto Administration.
135. Ibid.
136. Bundesarchiv Berlin-Lichterfelde (BArch) R59/229, 46: Arbeits- und Tätigkeitsberichte. Arbeitsbericht des Einsatzstabes Litzmannstadt für das Jahr 1942.
137. Montague, *Chełmno and the Holocaust*, 185–8.
138. *Aktion Reinhardt* was the plan for the extermination of Jews in the General Government at the extermination camps Bełżec, Sobibór, Treblinka, and also Majdanek and Auschwitz-Birkenau.
139. BArch R59/229, 46: Arbeitsbericht des Einsatzstabes Litzmannstadt für das Jahr 1942.
140. Ulrike Jureit, "Ordering Space: Intersections of Space, Racism, and Extermination," *Journal of Holocaust Research* 33, no.1 (2019): 65–6. See also Ulrike Jureit, *Das Ordnen von Räumen: Territorium und Lebensraum im 19. und 20. Jahrhundert* (Hamburg: Hamburger Edition, 2012).
141. Jureit, "Ordering Space," 81.
142. See Lorenzo Veracini, "Introduction: Settler Colonialism as a Distinct Mode of Domination," in *The Routledge Handbook of the History of Settler Colonialism*, ed. Edward Cavanagh and Lorenzo Veracini (London: Routledge, 2017), 3–5.
143. Patrick Wolfe, "Settler Colonialism and the Elimination of the Native," *Journal of Genocide Research* 8, no. 4 (2006): 388, 403; see also Patrick Wolfe, *Settler Colonialism and the Transformation of Anthropology: The Politics and Poetics of an Ethnographic Event* (London: Cassell, 1999).
144. David Furber and Wendy Lower have previously argued this point and highlighted that the Poles (and also Ukrainians) were therefore more comparable to the stereotypical colonial native than the Jews were. David Furber and Wendy Lower, "Colonialism and Genocide in Nazi-Occupied Poland and Ukraine," in *Empire, Colony, Genocide: Conquest, Occupation, and Subaltern Resistance in World History* ed. A. Dirk Moses (New York: Berghahn Books, 2008), 372–402.

145. Caroline Elkins and Susan Pederson, "Introduction Settler Colonialism: A Concept and Its Uses," in *Settler Colonialism in the Twentieth Century: Projects, Practices, Legacies*, ed. Caroline Elkins and Susan Pederson (New York: Routledge, 2005), 14. In her contribution to Elkins' and Pederson's volume, Elizabeth Harvey shows that ethnic German resettlers were the "human material" for the Nazi settler-colonial project given the high level of state control and involvement but the relatively low level of resettler power and influence in governance, Harvey, "Management and Manipulation: Nazi Settlement Planners and Ethnic German Settlers in Occupied Poland," in *Settler Colonialism in the Twentieth Century*, 95.
146. See for example Kakel, *The American West and the Nazi East* and Kakel, "Patterns and Crimes of Empire: Comparative Perspectives on Fascist and Non-Fascist Extermination," *Journal of Holocaust Research* 33, no. 1 (2019): 4–21. On the American West and comparisons with Nazi Germany's eastern expansion, see also Edward B. Westermann, *Hitler's Ostkrieg and the Indian Wars: Comparing Genocide and Conquest* (Norman: University of Oklahoma Press, 2016).
147. Lorenzo Veracini, *Settler Colonialism: A Theoretical Overview* (London: Palgrave Macmillan, 2010), 33, 34.
148. "Necropolitics," a term explored by Achille Mbembe, is the social and political power to have the capacity to decide how certain people may live and how certain people must die. See Achille Mbembe, "Necropolitics," *Public Culture* 15, no. 1 (2003): 11–40.
149. Veracini, *Settler Colonialism*, 35, 49.
150. Ibid., 38–9.
151. Ibid., 48.
152. Ann Laura Stoler, "Tense and Tender Ties: The Politics of Comparison in North American History and (Post) Colonial Studies," in *Haunted by Empire: Geographies of Intimacy in North American History*, ed. Ann Laura Stoler (Durham: Duke University Press, 2006), 55.
153. In relation to the German Jews who were moved from the *Altreich* to the annexed territories, although they were not originating from an area which was outside of the *Altreich*, Nazi Germany would solve the supposed problem of their existence within the annexed territories by using the removal methods which were already in use there.
154. Ingo Loose, "Wartheland," in *The Greater German Reich and the Jews: Nazi Persecution Policies in the Annexed Territories, 1939–1945*, ed. Wolf Gruner and Jörg Osterloh, trans. Bernard Heise (New York: Berghahn Books, 2015), 210.
155. Zygmunt Bauman, "Making and Unmaking of Strangers," *Thesis Eleven* 43 (1995): 2. Emphasis in original. Veracini also quotes Bauman, see Veracini, *Settler Colonialism*, 50–1.

5 "To Colonize Is to Cultivate": Colonial Overlaps between Africa and Poland

The quote in the chapter title is taken from Institut für Zeitgeschichte Archiv, München (IfZ): Franz Ritter von Epp, *Der deutsche Standpunkt in der Kolonialfrage: Rede, gehalten bei der kolonialen Großkundgebung im Sportspalast Berlin am 6. Dezember 1937* (München: Müller, 1937), 10.

1. Wolfe W. Schmokel, *Dream of Empire: German Colonialism, 1919-1945* (New Haven: Yale University Press, 1964), 160.
2. Geoff Eley, "Empire by Land or Sea? Germany's Colonial Imaginary, 1840-1945," in *German Colonialism in a Global Age*, ed. Bradley Naranch and Geoff Eley (London: Duke University Press, 2014), 20.
3. See, for example, Karsten Linne, *Deutschland jenseits des Äquators? Die NS-Kolonialplanungen für Afrika* (Berlin: Ch. Links Verlag, 2008); Willeke Sandler, *Empire in the Heimat: Colonialism and Public Culture in the Third Reich* (Oxford: Oxford University Press, 2018); Britta Schilling, *Postcolonial Germany: Memories of Empire in a Decolonised Nation* (Oxford: Oxford University Press, 2014); Birthe Kundrus (ed.), *Phantasiereiche: Zur Kulturgeschichte des deutschen Kolonialismus* (Frankfurt: Campus, 2003). See also, Eric Ames, Marcia Klotz, and Lora Wildenthal, eds., *Germany's Colonial Pasts* (Lincoln: University of Nebraska, 2005) and the contributions to the edited collection Bradley Naranch and Geoff Eley, eds., *German Colonialism in a Global Age*.
4. Jens-Uwe Guettel, *German Expansionism, Imperial Liberalism and the United States, 1776-1945* (New York: Cambridge University Press, 2012), 190.
5. Adolf Hitler, *Mein Kampf*, ed. and trans. John Chamberlain et al (New York: Reynal & Hitchcock, 1939), 938.
6. Hitler, *Mein Kampf*, 181, 950.
7. See, Chantal Metzger, *L'Empire colonial français dans la stratégie du Troisième Reich, 1936-1945* (New York: Peter Lang, 2002).
8. Schmokel, *Dream of Empire*, 21.
9. Franz Xaver Epp was born in 1868 in Munich. For more on his biography, see Katja-Maria Wächter, *Die Macht der Ohnmacht: Leben und Politik des Franz Xaver Ritter von Epp (1868-1946)* (Frankfurt am Main: Peter Lang GmbH, 1999).
10. Franz Ritter von Epp, *Deutschlands kolonial Forderung* (München: Buchgewerbehaus M. Müller & Sohn, 1939), 7.
11. Linne, *Deutschland jenseits des Äquators?*, 30.
12. Memorandum reproduced in Klaus Hildebrand, *Vom Reich zum Weltreich. Hitler, NSDAP und koloniale Frage 1919-1945* (Munich: W. Fink, 1969), 863.
13. Hans Heinrich Lammers was born in Lubliniec (Lublinitz), Upper Silesia in 1879. He joined the National Socialist Party in 1932 and was appointed Secretary of State and Chief of the Reich Chancellery in 1933.
14. IfZ MA 190/3, Oberkommando der Wehrmacht (OKW); Feldwirtschaftsamt, 579-80: Vertrauliches Schreiben Lammers an Reichsleiter General von Epp (March 9, 1939).
15. BayHStA Polizeischule Fürstenfeldbruck 188, 17: Letter from the *Staatsministerium des Inneren* received by the *Pol.-Offizier-u. Schutz Polizeischule*, Fürstenfeldbruck (December 7, 1937). For example, the letter was sent to the police school in Fürstenfeldbruck and the Police Headquarters in Munich and Augsburg.
16. BayHStA Polizeischule Fürstenfeldbruck 188, 17-18.
17. Schmokel, *Dream of Empire*, 32.
18. Ibid., 144. It is unclear if Schmokel adjusted these figures for inflation; however, regardless of the amount, new budgets were allocated.
19. Linne, *Deutschland jenseits des Äquators?* 86.
20. IfZ: "Wanderung - Reiseverbindungen von und nach den deutschen Schutzgebieten," *Deutsche Kolonial-Zeitung. Monatsschrift des Reichkolonialbundes* 51, no.2 (1939) (München: Verlag des Reichkolonialbundes, 1939), 57.

21. See, for example, Jens Ruppenthal, *Kolonialismus als „Wissenschaft und Technik": Das Hamburgische Kolonialinstitut 1908 bis 1919* (Stuttgart: Franz Steiner Verlag, 2007).
22. "Am Tage des Universitätsjubiläums: Hamburgs Kolonialinstitut nahm seine Arbeit wieder auf," *Hamburger Anzeiger* (May 10, 1940).
23. For more information, see the in-depth study Karsten Linne, *Von Witzenhausen in die Welt: Ausbildung und Arbeit von Tropenlandwirten 1898 bis 1971* (Göttingen: Wallstein Verlag, 2017). Other *Kolonialschule* also existed in Germany, for example, in Carthaus und Bad Weilbach.
24. "Der deutsche Kolonialgeist lebt! Afrika in Witzenhausen, Europas einzige Kolonialschule," *Hamburger Nachrichten* (September 13, 1933), 11.
25. Another colonial school was opened in Bad Weilbach in 1911. In addition to the colonial schools, many agriculture schools existed throughout Germany, for example, in Berlin, Bonn, Kiel, Munich, Leipzig, and Hohenheim. For further information on overseas colonial education in the Third Reich see Willeke Sandler, "Colonial Education in the Third Reich: The Witzenhausen Colonial School and the Rendsburg Colonial School for Women," *Central European History* 49, no.2 (2016), 181–207.
26. Sandler, "Colonizers Are Born, Not Made," 438–9.
27. Hanna Reitsch, *Das Unzerstörbare in meinem Leben* (München: F. A. Herbig, 1979), 55. Reitsch was the only female to be awarded the Iron Cross First Class. She participated in numerous test flights for the *Luftwaffe* during the war and held many world records at the time.
28. "Colonial training for women," *The Guardian* (November 14, 1902) https://www.theguardian.com/theguardian/2013/nov/14/colonies-women-training-empire, accessed February 24, 2016.
29. "Der deutsche Kolonialgeist lebt!," 11.
30. Ibid.
31. "Verachtung des bequemen Lebens: Bericht über die koloniale Frauenschule in Rendsburg," *Hamburger Anzeiger* (June 28/29, 1941), 5.
32. Ibid.
33. Liebernez (1893–1954) had also produced other films with colonialism as the subject; for example, *Mensch und Tier im Urwald* (1924) and *Auf Tierfang in Afrika* (1926). He also worked as a cameraman for the 1934 Leni Riefenstahl film *Triumph des Willens*.
34. See, for example, Marion Hulverscheidt, "Der Weg in die Welt: Propagandafilme für deutsche Kolonialschulen," in *Das Vorprogramm: Lehrfilm/Gebrauchsfilm/Propagandafilm/unveröffentlichter Film in Kinos und Archiven am Oberrhein 1900–1970*, ed. Philipp Osten, Gabriele Moser, Christian Bonah, Alexandre Sumpf, Tricia Close-Koenig, and Joël Danet (Heidelberg: A25 Rhinfilm, 2015), 337–59. Colonialism and imperialism as film topics were not uncommon during the Third Reich; however, such film themes were often used within the context of British imperial violence in an effort to stir up anti-British sentiment. For example, *Ohm Krüger* (1941), which was directed by Hans Steinhoff depicted British crimes against the Boers during the Second Boer War of 1899–1902. Similarly, Max W. Kimmich's films *Der Fuchs von Glenarvon* (The Fox of Glenarvon) released in 1940 and *Mein Leben für Irland* (My Life for Ireland) released in 1941 depicted Irish suffering at the hands of the British Empire. For more on portrayals of foreign concentration camps in Nazi Germany, see Paul Moore, '"And What Concentration Camps Those Were!': Foreign Concentration Camps in Nazi Propaganda, 1933-9," *Journal of Contemporary History*, 45, no. 3 (2010): 649–74.

35. *Die Deutsche Frauen-Kolonialschule Rendsburg* 1937, Produktion Paul Lieberenz, Release Date: 1974 by IWF Wissen und Medien gGmbH Göttingen.
36. Irina Scheidgen, "Frauenbilder im Spielfilm, Kulturfilm und in der Wochenschau des Dritten Reiches," in *Nationalsozialismus und Geschlecht: Zur Politisierung und Ästhetisierung von Körper, Rasse und Sexualität im Dritten Reich und nach 1945*, ed. Elke Frietsch and Christina Herkommer (Bielefeld: Transcript Verlag, 2009), 273.
37. Katharina Walgenbach, *"Die Weiße Frau als Trägerin deutscher Kultur"*: *Kolonial Diskurse über Geschlecht, "Rasse" und Klasse im Kaiserreich* (Frankfurt: Campus Verlag, 2005), 125–7.
38. For more on comparisons between role of women in Poland and overseas colonies through the lens of film, see Rachel O'Sullivan, "The German Mission in Africa and Poland: Women, Expansion, and Colonial Training During the Third Reich," *Journal of Colonialism and Colonial History* 22, no. 2, 2021. muse.jhu.edu/article/801556.
39. Hildebrand, *Vom Reich zum Weltreich*, 428.
40. As Willeke Sandler highlights, overseas colonial enthusiasts in Germany generally promoted a whitewashed history of German colonialism in Africa, especially regarding the Herero and Nama Wars (1904–7). German colonialists were portrayed "as capable-but not brutal-colonisers." Sandler, *Empire in the Heimat*, 122–3; see also Andreas Eckl, "Zu leben, nur um da zu sein, hat niemand ein Recht': Der Kolonialkrieg mit dem Volk der Herero 1904 im Spiegel kolonialpropagandistischer Literatur der NS-Zeit," in *Afrika—Kultur und Gewalt: Hintergründe und Aktualität des Kolonialkriegs in Deutsch-Südwestafrika; seine Rezeption in Literatur, Wissenschaft und Populärkultur (1904–2004)*, ed. Christof Hamann (Iserlohn: Inst. für Kirche und Gesellschaft, 2005), 159–89.
41. IfZ: *Deutsche Kolonial-Ausstellung Köln 1934 1. Juli- 2. Sept* (Köln: Ernst Stauf Verlag, 1934), 7.
42. IfZ: *Großdeutschland - Deine Kolonien: Festschrift zur Reichstagung des Reichskolonialbundes in Bremen vom 24. Bis 29. Mai 1938* (Berlin: Wilhelm Limpert, Druck- und Verlagshaus, 1938), 53, 56–7.
43. Eckard Michels, "Paul von Lettow-Vorbeck," in *Kein Platz an der Sonne: Erinnerungsorte der deutschen Kolonialgeschichte*, ed. Jürgen Zimmerer (Frankfurt: Campus Verlag, 2013), 374.
44. Ibid.
45. BayHStA Kriegsabteilung V, (Offiziersakte) Op 271 Franz Ritter von Epp: General Ritter von Epp 50 Jahre Soldat, " *Völkischer Beobachter - Münchner Ausgabe* (August 15, 1937), 1–2.
46. BayHStA Kriegsabteilung V, Op 271 Franz Ritter von Epp: Ein Jubiläum des Reichsstatthalters in Bayern," *Völkischer Beobachter* (November 7, 1942), „Ritter von Epp 75 Jahre alt," *Münchner Neuste Nachrichten* (October 15, 1943).
47. Schilling, *Postcolonial Germany*, 46–7.
48. The joint publishers of the poster were the RKB and the *Deutsches Theater*, which implies that the RKB organized the ball.
49. Bayerisches Hauptstaatsarchiv (BayHStA) Abt. V, Plakatsammlung Kultur- und Werbeplakate bis 1945-21340: "Auf Safari," Anton M. Kolnberger. Printed by C. Wolf and Sohn (Munich, February 1936); BayHStA Abt. V, 21424: "Auf Safari," Anton M. Kolnberger. Printed by Köhler and Sohn (Munich, February 1939).
50. BayHStA Abt. V, 21371: "Kolonial-Ball," Philipp Waizmann (Munich, February 1937). Ngoma is an area in present-day Namibia. As well as the aforementioned colonial balls, another colonial event was held during the Nazi regime. The *Deutsche*

Afrika-Schau (German Africa Show), which ran from 1934 until 1940, is particularly notable in that it was actually supported by the National Socialist Party during its years of operation. The Show, which was originally privately ran, became sanctioned by such offices as the KPA and the Ministry of Propaganda. This was most probably because the idea of possibly regaining the former German African colonies was a useful propaganda tool at the time; however, it does demonstrate an official acceptance of colonial propaganda by Nazi government officials. See Elisa von Joeden-Forgey, "Race Power in Postcolonial Germany: The German Africa Show and the National Socialist State, 1935–1940," in *Germany's Colonial Pasts*, ed. Eric Ames, Marcia Klotz, and Lora Wildenthal (Lincoln: University of Nebraska, 2005), 167–88.

51. Henry Picker, *Hitlers Tischgespräche im Führerhauptquartier* (Stuttgart: Seewald, 1977), 465 and Adolf Hitler, *Monologe im Führerhauptquartier 1941–1944. Die Aufzeichnungen Heinrich Heims*, ed. Werner Jochmann (Hamburg: Albrecht Knaus Verlag, 1980), 389 quoted in Linne, *Deutschland jenseits des Äquators?*, 147–8.
52. Both examples from Linne, *Deutschland jenseits des Äquators?*, 148.
53. Schmokel, *Dream of Empire*, 150.
54. Richard Walther Darré was born in Argentina on July 14, 1895, to a German father and half-German mother. The family moved back to Germany in the lead up to the First World War and in 1914, Darré enrolled in the boys' colonial school in Witzenhausen. With the outbreak of the First World War, Darré volunteered for the army and fought on the Western Front. He returned to Witzenhausen in 1920 to finish his education. Darré was expelled from the school that year on charges of lying but was later awarded his degree in 1930 when the verdict was overturned. He began a degree in agriculture in 1922 and completed his doctorate in 1929. Darré became a member of the National Socialist Party and the SS in 1930 and he was well-known for his beliefs surrounding agrarianism and race. Darré was a strong proponent of the *Blut und Boden* ideology and contributed to its literature with books such as *Das Bauerntum als Lebensquell der nordischen Rasse* (The Peasantry as the Source of the Nordic Race, 1928) and *Neuadel aus Blut und Boden* (A New Nobility from Blood and Soil, 1930).
55. R. Walther Darré, "Stellung und Aufgaben des Landstandes in einem nach lebensgesetzlichen Gesichtspunkten aufgebauten deutsche Staate (September 1930)," in *Erkenntnisse und Werden: Aufsätze aus der Zeit vor der Machtergreifung*, ed. Marie Adelheid Prinzessin Reuß-zur Lippe, 2nd ed. (Goslar: Verlag Blut und Boden, 1940), 160–1. The editor of the book, Marie Adelheid Prinzessin Reuß-zur Lippe, was a member of the aristocracy and a supporter of the Nazi Regime. She had a close relationship with Darré and was one of his earliest supporters. See Lionel Gossman, *Brownshirt Princess: A Study of the "Nazi Conscience"* (Open Book Publishers: Cambridge, 2009).
56. R. Walther Darré, "Ostraumgedanke oder Rückforderung unserer Kolonien," *Bayerische Hochschulzeitung*, May 21, 1931. The article was first published in the *Völkischer Beobachter* on May 9, 1931.
57. Ibid.
58. "The Ministries Trail, October 1946–April 1949," *Trials of War Criminals before the Nuremberg Military Tribunals under Control Council Law No. 10*, Vol. XIV (Washington, DC: U S Government Printing Office, 1949–1953), 559.
59. Anna Bramwell, *Blood and Soil: Walther Darré and Hitler's "Green Party"* (Bourne End: Kensal Press, 1985), 146–7.
60. Hildebrand, *Vom Reich zum Weltreich*, 333.

61. See, for example, IfZ: Rudolf Ibel (ed.), *Deutschland braucht Kolonien* (Hamburg: Köbner & Co Verlag, 1936), 41.
62. Benjamin Madley and Jürgen Zimmerer include Epp in their arguments for the existence of individuals who served as a link between the German colonialism of the past and the German colonialism of the future. Although Epp is certainly an interesting figure given his military background, long-standing relationship with the National Socialist Party, and his passion for German colonialism in Africa, the extent of Epp's direct impact on other Nazi leaders should be approached with caution. Madley's argument that Epp was an influence on leading Nazi figures is problematic given that ascertaining exactly how a person influenced another or exactly what areas of the person's life was effected by the influence is an extremely difficult factor to pinpoint. Similarly, the exact impact Epp made or did not make on Hitler or on Nazi policies cannot be conclusively seen. See Madley, "From Africa to Auschwitz," 450–3 and Zimmerer, "The birth of the *Ostland*," 211–14.
63. Wächter, *Die Macht der Ohnmacht*, 205.
64. Epp quoted in Schmokel, *Dream of Empire*, 50.
65. Epp's speech on August 4, 1933 in Leipzig quoted in Wächter, *Die Macht der Ohnmacht*, 210. This was possibly a reaction to Darré, a supporter of Eastern settlement, being appointed as Minister for Food and Agriculture in June of that year.
66. This mentality can be compared to the BDM lecturer (discussed in the *Koloniale Frauenschule* section) who told the students of the *Koloniale Frauenschule* they could test their skills in the East. The implication being that the European East could be a practice ground for overseas colonial activities.
67. Letter from Epp to Weigelt (November 20, 1941) quoted in Linne, *Deutschland jenseits des Äquators?*, 117. Letter also partially quoted in Zimmerer, "The birth of the *Ostland*," 214. Kurt Weigelt was born on June 4, 1884, in Berlin. He would later become the director of Deutsche Bank in 1923, a patron member of the SS (*Förderndes Mitglied der SS*) in 1934 and a member of the NSDAP in 1937. Additionally, Weigelt was involved in numerous colonial institutions such as the *Deutsch-Ostafrikanische Gesellschaft* (German East Africa Society), the Hamburg Colonial Institute, the colonial council of the RKB and the *Gruppe Deutscher Kolonialwirtschaftlicher* Unternehmungen (Colonial Economic Enterprise Group), of which he was the head.
68. Linne, *Deutschland jenseits des Äquators?*, 166.
69. For example, Konrad Meyer was born in 1901 meaning he was more than thirty years younger than Epp.
70. Sandler, "Colonizers Are Born, Not Made," 440.
71. Hulda Rautenberg and Mechtild Rommel, "Die Koloniale Frauenschule in Rendsburg von 1926–1945," in *Die Kolonialen Frauenschulen von 1908–1945* (Witzenhausen: Gesamthochschule Kassel, 1983), 87.
72. Rautenberg and Rommel, "Die Koloniale Frauenschule in Rendsburg von 1926–1945," 74.
73. Lora Wildenthal, *German Women for Empire, 1884–1945* (Durham: Duke University Press, 2001), 198.
74. Dorothea Siegle, *"Trägerinnen echten Deutschtums." Die Koloniale Frauenschule Rendsburg* (Rendsburg: Wachholtz Verlag, 2004), 107.
75. Elizabeth Harvey, *Women and the Nazi East: Agents and Witnesses of Germanization* (New Haven: Yale University Press, 2003), 109.

76. "Kolonialschulerinnen können sich im Warthegau erproben," *Hamburger Anzeiger* (December 3, 1940), 3.
77. Quoted in Sandler, "Colonizers Are Born, Not Made," 441.
78. Wildenthal, *German Women for Empire*, 199.
79. Ibid.
80. Jürgen Zimmerer, "The First Genocide of the Twentieth Century: The German War of Destruction in South West Africa (1904–1908) and the Global History of Genocide," in *Lessons and Legacies VIII: From Generation to Generation* ed. Doris L. Bergen (Evanston: Northwestern University Press, 2008), 36, 56. A number of Zimmerer's articles have been compiled in the book Zimmerer, *Von Windhuk nach Auschwitz?* Gerwarth and Malinowski, "Hannah Arendt's Ghosts," 287; Kühne, "Colonialism and the Holocaust," 344–5.
81. Christoph Kienemann, *Der koloniale Blick gen Osten: Osteuropa im Diskurs des Deutschen Kaiserreiches von 1871* (Paderborn: Ferdinand Schöningh, 2018), 265–6.
82. IfZ: Ibel (ed.), *Deutschland braucht Kolonien*, 41.
83. Quote by Franz Ritter von Epp in G. W. Filcher, "Auf, zum Kampf um Deutschlands koloniale Ehre!" in *Deutsche Kolonialarbeit in Vergangenheit und Zukunft: Ein Kapitel Deutsche Ehre* (Königsberg: Reichskolonialbund Kreisverband Königsberg-Stadt, 1938), 3.
84. IfZ: *Deutsche Kolonial-Ausstellung Köln 1934*, 7.
85. Ibid.
86. IfZ: Ibel (ed.), *Deutschland braucht Kolonien*, 43.
87. Paul Leßner, *Was müssen wir von unseren Kolonien wissen?* (Leipzig: Friedrich M. Hörhold-Verlag, 1938), 11. Paul Leßner was an *Oberstleutnant* in the *Schutztruppe* in Cameron. For more biographical information, see Florian Hoffmann, *Okkupation und Militärverwaltung in Kamerun: Etablierung und Institutionalisierung des kolonialen Gewaltmonopols. Teil II - Die kaiserliche Schutztruppe und ihr Offizierkorps* (Göttingen: Cuvillier Verlag, 2007), 129–30.
88. IfZ: Heinrich Schnee, *Deutschlands koloniale Forderung, Zeitfragen deutscher Kultur*. Vol. 3 (Berlin: Hermann Wendt Gmbh, 1937), 7, 8, 10, 30. The publication series was released by the *Gesellschaft der Berliner Freunde der Deutschen Akademie* and edited by Fritz Behrend.
89. *Zeitfragen deutscher Kultur*, 30.
90. Adolf von Duisburg, *Wer will in die Kolonien? Ein Wegweiser zur kolonialen Arbeit* (Berlin: Dr. Hans Riegler Verlag für vaterländische Literatur, 1938), 11.
91. Ingo Haar, "German *Ostforschung* and Anti-Semitism," in *German Scholars and Ethnic Cleansing, 1920–1945*, ed. Ingo Haar and Michael Fahlbusch (New York: Berghahn Books, 2005), 12.
92. Hermann Aubin, "Die historisch-geographischen Grundlagen der deutsch-polnischen Beziehungen," in *Deutschland und Polen – Beiträge zu ihren geschichtlichen Beziehungen*, ed. Albert Brackmann (Munich and Berlin: Verlag von R. Oldenbourg, 1933), 25. Aubin was born in 1885 in Liberec in the Czech Republic (then known as Reichenberg and part of the Habsburg Monarchy). He studied history and economics in Munich and Freiburg. For more in-depth information on Aubin, see Eduard Mühle's very comprehensive study: Eduard Mühle, *Für Volk und deutschen Osten: Der Historiker Hermann Aubin und die deutsche Ostforschung* (Droste Verlag: Düsseldorf, 2005).
93. See, for example, Ibel (ed.), *Deutschland braucht Kolonien*, 43.

94. A. Hillen Ziegfeld, "Die Lebensgesetze des deutschen Ostens," in *Der Deutsche Osten: Seine Geschichte, sein Wesen und seine Aufgabe*, ed. Karl. E. Thalheim and A. Hillen Ziegfeld (Berlin: Propyläen Verlag, 1936), 602.
95. Otto Fitzner, "Die kommenden Aufgaben der Wirtschaft im Osten," in *Breslau und deutscher Osten*, ed. W. Foerst (Otto v. Holten: Berlin, 1941), 50. Fitzner does not provide the exact coordinates of where he believes West, Central, and East Germany to be located but his main point is that in the East areas, the population had more space. Fitzner was a member of the NSDAP since 1931 and was named economic advisor for the *Gau* of Lower Silesia in 1941.
96. Geoff Eley, "Commentary: Empire, Ideology and the East: Thoughts on Nazism"'s Spatial Imaginary," in *Heimat, Region, and Empire: Spatial Identities under National Socialism*, ed. Claus-Christian W. Szejnmann and Maiken Umbach (Basingstoke: Palgrave Macmillan, 2012), 259.
97. Eduard Mühle, "The Mental Map of German *Ostforschung*," in *Germany and the European East in the Twentieth Century*, ed. Eduard Mühle (Oxford: Berg, 2003), 117.
98. Eduard Mühle, "Putting the East in Order: German Historians and their Attempts to Rationalize German Eastward Expansion during the 1930s and 1940s," in *Germans, Poland, and Colonial Expansion to the East: 1800 Through the Present*, ed. Robert Nelson (Basingstoke: Palgrave Macmillan, 2009), 101.
99. Hermann Aubin, "Zur Erforschung der deutschen Ostbewegung," in *Deutsche Schriften zur Landes- und Volksforschung*, ed. E. Meynen (Leipzig: S. Hirzel, 1939), 89.
100. IfZ: Franz Ritter von Epp, *Der deutsche Standpunkt in der Kolonialfrage*, 12–13.
101. Birthe Kundrus has also alluded to how woman provided a similar cultural influence in East Prussia. See Birthe Kundrus, "Weiblicher Kulturimperialismus: Die imperialistischen Frauenverbände des Kaiserreiches," in *Das Kaiserreich transnational: Deutschland in der Welt 1871–1914*, ed. Sebastian Conrad und Jürgen Osterhammel (Göttingen: Vandenhoeck & Ruprecht, 2004), 226.
102. Duisburg, *Wer will in die Kolonien?*, 76–7.
103. IfZ: *Richtlinien für die kolonialpolitische Ausbildung*, Schulungsamt des kolonialpolitischen Amtes der NSDAP, Reichsleitung (Berlin, August 1939).
104. IfZ: Eva MacLean, "Die Aufgaben der deutsche Frau in den Kolonien," in *Koloniales Taschenbuch 1941*, ed. Bundesführung des Reichskolonialbundes, Berlin (München: Buchgewerbehaus M. Müller & Sohn, 1941), 42.
105. Max Hildebert Boehm, "Der deutsche Osten und das Reich," in *Der Deutsche Osten: Seine Geschichte, sein Wesen und seine Aufgabe*, ed. Karl. E. Thalheim and A. Hillen Ziegfeld (Berlin: Propyläen Verlag, 1936), 3.
106. A. Hillen Ziegfeld, "Die Lebensgesetze des deutschen Ostens," 602.
107. Albert Brackmann, *Krisis und Aufbau in Osteuropa. Ein weltgeschichtliches Bild* (Berlin: Ahnenerbe-Stiftung Verlag: 1939), 6. Albert Brackmann (1871–1952), born in Hanover, was a nationalist historian who is well-known for his involvement in the *Ostforschung* movement. Brackmann was also the director of the Prussian State archives from 1929 and was the first director of the Prussian Institute of Archival Sciences.
108. Brackmann, *Krisis und Aufbau in Osteuropa*.
109. Otto Fitzner, "Die kommenden Aufgaben der Wirtschaft im Osten," 50.
110. Hans Rothfels, "The Problem of Nationalism in the East," in *Germany and Poland in Their Historical Relations*, ed. Albert Brackmann, trans. S. Miles Bouton (Munich and Berlin: R. Oldenbourg, 1934), 262. This was the English translation of *Deutschland*

und Polen released one year later. Rothfels was a German historian born in Kassel in 1891. Despite his initial support of right-wing policies and potentially the Nazi Party, Rothfels was forced to leave Germany in 1938 due to his Jewish ancestry. For further discussion on Hans Rothfels support of National Socialist policies, see Karl Heinz Roth, "Richtung Halten" Hans Rothfels and Neoconservative Historiography on Both Sides of the Atlantic," in *German Scholars and Ethnic Cleansing*, ed. Haar and Fahlbusch, 236–59.

111. Haar, *Historiker im Nationalsozialismus*, 90.
112. As explained in Chapter 2, the racial and health screening of ethnic Germans demonstrated a degree of suspicion toward them.
113. IfZ: *Reichskolonialbund - Deutschland, deine Kolonien!*, Nr. 2 (Duderstadt: Friedrich Wagner, 1937), 2.
114. *Der Führer hat uns gerufen* (Berlin-Luck: VoMi-Berlin, Deutsches Kommando für die Umsiedlung der Deutschen aus Galizien, Wolhynien und Bialystok., 1940), 16.
115. Willeke Sandler, "Deutsche Heimat in Afrika: Colonial Revisionism and the Construction of Germanness through Photography," *Journal of Women's History* 25, no. 1 (2013): 41.
116. Paul H. Kuntze *Das neue Volksbuch der Kolonien* (Leipzig: Georg Dollheimer Verlag, 1941), Illustration 61 (Photographer: Ilse Steinhoff).
117. The South West African Scouts Association was merged with the Hitler Youth in 1934 but were banned by the South African League of Nations mandate authorities. In 1935, the scouts were reformed under a slightly different name before being banned in 1939 after the outbreak of the Second World War. See the *Arbeitsgemeinschaft Pfadfinder e.V.* website for more information, https://www.arge-pfadfinder.org/dt.-pfadf.-in-swa.html, accessed October 10, 2022.
118. Kuntze, *Das neue Volksbuch der Kolonien*, Illustration 60 (Photographer: Ilse Steinhoff).
119. IfZ: *Reichskolonialbund - Deutschland, deine Kolonien!*, 1, 6–7.
120. See also the work of Reinhard Wittram discussed in Jörg Hackmann, "Narrating the Building of a Small Nation: Divergence and Convergence in the Historiography of Estonian 'National Awakening,' 1868–2005," in *Nationalizing the Past: Historians as Nation Builders in Modern Europe*, ed. Stefan Berger and Chris Lorenz (Basingstoke: Palgrave Macmillan, 2010), 181.
121. Erich Keyser, "Die Erforschung der Bevölkerungsgeschichte des deutschen Ostens," in *Deutsche Ostforschung: Ergebnisse und Aufgaben seit dem ersten Weltkrieg*, ed. Hermann Aubin, Otto Brunner, Wolfgang Kohte, and Johannes Papritz (Leipzig: Verlang von S. Hirzel, 1942), 90. Erich Keyser (1893–1968) was a German historian born in Danzig. He was the creator and director of the State Regional Museum of Danzig History in Danzig-Olivia and he was the director of a research unit in Königsberg which was linked to the *Nord- und Ostdeutsche Forschungsgemeinschaft* (NODFG). Keyser also participated in the compilation of the *Deutsche Volksliste* in the *Reichsgau* Danzig-West Prussia. For more information, see Alexander Pinwinkler, "*Volk, Bevölkerung, Rasse*, And *Raum*: Erich Keyser's Ambiguous Concept of a German History of Population, ca. 1918–1955," in *German Scholars and Ethnic Cleansing*: 86–99.
122. Keyser, "Die Erforschung der Bevölkerungsgeschichte des deutschen Ostens," 104.
123. Brackmann, *Krisis und Aufbau in Osteuropa*, 64–5.
124. Ibid., 65.

125. Karl Thalheim, "Deutsches Vorfeld im Osten," *Der Deutsche Osten*, 305. Thalheim (1900–1993) was a German economist and at the time of editing *Der Deutsche Osten*, he was a lecturer at the *Handelshochschule* in Lepzig. His claim that ethnic Germans still had the dialect of their ancestors may have been true in some cases; however, as mentioned in Chapter 2, many of the ethnic Germans could not speak German, let alone speak with a German dialect.
126. Erich Ludow, "Danzig," in *Der Deutsche Osten*, 97.
127. H. W. Bauer, *Kolonien oder nicht? Die Einstellung von Partei und Staat zum kolonialen Gedanken* (Leipzig: Richard Bauer Verlag, 1935), 48.
128. *Zeitfragen deutscher Kultur*, Heft 3, 48.
129. Senta Dinglreiter, *Wann kommen die deutschen endlich wieder? Eine Reise durch unsere Kolonien in Afrika* (Leipzig: Koehler & Ameland, 1935), 57.
130. The aspect of bringing German culture to Poland echoed Bismarck's policy of *Kulturkampf*.
131. Boehm, "Der deutsche Osten und das Reich," 3.
132. Hans Rothfels, "Das Problem des Nationalismus im Osten," in *Deutschland und Polen – Beiträge zu ihren geschichtlichen Beziehungen*, ed. Albert Brackmann (Munich: Verlag von R. Oldenbourg, 1933), 269.
133. Curt von Ulrich, "Mitteldeutschland und die Ostkolonisation," *Raumforschung und Raumordnung: Monatsschrift der Reichsarbeitsgemeinschaft für Raumforschung* (1940) 4, no. 1/2: 4. Von Ulrich was the Chairman of the *Landesplanungsgemeinschaft Provinz Sachsen-Land Anhalt* (Provincial Planning Association of Saxony-Anhalt).
134. IfZ: Epp, *Der deutsche Standpunkt in der Kolonialfrage*, 3–4.
135. Dinglreiter, *Wann kommen die deutschen endlich wieder?*, 6.
136. Ernst Gerhard Jacob, "Der Kampf gegen die koloniale Schuldlüge," *Deutsches Ringen um kolonialen Raum* 7 (Hamburg: Paul Hartung Verlag, 1938), 4.
137. Ibid., 47.
138. Paul Ritter, ed., *Unvergessenes deutsches Land* (Berlin: Verlag und Vertriebs-Gesellschaft, 1936), 3.
139. Zabełków is located in the Silesian Voivodeship, in southern Poland.
140. Eduard Mühle, "The Mental Map of German *Ostforschung*," 121–3. Mühle's quotes by Aubin are abstracts from Aubin, "Das Deutsche Reich und die Völker des Ostens," *Die Burg*, 1: 7–20.
141. Brackmann, *Krisis und Aufbau in Osteuropa*, 11.
142. Heinrich Felix Schmid, "German Law in Poland," in *Germany and Poland*, 77. Schmid was born in 1896 in Berlin and died in 1963 in Vspaceienna. At the time of writing his chapter, he was a Professor of Slavic Philology at the University of Graz.
143. Hermann Aubin, "Wirtschaftsgeschichtliche Bemerkungen zur ostdeutschen Kolonisation (1927)," in *Von Raum und Grenzen des deutschen Volkes: Studien zur Volksgeschichte* (Breslau: Verlag Priebatschs Buchhandlung, 1938), 155.
144. Karl. E. Thalheim and A. Hillen Ziegfeld, "Vorwart," in *Der Deutsche Osten*, xi.
145. Hermann Aubin, "Brief: An den Verlag Volk und Reich, 13.11.1936," in *Briefe des Ostforschers Hermann Aubin aus den Jahren 1910 – 1968*, ed. Eduard Mühle (Marburg: Herder-Institut, 2008), 228.
146. For example, Otto Reche (1879–1966) an anthropologist and lecturer who joined the Hamburg South Seas Expedition from 1908 to 1909 had previously conducted anthropological research in what was then partially the German colony of New Guinea. Reche joined the National Socialist Party in May 1937 and in September 1939, he became the *Nord-und Ostdeutsche Forschungsgemeinschaft* (NODFG) expert

advisor on racial studies. Reche also worked from 1939 directly with the RuSHA as an advisor. Günther Pancke, the then leader of the RuSHA, commissioned Reche to assist with the racial screening of ethnic German resettlers. In this capacity, Reche acted as a "one-man judge." Burleigh, *Germany Turns Eastwards*, 121; Haar, *Historiker im Nationalsozialismus*, 337. For further information on the SS racial advisors see Heinemann, *Rasse, Siedlung, deutsches Blut*. Jürgen Zimmerer also mentions Reche in his article due to Reche's experience in the colonies and then his work in Nazi Germany; however, Zimmerer does not go into detail on Reche's prior experience nor his contribution to population policy in Poland. See Zimmerer, "The birth of the *Ostland,*" *Patterns of Prejudice*, 213.
147. As mentioned by Karen Schönwälder, the scholarship of *Ostforschung* saw itself as a "guardian of national interest" and it was now its turn to inform the German nation that the Nazi regime was itself completing a historic task. Karen Schönwälder, "The Fascination of Power: Historical Scholarship in Nazi Germany," *History Workshop Journal* 43, no. 1 (1997), 148.
148. See Dirk van Laak, 'Ist je ein Reich, das es nicht gab, so gut verwaltet worden?' Der imaginäre Ausbau der imperialen Infrastruktur in Deutschland nach 1918," in *Phantasiereiche*, 71–90. See also Laak, *Imperiale Infrastruktur: Deutsche Planungen für die Erschließung Afrikas 1880–1960* (Paderborn: Ferdinand Schöningh Verlag, 2004).

Conclusion

1. Polish Research Centre London, ed., *German Failures in Poland: Natural Obstacles to Nazi Population Policy* (London: Cornwall Press, 1942), 29.
2. Contributions that challenge the notion of the racial state include, for example, Devin O. Pendas, Mark Roseman, and Richard F. Wetzell, eds., *Beyond the Racial State: Rethinking Nazi Germany: Rethinking Nazi Germany* (Cambridge: Cambridge University Press, 2017).
3. Frederick Cooper, *Colonialism in Question: Theory, Knowledge, History* (Berkeley: University of California Press, 2005), 201.
4. Ibid., 194.
5. Gerwarth and Malinowski, "Hannah Arendt's Ghosts," 287; Kühne, "Colonialism and the Holocaust," 344–5. I would suggest the theory of a "colonial archive" is more helpful as an analytical tool for historians than it is for suggesting continuity.
6. See Gerhard Wolf, *Ideologie und Herrschaftsrationalität: Nationalsozialistische Germanisierungspolitik in Polen* (Hamburg: Hamburger Edition, 2012).
7. See, for example, Frank Bajohr und Andrea Löw, "Tendenzen und Probleme der neueren Holocaust-Forschung: Eine Einführung," in *Der Holocaust: Ergebnisse und neue Fragen der Forschung*, ed. Frank Bajohr and Andrea Löw (Frankfurt am Main: S. Fischer Verlag GmbH, 2015), 9–30; Christian Gerlach, *The Extermination of the European Jews* (Cambridge: Cambridge University Press, 2016), 119–22.
8. Michelle Gordon, "Colonial violence and Holocaust studies," *Holocaust Studies* 21, no. 4 (2015): 279. Historians such as Zimmerer have also alluded to this point in relation to colonial similarities. See for example, Zimmerer, *Von Windhuk nach Auschwitz*, 194.
9. See Chapter 4; see also Lorenzo Veracini, *Settler Colonialism: A Theoretical Overview* (London: Palgrave Macmillan, 2010).

10. Dan Stone, *Histories of the Holocaust* (Oxford: Oxford University Press, 2010), 243.
11. Ann Laura Stoler, "Tense and Tender Ties: The Politics of Comparison in North American History and (Post) Colonial Studies," in *Haunted by Empire: Geographies of Intimacy in North American History*, ed. Ann Laura Stoler (Durham: Duke University Press, 2006), 55.
12. Here, I recall the United Nations definition of genocide. See Convention on the Prevention and Punishment of the Crime of Genocide, Article II, https://www.un.org/en/genocideprevention/genocide.shtml, accessed August 30, 2021.
13. See Roberta Pergher and Mark Roseman, "The Holocaust—An Imperial Genocide?," *Dapim—Studies on the Holocaust* 27, no. 1 (2013): 42–9.
14. For example, Ireland has long been perceived as a victim of the British Empire in the public sphere. However, recently academic scholarship is beginning to address how Irish people and institutions also contributed to colonial and imperial practices. See for example, the "Trinity Colonial Legacies" project at Trinity College Dublin, https://www.trinitycoloniallegacies.com/, accessed February 22, 2023.
15. Michael Rothberg, *Multidirectional Memory: Remembering the Holocaust in the Age of Decolonization* (Stanford: Stanford University Press, 2009), 3.
16. Joseph Conrad, *Heart of Darkness*, new ed. (Oxford: Oxford University Press, 2008), 34.

Bibliography

Primary Sources

Archival Material

Germany

Bayerisches Hauptstaatsarchiv (BayHStA)

Abteilung II:
Polizeischule Fürstenfeldbruck 188.
Abteilung V, Plakatsammlung Kultur- und Werbeplakate bis 1945:
21340 "Auf Safari," Anton M. Kolnberger. Printed by C. Wolf and Sohn. Munich, February 1936.
21371 "Kolonial-Ball," Philipp Waizmann. Munich, February 1937.
21424 "Auf Safari," Anton M. Kolnberger. Printed by Köhler and Sohn. Munich, February 1939.

Kriegsabteilung V:
(Offiziersakte) Op 271 Franz Ritter von Epp.

Bundesarchiv Berlin-Lichterfelde (BArch)

R 49 Reichskommissar für die Festigung deutschen Volkstums:
R 49 Bild-0705 Karte.- Übersicht zur Herkunft deutschstämmiger Umsiedler im Wartheland (ca. 1939/1941).
R 49/12 Befehle und Rundschreiben des RKFV (Erlasse und Verordnungen sowie Besprechungsvermerke über Fragen der Umsiedlung 1939–42).
R 49/20 Bd. 1 1939–1942 Reden führender Personen über die Umsiedlungsaktion, 1939–1942.
R 49/117 Ansiedlung von Wolhynien- und Galiziendeutschen im Regierungsbezirk Zichenau.
R 49/157 Planungsgrundlagen für den Aufbau der Ostgebiete. Bericht der Planungshauptabteilung des RKFV.
R 49/157a Generalplan Ost. Rechtliche, wirtschaftliche und räumliche Grundlagen des Ostaufbaus von Prof. Dr Konrad Meyer.
R 49/2355 Presseberichte zur Umsiedlung Volksdeutscher.
R 49/3057 Generalbericht vom studentischen Osteinsatz im Warthegau und Oberschlesien von der Einsatzleitung Ost der Reichsstudentenführung.
R 49/3082 Umsiedlerbetreuung. Zeitungsausschnittsammlung der Gaufrauenschaftsleitung Danzig-Langfuhr der NS-Frauenschaft Danzig (Fotokopien).
R 49/3084 Lage und Stimmung der Umsiedler im Reichsgau Danzig-Westpreußen.- Tätigkeitsberichte von Ansiedlerbetreuerinnen.

R 59 Volksdeutsche Mittelstelle:
R 59/229 Arbeits- und Tatigkeitberichte

R 69 Einwandererzentralstelle Litzmannstadt:
R 69/281 Volksdeutsche aus Wolhynien und Galizien.

R 1001 Reichskolonialamt:
R 1001/6339 Ausstellungen. Allgemeines.
R 1001/6726m Verschiedene Gesellschaften und Vereine 1890-1937.
R 1001/6914 Errichtung von Kolonialkriegsdenkmälern in Deutschland.
R 8023 Deutsche Kolonialgesellschaft:
R 8023/74 Jubiläumstagung zum 50-jährigen Bestehen der Deutschen Kolonialgesellschaft am 14. 10. 1932 in Berlin.

Institut für Zeitgeschichte Archiv, Munich (IfZ)

MA 225/1 NS-Frauenschaft/Gau Wartheland: Betreuung der volksdeutschen Umsiedler, 1940-1942.
MA 190/3 Oberkommando der Wehrmacht (OKW); Feldwirtschaftsamt.

Publications held in the IfZ archive:
Deutsche Kolonial-Ausstellung Köln 1934 1. Juli- 2. Sept. Köln: Ernst Stauf Verlag, 1934.
Deutsche Kolonial-Zeitung. Monatsschrift des Reichkolonialbundes 51, no. 2, 1939.
Epp, Franz Ritter von. *Der deutsche Standpunkt in der Kolonialfrage: Rede, gehalten bei der kolonialen Großkundgebung im Sportspalast Berlin am 6. Dezember 1937.* München: Müller, 1937.
Großdeutschland - Deine Kolonien: Festschrift zur Reichstagung des Reichkolonialbundes in Bremen vom 24. Bis 29. Mai 1938. Berlin: Wilhelm Limpert, Druck- und Verlagshaus, 1938.
Ibel, Rudolf (ed.). *Deutschland braucht Kolonien.* Hamburg: Köbner & Co Verlag, 1936.
Koloniales Taschenbuch 1941. Edited by the Bundesführung des Reichskolonialbundes. Berlin. München: Buchgewerbehaus M. Müller & Sohn, 1941.
Reichskolonialbund - Deutschland, deine Kolonien!, Nr. 2. Duderstadt: Friedrich Wagner, 1937.
Richtlinien für die kolonialpolitische Ausbildung. Berlin: Schulungsamt des kolonialpolitischen Amtes der NSDAP (Reichsleitung), August 1939.
Schnee, Heinrich. *Deutschlands koloniale Forderung, Zeitfragen deutscher Kultur. Volume 3.* Berlin: Hermann Wendt Gmbh, 1937.

Poland

Archivum Instytut Zachodni Poznań (AIZ)

Dok. I-9: Położenie prawne Polaków w Kraju Warty.
Dok. I-12: Szkolnictwo niemieckie dla Polaków w Kraju Warty.
Dok. I-25: Wysiedlanie Polaków z powiatu międzychodzkiego i osiedlanie Niemców.
Dok. I-27: Różne afisze niemieckie z czasów okupacji dot. Poznania i ziem wcielonych do Rzeszy.
Dok. I-31: Nakaz obowiązkowego noszenia oznak przez Niemców w "Kraju Warty."

Dok. I-32: Niedostateczne opanowanie języka niemieckiego przez zatrudnionych na poczcie dzieci Volksdeutschów.
Dok. I-69: Okólnik Greisera w sprawie używania języka polskiego przez Polaków.
Dok. I-109: Różne dokumenty w sprawie akcji wysiedleńczej wobec Polaków oraz odrębnego traktowania Polaków nadających się do zniemczenia.
Dok. I-120: Wysiedlanie Polaków.
Dok. I-200 Traktowanie Polaków (także Żydów) - również sprawy wysiedlenia.
Dok. I-423: Używanie rowerów przez Polaków w okręgu regencyjnym Poznań.
Dok. I-424: Korzystanie z publicznych środków lokomocji przez Polaków.
Dok. I-586: Nastrój Volksdeutschów w stosunku do Reichsdeutschów w marcu 1940 w powiecie bydgoskim.
Dok. I-616: Sprawozdanie o nastroju i postawie ludności polskiej i "eindeutschowanej" na Pomorzu.

Archiwum Państwowe w Gdańsku (APG)

10/4498 Korespondencja.

Archiwum Państwowe w Łodzi (APL)

39/741: Graphische Aufstellung der Todesfälle für den Monat Mai 1940 in Litzmannstadt-Ghetto.
39/29181: Organizacja, obszar Getta.
39/31870: Beurteilung wiedereizudeutscher Polen.

Archiwum Państwowe w Poznaniu (APP)

53/68 Weltanschauliche Erziehung der Ordnungspolizei.
53/1158 (Microfilm O-60010): Reichsstatthalter-Posen- "Schaffung Deutscher Häuser im Warthegau."
53/2202 (Microfilm O-61044): Umsiedlerkreisfürsorge.
53/2379 (Microfilm O-61221): Besichtigung deutscher Schulen durch auswärtige Besucher. Schulstreik 1906–1909- Ausstellung "Kampf und Aufbau im Wartheland."
53/2609 (Microfilm: O-61451): Kaiser-Friedrich-Museum-Landesmuseum des Reichsgaus Wartheland-in Posen.
53/2817 (Microfilm O-61659): Wirtschaft des Warthelandes in den Zeitschriften.
53/2824 (Microfilm O-61666): Protokoły zebrań zespołu "Baugestaltung und Baupflege im Reichsgau Wartheland."
53/3383 (Microfilm O-62225): Sprawozdania i korespondencja w sprawie rejestracji dzieł sztuki na terenie Kraju Warty.

Instytut Pamięci Narodowej (IPN)

BU 2586 Zbiór akt z postępowań karnych dotyczących zbrodni nazistowskich:
BU 2586/168
BU 2586/179
BU 2586/200

Proces Artura Greiser:
Sygn. GK 196/16
Sygn. GK 196/36

Published Primary Sources

Books

Aubin, Hermann. *Briefe des Ostforschers Hermann Aubin aus den Jahren 1910—1968*, edited by Eduard Mühle. Marburg: Herder-Institut, 2008.

Aubin, Hermann. "Die historisch-geographischen Grundlagen der deutsch-polnischen Beziehungen." In *Deutschland und Polen – Beiträge zu ihren geschichtlichen Beziehungen*, edited by Albert Brackmann, 13–25. Munich and Berlin: Verlag von R. Oldenbourg, 1933.

Aubin, Hermann. "Wirtschaftsgeschichtliche Bemerkungen zur ostdeutschen Kolonisation (1927)." In *Von Raum und Grenzen des deutschen Volkes: Studien zur Volksgeschichte*, 155–74. Breslau: Verlag Priebatschs Buchhandlung, 1938.

Aubin, Hermann. "Zur Erforschung der deutschen Ostbewegung." In *Deutsche Schriften zur Landes- und Volksforschung*, edited by E. Meynen, 1–90. Leipzig: S. Hirzel, 1939.

Baeskow, C., and H. Schrader. "Als NSV.-Schwestern bei der Umsiedlung der Bessarabiendeutschen." In *Heimkehr der Bessarabiendeutschen*, edited by Andreas Pampuch, 210–13. Breslau: Schlesien-Verlag, 1941.

Bauer, H. W. *Kolonien oder nicht? Die Einstellung von Partei und Staat zum kolonialen Gedanken*. Leipzig: Richard Bauer Verlag, 1935.

Blohm, Georg. *Siedlung und Landwirtschaft im Reichsgau Danzig-Westpreußen*. Berlin: Deutsche Landbuchhaltung Sohnrey, 1941.

Boehm, Max Hildebert. "Der deutsche Osten und das Reich." In *Der Deutsche Osten: Seine Geschichte, sein Wesen und seine Aufgabe*, edited by Karl. E. Thalheim and A. Hillen Ziegfeld, 1–18. Berlin: Propyläen Verlag, 1936.

Brackmann, Albert. *Krisis und Aufbau in Osteuropa. Ein weltgeschichtliches Bild*. Berlin: Ahnenerbe-Stiftung Verlag, 1939.

Darré, R. Walther. *Erkenntnisse und Werden: Aufsätze aus der Zeit vor der Machtergreifung*, edited by Marie Adelheid Prinzessin Reuß-zur Lippe. 2nd ed., Goslar: Verlag Blut und Boden, 1940.

Decken, Carl Claus von der. *Reisen in Ost-Afrika in den Jahren 1859 bis 1865*. Leipzig: Winter'sche Verlagshandlung, 1869.

Der Führer hat uns gerufen. Berlin-Luck: VoMi-Berlin, Deutsches Kommando für die Umsiedlung der Deutschen aus Galizien, Wolhynien und Bialystok., 1940.

Diewerge, Wolfgang. *Der neue Reichsgau Danzig-Westpreußen*. Berlin: Junker und Dünnhaupt Verlag, 1940.

Dinglreiter, Senta. *Wann kommen die deutschen endlich wieder? Eine Reise durch unsere Kolonien in Afrika*. Leipzig: Koehler & Ameland, 1935.

Duisburg, Adolf von. *Wer will in die Kolonien? Ein Wegweiser zur kolonialen Arbeit*. Berlin: Dr. Hans Riegler Verlag für vaterländische Literatur, 1938.

Engelhardt-Kyffhäuser, Otto. "Aus meinem Tagebuch." In *Das Buch vom großen Treck*, edited by Otto Engelhardt-Kyffhäuser, 30–48. Berlin: Verlag Grenze und Ausland GmbH, 1940.

Engelhardt-Kyffhäuser, Otto. *Der große Treck: Die Heimkehr der deutschen Bauern aus Galizien und Wolhynien. Führer durch die Ausstellung Im Haus der Kunst.* Berlin: Thormann & Goetsch, 1940.

Epp, Franz Ritter von. *Deutschlands kolonial Forderung.* München: Buchgewerbehaus M. Müller & Sohn, 1939.

Essig, Luise. "Unsere Ziele für die Mädchen und Frauen des Landvolks." In *Landvolk im Werden: Material zum ländlichen Aufbau in den neuen Ostgebieten und zur Gestaltung des dörflichen Lebens,* edited by Konrad Meyer. Berlin: Deutsche Landbuchhandlung, 1941.

Filcher, G. W. "Auf, zum Kampf um Deutschlands koloniale Ehre!." In *Deutsche Kolonialarbeit in Vergangenheit und Zukunft: Ein Kapitel Deutsche Ehre,* 3–10. Königsberg: Reichskolonialbund Kreisverband Königsberg-Stadt, 1938.

Fitzner, Otto. "Die kommenden Aufgaben der Wirtschaft im Osten." In *Breslau und deutscher Osten,* edited by W. Foerst, 50–8. Berlin: Otto v. Holten, 1941.

Frymann, Daniel. [Heinrich Claß]. *Wenn ich der Kaiser wär'. Politische Wahrheiten und Notwendigkeiten.* Leipzig: Dieterich'schen Verlagsbuchhandlung, 1913.

Geisler, Walter. *Deutscher! Der Osten ruft dich!* Berlin: Volk und Reich Verlag, 1942.

Gissibl, Fritz (ed.). *Der Osten des Warthelands.* Stuttgart: Stähle & Friedel, 1941.

Gronauer, Wilhelm. "Gesundheitszustand und Krankheiten der Eingeborenen. Ernährung. Bekleidung. Ärztlicher Kontrolle. Ärztlicher Bericht." In *Deutschland und seine Kolonien im Jahre 1896,* edited by Gustav Meinke, 43–50. Berlin: Verlag von Dietrich Reimer, 1897.

Hitler, Adolf. *Mein Kampf,* edited and translated by John Chamberlain, Sidney B. Fay, John Gunther, and Carlton J. H. Hayes. New York: Reynal & Hitchcock, 1939.

Hohenstein, Alexander [Franz Heinrich Bock]. *Wartheländisches Tagebuch aus den Jahren 1941/1942.* Stuttgart: Deutsche Verlags-Anstalt, 1961.

Jacob, Ernst Gerhard. "Der Kampf gegen die koloniale Schuldlüge," *Deutsches Ringen um kolonialen Raum* 7. Hamburg: Paul Hartung Verlag, 1938.

Kargel, Adolf. "Das Litzmannstadt Gebiet ist germanische Urheimat." In *Der Osten des Warthelands,* edited by Fritz Gissibl, 30–5. Stuttgart: Stähle & Friedel, 1941.

Keyser, Erich. "Die Erforschung der Bevölkerungsgeschichte des deutschen Ostens." In *Deutsche Ostforschung: Ergebnisse und Aufgaben seit dem ersten Weltkrieg,* edited by Hermann Aubin, Otto Brunner, Wolfgang Kohte, and Johannes Papritz, 90–104. Leipzig: Verlang von S. Hirzel, 1942.

Kipling, Rudyard. "The White Man's Burden." *McClure's Magazine* XII, no. 4. February, 1899.

Krieg, Hans (ed.). *Baltenbriefe zur Rückkehr ins Reich.* Berlin: Nibelungen-Verlag, 1940.

Kuntze, Paul H. *Das neue Volksbuch der Kolonien.* Leipzig: Georg Dollheimer Verlag, 1941.

Leßner, Paul. *Was müssen wir von unseren Kolonien wissen?* Leipzig: Friedrich M. Hörhold-Verlag, 1938.

Löbsack, Wilhelm. *Albert Forster, Gauleiter und Reichsstatthalter im Reichsgau Danzig-Westpreußen.* Danzig: Danziger Verlags-Gesellschaft m.b.H (Paul Rosenburg), 1940.

Lorenz, Werner (ed.). *Der Zug der Volksdeutschen aus Bessarabien und dem Nord-Buchenland.* Berlin: Volk und Reich Verlag GmbH, 1942.

Pampuch, Andreas. "Dös hab i net gewußt!" In *Heimkehr der Bessarabiendeutschen,* edited by Andreas Pampuch, 118–19. Breslau: Schlesien-Verlag, 1941.

Polish Research Centre London. Editors. *German Failures in Poland: Natural Obstacles to Nazi Population Policy.* London: Cornwall Press, 1942.

Reitsch, Hanna. *Das Unzerstörbare in meinem Leben.* München: F. A. Herbig, 1979.

Rohlfs, Gerhard. *Land und Volk in Afrika: Berichte aus den Jahren 1865–1870*. Bremen: J. Kühtmann Verlagshandlung, 1870.

Rothfels, Hans. "Das Problem des Nationalismus im Osten." In *Deutschland und Polen— Beiträge zu ihren geschichtlichen Beziehungen*, edited by Albert Brackmann, 259–69. Munich: Verlag von R. Oldenbourg, 1933.

Rothfels, Hans. "The Problem of Nationalism in the East." In *Germany and Poland in Their Historical Relations*, edited by Albert Brackmann, translated by S. Miles Bouton, 252–62. Munich: R. Oldenbourg, 1934.

Ritter, Paul (ed.). *Unvergessenes deutsches Land*. Berlin: Verlag und Vertriebs-Gesellschaft, 1936.

Schacht, Hjalmar. *The End of Reparations*, translated by Lewis Gannett. New York: Jonathan Cape & Harrison Smith, 1931.

Schmid, Heinrich Felix. "German Law in Poland." In *Germany and Poland in Their Historical Relations*, edited by Albert Brackmann, translated by S. Miles Bouton, 63–79. Munich: R. Oldenbourg, 1934.

Sering, Max. *Die innere Kolonisation im östlichen Deutschland*. Leipzig: Duncker and Humblot, 1893.

Sommer, Hellmut. *135,000 gewannen das Vaterland*. Berlin: Nibelungen Verlag, 1940.

Sommer, Hellmut. *Völkerwanderung im 20. Jahrhundert: Die große Heimkehr der Volksdeutschen ins Reich*. Berlin: Wilhelm Limpert-Verlag, 1940.

Thalheim, Karl E. "Deutsches Vorfeld im Osten." In *Der Deutsche Osten: Seine Geschichte, sein Wesen und seine Aufgabe*, edited by Karl. E. Thalheim and A. Hillen Ziegfeld, 305–34. Berlin: Propyläen Verlag, 1936.

Thalheim, Karl. E., and Ziegfeld, A. Hillen. "Vorwort." In *Der Deutsche Osten: Seine Geschichte, sein Wesen und seine Aufgabe*, edited by Karl. E. Thalheim and A. Hillen Ziegfeld, xi–xii. Berlin: Propyläen Verlag, 1936.

"The Ministries Case, October 1946–April 1949." *Trials of War Criminals before the Nuremberg Military Tribunals under Control Council Law No. 10*. Vol. XIV. Washington DC: US Government Printing Office, 1949–1953.

Wolff, Ludwig. "Der Volkstumskampf des Deutschtums im Osten des Warthelandes." In *Der Osten des Warthelands*, edited by Fritz Gissibl, 176–95. Stuttgart: Stähle & Friedel, 1941.

Ziegfeld, A. Hillen. "Die Lebensgesetze des deutschen Ostens." In *Der Deutsche Osten: Seine Geschichte, sein Wesen und seine Aufgabe*, edited by Karl. E. Thalheim and A. Hillen Ziegfeld, 595–602. Berlin: Propyläen Verlag, 1936.

Journals

"Besiedlung im Inlande und in den Kolonien. Ein Vorwort zur Kolonialnummer." *Archiv für innere Kolonisation* 4, no. 5 (1912): 145–92.

Rohrbach, Paul. "Siedlungsbestrebungen in unseren afrikanischen Kolonien." *Archiv für innere Kolonisation* 3, no. 3 (1910): 71–86.

Thiele, Paul. "Deutsche Kolonialschule zu Witzenhausen a. d. Werra." Der Tropenpflanzer: Zeitschrift für Tropische Landwirtschaft 3 (January 1899): 7–12.

Ulrich, Curt von. "Mitteldeutschland und die Ostkolonisation," *Raumforschung und Raumordnung: Monatsschrift der Reichsarbeitsgemeinschaft für Raumforschung* (1940) 4, no. 1/2: 4–5.

Reports

Jahresbericht der Deutschen Kolonialgesellschaft 1897 (Berlin: Karl Heymanns Verlag, 1897).
Union of South Africa. *Report on the Natives of South West Africa and their Treatment by Germany.* London: HMSO, 1918.

Edited Primary Source Collections

Bömelburg, Hans-Jürgen and Marlene Klatt (eds.). *Lodz im Zweiten Weltkrieg: Deutsche Selbstzeugnisse über Alltag, Lebenswelten und NS-Germanisierungspolitik in einer multiethnischen Stadt.* Ösnabrück: Fibre Verlag, 2015.
Bopp, Dominika, Sascha Feuchert, Andrea Löw, Jörg Riecke, Markus Roth, and Elisabeth Turvold (eds.). *Die Enzyklopädie des Gettos Lodz/Litzmannstadt.* Göttingen: Wallstein Verlag, 2020.
Loose, Ingo (ed.). *Die Verfolgung und Ermordung der europäischen Juden durch das nationalsozialistische Deutschland, 1933–1945: Band 10, Polen: Eingegliederte Gebiete August 1941–1945* (VEJ 10). Berlin: De Gruyter, 2020.
Łuczak, Czesław (ed.). *Wysiedlenia ludności polskiej na tzw. Ziemiach wcielonych do Rzeszy 1939–1945, Documenta Occupationis.* Volume VIII. Poznań: Instytut Zachodni, 1969.
Madajczyk, Czesław (ed.). *Vom Generalplan Ost zum Generalsiedlungsplan: Dokumente.* Munich: K. G. Saur, 1994.
United Nations War Crimes Commission. Editor. "Case No. 74, Trial of Artur [sic] Greiser: Supreme National Tribunal of Poland, 21 June–7 July 1946." In *Law Reports of Trials of War Criminals.* Volume XIII, 70–117. London: His Majesty's Stationary Office, 1949.

Newspapers

Alldeutsche Blätter
Altonaer Nachrichten
Bayerische Hochschulzeitung
Deutsches Nachrichtenbüro
Die Zeit
Frankfurter Allgemeine Zeitung
Freiburger Zeitung
Hamburger Anzeiger
Hamburgischer Correspondent
Hamburger Nachrichten
Litzmannstädter Zeitung
The Guardian

Films

Die Deutsche Frauen-Kolonialschule Rendsburg 1937, Produktion Paul Lieberenz, Release Date: 1974 by IWF Wissen und Medien gGmbH Göttingen.

Bundesarchiv Berlin-Lichterfelde (BArch)

12611–1, *Die Deutsche Wochenschau*, 534 / - / 49 / 1940 / - (Berlin: Universum Film AG, 1940).

K 136099–1, *Die Deutsche Wochenschau*, 552 / - / 15 / 1941 / - (Berlin: Universum Film AG, 1941).

K 152565–2, *Heimkehr*, Director: Gustav Ucicky (Berlin: Universum Film AG, 1941).

22066–2, *Die Deutsche Wochenschau*, 528 / - / 43 / 1940 / - (Berlin: Universum Film AG, 1940).

United States Holocaust Memorial Museum (USHMM), Steven Spielberg Film and Video Archive

Film ID: 2559 "Mädel verlassen die Stadt." http://www.ushmm.org/online/film/display/detail.php?file_num=521, accessed February 13, 2016.

Film ID: 2628 "Ostland – deutsches Land." http://www.ushmm.org/online/film/display/detail.php?file_num=3877, accessed February 13, 2016.

Recorded Interviews

United States Holocaust Memorial Museum (USHMM), Steven Spielberg Film and Video Archive- Claude Lanzmann Shoah Collection

Film ID: 3352–3354 "Interview with Martha Michelsohn." http://www.ushmm.org/online/film/display/detail.php?file_num=5134, accessed February 12, 2016. (Full German interview transcript used for quotations and references.)

Websites

Aly, Götz. "Es gibt nichts, das deckungsgleich mit dem Holocaust wäre." Interview with Deutschlandfunk Kultur (July 13, 2021). https://www.deutschlandfunkkultur.de/goetz-aly-es-gibt-nichts-das-deckungsgleich-mit-dem-100.html, accessed October 6, 2022.

Arbeitsgemeinschaft Pfadfinder e.V. https://www.arge-pfadfinder.org/dt.-pfadf.-in-swa.html, accessed October 10, 2022.

Gründungsmanifest der Gesellschaft für Deutsche Kolonisation (March 28, 1885). German History in Documents and Images. http://ghdi.ghi-dc.org/docpage.cfm?docpage_id=1045, accessed April 1, 2020.

Moses, A. Dirk. "The German Catechism," *Geschichte der Gegenwart*. https://geschichtedergegenwart.ch/the-german-catechism/, accessed August 9, 2021.

Stadtplan von Bromberg (1941). Landkartenarchiv. https://landkartenarchiv.de/vollbild_stadtplansammlung.php?q=stadtplan_bromberg_25T_1941, accessed October 26, 2019.

Stadtplan von Litzmannstadt (1942). Sächsische Landesbibliothek, Staats- und Universitätsbibliothek, Dresden. http://www.deutschefotothek.de/documents/obj/90066471/df_dk_0009664, accessed October 26, 2019.

Stadtplan von Posen (1939). Sächsische Landesbibliothek, Staats- und Universitätsbibliothek, Dresden. http://www.deutschefotothek.de/documents/obj/90061895/df_dk_0011894, accessed October 26, 2019.

Trinity Colonial Legacies" project, Trinity College Dublin. https://www.trinitycoloniall egacies.com/, accessed February 22, 2023.
United Nations Convention on the Prevention and Punishment of the Crime of Genocide. Article II. https://www.un.org/en/genocideprevention/documents/atrocity-crimes/ Doc.1_Convention%20on%20the%20Prevention%20and%20Punishment%20of%20 the%20Crime%20of%20Genocide.pdf, accessed May 26, 2021.

Secondary Sources

Books

Ahonen, Pertti, Jerzy Kochanowski, Gustavo Corni, Tamás Stark, Rainer Schulze, and Barbara Stelzl-Marx. *People on the Move: Forced Population Movements in Europe in the Second World War and its Aftermaths*. Oxford: Berg, 2008.

Aitken, Robbie. *Exclusion and Inclusion: Gradations of Whiteness and Socio-Economic Engineering in German Southwest Africa, 1884–1914*. Oxford: Perter Land, 2007

Alberti, Michael. *Die Verfolgung und Vernichtung der Juden im Reichsgau Wartheland 1939–1945*. Wiesbaden: Harrassowitz Verlag, 2006.

Aly, Götz. *Final Solution: Nazi Population Policy and Murder of the European Jews*. London: Arnold, 1999.

Aly, Götz and Heim, Susanne. *Architects of Annihilation: Auschwitz and the Logic of Destruction*. Translated by Allan Blunden. London: Phoenix, 2003.

Anderson, Benedict. *Imagined Communities: Reflections on the Origin and Spread of Nationalism*. London: Verso, 1991.

Angrick, Andrej. *Besatzungspolitik und Massenmord. Die Einsatzgruppe D in der südlichen Sowjetunion 1941–1943*. Hamburg: Hamburger Edition, 2003.

Arani, Miriam Y. "Photojournalism as a means of deception in Nazi-occupied Poland, 1939–45." In *Visual Histories of Occupation: A Transcultural Dialogue*, edited by Jeremy E. Taylor, 159–82. London: Bloomsbury Academic, 2021.

Arendt, Hannah. *The Origins of Totalitarianism*. 4th ed. New York: Harcourt, 1973.

Ashcroft, Bill, Gareth Griffiths, and Helen Tiffin (eds.). *Post-Colonial Studies: The Key Concepts*. London: Routledge, 2000.

Bajohr, Frank, and Andrea Löw. "Tendenzen und Probleme der neueren Holocaust-Forschung: Eine Einführung." In *Der Holocaust: Ergebnisse und neue Fragen der Forschung*, edited by Frank Bajohr and Andrea Löw, 9–30. Frankfurt am Main: S. Fischer Verlag GmbH, 2015.

Baranowski, Shelley. *Nazi Empire: German Colonialism and Imperialism from Bismarck to Hitler*. New York: Cambridge University Press. 2011.

Barth, Boris, and Jürgen Osterhammel (eds.). *Zivilisierungsmissionen. Imperiale Weltverbesserung seit dem 18. Jahrhundert*. Konstanz: UVK Verlagsgesellschaft, 2005.

Benz, Wolfgang, and Barbara Distel (eds.). *Der Ort des Terrors. Geschichte der nationalsozialistischen Konzentrationslager: Natzweiler, Groß-Rosen, Stutthof*. Volume 6, Munich: C.H. Beck, 2007.

Biskupska, Jadwiga. "Zamość Experiments: SS Settler Colonialism and Violence in Eastern Poland." In *Colonial Paradigms of Violence: Comparative Analysis of the Holocaust, Genocide, and Mass Killing*, edited by Michelle Gordon and Rachel O'Sullivan, 161–84. Göttingen: Wallstein Verlag, 2022.

Blackbourn, David. "Das Kaiserreich transnational. Eine Skizze." In *Das Kaiserreich transnational. Deutschland in der Welt 1871–1914*, edited by Sebastian Conrad and Jürgen Osterhammel, 302–25. Göttingen: Vandenhoeck & Ruprecht, 2004.

Bley, Helmut. *Kolonialherrschaft und Sozialstruktur in Deutsch-Südwestafrika 1894–1914*. Hamburg: Leibniz Verlag, 1968.

Bloxham, Donald. *The Final Solution: A Genocide*. Oxford: Oxford University Press, 2009.

Bosse, Jana Elena. "Siebzig Jahre nach der Umsiedlung—deutschbaltische Zeitzeugen erinnern sich." In *Umgesiedelt – Vertrieben: Deutschbalten und Polen 1939–1945 im Warthegau*, edited by Eckhart Neander and Andrzej Sakson, 30–42. Marburg: Verlag Herder-Institut, 2010.

Bowersox, Jeff. "Boy's and Girl's Own Empires: Gender and the Uses of the Colonial World in *Kaiserreich* Youth Magazines." In *German Colonialism and National Identity*, 57–68, edited by Michael Perraudin and Jürgen Zimmerer. New York: Routledge, 2011.

Bowersox, Jeff. *Raising Germans in the Age of Empire: Youth and Colonial Culture, 1871–1914*. Oxford: Oxford University Press, 2013.

Bramwell, Anna. *Blood and Soil: Walther Darré and Hitler's "Green Party."* Bourne End: Kensal Press, 1985.

Brendon, Piers. *The Decline And Fall of the British Empire 1781–1997*. London: Vintage Books, 2008.

Burleigh, Michael. *Germany Turns Eastwards: A Study of Ostforschung in the Third Reich*. London: Pan Macmillan, 2002.

Çelik, Zeynep. *Urban Forms and Colonial Confrontations: Algiers Under French Rule*. Berkeley: University of California Press, 1997.

Césaire, Aimé. *Discours sur le colonialisme*. Paris: Présence Africaine, 1955.

Chickering, Roger. *We Men Who Feel Most German: A Cultural Study of the Pan-German League, 1886–1914*. Boston: Allen & Unwin, 1984.

Chu, Winson. *The German Minority in Interwar Poland*. Cambridge: Cambridge University Press, 2012.

Ciarlo, David. *Advertising Empire: Race and Visual Culture in Imperial Germany*. Cambridge, MA: Harvard University Press, 2011.

Conrad, Joseph *Heart of Darkness*. New Edition. Oxford: Oxford University Press, 2008.

Conrad, Sebastian. *German Colonialism: A Short Introduction*, translated by Sorcha O'Hagan. Cambridge: Cambridge University Press, 2012.

Conrad, Sebastian. *Globalisation and the Nation in Imperial Germany*, translated by Sorcha O'Hagan. Cambridge: Cambridge University Press, 2010.

Conrad, Sebastian. "Internal Colonialism in Germany: Culture Wars, Germanification of the Soil, and the Global Market Imaginary." In *German Colonialism in a Global Age*, edited by Bradley Naranch and Geoff Eley, 246–64. London: Duke University Press, 2014.

Cooper, Frederick. *Colonialism in Question: Theory, Knowledge, History*. Berkeley: University of California Press, 2005.

Cooper, Frederick, and Ann Laura Stoler (eds). *Tensions of Empire: Colonial Cultures in a Bourgeois World*. Berkeley: University of California Press, 1997.

Cornils, Ingo. "Denkmalsturz: The German Student Movement and German Colonialism." In *German Colonialism and National Identity*, 197–212, edited by Michael Perraudin and Jürgen Zimmerer. New York: Routledge, 2011.

Döring, Stephan. *Die Umsiedlung der Wolhyniendeutschen in den Jahren 1939 bis 1940*. Frankfurt am Main: Peter Lang, 2001.

Drummond, Elizabeth A. "From 'verloren gehen' to 'verloren bleiben': Changing German Discourses on Nation and Nationalism in Poznańia." In *The Germans and the East*,

edited by Charles W. Ingrao and Franz A. J. Szabo, 226–40. West Lafayette: Purdue University Press, 2008.
Drywa, Danuta. *The Extermination of Jews in Stutthof Concentration Camp*. Gdańsk: Stutthof Museum in Sztutowo, 2004.
Du Bois, W. E. B. *The World and Africa: An Inquiry into the Part Which Africa Has Played in World History*. New York: Viking, 1947.
Eckl, Andreas. "'Zu leben, nur um da zu sein, hat niemand ein Recht': Der Kolonialkrieg mit dem Volk der Herero 1904 im Spiegel kolonialpropagandistischer Literatur der NS-Zeit." In *Afrika - Kultur und Gewalt. Hintergründe und Aktualität des Kolonialkriegs in Deutsch-Südwestafrika; seine Rezeption in Literatur, Wissenschaft und Populärkultur (1904–2004)*, edited by Christof Hamann, 159–89. Iserlohn: Inst. für Kirche und Gesellschaft, 2005.
Eddie, Scott M. "The Prussian Settlement Commission and Its Activities in the Land Market, 1886–1918." In *Germans, Poland, and Colonial Expansion to the East: 1850 Through the Present*, edited by Robert L. Nelson, 39–64. Basingstoke: Palgrave Macmillan, 2009.
Eigler, Friederike. "Engendering German Nationalism: Gender and Race in Frieda von Bülows Colonial Writings." In *The Imperialist Imagination: German Colonialism and Its Legacy*, edited by Sara Friedrichsmeyer, Sara Lennox, and Susanne Zantop, 68–85. Ann Arbour: University of Michigan Press, 1998.
Eley, Geoff. "Commentary: Empire, Ideology and the East: Thoughts on Nazism's Spatial Imaginary." In *Heimat, Region, and Empire: Spatial Identities under National Socialism*, edited by Claus-Christian W. Szejnmann and Maiken Umbach, 252–75. Basingstoke: Palgrave Macmillan, 2012.
Eley, Geoff. "Empire by Land or Sea? Germany's Colonial Imaginary, 1840–1945." In *German Colonialism in a Global Age*, edited by Bradley Naranch and Geoff Eley, 19–45. London: Duke University Press, 2014.
Elkins, Caroline, and Pederson, Susan. "Introduction Settler Colonialism: A Concept and Its Uses." In *Settler Colonialism in the Twentieth Century: Projects, Practices, Legacies*, edited by Caroline Elkins and Susan Pederson, 1–20. New York: Routledge, 2005.
Epstein, Catherine. "Germanization in the Warthegau: Germans, Jews and Poles and the Making of a 'German' Gau." In *Heimat, Region, and Empire: Spatial Identities under National Socialism*, edited by Claus-Christian W. Szejnmann and Maiken Umbach, 93–111. New York: Palgrave Macmillan, 2012.
Epstein, Catherine. *Model Nazi: Arthur Greiser and the Occupation of Western Poland*. Oxford: Oxford University Press, 2010.
Erichsen, Casper W. "Zwangsarbeit im Konzentrationslager auf der Haifischinsel." In *Völkermord in Deutsch-Südwestafrika. Der Kolonialkrieg (1904–1908) in Namibia und seine Folgen*, edited by Jürgen Zimmerer and Joachim Zeller, 80–5. Berlin: Christoph Links Verlag GmbH, 2016.
Ertola, Emanuele. "The Italian fascist settler empire in Ethiopia, 1936–1941." In *The Routledge Handbook of the History of Settler Colonialism*, edited by Edward Cavanagh and Lorenzo Veracini, 263–76. London: Routledge, 2017.
Esch, Michael G. *"Gesunde Verhältnisse." Deutsche und polnische Bevölkerungspolitik in Ostmitteleuropa 1939–1950*. Marburg: Verlag Herder-Institut, 1998.
Fanon, Frantz. *Les Damnés de la terre*. Paris: François Maspero, 1961.
Fanon, Frantz. *The Wretched of the Earth*. Translated by Constance Farrington. New York: Grove Press, 1963.
Fiebrandt, Maria. *Auslese für die Siedlergesellschaft. Die Einbeziehung Volksdeutscher in die NS-Erbgesundheitspolitik im Kontext der Umsiedlungen 1939–1945*. Göttingen: Vandenhoeck & Ruprecht, 2014.

Fielitz, Wilhelm. *Das Stereotyp des Wolhyniendeutschen Umsiedlers. Popularisierungen zwischen Sprachinselforschung und Nationalsozialistischer Propaganda*. Marburg: N. G. Elwert Verlag, 2000.

Fisher, Gaëlle. "From Model to Warning: Narratives of Resettlement 'Home to the Reich' after World War II." In *German-Balkan Entangled Histories in the Twentieth Century*, edited by Mirna Zakić and Christopher A. Molnar, 180–201. Pittsburgh: University of Pittsburgh Press, 2020.

Fitzpatrick, Matthew P. *Liberal Imperialism in Germany: Expansionism and Nationalism, 1848–1884*. New York: Berghahn, 2008.

Fitzpatrick, Matthew P. *Purging the Empire: Mass Expulsions in Germany, 1871–1914*. Oxford: Oxford University Press, 2015.

Friedländer, Saul. *Nazi Germany and the Jews: The Years of Persecution, 1933–1939*. New York: HarperCollins, 1997.

Friedrichsmeyer, Sara, Sara Lennox, and Susanne Zantop (eds). *The Imperialist Imagination: German Colonialism and Its Legacy*. Ann Arbor: University of Michigan Press, 1998.

Furber, David and Lower, Wendy. "Colonialism and Genocide in Nazi-occupied Poland and Ukraine." In *Empire, Colony, Genocide: Conquest, Occupation, and Subaltern Resistance in World History*, edited by A. Dirk Moses, 372–400. New York: Berghahn Books, 2008.

Fuhrmann, Wolfgang. *Imperial Projections: Screening the German Colonies*. London: Berghahn, 2015.

Gann, L.H., and Peter Duignan. *The Rulers of German Africa, 1884–1914*. Stanford: Stanford University Press, 1977.

Gerber, David A., and Alan M. Kraut. "Introduction: Becoming White: Irish Immigrants in the Nineteenth Century." In *American Immigration and Ethnicity*, edited by Geber and Kraut, 161–8. Basingstoke: Palgrave Macmillan, 2005.

Gerlach, Christian. *The Extermination of the European Jews*. Cambridge: Cambridge University Press, 2016.

Gippert, Wolfgang. "Danzig-West Prussia." In *The Greater German Reich and the Jews: Nazi Persecution Policies in the Annexed Territories 1935–1945*, edited by Wolf Gruner and Jörg Osterloh. Translated by Bernard Heise, 157–88. New York: Berghahn Books, 2015.

Gordon, Michelle. *Extreme Violence and the "British Way": Colonial Warfare in Perak, Sierra Leone and Sudan*. London: Bloomsbury, 2020.

Gordon, Michelle and Rachel O'Sullivan. "Introduction: Colonial Paradigms of Violence." In *Colonial Paradigms of Violence: Comparative Analysis of the Holocaust, Genocide, and Mass Killing*, edited by Michelle Gordon and Rachel O'Sullivan, 9–30. Göttingen: Wallstein Verlag, 2022.

Gossman, Lionel. *Brownshirt Princess: A Study of the "Nazi Conscience."* Cambridge: Open Book Publishers, 2009.

Grabowski, Jan. *Hunt for the Jews: Betrayal and Murder in German-Occupied Poland*. Bloomington: Indiana University Press, 2013.

Grosse, Pascal. *Kolonialismus, Eugenik und bürgerliche Gesellschaft in Deutschland: 1850–1918*. Frankfurt a. M.: Campus, 2000.

Grosse, Pascal. "What Does German Colonialism Have to Do with National Socialism?" In *Germany's Colonial Pasts*, edited by Eric Ames, Marcia Klotz and Lora Wildenthal, 115–34. Lincoln: University of Nebraska, 2005.

Gründer, Horst. *Geschichte der deutschen Kolonien*. 7th ed. Paderborn: Verlag Ferdinand Schöningh, 2018.
Guettel, Jens-Uwe. *German Expansionism, Imperial Liberalism and the United States, 1776–1945*. New York: Cambridge University Press, 2012.
Gutschow, Niels. *Ordnungswahn: Architekten planen im „eingedeutschten Osten' 1939–1945*. Basel: Birkhäuser, 2001.
Ha, Marie-Paule. *French Women and the Empire: The Case of Indochina*. Oxford: Oxford University Press, 2014.
Haar, Ingo. "German *Ostforschung* and Anti-Semitism." In *German Scholars and Ethnic Cleansing, 1920–1945*, edited by Ingo Haar and Michael Fahlbusch, 1–27. New York: Berghahn Books, 2005.
Haar, Ingo. *Historiker im Nationalsozialismus. Deutsche Geschichtswissenschaft und der "Volkstumskampf" im Osten*. Göttingen: Vandenhoeck und Ruprecht, 2000.
Hackmann, Jörg. "Narrating the Building of a Small Nation: Divergence and Convergence in the Historiography of Estonian 'National Awakening,' 1868–2005." In *Nationalizing the Past: Historians as Nation Builders in Modern Europe*, edited by Stefan Berger and Chris Lorenz, 170–91. Basingstoke: Palgrave Macmillan, 2010.
Hagen, Joshua and Robert C. Ostergren. *Building Nazi Germany: Place, Space, Architecture, and Ideology*. London: Rowman & Littlefield, 2020.
Hahn, Hans Henning and Eva Hahn. *Die Vertreibung im deutschen Erinnern. Legenden, Mythos, Geschichte*. Paderborn: Verlag Ferdinand Schöningh GmbH, 2010.
Hardach, Gerd. *The First World War, 1914–1918*. Berkeley: University of California Press, 1981.
Hartwig, Edgar. "Deutsche Kolonialgesellschaft (DKG) 1887–1936." In *Lexikon zur Parteiengeschichte 1789–1945. Die bürgerlichen und kleinbürgerlichen Parteien und Verbände in Deutschland*, Volume 1, edited by Dieter Fricke, Werner Fritsch, Herber Gottwald, Siegfried Schmidt, and Manfred Weißbecker. Leipzig: VEB Bibliographisches Institut, 1985.
Harvey, Elizabeth. "Documenting *Heimkehr*: Photography, Displacement and 'Homecoming' in the Nazi Resettlement of the Ethnic Germans, 1939–1940." In *The Ethics of Seeing: Photography and Twentieth-Century German History*, edited by Jennifer Evans, Paul Betts, and Stefan-Ludwig Hoffmann, 79–107. New York. Berghahn Books, 2018.
Harvey, Elizabeth. "Management and Manipulation: Nazi Settlement Planners and Ethnic German Settlers in Occupied Poland." In *Settler Colonialism in the Twentieth Century: Projects, Practices, Legacies*, edited by Caroline Elkins, and Susan Pedersen, 95–112. New York: Routledge, 2015.
Harvey, Elizabeth. *Women and the Nazi East: Agents and Witnesses of Germanization*. New Haven: Yale University Press, 2003.
Heinemann, Isabel. *Rasse, Siedlung, deutsches Blut. Das Rasse- und Siedlungshauptamt der SS und die rassenpolitische Neuordnung Europas*. Göttingen: Wallstein Verlag, 2003.
Hering, Rainer. *Konstruierte Nation: Der Alldeutsche Verband 1890 bis 1939*. Hamburg: Christians, 2003.
Herwig, Holger H. *"Luxury" Fleet: The Imperial German Navy 1888–1918*. New York: Routledge, 1980.
Heyden, Ulrich van der. "Christian Missionary Societies in the German Colonies, 1884–85–1914/15." In *German Colonialism: Race, The Holocaust and Postwar Germany*, edited by Volker Langbehn and Mohammad Salma, 215–53. New York: Columbia University Press, 2011.

Heyningen, Elizabeth van. *The Concentration Camps of the Anglo-Boer War: A Social History*. Johannesburg: Jacana Media, 2013.

Hildebrand, Klaus. *Vom Reich zum Weltreich. Hitler, NSDAP und koloniale Frage 1919–1945*. Munich: W. Fink, 1969.

Hoffmann, Florian. *Okkupation und Militärverwaltung in Kamerun. Etablierung und Institutionalisierung des kolonialen Gewaltmonopols. Teil II - Die kaiserliche Schutztruppe und ihr Offizierkorps*. Göttingen: Cuvillier Verlag, 2007.

Honold, Alexander. "Afrikanisches Viertel: Straßennamen als kolonialer Gedächtnisraum." In *Phantasiereiche. Zur Kulturgeschichte des deutschen Kolonialismus*, edited by Birthe Kundrus, 305–21. Frankfurt: Campus Verlag, 2003.

Horwitz, Gordon J. *Ghettostadt: Łódź And the Making of a Nazi City*. Cambridge: Cambridge University Press, 2008.

Hull, Isabell V. *Absolute Destruction: Military Culture and the Practices of War in Imperial Germany*. Ithaca: Cornell University Press, 2005.

Hulverscheidt, Marion. "Der Weg in die Welt: Propagandafilme für deutsche Kolonialschulen." In *Das Vorprogramm: Lehrfilm /Gebrauchsfilm /Propagandafilm / unveröffentlichter Film in Kinos und Archiven am Oberrhein 1900–1970*, edited by Philipp Osten, Gabriele Moser, Christian Bonah, Alexandre Sumpf, Tricia Close-Koenig, and Joël Danet, 337–59. Heidelberg: A25 Rhinfilm, 2015.

Ignatiev, Noel. *How the Irish Became White*. New York: Routledge, 1995.

Ingrao, Christian. *The Promise of The East: Nazi Hopes and Genocide, 1939–43*. Translated by Andrew Brown. Cambridge: Polity Press, 2019.

Jackson, Will. "Not Seeking Certain Proof: Interracial Sex and Archival Haze in High-Imperial Natal." In *Subverting Empire: Deviance and Disorder in the British Colonial World*, edited by Will Jackson and Emily J. Manktelow, 185–204. London: Palgrave Macmillan, 2015.

Jinks, Rebecca. *Representing Genocide: The Holocaust as Paradigm?* London: Bloomsbury Academic, 2016.

Joeden-Forgey, Elisa von. "Race Power in Postcolonial Germany: The German Africa Show and the National Socialist State, 1935–1940." In *Germany's Colonial Pasts*, edited by Eric Ames, Marcia Klotz, and Lora Wildenthal, 167–88. Lincoln: University of Nebraska, 2005.

Jureit, Ulrike. *Das Ordnen von Räumen. Territorium und Lebensraum im 19. und 20. Jahrhundert*. Hamburg: Hamburger Edition, 2012.

Kakel, Carroll P. *The American West and the Nazi East: A Comparative and Interpretative Perspective*. New York: Palgrave Macmillan, 2011.

Keese, Alexander. *Living with Ambiguity: Integrating an African Elite in French and Portuguese Africa, 1930–61*. Stuttgart: Franz Steiner Verlag, 2007.

Ketelsen, Uwe-K. "Der koloniale Diskurs und die Öffnung des europäischen Ostens im deutschen Roman." In *Kolonialismus: Kolonialdiskurs und Genozid*, edited by Mihran Dabag, Horst Gründer, and Uwe-K. Ketelsen, 67–94. Munich: Wilhelm Fink Verlag, 2004.

Kienemann, Christoph. *Der koloniale Blick gen Osten: Osteuropa im Diskurs des Deutschen Kaiserreiches von 1871*. Paderborn: Ferdinand Schöningh 2018.

Kissi, Edward. *Africans and the Holocaust: Perceptions and Responses of Colonized and Sovereign Peoples*. London: Routledge, 2020.

Klävers, Steffen. *Decolonizing Auschwitz?: Komparativ-postkoloniale Ansätze in Der Holocaustforschung*. Berlin: de Gruyter, 2019.

Klein, Peter (ed.). *Die Einsatzgruppen in der besetzten Sowjetunion 1941/42. Die Tätigkeits- und Lageberichte des Chefs der Sicherheitspolizei und des SD.* Berlin: Wannsee-Haus, 1997.

Klein, Peter. *Die 'Ghettoverwaltung Litzmannstadt' 1940 bis 1944: Eine Dienststelle im Spannungsfeld von Kommunalbürokratie und staatlicher Verfolgungspolitik.* Hamburg: Hamburger Edition, 2009.

Koehl, Robert L. *RKFDV: German Resettlement and Population Policy, 1939–1945: A history of the Reich Commission for the Strengthening of Germandom.* Cambridge, MA: Harvard University Press, 1957.

Kopp, Kristin. *Germany's Wild East: Constructing Poland as Colonial Space.* Ann Arbor: University of Michigan Press, 2012.

Knight, Alan. *Mexico: Volume 2, The Colonial Era.* Cambridge: Cambridge University Press, 2002.

Kreienbaum, Jonas. *A Sad Fiasco: Colonial Concentration Camps in Southern Africa, 1900–1908.* Translated by Elizabeth Janik. New York: Berghahn Books, 2019.

Kruck, Alfred. *Die Geschichte des Alldeutschen Verbandes 1890–1939.* Wiesbaden: Steiner, 1954.

Kühne, Thomas. *Belonging and Genocide. Hitler's Community, 1918–1945.* New Haven: Yale University Press, 2010.

Kundrus, Birthe. "Colonialism, Imperialism, National Socialism: How Imperial Was the Third Reich?" In *German Colonialism in a Global Age*, edited by Bradley Naranch and Geoff Eley, 330–406. Durham: Duke University Press, 2014.

Kundrus, Birthe (ed.). *Phantasiereiche. Zur Kulturgeschichte des deutschen Kolonialismus.* Frankfurt: Campus, 2003.

Kundrus, Birthe. "Regime der Differenz: Volkstumspolitische Inklusionen und Exklusionen im Warthegau und im Generalgouvernement 1939–1944." In *Volksgemeinschaft: Neue Forschungen zur Gesellschaft des Nationalsozialismus*, edited by Frank Bajohr and Michael Wildt, 105–23. Frankfurt am Main: Fischer, 2009.

Kundrus, Birthe. "Weiblicher Kulturimperialismus: Die imperialistischen Frauenverbände des Kaiserreichs." In *Das Kaiserreich transnational. Deutschland in der Welt 1871–1914*, edited by Sebastian Conrad und Jürgen Osterhammel, 213–35. Göttingen: Vandenhoeck & Ruprecht, 2004.

Kunz, Rudibert and Rolf-Dieter Müller. *Giftgas gegen Abd el Krim: Deutschland, Spanien und der Gaskrieg in Spanisch- Marokko 1922-1927.* Freiburg: Verlag Rombach, 1990.

Laak, Dirk van. *Imperiale Infrastruktur: Deutsche Planungen für die Erschließung Afrikas 1880–1960.* Paderborn: Ferdinand Schöningh Verlag, 2004.

Laak, Dirk van. "'Ist je ein Reich, das es nicht gab, so gut verwaltet worden?' Der imaginäre Ausbau der imperialen Infrastruktur in Deutschland nach 1918." In *Phantasiereiche. Zur Kulturgeschichte des deutschen Kolonialismu*, edited by Birthe Kundrus, 71–90. Frankfurt: Campus, 2003.

Lehnstaedt, Stephan. "Deutsche in Warschau: Das Alltagsleben der Besatzer 1939–1944." In *Gewalt und Alltag im besetzten Polen, 1939–1945*, edited by Jochen Böhler and Stephan Lehnstaedt, 205–31. Osnabrück: Fibre Verlag, 2012.

Lehnstaedt, Stephan. *Imperiale Polenpolitik in den Weltkriegen. Eine vergleichende Studie zu den Mittelmächten und zu NS-Deutschland.* Osnabrück: Fibre Verlag, 2017.

Lemkin, Raphael. *Axis Rule in Occupied Europe: Laws of Occupation, Analysis of Government, Proposals for Redress.* Clark: Lawbook Exchange Ltd, 2008.

Leniger, Markus. *Nationalsozialistische "Volkstumsarbeit" und Umsiedlungspolitik 1933–1945. Von der Minderheitenbetreuung zur Siedlerauslese.* Berlin: Frank & Timme, 2006.

Lerp, Dörte. *Imperiale Grenzräume: Bevölkerungspolitiken in Deutsch-Südwestafrika und den östlichen Provinzen Preußens 1884–1914*. Frankfurt a. Main: Campus, 2016.

Lindner, Ulrike and Lerp, Dörte. "Introduction: Gendered Imperial Formations." In *New Perspectives on the History of Gender and Empire; Comparative and Global Approaches*, edited by Ulrike Lindner and Dörte Lerp, 1–30. London: Bloomsbury, 2018.

Linne, Karsten. *Deutschland jenseits des Äquators? Die NS-Kolonialplanungen für Afrika*. Berlin: Ch. Links Verlag, 2008.

Linne, Karsten. *Von Witzenhausen in die Welt: Ausbildung und Arbeit von Tropenlandwirten 1898 bis 1971*. Göttingen: Wallstein Verlag, 2017.

Liulevicius, Vejas Gabriel. *The German Myth of the East: 1800 to the Present*. Oxford: Oxford University Press, 2009.

Liulevicius, Vejas Gabriel. *War Land on the Eastern Front: Culture, National Identity, and German Occupation in World War I*. Cambridge: Cambridge University Press, 2000.

Longerich, Peter. *Holocaust: The Nazi Persecution and Murder of the Jews*. Oxford: Oxford University Press, 2010.

Loose, Ingo. "Die Enteignung der Juden im besetzten Polen 1939–1945." In *Vor der Vernichtung. Die staatliche Enteignung der Juden im Nationalsozialismus*, edited by Katharina Stengel, 283–307. Frankfurt am M: Campus Verlag, 2007.

Loose, Ingo. "Wartheland." In *The Greater German Reich and the Jews: Nazi Persecution Policies in the Annexed Territories, 1939–1945*, edited by Wolf Gruner and Jörg Osterloh. Translated by Bernard Heise, 189–218. New York: Berghahn Books, 2015.

Löw, Andrea. "'Ein Verbrechen, dessen Grauen mit nichts zu vergleichen ist': Die Ursprünge der Debatte über die Singularität des Holocaust." *Holocaust und Völkermorde: Die Reichweite des Vergleichs*, edited by Sybille Steinbacher, 125–43. Frankfurt am Main: Campus, 2012.

Löw, Andrea. *Juden im Getto Litzmannstadt: Lebensbedingungen, Selbstwahrnehmung, Verhalten*. Göttingen: Wallstein Verlag, 2006.

Lower, Wendy. *Hitler's Furies: German Women in the Nazi Killing Fields*. London: Chatto & Windus, 2013.

Lumans, Valdis O. *Himmler's Auxiliaries: The Volksdeutsche Mittelstelle and the German National Minorities of Europe, 1933–1945*. Chapel Hill: University of North Carolina Press, 1993.

MacLeod, Roy. "Preface," in *Disease, Medicine, and Empire: Perspectives on Western Medicine and the Experience of European Expansion*, edited by Roy MacLeod and Milton Lewis, i-xii. London: Routledge, 1988.

Madajczyk, Czesław. *Die Okkupationspolitik Nazideutschlands in Polen 1939–1945*. Cologne: Pahl-Rugenstein Verlag GmbH, 1988.

Majer, Diemut. *Fremdvölkische im Dritten Reich. Ein Beitrag zur nationalsozialistischen Rechtssetzung und Rechtspraxis in Verwaltung und Justiz unter besonderer Berücksichtigung der eingegliederten Ostgebiete und des Generalgouvernements*. Munich: Oldenbourg, 1993.

Majer, Diemut. *"Non-Germans" under the Third Reich: The Nazi Judicial and Administrative System in Germany and Occupied Eastern Europe, with Special Regard to Occupied Poland, 1939–1945*, translated by Peter Thomas Hill, Edward Vance Humphrey, and Brian Levin. Lubbock: Texas Tech University Press, 2013.

Mallmann, Klaus-Michael, Jochen Böhler, and Jürgen Matthäus (eds). *Einsatzgruppen in Polen. Darstellung und Dokumentation*. Darmstadt: Wissenschaftliche Buchgesellschaft, 2008.

Mazower, Mark. *Hitler's Empire: Nazi Rule in Occupied Europe*. London: Allen Lane, 2008.

Meier, Anna. *Die Intelligenzaktion: Die Vernichtung der Polnischen Oberschicht Im Gau Danzig-Westpreußen*. Saarbrücken: VDM Verlag Dr. Müller, 2008.
Metzger, Chantal. *L'Empire colonial français dans la stratégie du Troisième Reich, 1936–1945*. New York: Peter Lang, 2002.
Michels, Eckard. "Paul von Lettow-Vorbeck." In *Kein Platz an der Sonne: Erinnerungsorte der deutschen Kolonialgeschichte*, edited by Jürgen Zimmerer, 373–85. Frankfurt: Campus Verlag, 2013.
Mikel-Arieli, Roni. *Remembering the Holocaust in a Racial State: Holocaust Memory in South Africa from Apartheid to Democracy (1948–1994)*. Oldenbourg: De Gruyter, 2022.
Millet, Kitty. *The Victims of Slavery, Colonization and the Holocaust: A Comparative History of Persecution*. London: Bloomsbury Academic, 2017.
Molnar, Claudia. *Von der bürgerlichen Villa zur NS-Kunsthalle: Die Berliner Hardenbergstraße 21–23*. Norderstadt: BoD Books on Demand, 2018.
Montague, Patrick. *Chełmno and the Holocaust: The History of Hitler's First Death Camp*. London: I.B: Tauris, 2012.
Moses, A. Dirk. "Empire, Colony, Genocide: Keynotes and the Philosophy of History." In *Empire, Colony, Genocide: Conquest, Occupation, and Subaltern Resistance in World History*, edited by A. Dirk Moses, 3–54. New York: Berghahn Books, 2008.
Moses, A. Dirk. "Raphael Lemkin, Culture, and the Concept of Genocide." In *The Oxford Handbook of Genocide Studies*, edited by Donald Bloxham and A. Dirk Moses, 19–41. Oxford: Oxford University Press, 2010.
Moses, A. Dirk. "The Holocaust and Genocide." In *The Historiography of the Holocaust*, edited by Dan Stone, 533–55. New York: Palgrave Macmillan, 2004.
Moses, A. Dirk. *The Problems of Genocide: Permanent Security and the Language of Transgression*. Cambridge: Cambridge University Press, 2021.
Mühle, Eduard. *Für Volk und deutschen Osten. Der Historiker Hermann Aubin und die deutsche Ostforschung*. Düsseldorf: Droste Verlag, 2005.
Mühle, Eduard. "Putting the East in Order: German Historians and their Attempts to Rationalize German Eastward Expansion during the 1930s and 1940s." In *Germans, Poland, and Colonial Expansion to the East: 1800 Through the Present*, edited by Robert Nelson, 95–120. Bakingstoke: Palgrave Macmillan, 2009.
Mühle, Eduard. "The Mental Map of German *Ostforschung*." In *Germany and the European East in the Twentieth Century*, edited by Eduard Mühle, 107–30. Oxford: Berg, 2003.
Mühlenfeld, Daniel. "Reich Propaganda Offices and Political Mentoring of Ethnic German Resettlers." In *Heimat, Region, and Empire Spatial Identities under National Socialism*, edited by Claus-Christian W. Szejnmann, and Maiken Umbach, 199–212. Basingstoke: Palgrave Macmillan, 2012.
Müller, Rolf-Dieter. *Hitlers Ostkrieg und die deutsche Siedlungspolitik*. Frankfurt am Main: Fischer Taschenbuch Verlag GmbH, 1991.
Nelson, Robert L. "The Archive for Inner Colonisation, The German East, and World War I." In *Germans, Poland, and Colonial Expansion to the East: 1850 Through the Present*, edited by Robert L. Nelson, 65–93. Basingstoke: Palgrave Macmillan, 2009.
Nerdinger, Winfried (ed.). *Architektur und Verbrechen: Die Rolle von Architekten im Nationalsozialismus*. Göttingen: Wallstein Verlag, 2014.
O'Hara, Matthew D., and Andrew B. Fisher (eds). *Imperial Subjects: Race and Identity in Colonial Latin America*. London: Duke University Press, 2009.
Orski, Marek. "Organisation und Ordnungsprinzipien des Lagers Stutthofs." In *Die nationalsozialistischen Konzentrationslager: Entwicklung und Struktur*. Volume

1, edited by Ulrich Herbert, Karin Orth and Christoph Dieckmann, 285–308. Göttingen: Wallstein Verlag, 1998.
Osayimwese, Itohan. "Demystifying Colonial Settlement: Building Handbooks for Settlers, 1904–1930." In *German Colonialism, Visual Culture, and Modern Memory*, edited by Volker Langbehn, 124–47. Oxon: Routledge, 2010.
Osterhammel, Jürgen. *Colonialism: A Theoretical Overview*, translated by Shelley L. Frisch. Princeton: Markus Wiener Publications, 1997.
Pflanze, Otto. *Bismarck and the Development of Germany, Volume III: The Period of Fortification, 1880–1898*. Princeton: Princeton University Press, 1990.
Pendas, Devin O. "Racial States in Comparative Perspective." In *Beyond the Racial State: Rethinking Nazi Germany: Rethinking Nazi Germany*, edited by Devin O. Pendas, Mark Roseman, and Richard F. Wetzell, 116–47. Cambridge: Cambridge University Press, 2017.
Poley, Jared. *Decolonization in Germany: Weimar Narratives of Colonial Loss and Foreign Occupation*. Oxford: Peter Lang: 2005.
Rash, Felicity. *German Images of the Self and the Other: Nationalist, Colonialist and Anti-Semitic Discourse, 1871–1918*. Basingstoke: Palgrave Macmillan, 2012.
Rautenberg, Hulda and Mechtild Rommel. *Die Kolonialen Frauenschulen von 1908–1945*. Witzenhausen: Gesamthochschule Kassel, 1983.
Reagin, Nancy R. *Sweeping the German Nation: Domesticity and National Identity in Germany, 1870–1945*. Cambridge: Cambridge University Press, 2006.
Roediger, David R. "Whiteness and Race." In *The Oxford Handbook of American Immigration and Ethnicity*, edited by Ronald H. Bayor, 197–212. Oxford: Oxford University Press, 2016.
Röger, Maren. *Wartime Relations: Intimacy, Violence, and Prostitution in Occupied Poland, 1939–1945*, translated by Rachel Ward. Oxford: Oxford University Press, 2021.
Rössler, Mechtild and Sabine Schleiermacher (eds.). *Der "Generalplan Ost": Hauptlinien der nationalsozialistischen Planungs- und Vernichtungspolitik*. Berlin: Akademie, 1993.
Roth, Karl Heinz. "Richtung Halten" Hans Rothfels and Neoconservative Historiography on Both Sides of the Atlantic." In *German Scholars and Ethnic Cleansing, 1920–1945*, edited by Ingo Haar and Michael Fahlbusch, 236–59. New York: Berghahn Books, 2005.
Rothberg, Michael. *Multidirectional Memory: Remembering the Holocaust in the Age of Decolonization*. Stanford: Stanford University Press, 2009.
Rothberg, Michael. *Multidirektionale Erinnerung. Holocaustgedenken im Zeitalter der Dekolonisierung*. Berlin: Metropol Verlag, 2021.
Ruppenthal, Jens. *Kolonialismus als "Wissenschaft und Technik": Das Hamburgische Kolonialinstitut 1908 bis 1919*. Stuttgart: Franz Steiner Verlag, 2007.
Sakson, Andrzej. "Polnische Zeitzeugen berichten." In *Umgesiedelt – Vertrieben: Deutschbalten und Polen 1939–1945 im Warthegau*, edited by Eckhart Neander and Andrzej Sakson, 21–9. Marburg: Verlag Herder-Institut, 2010.
Said, Edward. *Orientalism*. London: Routledge & Kegan Paul, 1978/New York: Vintage Books, 1978.
Samson, Colin and Carlos Gigoux. *Indigenous Peoples and Colonialism: Global Perspectives*. Cambridge: Polity Press, 2017.
Sandler, Willeke. *Empire in the Heimat: Colonialism and Public Culture in the Third Reich*. Oxford: Oxford University Press, 2018.
Scheidgen, Irina. "Frauenbilder im Spielfilm, Kulturfilm und in der Wochenschau des Dritten Reiches." In *Nationalsozialismus und Geschlecht: Zur Politisierung und*

Ästhetisierung von Körper, Rasse und Sexualität im Dritten Reich und nach 1945, edited by Elke Frietsch and Christina Herkommer, 259-84. Bielefeld: Transcript Verlag, 2009.

Schilling, Britta. "Deutsche Frauen! Euch und euer Kinder geht es an!" Deutsche Frauen als Aktivistinnen für die koloniale Idee." In *Frauen in den deutschen Kolonien*, edited by Marianne Bechhaus-Gerst and Mechthild Leutner, 70-9. Berlin: C.H. Links Verlag, 2009.

Schilling, Britta. *Postcolonial Germany: Memories of Empire in a Decolonized Nation*. Oxford: Oxford University Press, 2014.

Schmokel, Wolfe W. *Dream of Empire: German Colonialism, 1919-1945*. New Haven: Yale University Press, 1964.

Schulze, Rainer. "Der Führer ruft!' Zur Rückholung der Volksdeutschen aus dem Osten." In *Die Volksdeutschen in Polen Frankreich Ungarn und der Tschechoslowakei*, edited by Jerzy Kochanowski and Maike Sach, 183-204. Osnabrück: Fibre Verlag, 2006.

Siegle, Dorothea. *"Trägerinnen echten Deutschtums." Die Koloniale Frauenschule Rendsburg*. Rendsburg: Wachholtz Verlag, 2004.

Smith, Woodruff D. *The Ideological Origins of Nazi Imperialism*. New York: Oxford University Press, 1986.

Speitkamp, Winfried. "Kolonialdenkmäler." In *Kein Platz an der Sonne: Erinnerungsorte der deutschen Kolonialgeschichte*, edited by Jürgen Zimmerer, 409-23. Frankfurt: Campus Verlag, 2013.

Stefanescu, Bogdan. *Postcommunism/Postcolonialism: Siblings of Subalternity*. Bucharest: Editura Universitatii din Bucuresti, 2013.

Steinbacher, Sybille. "Sonderweg, Kolonialismus, Genozide: Der Holocaust im Spannungsfeld von Kontinuitäten und Diskontinuitäten der deutschen Geschichte." In *Der Holocaust: Ergebnisse und neue Fragen der Forschung*, edited by Frank Bajohr and Andrea Löw, 83-101. Frankfurt am Main: S. Fischer Verlag Gmbh, 2015.

Stiller, Alexa. "Ethnic Germans." In *A Companion to Nazi Germany*, edited by Shelley Baranowski, Armin Nolzen, and Claus-Christian W. Szejnmann, 533-49. Oxford: Wiley Blackwell, 2018.

Stiller, Alexa. "On the Margins of Volksgemeinschaft: Criteria for Belonging to the Volk within the Nazi Germanization Policy in the Annexed Territories, 1939-1945." In *Heimat, Region, and Empire: Spatial Identities under National Socialism*, edited by Claus-Christian W. Szejnmann and Maiken Umbach, 235-51. Basingstoke: Palgrave Macmillan, 2012.

Stiller, Alexa. *Völkische Politik: Praktiken der Exklusion und Inklusion in polnischen, französischen und slowenischen Annexionsgebieten 1939-1945*. Göttingen: Wallstein Verlag, Forthcoming 2022.

Stoehr, Irene. "Von Max Sering zu Konrad Meyer - ein „machtergreifender" Generationswechsel in der Agrar- und Siedlungswissenschaft." In *Autarkie und Ostexpansion: Pflanzenzucht und Agrarforschung im Nationalsozialismus*, edited by Susanne Heim, 57-91. Göttingen: Walstein Verlag, 2002.

Stoler, Ann Laura. "Tense and Tender Ties: The Politics of Comparison in North American History and (Post) Colonial Studies." In *Haunted by Empire: Geographies of Intimacy in North American History*, edited by Ann Laura Stoler, 23-70. Durham: Duke University Press, 2006.

Stone, Dan. *Histories of the Holocaust*. Oxford: Oxford University Press, 2010.

Strippel, Andreas. *NS-Volkstumspolitik und die Neuordnung Europas: rassenpolitische Selektion der Einwandererzentralstelle des Chefs der Sicherheitspolizei und des SD 1939-1945*. Paderborn: Ferdinand Schöningh, 2011.

Strippel, Andreas. "Race, Regional Identity and Volksgemeinschaft: Naturalization of Ethnic German Resettlers in the Second World War by the Einwandererzentralstelle/Central Immigration Office of the SS." In *Heimat, Region, and Empire: Spatial Identities under National Socialism*, edited by Claus-Christian W. Szejnmann and Maiken Umbach, 185–98. Basingstoke: Palgrave Macmillan, 2012.

Suttner, Raymond. "Masculinities in the ANC-led liberation movement." In *From Boys to Men: Social Constructions of Masculinity in Contemporary Society*, edited by Tamara Shefer, Kopano Ratele, A. Strebel, and R. Buikema 195–224. Lansdowne: UCT Press, 2007.

Swartz, Rebecca. *Education and Empire: Children, Race and Humanitarianism in the British Settler Colonies, 1833–1880*. London: Palgrave Macmillan, 2019.

Sweeney, Dennis. "Pan-German Conceptions of Colonial Empire." In *German Colonialism in a Global Age*, edited by Bradley Naranch and Geoff Eley, 265–82. London: Duke University Press, 2014.

Tilse, Mark. *Transnationalism in the Prussian East: From National Conflict to Synthesis, 1871–1914*. Basingstoke: Palgrave Macmillan, 2011.

Trimmel, Gerald. *Heimkehr. Strategien eines nationalsozialistischen Films*. Vienna: W. Eichbauer Verlag, 1998.

Veracini, Lorenzo. "Introduction: Settler Colonialism as a Distinct Mode of Domination." In *The Routledge Handbook of the History of Settler Colonialism*, edited by Edward Cavanagh and Lorenzo Veracini, 1–8. London: Routledge, 2017.

Veracini, Lorenzo. *Settler Colonialism: A Theoretical Overview*. London: Palgrave Macmillan, 2010.

Wachsmann, Nikolaus. *KL: Die Geschichte der nationalsozialistischen Konzentrationslager*. Munich: Siedler Verlag, 2016.

Wächter, Katja-Maria. *Die Macht der Ohnmacht: Leben und Politik des Franz Xaver Ritter von Epp (1868–1946)*. Frankfurt am Main: Peter Lang GmbH, 1999.

Walkenhorst, Peter. *Nation-Volk-Rasse: Radikaler Nationalismus im Deutschen Kaiserreich 1890–1914*. Göttingen: Vandenhoeck & Ruprecht, 2007.

Walgenbach, Katharina. *"Die Weiße Frau als Trägerin deutscher Kultur": Kolonial Diskurse über Geschlecht, Rasse und Klasse im Kaiserreich*. Frankfurt: Campus Verlag, 2005.

Walsh, Tom. "The National System of Education, 1831–2000." In *Essays in the History of Irish Education*, edited by Brendan Walsh, 7–43. London: Palgrave Macmillan, 2016.

Weber, Eugen. *Peasants into Frenchmen: The Modernization of Rural France, 1870–1914*. Stanford: Stanford University Press, 1976.

Wempe, Sean Andrew. *Revenants of the German Empire: Colonial Germans, Imperialism, and the League of Nations*. Oxford: Oxford University Press, 2019.

Westermann, Edward B. *Hitler's Ostkrieg and the Indian Wars: Comparing Genocide and Conquest*. Norman: University of Oklahoma Press, 2016.

Wildenthal, Lora. *German Women for Empire, 1884–1945*. Durham: Duke University Press, 2001.

Wildenthal, Lora. "Race, Gender, and Citizenship in the German Colonial Empire." In *Tensions of Empire: Colonial Cultures in a Bourgeois World*, edited by Frederick Cooper and Ann Laura Stoler. 263–83. Berkeley: University of California Press, 1997.

Williams, Robert C. *Horace Greeley: Champion of American Freedom*. New York: New York University Press, 2006.

Wolf, Gerhard. *Ideologie und Herrschaftsrationalität: Nationalsozialistische Germanisierungspolitik in Polen*. Hamburg: Hamburger Edition, 2012.

Wolfe, Patrick. *Settler Colonialism and the Transformation of Anthropology: The Politics and Poetics of an Ethnographic Event*. London: Cassell, 1999.

Zantop, Susanne. *Colonial Fantasies: Conquest, Family, and Nation in Precolonial Germany, 1770–1870*. Durham: Duke University Press, 1997.

Zeller, Joachim. "Decolonization of the Public Space? (Post)colonial Culture of Remembrance in Germany." In *Hybrid Cultures, Nervous States: Britain and Germany in a (Post)Colonial World*, edited by Ulrike Lindner, Maren Möhring, Mark Stein, and Silke Stroh, 65–88. Amsterdam: Rodophi, 2010.

Zeller, Joachim. "'Ombepera I koza - Die Kälte tötet mich,' Zur Geschichte des Konzentrationslagers in Swakopmund." In *Völkermord in Deutsch-Südwestafrika: Der Kolonialkrieg (1904–1908) in Namibia und seine Folgen*, edited by Jürgen Zimmerer and Joachim Zeller, 192–208. Berlin: Christoph Links Verlag GmbH, 2016.

Zimmerer, Jürgen. "The First Genocide of the Twentieth Century: The German War of Destruction in South West Africa (1904–1908) and the Global History of Genocide." In *Lessons and Legacies VIII: From Generation to Generation*, edited by Doris L. Bergen, 34–64. Evanston: Northwestern University Press, 2008.

Zimmerer, Jürgen. *Von Windhuk nach Auschwitz? Beiträge zum Verhältnis von Kolonialismus und Holocaust*. Münster: LIT, 2011.

Journal Articles

Bajohr, Frank and Rachel O'Sullivan. "Holocaust, Kolonialismus und NS-Imperialismus: Wissenschaftliche Forschung im Schatten einer polemischen Debatte." *Vierteljahrshefte für Zeitgeschichte* 70, no. 1 (2022): 191–202.

Baranowski, Shelly. "Scholar's Forum: The Holocaust—a colonial genocide?" *Dapim: Studies on the Holocaust* 25, no. 1 (2013): 58–61.

Barteaux, Jillian. "Urban Planning as Colonial Marketing Strategy for the Swan River Settlement, Western Australia." *Australasian Historical Archaeology* 34 (2016): 22–31.

Bartrop, Paul R. "The Holocaust, the Aborigines, and the Bureaucracy of Destruction: An Australian Dmension of Genocide." *Journal of Genocide Research* 3, no. 1 (2001): 75–87.

Bauman, Zygmunt. "Making and Unmaking of Strangers." *Thesis Eleven* 43 (1995): 1–16.

Bellamy, Alex J. "Mass Killing and the Politics of Legitimacy: Empire and the Ideology of Selective Extermination." *Australian Journal of Politics and History* 58, no. 2 (2012): 159–80.

Bergen, Doris L. "The Nazi Concept of 'Volksdeutsche' and the Exacerbation of Anti-Semitism in Eastern Europe, 1939–45." *Journal of Contemporary History* 29, no. 4 (1994): 569–82.

Bernhard, Patrick. "Borrowing from Mussolini: Nazi Germany's Colonial Aspirations in the Shadow of Italian Expansionism." *Journal of Imperial and Commonwealth History* 41, no. 4 (2013): 617–43.

Bernhard, Patrick. "Hitler's Africa in the East: Italian Colonialism as a Model for German Planning in Eastern Europe." *Journal of Contemporary History* 51, no. 1 (2016): 61–90.

Best, Jeremy. "Godly, International, and Independent: German Protestant Missionary Loyalties before World War I." *Central European History* 47, no. 3 (September 2014): 585–611.

Carsten, Francis L. "Volk ohne Raum: A Note on Hans Grimm." *Journal of Contemporary History* 2, no. 2 (1967): 221–7.
Cohen, William B. "The Colonized as Child: British and French Colonial Rule." *African Historical Studies* 3, no. 2 (1970): 427–31.
Djiar, Kahina Amal. "Locating Architecture, Post-Colonialism and Culture: Contextualisation in Algiers." *Journal of Architecture* 14, no. 2 (2009): 161–83.
Edmonds, Penelope and Anna Johnston. "Empire, Humanitarianism and Violence in the Colonies." *Journal of Colonialism and Colonial History* 17 (2016): https://muse.jhu.edu/article/613279
Fitzpatrick, Matthew. "The Pre-History of the Holocaust? The *Sonderweg* and *Historikerstreit* Debates and the Abject Colonial Past." *Central European History* 41, no. 3 (2008): 477–503.
Fortier, Craig and Edward Hon-Sing Wong. "The Settler Colonialism of Social Work and the Social Work of Settler Colonialism." *Settler Colonial Studies* 9, no. 4 (2019): 437–56.
Foster, Robert. "Rations, Coexistence, and the Colonization of Aboriginal Labour in the South Australian Pastoral Industry, 1860–1911." *Aboriginal History* 24 (2000): 1–26.
Furber, David. "Near as Far in the Colonies: The Nazi Occupation of Poland." *International History Review* 26, no. 3 (2004): 541–79.
Gerwarth, Robert and Stephan Malinowski. "Hannah Arendt's Ghosts: Reflections on the Disputable Path from Windhoek to Auschwitz." *Central European History* 42, no. 2 (2009): 279–300.
Gordon, Michelle. "Colonial Violence and Holocaust Studies." *Holocaust Studies* 21, no. 4 (2015): 272–91.
Grewling, Nicole. "Blood Brothers? Indians and the Construction of a German Colonial Self in Friedrich Gerstäcker's Fiction." *Arkansas Historical Quarterly* 73, no. 1 (Spring 2014): 90–101.
Howell, Jessica M. "Nurse going native: Language and Identity in Letters From Africa and the British West Indies." *Journal of Commonwealth Literature* 51, no. 1 (2016): 165–81.
Hom, Stephanie Malia. "Empires of Tourism: Travel and Rhetoric in Italian Colonial Libya and Albania, 1911–1943." *Journal of Tourism History* 4, no. 3 (2012): 281–300.
Jaworska, Sylvia. "Anti-Slavic Imagery in German Radical Nationalist Discourse at the Turn of the Twentieth Century: A Prelude to Nazi Ideology?" *Patterns of Prejudice* 45, no. 5 (2011): 435–52.
Joon-Hai Lee, Christopher. "The 'Native' Undefined: Colonial Categories, Anglo-African Status and the Politics of Kinship in British Central Africa, 1929–38." *Journal of African History* 46, no. 3 (2005): 455–78.
Jureit, Ulrike. "Ordering Space: Intersections of Space, Racism, and Extermination." *Journal of Holocaust Research* 33, no.1 (2019): 64–82.
Kakel, Carroll P. "Patterns and Crimes of Empire: Comparative Perspectives on Fascist and Non-Fascist Extermination." *Journal of Holocaust Research* 33, no. 1 (2019): 4–21.
Kettler, Mark T. "What Did Paul Rohrbach Actually Learn in Africa? The Influence of Colonial Experience on a Publicist's Imperial Fantasies in Eastern Europe." *German History* 38, no. 2 (2020): 240–62.
Kühne, Thomas. "Colonialism and the Holocaust: Continuities, Causations, and Complexities." *Journal of Genocide Research* 15, no. 3 (2013): 339–62.
Lisner, Wiebke. "Midwifery and Racial Segregation in Occupied Western Poland, 1939–1945." *German History* 35, no. 1 (2017): 229–46.
Madajczyk, Czesław. "Generalplan Ost." *Polish Western Affairs* 3 (1962): 391–442.

Madley, Benjamin. "From Africa to Auschwitz: How German South West Africa Incubated Ideas and Methods Adopted and Developed by the Nazis in Eastern Europe." *European History Quarterly* 35, no. 3 (2005): 429–62.

Mailänder Koslov, Elissa. "'Going east': Colonial Experiences and Practices of Violence Among Female and Male Majdanek Camp Guards (1941–44)." *Journal of Genocide Research* 10, no. 4 (2008): 563–82.

Mbembe, Achille. "Necropolitics." *Public Culture* 15, no. 1 (2003): 11–40.

Moore, Paul. "'And What Concentration Camps Those Were!': Foreign Concentration Camps in Nazi Propaganda, 1933–9." *Journal of Contemporary History* 45, no. 3 (2010): 649–74.

Moses, A. Dirk. "Conceptual Blockages and Definitional Dilemmas in the 'Racial Century': Genocides of Indigenous Peoples and the Holocaust." *Patterns of Prejudice* 36, no. 4 (2002): 7–36.

Nichols, Bradley J. "The Re-Germanization Procedure: A Domestic Model for Nazi Empire-Building." *German Historical Institute Bulletin* (2018): 61–91.

O'Sullivan, Rachel. "Integration and Division: Nazi Germany and the "Colonial Other" in Annexed Poland." *Journal of Genocide Research* 22, no. 4 (2020): 437–58.

O'Sullivan, Rachel. "The German Mission in Africa and Poland: Women, Expansion, and Colonial Training During the Third Reich." *Journal of Colonialism and Colonial History* 22, no. 2, 2021: muse.jhu.edu/article/801556.

Pergher, Roberta and Mark Roseman. "The Holocaust– An Imperial Genocide?," *Dapim—Studies on the Holocaust* 27, no. 1 (2013): 42–9.

Pretelli, Matteo. "Education in the Italian Colonies During the Interwar Period." *Modern Italy* 16, no. 3 (2011): 275–93.

Röger, Maren. "The Sexual Policies and Sexual Realities of the German Occupiers in Poland in the Second World War." *Contemporary European History* 23, no. 1 (2014): 1–21.

Rosenfeld, Gavriel D. "The Politics of Uniqueness: Reflections on the Recent Polemical Turn in Holocaust and Genocide Scholarship." *Holocaust and Genocide Studies* 13, no. 1 (1999): 28–61.

Russell, Penny "Unhomely Moments": Civilising Domestic Worlds in Colonial Australia." *History of the Family* 14, no. 4 (2009): 327–39.

Sandler, Willeke. "Colonial Education in the Third Reich: The Witzenhausen Colonial School and the Rendsburg Colonial School for Women." *Central European History* 49, no. 2 (2016): 181–207.

Sandler, Willeke. "Deutsche Heimat in Afrika: Colonial Revisionism and the Construction of Germanness through Photography." *Journal of Women's History* 25, no. 1 (2013): 37–61.

Schönwälder, Karen. "The Fascination of Power: Historical Scholarship in Nazi Germany." *History Workshop Journal* 43, no. 1 (Spring, 1997): 133–53.

Sinha, Mrinalini. "Britishness, Clubbability, and the Colonial Public Sphere: The Genealogy of an Imperial Institution in Colonial India." *Journal of British Studies* 40, no. 4 (2001): 489–521.

Smith, Iain R. and Andreas Stucki. "The Colonial Development of Concentration Camps (1868–1902)." *Journal of Imperial and Commonwealth History* 39, no. 3 (2011): 417–37.

Spodek, Howard. "City Planning in India under British Rule." *Economic and Political Weekly* 48, no. 4 (2013): 53–61.

Steinweis, Alan E. "Eastern Europe and the Notion of the 'Frontier' in Germany to 1945." *Yearbook of European Studies* 13 (1999): 56–69.

Stiller, Alexa. "Völkischer Kapitalismus: Theoretische Überlegungen anhand des empirischen Beispiels der Deutschen Umsiedlungs-Treuhandgesellschaft 1939–1945." *Zeitschrift für Geschichtswissenschaft* 66, no. 6 (2018): 505–23.

Stoler, Ann Laura. "Making Empire Respectable: The Politics of Race and Sexual Morality in 20th-Century Colonial Cultures." *American Ethnologist* 16, no. 4 (1989): 634–60.

Stoler, Ann Laura. "Rethinking Colonial Categories: European Communities and the Boundaries of Rule." *Comparative Studies in Society and History* 31, no. 1 (1989): 134–61.

Surynt, Izabela. "Postcolonial Studies and the "Second World": Twentieth-Century German Nationalist-Colonial Constructs." *Werkwinkel* 3, no. 1 (2008): 61–87.

Szczepan, Aleksandra. "Terra Incognita? Othering East-Central Europe in Holocaust Studies," in *Colonial Paradigms of Violence: Comparative Analysis of the Holocaust, Genocide, and Mass Killing*, edited by Michelle Gordon and Rachel O'Sullivan, 185–7, Göttingen: Wallstein, 2022.

Wildt, Michael. "Was heißt: Singularität des Holocaust?" *Zeithistorische Forschungen/ Studies in Contemporary History* 19 (2022): 126–47.

Wolf, Gerhard. "Negotiating Germanness: National Socialist Germanization policy in the Wartheland." *Journal of Genocide Research* 19, no. 2 (2017): 214–39.

Wolf, Gerhard. "The Wannsee Conference in 1942 and the National Socialist Living Space Dystopia." *Journal of Genocide Research* 17, no.2 (2015): 153–75.

Wolfe, Patrick. "Settler Colonialism and the Elimination of the Native." *Journal of Genocide Research* 8, no. 4 (2006): 387–409.

Zimmerer, Jürgen. "The Birth of the Ostland Out of the Spirit of Colonialism: A Postcolonial Perspective on the Nazi Policy of Conquest and Extermination." *Patterns of Prejudice* 39, no. 2 (2005): 197–219.

Dissertations

Furber, David. "Going East: Colonialism and German Life in Nazi-Occupied Poland." PhD diss., University of New York, 2003.

Gangelmayer, Franz Josef. "Das Parteiarchivwesen der NSDAP Rekonstruktionsversuch des Gauarchivs der NSDAP-Wien." PhD diss., Universität Wien, 2010.

Holston, Keith. "A Measure of the Nation: Politics, Colonial Enthusiasm and Education in Germany, 1896–1933." PhD diss., University of Pennsylvania: 1996.

Kopp, Kristin. "Contesting Borders: German Colonial Discourse and the Polish Eastern Territories." PhD diss., University of California, Berkeley, 2001.

Nichols, Bradley J. "The Hunt for Lost Blood: Nazi Germanization Policy in Occupied Europe." PhD diss., University of Tennessee, 2016.

Plavnieks, Richards Olafs. "'Wall of Blood': The Baltic German Case Study in National Socialist Wartime Population Policy, 1939–1945." MA diss., University of North Carolina, 2008.

Sandler, Willeke. "'Colonizers Are Born, Not Made': Creating a Colonialist Identity in Nazi Germany, 1933–1945." PhD. diss., Duke University, 2012.

Stiller, Alexa. "Germanisierung und Gewalt: Nationalsozialistische Politik in den annektierten Gebieten Polens, Frankreichs und Sloweniens, 1939–1945." PhD diss., Historisches Institut Bern, 2014/2015.

Index

accommodation 57, 115
  allocation for ethnic Germans 50, 54
  lack of 54
  provision department 97
advertisements
  colonial events 32, 145
  colonial products 28, 68
  colonial reference 25, 26, 33, 45
  East 90–6
  former German colonies in Africa 140
  job vacancies 80, 99
  Kampf und Aufbau exhibition 82, 83
  personal 79
Africa/African continent, *see also* advertisements; schools; irredentism
  assimilation policies 73
  books, see *Afrikabücher*
  films 33
  former German colonies 6, 21, 34, 141, 148, 158–9, 161–2
  German expansion 8, 17, 18, 22, 24, 146–8, 153
  German settlement 25, 39, 40, 87, 140, 146, 150, 161
  German settlers 156
  German women 106, 150, 154
  loss of German colonies 28
  museum 26
  reclamation of German colonies 17, 21, 31, 138, 140, 144–5, 150–1, 155, 157–8, 161–2, 166
  resources 146
  toys 27
  trade 23, 24
Afrikabücher 28–9, 33, 37, 150–60
agriculture, *see also* films
  Africa 159
  assigned work 55
  ethnic German farmers 49, 63–4, 70, 94
  farms 5, 36, 42, 50, 54, 56, 59, 62, 72, 82, 92, 104, 113, 128, 131, 160
  German farmers 84, 93, 140
  methods 99
  Polish buildings 84
  Reich Minister for Food and Agriculture, *see* Darré, Richard Walther
  training 141 (see also *Koloniale Frauenschule*; Witzenhausen)
  women 149 (see also *Koloniale Frauenschule*)
Alldeutscher Verband, *see* Pan-German League
Altreich (old Reich), 60, 85, 87, 88, 108, 118, *see also* architecture
  classification 54
  deportations to 113–14
  Germans 3, 50, 63, 67–8, 72, 92, 96, 100, 105
  Jews 108, 128
  society 76, 103
Anglo-Boer Wars (1880–1, 1899–1902) 29
  Second Anglo-Boer War (1899–1902) 123–4 (*see also* camps)
anti-Semitism 2, 9, 11, 170
  ideology 41–2, 44, 170
  policies 7, 108, 115
architecture
  Altreich 80–1
  Annexed Poland 79–81, 85, 87
  colonial territory 87–8
  journals 81
Archiv für innere Kolonisation (Archive for Inner Colonization, AfiK) 38–40, 44, 81
  eastern settlement 39–40
  First World War 40
  German overseas settlement 39
  Nazi regime 40
assimilation 3, 16, 50, 60, 75, 107, 130, 166–7
Australia 74

Index

British Empire 73
   colonial 61, 73–4, 75–6, 122, 166–7
   Deutsche Volksliste 4, 71–4, 76, 132, 169
   ethnic Germans 17, 61, 75, 167 (*see also* Germanization)
   French Empire 73
   Portuguese Empire 73
   Prussia 36
   settler colonialism 13, 130–3, 168
   Wiedereindeutschungsverfahren (re-Germanization procedure, WED) 72–4, 76, 132 (see also *Wiedereindeutschungsverfahren*)
Aubin, Hermann 152–3, 159–60
Aufgabe (task), German 28
   Annexed Poland 80, 92–3, 96, 98, 104–6, 143, 148–9
   colonial 104, 148, 153
   Ostforschung 154–6
   women 94, 101, 142–3, 148, 154
Auschwitz 118, 124, 126
   Auschwitz-Birkenau 100, 126 (*see also* Holocaust)
   debates 6
   gas chambers 126, 133, 168
Australia 74, 76, 87

Baltic Germans 51–2, 57, 65, 69–70
Baltic States 1, 4, 50, 98, 118
Bessarabia 1, 52, 63
Bessarabian Germans 63, 66, 91–2
Bismarck, Otto von 22–4, 36, 139
Bock, Franz Heinrich [Alexander Hohenstein] 99–100
Boers 69, 124
Brackmann, Albert 89, 154–5, 157, 159
British Empire 41, 74, 76, 88, 152, *see also* assimilation
   schools 60
   violence 127
Bromberger Blutsonntag (Bromberg Bloody Sunday) 69, 92
Bukovina 4, 52, 55, 56
Bund Deutscher Mädel (BDM, League of German Girls) 56, 58, 149, 154, 156, *see also* women
Bydgoszcz (Bromberg) 65, 69, 87, 109, 118, see also *Bromberger Blutsonntag*

Cameroon 23, 24, 28, 32, 141, 147, 152
camps, *see also* Auschwitz; Chełmno nad Nerem; Stutthof
   colonial 123, 124–5
   ethnic German resettler 51–2, 54–6, 57, 62–4, 82, 92, 114
   extermination 115, 119, 124, 125–6
   labor 117–18
   Nazi Germany concentration 101, 113, 118, 124, 125, 129
   Second Anglo-Boer War 123–4
categorization, 4, 24, 15, 70–1, 74–7, 121, 123, 127, 132, 168–9
   Deutsche Volksliste 71–2, 74–5
   ethnic Germans 4, 53–4, 70, 109, 121, 128, 132, 162, 169
   Jews 132, 170
   Poles 15, 109, 121, 132, 162, 169
   racialization 131, 132
Chełmno nad Nerem (Kulmhof an der Nehr) 64
   extermination camp 5, 115–19, 124–6, 129, 168
children 65, 68, 74
   colonial contexts 120–2, 125, 156, 159
   ethnic Germans 54, 57–60, 63, 66, 71–2, 91, 102–3, 111–12
   Jewish 116
   Kaiserreich 26–7, 29
   Polish 58, 108, 111–12, 118, 122
citizenship
   colonial contexts 169
   German 7, 52–3, 60, 69–71
   provisional German 71
   Prussian 7, 35
civilising mission, 9, *see also* humanitarian mission
   Annexed Poland 61, 70, 105, 154, 166–7
   colonial 61, 68, 70, 87, 102, 105, 107, 130, 167
   Kaiserreich 28, 38, 44, 45
Claß, Heinrich [Daniel Frymann] 41–3
classification, *see* categorization
clothing, 67, 73, 93, 115, 123
   ethnic Germans 67
   redistribution 129–30
   shoe repair 116
colonial archive 150, 166

Colonial Other
  Africa 26
  Annexed Poland 37, 45, 56–61, 76–7, 87, 150
  othering 125, 128
colonialism
  continental, internal 16, 42, 61, 77, 95, 138, 150, 154, 163
  definition 13
  European 96, 163
  overseas 6, 8, 16–17, 28, 89, 137–8, 143, 145, 147, 148, 150, 152, 161–2, 166
  settler colonialism (*see* settler colonialism)
comparative debate 2, 4, 6, 8–12, 59, 75, 107, 126, 133, 162, 166–7
  continuity thesis 6, 8, 9, 11, 16, 45, 59, 126, 162, 166
curfew
  Annexed Poland 110
  colonial territories 121–2

Danzig (Gdańsk) 87, 90, 93, 114–15, 157
Danzig-West Prussia 2, 4–5, 13–14, 57, 69, 80, 94, 103, 109, 121, 133, 149, 165
  annexation 13, 123, 127
  concentration camps 118
  Deutsche Volksliste 72
  economy 93
  ghettos 114
  irredentism 95
  settlement 16, 51, 56, 107, 155
Darré, Richard Walther 40, 146–7
deportation 101, 106, 117, 126
  Annexed Poland 3, 5, 16, 56, 59, 89, 112–15, 128, 133–4, 152
  colonial 123, 128
  Generalplan Ost 119–20
  settler colonial 131, 168
Deutsche Kolonialgesellschaft (German Colonial Society, DKG) 21, 23–5, 29, 31–3, 41, 45, 138, 143
Deutsche Häuser (German Houses) 86, 88
Deutsche Volksliste (German Peoples' List, DVL) 4, 15, 71–7, 109, 119, 127, 130, 132, 169
developmental mission, *see* civilising mission; humanitarian mission
discourse 17, 38, 43–5, 151
  colonial 17–18, 88, 150–1, 150–63, 166

German expansion 56, 151
  irredentist 95, 157, 159, 160–1
  overlaps 8, 17, 150–63, 166
  Poland 38, 41–2, 95, 155, 150–63, 166

education 53, 122, 124, *see also* schools
  colonial 6, 26–8, 33, 137, 140–3, 147 (see also *Koloniale Frauenschule*; Witzenhausen)
  colonial territories 60, 104–5, 122
  ethnic Germans 58–60, 66, 68, 102, 104–5, 112
  Kaiserreich 6, 26–8
  Polish 111–12, 122
  Prussia 35
Einsatzgruppen 116, 119
Einwandererzentralstelle (Central Immigration Office, EWZ) 51–4, 99
Engelhardt-Kyffhäuser, Otto 49, 62–3, 67
Epp, Franz Xaver Ritter von 139–40, 144–8, 150–1, 153, 159, 161
Estonia 51–3
ethnic Germans (*Volksdeutsche*), *see also* resettlement
  assimilation (*see under* assimilation)
  categorization (*see under* categorization)
  definition/concept 52
  differentiation between groups of 69–70
  Germanization (*see* Germanization)
  Polish/local 4, 15, 50, 61, 66, 69, 71, 73, 76, 85, 87, 99, 102, 103, 111, 132
  screening, of (*see under* screening)
eviction 3, 5, 50–1, 56–7, 59, 98, 113–15, 129
exhibitions 15, 32, 45, 49–50, 59, 61–2, 79, 82, 84, 96, 143–4, 151–2, 170
  Das deutsche Wartheland (The German Wartheland) 82
  Der Osten des Warthelands (The East of the Wartheland) 95
  Deutsche Kolonialausstellung (German Colonial Exhibition) 25–6
  Kampf und Aufbau im Wartheland (Struggle and Development in the Wartheland) 82–3
  Planung und Aufbau im Osten (Planning and Development in the East) 84–5

films 10, 15, 96, 104, 143, 151
  colonial subject 28, 33, 79, 143

Der Weg in die Welt (The Pathway to the World) 142
Die Deutsche Frauen-Kolonialschule Rendsburg (The German Women's Colonial School Rendsburg) 142–3
Heimkehr (Homecoming) 92–3
Mädel verlassen die Stadt (Girls Leave the City) 91, 143
Ostland—deutsches Land (Eastern land—German land) 92
First World War (1914–1918) 7, 21, 27–9, 31–2, 40, 43, 45, 52, 87, 139, 156, 166
Forster, Albert 51, 80, 93
France 24, 27–8, 60–1, 101, 128, 152
 French Empire 59, 73, 76, 88, 122
 women 59

Galicia 42, 49, 51, 113
gas chambers 126, 128, 168, *see under* Auschwitz
 Stutthof 118
General Government 86, 149
 deportations to 54, 113–15
Generalplan Ost (General Plan East, GPO) 85, 119–20, 130, 145, 165
genocide 9–10, 127–8, 131
 colonial 2, 6, 10, 127–8, 134, 168, 170
 first definition 2, 127
 Herero and Nama 6
 Holocaust 9–10, 128, 134, 168, 170
 United Nations definition (1948) 2, 127
German East Africa 22, 24, 28, 29, 30–2, 120, 152
Germanization 3, 15, 130, 149, *see also* assimilation; *Deutsche Volksliste*; *Wiedereindeutschungsverfahren*
 ethnic Germans 56–8, 60–1, 64, 66–7, 72–3, 76, 79, 103, 130, 132, 143, 167
 Generalplan Ost 120, 165
 Poles 118, 120, 130, 132, 143
 Prussia 35
German South West Africa 6, 28–30, 39, 42, 74, 120, 139, 156, 170
 Blue Book 27
 camps 123–5
 genocide 6
 settlement 24, 70–1

Gesellschaft für Deutsche Kolonisation (Society for German Colonization) 23, 41
Gesellschaft zur Förderung der inneren Kolonisation (Society for the Advancement of Inner Colonization, GFK) 38–41, 43, 44–5, see also *Archiv für innere Kolonisation*; internal colonization
ghetto 101, 124–6, 133, *see also* Łódź (Litzmannstadt) ghetto
 Warsaw 114
 Wartheland 114–18
Gostynin (Waldrode) 66, 103
Greiser, Arthur 54, 81–2, 84, 86, 108, 111, 114, 116–17
Grimm, Hans 29–30, 146

Hauptamt Volksdeutsche Mittlestelle (Main Welfare Office for Ethnic Germans, VoMi) 49, 52, 62, 129, 155–6
 resettler camps 51–2, 54, 57, 92
healthcare
 Annexed Poland 58, 60, 68, 79, 104
 colonial territories 59, 102, 105, 144, 158
 doctors 53, 58, 61, 79, 99, 105, 108, 113, 117, 143
 nurses 4, 66–8, 79, 98, 101–2, 105–6, 154, 167
Heim ins Reich (Home to the Reich) policy 4, 50, 56, 70, 89
Herero and Nama 6
 Herero and Nama Wars (1904–8) 6, 26–7, 30, 139
Heydrich, Reinhard 112, 116, 119, 126
hierarchy, 67, 71, 107, 127, 130
 colonial 121–2, 133, 169
 cultural 5
 ethnic/racial 61, 70, 76, 121, 165, 169
 settler 68
 societal 17, 50, 86, 88, 96, 99, 102–3, 111–12, 121, 133, 168–9
Himmler, Heinrich 53, 55, 95, 129, 139, 144, 165
 Generalplan Ost 119–20 (*see also* *Generalplan Ost*)
 Jewish deportations 113
 Koloniale Frauenschule 149
 murder of Jews 116–17

Reichskommissariat für die Festigung deutschen Volkstums 4, 50–1, 147
Hitler, Adolf 2, 9, 11, 21, 49, 50, 52, 57, 62–3, 82, 101, 105, 144–5, 147–8, 150–1, 153
  colonial rhetoric 75, 90
  German overseas colonialism 138, 139–40, 145–6, 148, 156
  murder of Jews 116
Hitler Youth (*Hitler Jugend*) 86, 92
Holocaust, 2, 3, 12, 99, 107, 126, 128, 134, 137, 168, 170–1, *see also* genocide; settler colonialism; Wartheland
  Annexed Poland 5, 17, 128, 133–4, 168–9
  Auschwitz-Birkenau 126
  colonial comparison debate 4, 9–11, 127–8, 133, 151, 166, 168, 170–1
  continuity thesis 6
  memory 10, 170
  uniqueness/singularity 8–9, 11, 168
homogenous society, fantasy of 74
  Annexed Poland 17, 67, 69, 72–3, 76, 132, 134, 165
  colonial 73–4, 121, 130, 165
  Germany 41, 44, 72–3
  Prussia 42
Hottentot, term 25, 65, 70
humanitarian missions, notion of
  Annexed Poland 5, 17, 68, 75–7, 85, 96, 103–5, 162, 167, 169
  colonial 5, 17, 59, 73, 75–7, 103–6, 159, 161–3, 167, 169
  Nazi Germany's lack of 75, 158, 166
  Ostforschung 158, 161, 163

imperialism 1, 2, 4, 9, 10, 12, 60, 73–4, 87–8, 90, 101, 121, 147, 165, 170–1, see also *Kaiserreich*
  definition 13
  German overseas 6, 26, 41, 137
  Prussia 36
  violence 2, 130
infrastructure 16–17, 80–1, 84, 86–7, 107, 150, 161
  colonial territory 87, 105, 159
inner colonization (internal) 36, 38, 39, 42–3, 77, 95

interwar period 7, 12, 15–16, 21–2, 34, 38, 40, 58, 151–2, 161
  decline of former German territories, notion of 58, 94
  memories of overseas colonialism 16, 22, 33–4, 45, 147, 166
Ireland 60, 122, 147, 170
  Irish in America 123
irredentism 95
  former German colonies in Africa 13, 159, 161, 166
  Poland 13, 79, 94–5, 157, 159–61, 166
Italian empire 89, 90, 95–6, 120–2

Koło (Warthbrücken) 64, 98, 114, 116
Kolonialball (Colonial Ball) 32–3, 145
Koloniale Frauenschule (Colonial Women's School), Rendsburg 141–3, 148–50, 161, *see also* films
Kolonialfrage (colonial question) 139, 153
Kolonialpolitisches Amt der NSDAP (NSDAP Office of Colonial Policy, KPA) 139–40, 144–6, 148–9
Kolonialschuldlüge (Colonial Guilt Lie) 30, 140
Königlich Preußische Ansiedlungskommission in den Provinzen Westpreußen und Posen, *see* Prussian Settlement Commission
Koppe, Wilhelm 112, 116–17
Kulturfilm (culture film), *see* films
Kulturkampf (culture struggle) 7, 35
Kulturträger (culture bringers) 36, 70, 84, 105, 160, *see also* civilizing mission

labor 8, 54, 102, 112, 113, 116, 122, 124, 130, 137, 159
  colonial territories 13, 122, 124–5, 127, 130, 168
  domestic 102, 110
  forced 1, 108, 112, 117–18, 120, 125, 127, 129–30, 133
language 35, 70, 90, 141–2, 165
  colonial destruction of 5, 122
  colonial territories 70, 73–4, 87, 130
  German 4, 42, 52–3, 55, 63, 66, 71, 73, 79, 99, 111, 122, 155–6
  Polish 7, 35–6, 44, 53, 95, 111, 160, 165
  Russian 53, 148

Latvia 51–3, 55
laws
  anti-Jewish 76, 108
  anti-Polish 103, 108–9, 112, 121–2, 132, 169
  colonial 103, 120–2, 133, 169
  Jim Crow 122
  land 147
  Nuremberg Laws (1935) 76
  Prussia 35
Lebensraum 41, 43, 80, 130–1
  Eastern Europe 42, 45, 148, 151, 153, 155, 160
  overseas 42, 45, 147, 151–3
Lemkin, Raphael 2, 127, *see also* genocide
Lettow-Vorbeck, Paul von 29, 32–3, 144
Libya 95–6, 122
Łódź (Litzmannstadt) 31, 51–2, 62, 69, 72, 84–5, 87, 89, 91, 95, 97, 100, 109–10, 113, 129, 130, *see also* Łódź ghetto
Łódź (Litzmannstadt) ghetto 5, 114–18, 125

marriage 109–10, 112, 132, 144
  applications 109–10
  colonial territories 120–1, 132
  Germans and Poles 108–9, 120–1
May, Karl 27, 37
medicine, *see* healthcare
Meyer (also Meyer-Hetling), Konrad
  Generalplan Ost 119–20
  Neues Bauerntum, editor of 40
  Planning Department 84, 86, 119
Michelsohn, Martha 64, 100–1
Molotov–Ribbentrop Pact (1939) 50, 56
monuments 34, 81, 84, 105
  colonial 21, 31–3, 45
murder, 69, 92, 101 *see also* genocide; Holocaust
  Annexed Poland 3, 5, 13, 16, 74, 106–8, 112, 115–19, 125–30, 132–4, 168
  apathetic, indirect methods 128, 168
  colonial 107, 127–8, 130, 168
  intentional, direct methods 125, 128, 168
  settler colonial 130–4, 168

Namibia 22, 24, 28
National Socialist Party 22, 33, 44–5, 65, 98, 115, 139, 144–5

nationalization 60–1
Nationalsozialistische Volkswohlfahrt (National Socialist People's Welfare, NSV) 66–7, 81, 129
Neues Bauerntum: fachwissenschaftliche Zeitschrift für das ländliche Siedlungswesen (New Peasantry: Scientific Journal for Rural Settlement), 40, 81
New Guinea 24–5
NS–Frauenschaft (National Socialist Women's League) 56–7, 69, 94, *see also* women

Ober Ost 40
Osteinsatz (Eastern Work Placement) 56, 58–9, 101–2, 105, 149, 154
Ostforschung (Eastern Research), 7–8, 16, 89, 151–6, 158–62, 166, *see also* interwar period
Ostmarkenromane (Eastern Marches Novels) 37–8

Pampuch, Andreas 63, 66
Pan-German League 41–5
Peters, Carl 22–3, 30–1, 41
  film 143
Polish Research Centre, London 1, 165
Portuguese Empire 73
Poznań (Posen) 31, 53, 55, 62, 65, 82, 84, 86–7, 92, 97, 110, 117
Prussia 7, 34–8, 41–5, 70, 89
Prussian Settlement Commission, 7, 36, 38–9

race, *see also* hierarchy; screening
  construct 74, 123, 132, 170
Radegast (Radogoszcz) train station 117
Rasse- und Siedlungshauptamt-SS (SS Race and Settlement Main Office, RuSHA) 4, 51, 53, 72, 128
relations, sexual, *see* relationships
relationships 72, 108–9, 110, 121
  colonial territories 120–1
Reichsarbeitsdienst der weiblichen Jugend (Women's Youth Labor Service, RADwJ) 56, 91
Reich Germans (*Reichsdeutsche*), *see also* settlement advisors

attitude towards ethnic Germans 16, 58, 60–1, 64–71, 73, 155
concept/term 3, 15, 52
experiences 16, 17, 80, 88, 96–100, 102–3, 106
humanitarian mission, self-conceived (*see* humanitarian mission)
propaganda related to 90, 92–3, 96
settlement 13, 96, 99, 108
shortages, personnel 98–9
Reichskolonialbund (Reich Colonial League, RKB) 139–40, 143–6, 148, 151, 155–6
Reichskommissariat für die Festigung deutschen Volkstums (Reich Commission for the Consolidation of Germandom, RKFDV), 4, 40, 51, 58–9, 82, 147–8
Himmler, Heinrich (*see* Himmler, Heinrich)
Planning Department (see Meyer, Konrad)
tasks 50–1
Reichssicherheitshauptamt (Reich Security Main Office, RSHA) 112, 119, 126, 148, 150
Rendsburg, see *Koloniale Frauenschule*
resettlement (*Umsiedlung*)
first resettlements 50–2
paintings of 49–50, 62
policy 4, 50, 162
problems 55–7, 99, 167
propaganda related to 61–4, 66–8, 82, 84–5, 90, 92–3, 96, 143, 145
term, creation of 89
Roma 5, 116, 119, 124, 128, 133, 168

Samoa 24, 120
Schnee, Heinrich 30, 138, 143, 151–2, 158
schools, 54, 59, 66, 68, 71–2, 75, 79, 85, 93, 102, 122, 160, 170 *see also* education
colonies 60, 74, 122, 156
Kaiserreich 26–8, 45
Koloniale Frauenschule (*see Koloniale Frauenschule*)
mother's schools, 57–58 (*see also* settlement advisors)
Polish 58, 111–12
Prussia 35

Wartheland, number in 58
Witzenhausen Colonial School (*see* Witzenhausen)
Schwerin, Friedrich von 38, 40
screening, of
ethnic Germans 4, 50–3, 56, 57, 61, 70, 76
Poles, for *Deutsche Volksliste* 4, 50, 71–3, 76
settlers, colonial 70
Second Anglo–Boer War (1899–1902), *see* Anglo–Boer Wars
Sering, Max 38–9
settlement advisors 4, 56, 58–60, 64, 69, 98, 106, 149, 167, *see also* women
experiences 64–6, 103–4
home visits 57
settler colonialism 13, 17, 104, 130–2, 168
removal/transfer strategies 131–2, 168
Sinti 5, 116, 119, 124, 128, 133, 168
skin color 43, 74–5, 122–3, 127, 170
Sonderweg (special path) 18
South Africa 10–11, 22, 27–9, 69, 122, 124
Soviet Union 50, 53, 76, 145
street names
colonial 31, 45, 87
renaming in Annexed Poland 81, 85, 87–8, 105
Stutthof (Sztutowo) 14
camp 118, 129

taxonomic 132, 169
Togo 24–5, 28
street name 31
Togoland 24
transport, public 122
restrictions on Poles 100, 110, 112
Treaty of Versailles 4, 7, 13, 16, 27–8, 31, 34, 36, 40, 43, 50, 90, 94, 137–8, 150, 152, 155
trek (concept) 49, 68–9, 82

Upper Silesia 36, 100, 105, 110
Umwandererzentralstelle (Central Emigration Office, UWZ) 113–14, 129

Volhynia 16, 49, 51, 62, 92
Volhynian Germans 49, 62, 63–5, 68–70, 94, 113, 129

Volk ohne Raum (People without Space) 29–30, 89, 146, 152, *see also* Grimm, Hans
Völkischer Beobachter 85, 145
Volksdeutsche, *see* ethnic Germans
Volksgemeinschaft (people's community) 51, 57, 86, 96, 133, 156

Wartheland 2, 4–5, 13, 31, 49, 56, 58, 64, 66, 69, 91, 93, 97, 100, 103, 105, 115, 149, 155
  administration in 98
  annexation 13, 123, 127, 165
  badges for Germans 110–11
  building and construction 81, 85, 86
  deportations from 112–14
  Deutsche Volksliste 71–2
  exhibitions about 82–4, 95
  ghettos 115–18
  Holocaust 5, 116–18, 133
  language 111
  marriages (*see* marriage)
  schools (*see under* schools)
  settlement 13, 16, 51, 54, 57, 63, 107, 134
  transport (*see* transport)
  Warthelåndisches Tagebuch (see *Warthelåndisches Tagebuch*)
Warthelåndisches Tagebuch (Watheland Diary) 99–100
Wehrmacht 72, 93, 108–9, 119
Wetzel, Erhard 119–20
women, 36, 54, 57–8, 62–3, 67, 108–9, 115–16, 118, 155, see also *Aufgabe*; settlement advisors
  Annexed Poland, Germans in 4, 56–8, 67, 69, 80, 91–2, 94, 98, 101–2, 104–6, 143, 149–50, 154, 187
  colonialism 29, 32–3, 59, 102, 104, 121, 125, 141–3, 145, 150, 154, 167 (see also *Koloniale Frauenschule*)
  domestic sphere 60, 66, 91–2, 94, 102, 106, 154, 167
  nurses (*see under* healthcare)
Wiedereindeutschungsverfahren (re-Germanization procedure, WED) 72–7, 131–2
Witzenhausen, colonial school 26, 141–2, 146–7, 152, *see also* films

www.ingramcontent.com/pod-product-compliance
Lightning Source LLC
Chambersburg PA
CBHW071818300426
44116CB00009B/1362